# International Finance and Financial Crises

Essays in Honor of Robert P. Flood, Jr.

# International Finance and Financial Crises

Essays in Honor of Robert P. Flood, Jr.

*Edited by*

**Peter Isard, Assaf Razin and Andrew K. Rose**

Partly reprinted from *International Tax and Public Finance*, Volume 6, No. 4 (1999)

SPRINGER SCIENCE
+BUSINESS MEDIA, LLC

INTERNATIONAL MONETARY FUND
Washington, D. C.

**Library of Congress Cataloging-in-Publication Data**

International finance and financial crises : essays in honor of Robert P. Flood, Jr. / edited by Peter Isard, Assaf Razin, and Andrew K. Rose.
p. cm.
Proceedings of a conference.
"Partly reprinted from the International tax and public finance. volume 6. no. 4 (1999)."
Includes bibliographical references.
**ISBN 978-94-010-5770-7** **ISBN 978-94-011-4004-1 (eBook)**
**DOI 10.1007/978-94-011-4004-1**
P. I. Flood, Robert P. II. Isard, Peter. III. Razin, Assaf. IV. Rose, Andrew, 1959- . V. International tax and public finance.
HG3881.I6027 2000
332-dc21 99-40806
CIP



*Printed on acid-free paper.*

to Bob's parents, Robert and Nancy Flood,

and to Ofair Razin

# Contents

# Preface

This book contains the proceedings of a conference held in honor of Robert P. Flood, Jr.

The "Floodfest" took place at the International Monetary Fund in Washington, DC on the occasion of Bob's fiftieth birthday in January 1999. The idea arose some two years earlier in a conversation between Peter Garber (Bob's longtime co-author) and Assaf Razin (an old friend and colleague). The sad origin of the event was the untimely and tragic death of Assaf's son Ofair from complications arising from Multiple Sclerosis, the same disease that continues to affect Flood. Razin and Garber quickly asked Andy Rose (another collaborator and friend of Bob's) to join the organizing team. The Research Department of the International Monetary Fund, under the leadership of Michael Mussa, then generously offered to provide both financial and logistic support for the conference, including the organizing talents of Peter Isard (yet another friend and co-author of Bob's) and his administrative assistant, Norma Alvarado.

A number of Bob's many friends and colleagues over the years were asked to consider contributing to the academic festivities. The request met with a gratifying response, as this book amply shows. Indeed, to accommodate the long list of people who wished to honor Bob, the program provided scope for a round table discussion on policy matters, two discussants for most of the papers, session chairs, and opportunities to participate from the audience.

Bob has written on a variety of subjects over the years, including regime switching, speculative attacks, bubbles, stock market volatility, macro models with nominal rigidities, dual exchange rates, and target zones. Most of these topics are represented in this volume, the "Floodschrift" counterpart of the "Floodfest" conference. The volume begins with Stanley Fischer's tribute to Flood's scholarly contributions and also contains Bob's vitae as an appendix.

The enthusiasm of the profession to honor Bob's achievements is one of the many signs of the affection and esteem with which we regard him. To many of us, Bob has offered much more than just academic scholarship and new ways of tackling economic problems. He has been an intellectual mentor, who has inspired us to think about economics in a whimsical way. He has encouraged us to think long and hard about both theory and empirics, trying to confront mathematical conjectures with the messy facts—and vice versa! And he has invited us into his home to meet his delightful family—his wife, Petrice (Pete), and children, Greg and Kate—inspiring us by the way he has confronted his disease without surrendering his enjoyment in life and work.

Contributors and Conference Participants

**Pierre-Richard Agénor**,[1] World Bank
**Joshua Aizenman**, Dartmouth College
**Tamim Bayoumi**,[1] International Monetary Fund
**Jagdeep Bhandari**,[1] Florida Coastal School of Law
**James M. Boughton**, International Monetary Fund
**Edwin Burmeister**, Duke University
**Matthew Canzoneri**,[1] Georgetown University
**Michael P. Dooley**, University of California at Santa Cruz
**Rudiger Dornbusch**, Massachusetts Institute of Technology
**Ann-Charlotte Eliasson**, Stockholm University
**Charles Engel**, University of Washington
**Stanley Fischer**, International Monetary Fund
**Marjorie Flavin**,[1] University of California at San Diego
**Robert P. Flood, Jr.**, International Monetary Fund
**David Folkerts-Landau**, Deutsche Morgan Grenfell
**Jacob A. Frenkel**, Bank of Israel
**Peter Garber**, Deutsche Morgan Grenfell
**Jo Anna Gray**, University of Oregon
**Dale W. Henderson**, Federal Reserve Board
**Robert J. Hodrick**, Columbia University
**Peter Isard**, International Monetary Fund
**Olivier Jeanne**, International Monetary Fund
**Paul D. Kaplan**, Ibbotson Associates
**Jinill Kim**, University of Virginia
**Paul Krugman**, Massachusetts Institute of Technology
**Douglas Laxton**, International Monetary Fund
**Nancy P. Marion**, Dartmouth College
**Donald J. Mathieson**, International Monetary Fund
**Bennett T. McCallum**, Carnegie-Mellon University
**Richard A. Meese**, Barclays Global Investors
**Michael Mussa**, International Monetary Fund
**David Tat-Chee Ng**, Columbia University
**Maurice Obstfeld**,[2] University of California at Berkeley
**Alessandro Prati**, International Monetary Fund
**Assaf Razin**, Tel Aviv University and Stanford University
**Carmen M. Reinhart**, University of Maryland
**Andrew K. Rose**,[1] University of California at Berkeley
**Efraim Sadka**, Tel Aviv University
**Garry Schinasi**,[1] International Monetary Fund
**Louis Scott**, Morgan Stanley Dean Witter
**Paul Sengmueller**, Columbia University
**Lars E. O. Svensson**, Institute for International Economic Studies, Stockholm University
**Chi-Wa Yuen**, University of Hong Kong

[1] Chair of conference session.
[2] Presented the paper by Paul Krugman.

Robert P. Flood, Jr.

# A Tribute to Robert P. Flood, Jr.

STANLEY FISCHER

Bob Flood received his B.A. from Wake Forest College, which he attended on a golf scholarship. Spurning the lure of professional sports—or having understood the theory of comparative advantage—he turned to more intellectual pursuits, enrolling in the Ph.D. program at the University of Rochester. At Rochester he met the young Mike Mussa and the young Rudi Dornbusch and, impressed and inspired by them, chose to specialize in international monetary economics.

Under Mike Mussa's supervision, Bob wrote a thesis entitled "Essays on Real and Monetary Aspects of Various Exchange Rate Systems." His Ph.D. was awarded in 1977, the same year that he published his first journal article ("Growth and the Balance of Payments," then a popular topic) in the *Canadian Journal of Economics*. In the fall of 1976, Bob joined the Department of Economics at the University of Virginia, where he was mentored by Ben McCallum. He left in 1980 to spend two and a half years visiting Dale Henderson's group in the International Finance Division at the Federal Reserve Board. After a brief return to Virginia, he moved in 1983 to Northwestern to join Bob Hodrick. And then in 1987, he was persuaded by Jacob Frenkel to join the Fund's Research Department—and the Fund has been benefiting ever since.

Bob has been a prolific scholar during the twenty-two years since his doctorate. He has published almost sixty papers, as well as a book and a number of comments and reviews. He remains an active scholar, and continues to be a lively contributor to the profession's never-ending debate on exchange rate regimes, as well as on speculative bubbles and currency crises. He has played an important role as mentor to some of the younger members of the IMF research community—and given his acceptance of the editorship of *IMF Staff Papers*, we very much hope and expect that role will grow substantially in the future.

At Virginia, Bob began an extensive collaboration with Peter Garber, which resulted in seminal contributions to the analysis of "process switching." Technically, this literature analyses how macroeconomic behavior is affected by the prospect and/or realization of changes in policy regimes that are triggered when the operation of an initial regime induces relevant endogenous variables to move beyond certain thresholds and thus trigger a shift into another regime. The best known example is a switch in exchange rate regimes from fixed to floating. Flood and Garber's famous 1984 *Journal of International Economics* paper on collapsing exchange rate regimes formalized a model of speculative attacks in a linear setup. The model's clarity and simplicity both made it a hit from the start, and explain why it remains one of most highly cited JIE papers of all times. As a result, Bob is known as one of the founding fathers of the modern literature on currency crises. But the methodology is sufficiently general that it can be applied to a number of other examples, including the stabilization of hyper-inflations and currency reforms. This research program has proven invaluable in allowing the use of the same analytical and empirical framework to model economic behavior in a system that may exhibit either normal or crisis periods.

Bob is also well-known as one of the founders of the work on bubbles in markets with rational expectations. He and Garber developed the first empirical tests for price level bubbles. At Northwestern, he teamed up with Bob Hodrick to extend the work to asset price bubbles, allowing foreign exchange and stock markets to be dissected with much the same tools.

Much of Bob's other work is in international finance. He developed a well-known model of dual exchange rates, which led to collaboration with Nancy Marion on a number of papers addressing two-tier markets, speculative attacks, and related issues. Since joining the Fund, Bob has continued to focus on a variety of issues relating to exchange rate behavior and the macroeconomics of different exchange rate regimes. With Andy Rose he provided definitive empirical evidence against existing smooth-pasting models of exchange rate target zones and against standard macroeconomic models of exchange rate regimes; he has written with Peter Isard on rules versus discretion in monetary policy, introducing the concept of "escape clauses;" and the list of papers and co-authors stretches on.

Bob remains very active in generating frontline research that appears in the top journals. The academic community is looking forward, with particular interest, to his long-awaited paper with Garber on the economics of time zones!

Bob's students and colleagues have often remarked on the great enthusiasm he brings to discussions of economic issues and the exceptional generosity he displays in explaining concepts and providing helpful advice to others. His talents as an expositor are legendary. His outstanding abilities as a teacher have made him a regular lecturer at IMF Institute courses.

It came as great news that Bob would be willing to accept the editorship of *IMF Staff Papers*. He is just the man to revive the journal and help regenerate excitement about research at the Fund. An important part of his new role is to upgrade the caliber of feedback that Fund staff members receive on the research papers they submit for publication.

Bob is an excellent researcher and superb colleague, and we are very lucky to have him at the Fund. But beyond that, every one of us admires the extraordinary courage he has shown in dealing with his long battle with multiple sclerosis. He has remained productive and cheerful in the face of adversity as he continues to charge ahead, extending his scholarly contributions, and now taking on a major new challenge.

Bob: almost every one of your co-authors is here today; so are many of your teachers, and your colleagues. They are here to salute you, honor you, look forward to your future contributions, and to tell you how much you mean to all of us, and how much the example of your courage means to so many.

Thank you for all you have done—and Happy Birthday!

**Acknowledgment**

Editted version of luncheon remarks. I am grateful to Andrew Rose and Peter Isard for their assistance.

# Overview

Bob Flood has made important contributions to many areas of economic analysis, including regime switching, speculative attacks, bubbles, stock market volatility, macro models with nominal rigidities, dual exchange rates, target zones, and rules versus discretion in monetary policy. Contributors to the Floodfest were invited to address any of the topics that Bob has explored, or others of their choosing. The results, contained in this volume, include five papers on topics in international finance. Two of these papers, as well as the panel discussion, focus on speculative attacks and financial crises. The other three take new directions in exploring topics on which exisiting models leave much to be desired. Thus, most of the eight papers in this volume fit the title: *International Finance and Financial Crises*.

In Chapter 1, Nancy Marion reviews both the literature on the causes of speculative attacks on fixed exchange rates and the separate literature on the determinants of bank runs. Both types of crises involve attacks on asset price-fixing schemes. Marion draws a number of parallels between the two areas of analysis and examines some of the new insights that are emerging from a more integrated approach in the aftermath of the Asian financial crisis. Carmen Reinhart and Donald Mathieson provide comments.

The paper by Paul Krugman, in Chapter 2, argues that we badly need a "third-generation" crisis model to make sense of recent events and to help warn of crises to come. He is skeptical about whether either moral-hazard or Diamond-Dybvig types of bank-run stories really get at the essential nature of what went wrong in Asia, and he sketches a candidate for third-generation crisis modeling. Krugman's model emphasizes the role of companies' balance sheets in determining their ability to invest, and the role of capital flows in affecting the real exchange rate. Comments are provided by Peter Garber and Olivier Jeanne.

The Floodfest included a panel to solicit the views of some of the leading experts on "Financial Crises: What Have We Learned from Theory and Experience?" Chapter 3 summarizes the oral presentations of four of the panelists: Michael Dooley, Rudiger Dornbusch, David Folkerts-Landau, and Michael Mussa. It also includes written remarks by the fifth panelist, Jacob Frenkel.

The centerpiece of Chapter 4 is a paper in which Charles Engel derives expressions for the foreign exchange risk premium in four different specifications of sticky-price general equilibrium models. The models are distinguished by two basic types of pricing assumptions: pricing in the producer's currency and pricing to market (i.e., in the consumer's currency). Further model differentiation comes from two alternative assumptions about money demand: cash in advance, and real balances in the utility function. Among the interesting results, Engel finds that a pricing-to-market model with cash in advance is capable of explaining much larger risk premiums than the other three model variants. James Boughton and Richard Meese comment.

In Chapter 5, Assaf Razin, Efraim Sadka, and Chi-Wa Yuen provide an information-based model of foreign direct investment (FDI) that revisits the gains from trade. Their model emphasizes a feature of FDI that distinguishes it from other types of capital flows. In particular, FDI is viewed as an exercise in control and management, rather than merely buying an ownership share in the domestic firm, and the problem of channeling domestic saving into productive investment is analyzed in the presence of asymmetric information between the managing owners of firms and other portfolio stakeholders. Razin, Sadka, and Yuen emphasize that, in the absence of a well-developed domestic credit market, FDI can raise welfare through its double role of providing a vehicle to revive the domestic equity market and supplementing domestic saving with foreign saving; but in the presence of a well-developed credit market and asymmetric information, FDI can generate welfare losses. The paper is followed with comments by Joshua Aizenman.

In Chapter 6, Robert Hodrick, David Ng, and Paul Sengmueller extend John Campbell's asset-pricing model to investigate international equity returns. They also utilize and evaluate recent evidence on the predictability of stock returns. They find some evidence for the role of hedging demands in explaining stock returns and compare the predictions of the dynamic model to those from the static capital asset pricing model. Both models fail in their predictions of average returns on portfolios of high book-to-market stocks across countries. Comments are provided by Louis Scott and Paul Kaplan.

The next two chapters contain the three conference papers that do not address topics in international finance. Bennett McCallum's contribution, in Chapter 7, focuses on the fact that many dynamic models with rational expectations feature a multiplicity of paths that satisfy all of the conditions for intertemporal equilibrium. McCallum addresses several alternative criteria that have been proposed for selecting among the multiplicity of solution paths, makes the case for the minimum-state-variable (MSV) criterion, and demonstrates how unique MSV solutions can be defined and calculated in a very wide class of linear rational expectations models. Edwin Burmeister provides comments.

Chapter 8 includes two papers on monetary policy rules. Dale Henderson and Jinill Kim develop an optimizing-agent model of a closed economy that is sufficiently simple to allow exact utility calculations. The set-up includes one-period nominal contracts for wages, with prices either flexible or also governed by one-period contracts, as well as shocks that are unknown when contracts are signed. Alternative monetary policy rules for stabilizing the economy (including fully optimal rules and "naïve" and "sophisticated" simple rules) are evaluated and compared, under each type of price-level behavior, using the utility function of the representative agent. In the second paper, Peter Isard, Douglas Laxton, and Ann-Charlotte Eliasson use stochastic simulations and stability analysis to compare how different monetary policy rules perform in a moderately nonlinear model in which policymakers tend to make serially-correlated errors in estimating a time-varying NAIRU. They find that rules that work well in linear models but implicitly embody backward-looking measures of real interest rates (such as conventional Taylor rules) or substantial interest rate smoothing perform very poorly in their model. This is presented as a challenge to the general practice of evaluating policy rules on the basis of their performances in linear models. The chapter also includes comments by Jo Anna Gray, Lars Svensson, and Bennett McCallum.

# Some Parallels Between Currency and Banking Crises

NANCY P. MARION nancy.p.marion@dartmouth.edu
*Department of Economics, Dartmouth College, Hanover, NH 03755*

***Abstract***

There is a sizeable literature on the causes of speculative attacks on fixed exchange rates and a large literature on the determinants of bank runs. Surprisingly, these two literatures rarely overlap, even though both types of crises involve attacks on asset price-fixing schemes. This paper draws a number of parallels between the work on currency crises and the work on banking crises and examines some of the new insights that are coming out of a more integrated approach in the aftermath of the Asian financial crises.

## I. Introduction

Robert Flood has made important contributions to our understanding of speculative attacks on fixed exchange rates. Indeed, his many papers on currency crises have advanced a fruitful research agenda focused on the economics of process-switching. The "Floodfest" conference in his honor gives me the opportunity to take another look at the way economists think about crises and their causes.

In the 1990s, financial crises in emerging markets have been characterized by the collapse of both fixed exchange-rate regimes and financial intermediaries such as banks. While some have argued that these crises were essentially currency crises, others have pushed the view that the crises were fundamentally banking crises, where the fixed exchange-rate regime played no precipitating causal role. Still others have suggested that the currency and banking crises were closely intertwined.

The parallels between currency and banking crises are striking. Both involve attacks on asset price-fixing schemes. Both occur when the government can no longer credibly commit its assets in support of a fixed price, be it a fixed price between home and foreign currency or a fixed price between currency and bank deposits. Indeed, the government assets backing the exchange rate and bank deposits can ultimately be the same assets. Once the asset backing is gone, or the government chooses to halt its further depletion, price-fixing schemes collapse. Exchange rates can go into free fall and banks can become insolvent.

There is a large literature on the causes of speculative attacks on fixed exchange rates. (See the survey by Flood and Marion, 1997). There is also a substantial literature on the determinants of bank runs.[1] (See the survey by Calomiris and Gorton, 1991). Prior to the Asian crises, however, these two literatures rarely, if ever, overlapped. What we find are currency crisis models that ignore the private banking sector and bank-run models absent open-economy features. The lack of overlap is even more remarkable since both literatures embrace the same two approaches to explaining crises. Both literatures suggest that speculative attacks may be either the anticipated outcome of inconsistent policies or the unanticipated outcome of self-fulfilling changes in market expectations.

Since the 1997–98 financial crises in Asia, like some earlier crises, involved both foreign exchange markets and private financial intermediaries, economists have begun drawing from both currency and banking crisis literatures to enhance their understanding of these events.

In this essay, I first describe the main views about the causes of currency and banking crises and draw some parallels between the two. I then focus on some of the newer research. The Asian crisis has spawned efforts to consider bank-run models in an open-economy setting or suggest ways banking features such as moral hazard in international lending might lead to an eventual collapse of a fixed exchange rate. I take a look at this new crisis literature and stress the benefits of taking a more integrated approach.

## II. Crisis Causes

### A. *Causes of Currency Crises*

Twenty years ago, a "first generation" of currency crisis models pointed to inconsistent government policies as the cause of a speculative attack on a fixed exchange rate.[2] In most of this literature, the government fixes the price of foreign exchange but also monetizes a large fiscal deficit. Excessive domestic credit creation leads residents to exchange the unwanted domestic currency for foreign currency, reducing the government's stockpile of international reserves. The erosion of the reserve stockpile is problematic since, to maintain the fixed price of foreign exchange, a government must have sufficient reserves to sell whenever the price of foreign exchange is about to rise.

If speculators wait until reserves are naturally depleted on their own, then at that point the central bank must abandon the fixed exchange rate and the price of foreign exchange will jump up. Speculators foresee this potential opportunity for a capital gain and compete against each other for the profits. In doing so, they advance the date when reserves will be exhausted. At some point before reserves are exhausted on their own, an attack occurs as speculators rush to purchase the government's remaining stockpile of international reserves. The large transfer of real resources away from the government at the time of attack can be viewed as a penalty paid by the government for having pursued inconsistent policies.

Although this story tracks well with many past crises, it does not appear to characterize the recent one in Asia. During the mid-1990s, Asian governments were in approximate fiscal balance and not pursuing excessive credit creation. Nevertheless, it is important to remember that monetizing fiscal deficits when the exchange rate is fixed is just one example of inconsistent policies, albeit an historically relevant one. The main message of the first-generation model—that crises may be the predictable outcome of inconsistent policies—is still applicable today. Indeed, some of the new "third-generation" crisis models that focus on the role of government guarantees in promoting excessive investment have merely adapted the message of the first-generation model to a new set of policy inconsistencies.

A "second generation" of currency crisis models received considerable attention after the attacks on European currencies and the Mexican peso in the early 1990s. The second-generation models start from the premise that there is no underlying policy inconsistency before the crisis. Instead, these models consider an interaction between private sector behavior and government behavior that gives rise to several possible outcomes.[3] In principle, the economy can jump from one outcome to another. A jump from a "no-attack equilibrium" to an "attack equilibrium" can be triggered by a sudden and unpredictable shift in market expectations.

Often the root of the problem is an underlying tension among the government's multiple objectives. For example, the government may want to promote price stability or signal the markets of its intention to pursue a disciplined monetary policy in the future. It can advance these sorts of objectives with a fixed exchange rate. On the other had, the government may also wish to limit its debt service obligations, lower the rate of unemployment, or inject liquidity into a troubled banking system. These objectives can better be achieved if it abandons the fixed exchange rate to pursue monetary expansion.

As long as the benefits of the fixed exchange-rate policy exceed the costs, the fixed exchange rate is maintained. A shift in market expectations about the viability of the fixed exchange rate may alter the cost-benefit calculus, however. For example, if private agents start to give more weight to the probability of devaluation, interest rates or wage demands can increase, worsening the prospects for lower debt service, a sounder banking system or reduced unemployment. The government may then decide that maintaining the fixed exchange rate is too costly. The government's decision to devalue validates expectations, making expectations self-fulfilling.

Second-generation currency crisis models often illustrate the trade-offs faced by a government with a social loss function. For example, the government might conduct exchange-rate policy in order to minimize the deviation of prices and employment from their desired levels in the face of output shocks. If output shocks are small, the government will generally find it optimal to keep the exchange rate fixed even though employment deviates somewhat from its desired level.

While an economy may be fortunate enough to experience small shocks most of the time, it may nevertheless face large shocks every now and then. Consequently, it may be optimal for the government to follow a fixed exchange-rate rule most of the time but abandon the rule on occasion when disturbances to the economy are very large. Of course, the government must face a cost each time it invokes the "escape clause" or it will be tempted to break the rule (devalue) too often.[4]

Because of the way people form their expectations about the future value of the currency, there may be two (or more) values for the threshold disturbance that triggers the escape clause. Suppose the economy is at an equilibrium where only disturbances exceeding the largest threshold value can cause a crisis. If private expectations suddenly become more pessimistic, then the economy can jump to a different equilibrium where smaller shocks bring about a crisis.

In second-generation models of currency crises, the concept of "backing" for the fixed exchange-rate commitment is much broader than the international reserves on the government's balance sheet. Backing encompasses what the government is willing *to give up* in order to maintain the fixed exchange-rate policy. Not only must the government be willing to lose international reserves in defense of the fixed exchange rate, it must be willing to sacrifice other things as well—such as some employment or the solvency of some banks. Its willingness to give up these other goals depends on the state of the economy. It is harder to sacrifice further employment for the sake of defending the fixed exchange rate if unemployment is already high. It is harder to allow some banks to fail if it then puts many other banks and firms in financial jeopardy. Second-generation models therefore require that the economy's fundamentals be weak before a shift in expectations can pull the economy into a crisis.

Because the Asian economies enjoyed high growth, low unemployment and low inflation up until the crisis hit, some have questioned the applicability of the second-generation model to the Asian experience. Yet some Asian governments did face a worsening trade-off between the goal of maintaining a stable exchange rate and the desire to support fragile banks and indebted firms.

The key message of the second-generation model—that crises can be the unpredictable outcome of a change in market expectations—is an important one. Indeed, some "third-generation" crisis models developed in the aftermath of the Asian experience also rely on a shift in market expectations to trigger a crisis.

### *B. Causes of Banking Crises*

Almost twenty years ago, Flood and Garber adapted their perfect foresight model of a speculative attack on a fixed exchange to the case of a closed-economy bank run (Flood and Garber, 1981). They described a situation where commercial banks transform nominal deposit liabilities into both reserves and long-term bonds. The banks also make a commitment to a fixed nominal price. They agree to pay on demand one unit of high-powered money for each unit of home currency deposited with them. In the absence of deposit insurance, the banks can maintain this price-fixing scheme as long as their assets fully cover their deposits.[5]

Flood and Garber showed that a bank run can be the predictable outcome of inconsistent policies. In the example they constructed, a central bank policy of deflation undermines the commercial banks' commitment to redeem deposits at par.[6] To maintain the nominal value of their assets in a deflationary environment, banks must purchase new assets to offset the capital losses on their currently held assets. For a time, banks are willing to make these new purchases since the earnings on their asset holdings exceed the cost of managing their portfolio and the size of the asset valuation loss.

Over time, however, the deflation reduces asset earnings. Eventually, it is no longer profitable for banks to maintain the assets required for full backing of their deposit liabilities. At that point, there is a bank run. The attack occurs at the last instant when the banks can fulfill their obligation to convert demand deposits into currency at par.[7] Since the bank run occurs in a closed-economy environment without a lender of last resort, the run does not generate a claim on the central bank's domestic or international reserve assets. Rather, the run forces a transfer of real resources from the commercial banks to private agents.

While this early bank-run example lacks some desirable properties of later bank-run models, it nevertheless shows how a policy inconsistency that erodes the value of banks' net assets can generate a predictable bank run.[8] When banks can no longer maintain sufficient assets to meet their nominal liabilities, depositors, faced with incipient capital losses, run the banking system.

A sudden shift in expectations can also produce a bank run. Moreover, the possibility of a run arises because of the underlying tension between economic objectives—the need for flexibility and the economic pay-off from long-term commitment.[9] This tension is transparent in the closed-economy bank-run model of Diamond–Dybvig (1983), where banks transform deposits into high-yielding long-term assets that are costly to liquidate in the short term. Agents prefer the high returns associated with long-term investments but may have to consume at an earlier date due to unexpected shocks.

A bank permits private agents to achieve the optimal allocation of investment and consumption since it provides risk sharing among individuals who need to consume at different random times. The bank offers a positive return on deposits and allows deposit withdrawals on demand. The bank stores a fraction of the deposits and invests the rest in the long-term high-yield technology. By the law of large numbers, deposit withdrawals in the short term will generally equal the expected withdrawals of agents who discover they must consume early, and the bank can cover these withdrawals with its liquid reserves. This is the good outcome.

A second equilibrium outcome is a bank run. In the absence of deposit insurance, depositors in the short term may come to believe that the bank is unsafe and everyone else will be withdrawing their deposits. In that case, they will immediately attempt to withdraw their own funds. The bank is forced to liquidate its long-term investment, but since the liquidated value of bank assets is less than the amount people would like to withdraw, the bank fails. The shift to pessimistic expectations brings about the very event depositors feared.

As noted by Calomiris and Gorton (1991), the rush to withdraw arises because of the first-come-first-served rule of deposit withdrawals. Since those who wait may end up with nothing, depositors compete with each other to be the first to withdraw.[10] The run imposes real costs on the economy because it results in the early termination of productive investment.

The event that triggers the change in expectations and moves the economy from the "no-run equilibrium" to the "run equilibrium" is left unspecified. Not surprisingly, the Diamond–Dybvig approach is thus called the "random withdrawal" view of bank runs.

A number of researchers [e.g. Chari and Jagannathan (1988), Gorton (1985), Calomiris and Khan (1991) and Calomiris and Gorton (1991)] have suggested that any piece of news that leads depositors to view bank portfolios as riskier might trigger a bank run. Since banks hold nonmarketable assets that make their portfolios hard to monitor, depositors do not know which specific banks will be most affected by the bad news. Consequently, depositors may decide to withdraw a large volume of deposits from all banks. Banks then choose to suspend convertibility and sort out which of them are insolvent. Banks can accomplish this task because they have better information about each others' portfolios.

Bank runs may therefore resolve the information asymmetry between banks and depositors and help depositors monitor bank performance. This multiple equilibria story is called the "asymmetric information" view of bank runs. It argues that the economy's jump from the "no-run equilibrium" to the "run equilibrium" can be rationally triggered by movements in a noisy indicator related to the quality of bank assets. In empirical work, indicators correlated with returns on bank investments include the size of liabilities of failed non-financial businesses and the failure of a particularly large non-financial corporation.

## III. Parallels between Currency and Banking Crises

Some parallels between currency and banking crises are obvious, but worth emphasizing at the outset. Both crises are attacks on price-fixing policies. In one case, speculators bet that the government cannot maintain the fixed price for foreign currency and rush to purchase the government's remaining stockpile of international reserves before the fixed price is abandoned. In the other case, depositors believe the banks cannot maintain the fixed price between deposits and currency and rush to withdraw their deposits before the conversion rate is abandoned.

Both types of attacks occur when a finite stock of assets is still held by the institutions supporting the fixed-price scheme. Both types of runs produce a discontinuous drop in the asset holdings of the institution directly under attack. In a currency crisis, the assets of the monetary authority are depleted; in the case of a banking crisis where there is no deposit insurance, the banks' assets are depleted.

Currency and banking crises spring from the same two causes. They may be the predictable outcome of policy inconsistencies or the unpredictable outcome of sudden shifts in market expectations.

A predictable currency crisis can arise because the government fixes the price of foreign currency yet allows domestic credit growth to erode the stock of international reserves in a predictable way. More broadly, the crisis can result from pursuing any policy that depletes the reserves needed to back the fixed exchange-rate commitment. In the case of a predictable bank run, commercial banks promise to exchange currency for deposits at par on demand and yet the government pursues a policy that predictably erodes the value of the assets backing the commercial banks' commitment. By causing a predictable deterioration in the assets backing the nominal commitment, the policy inconsistency leads to the inevitable collapse of the fixed-price promise.

An important contribution of the literature on predictable runs is to show that a crisis need not be the result of irrational investors, market manipulators or big shocks to the economy. Rather, a crisis can be the outcome of rational agents who observe the deterioration in the resources backing the nominal commitment and try to profit from dismantling the underlying policy inconsistency.

In both types of predictable runs, the time of attack is motivated by profit opportunities. In a perfect-foresight attack on a fixed exchange rate, for example, speculators compete with each other for potential gains in the currency market and end up advancing the time of attack to where there are no realized profit opportunities. When there is uncertainty and the time of the attack can not be perfectly foreseen, successful speculators are awarded capital gains. In the perfect-foresight bank-run example, an attack occurs the moment banks no longer find it profitable to maintain full backing for their deposits.

Perfectly foreseen runs are sudden but orderly. The exchange of assets is consistent with the desires of private agents. Speculators attacking a fixed exchange rate obtain a stock of reserves that just matches the decrease in their demand to hold domestic currency. Depositors running the banks obtain a stock of liquid bank assets that just matches the value of their desired deposit withdrawals. When the exact time of a crisis is not perfectly foreseen, runs are characterized by a panic atmosphere in which agents queue up to acquire international reserves or bank assets according to a "first-come-first-served" criteria.

In both the currency and banking crisis literature, there is also a family of models that relies on an unpredictable shift in market expectations to trigger a crisis. When the markets become more pessimistic about the government's commitment to the fixed exchange rate, the government may decide to abandon the fixed exchange rate and validate market expectations. When the markets become more pessimistic about the bank's commitment to its fixed price for currency in terms of deposits, it can trigger a bank run that confirms people's fears.

In both cases, beliefs are shaped by more than the assets directly backing the fixed-price policy. In the currency crisis case, beliefs are also influenced by the government's willingness to give up other goals. In the banking crisis case, there is never sufficient asset backing in the short term to support the fixed-price promise, so a shift in expectations that triggers a run is either a random occurrence or a result of some generalized bad news.

Even though both currency and banking crises can be unpredictable, it is not necessarily true that crises "come out of the blue." In second-generation currency crisis models, a shift in expectations triggers a crisis if fundamentals are already weak. In some bank-run models, a shift in expectations generates a bank run only if it is preceded by bad news about the economy that implies an inability of some banks to support their fixed-price policy. Only the Diamond–Dybvig story of a bank run suggests that a random shift in expectations can precipitate a crisis.[11]

Moreover, both literatures on unpredictable runs face challenges about whether there really are viable multiple equilibria. If economic incentives are used to distinguish among equilibria in second-generation currency crisis models, then speculators who are awarded capital gains in a crisis may prefer to settle on the equilibrium where attacks are most frequent.[12] If uninsured banks never have sufficient backing in the short term to sustain their fixed-price policy, then the run equilibrium might be the only relevant equilibrium.

## IV. Banking Crises with Open-Economy Features

Since the start of the Asian crisis, economists have developed open-economy versions of predictable and unpredictable bank runs. We shall first describe key features of these models and then consider the new insights from adding open-economy features.

### A. *Predictable Bank Runs with Open-Economy Features*

Open-economy versions of predictable bank runs show how explicit or implicit government guarantees of resident foreign-currency liabilities can promote excessive investment, often in overly risky projects. Moreover, these guarantees increase the contingent claims on the government's international reserve assets. Once these claims on reserves increase to a certain threshold, capital inflows can suddenly become capital outflows and a crisis occurs.

The underlying policy inconsistency arises because the government provides an insurance guarantee for the currency-deposit conversion rate yet liberalizes and deregulates the financial sector so that the available backing to support new guarantees declines. The problem is exacerbated if the country has a fixed exchange rate since the international reserves available to support the guarantees must also be available to support the fixed exchange-rate policy.

One example of a predictable bank-run model with open-economy features is the one by Dooley (1997).[13] His model has two important features in common with the closed-economy bank-run model of Flood and Garber (1981). First, the price-fixing scheme to trade deposits for currency at par can only be supported as long as deposit liabilities are *fully* covered. Second, a policy inconsistency leads to a situation where deposits can no longer be fully covered, triggering a run.

In Dooley's set up, foreign-currency deposits are backed in part by private bank assets and in part by government insurance that is paid out using international reserves. Because the government insures poorly regulated domestic financial markets, banks increase their international financial liabilities at a more rapid pace than the government increases its reserve assets. When these liabilities are about to exceed their backing, a run is triggered.

The Dooley story has several attractive features. It rationalizes the international capital flows to emerging markets before the crisis by showing that a positive shock to the macroeconomic environment can turn government net reserves positive and thus create an insurance incentive for foreign investors. It also relies on the profit motive to explain the timing of the speculative international capital outflow that takes the form of a bank run. When foreign investors no longer earn above-market rates of return, they have an incentive to pull their funds out of the banks. It also shows that the speculative attack is an attack on the government's international reserve assets whether or not the country has a fixed exchange-rate regime.

The sequence of events can be illustrated with Dooley's diagram, labeled here as Figure 1. The positive vertical axis in the top panel measures government assets that could be liquidated in order to bail out resident banks if they should default. These are foreign-currency denominated assets, or international reserves, and they include some limited lines of credits from other governments or international organizations. The negative vertical axis measures the government's liabilities. These liabilities represent the government's *noncontingent* foreign liabilities—the foreign exchange the government owes its foreign creditors in the absence of bank runs—and its *contingent* liabilities—the foreign currency the government owes in case resident banks default. Initially, government assets are not even adequate to cover its noncontingent liabilities. As a result, foreign investors have no desire to deposit their funds in resident banks; government guarantees are not credible because there are no available assets to back them up.

Now suppose a change in the macroeconomic environment at time $t_1$, such as a drop in international interest rates, reduces the value of noncontingent government liabilities so that net assets become positive. (Net assets equal gross assets minus noncontingent liabilities.) These positive *net* assets can now support an implicit or explicit government insurance guarantee for bank liabilities.

The middle panel of Figure 1 shows the growth of insured liabilities over time (line D).[14] Once the government's net assets become positive, banks have an incentive to seek deposits

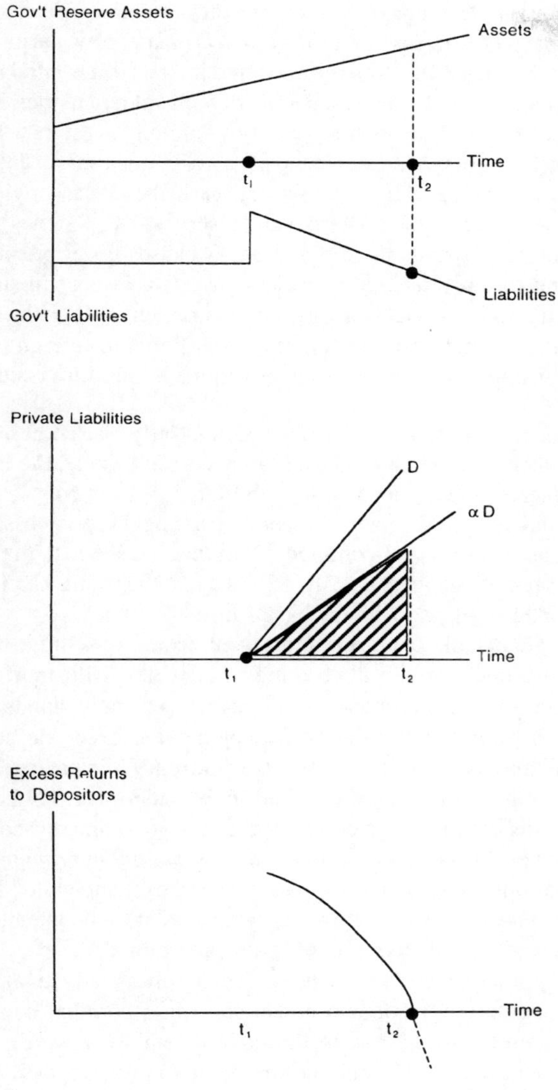


*Figure 1.* Dooley government guarantees on foreign borrowing.

from foreign investors. The reason is that they plan to pay back only a fraction $(1-\alpha)$ of these deposits and rely on government insurance to cover the remaining fraction, $\alpha$ $(0 < \alpha < 1)$. (Banks will appropriate $\alpha D$ of the proceeds for themselves.) The promise of a government bailout sets the stage for an ongoing erosion of the government's financial position. In poorly regulated and supervised financial markets, $\alpha$ may be a large fraction and the flow of new insured liabilities (the slope of line $D$) may also be large. Hence the government's required insurance payments in case of a run (line $\alpha D$) may grow alarmingly over time.

The bottom panel of Figure 1 illustrates the covered interest differential in favor of insured liabilities. Because banks do not plan on repaying the full amount of their insured liabilities, they can afford to offer an above-market yield to foreign investors. Essentially banks compete with each other to obtain foreign deposits by offering a share of their appropriation with foreign investors. As long as foreign investors earn above market yields, they have no incentive to mount an attack on the government's reserves.

The increase in foreign deposits in domestic banks causes government reserve assets to increase, but not one-for-one, since some reserve assets are spent in support of resident purchases of foreign goods, services or financial instruments. In addition, reserve assets earn the risk-free rate of return, not the higher return offered to foreign investors. The top panel of Figure 1 illustrates that the growth in government liabilities exceeds the growth in its reserve assets.

As long as the financial liabilities of banks are backed fully by a combination of bank and government assets, there will be no run. The run occurs at time $t_2$, the last moment when the government's reserve assets can cover its liabilities.[15]

In the Dooley model, the government stock of international reserve assets is lost because the government chooses to honor its contingent liabilities. Once lost, there are no reserves left to stabilize the nominal exchange rate. It follows that if the country had a fixed exchange-rate regime, it will likely collapse with the bank run.[16]

By considering a predictable bank run in an open-economy setting, the Dooley model and others along the same lines do three things. First, they illustrate the expansion of the government's nominal commitments. The government now stands ready to support the fixed rate between bank liabilities and currency and the fixed rate between home and foreign currency. If bank liabilities are in domestic currency, then a government bailout of the banks requires an injection of liquidity that might undermine the fixed exchange-rate policy. If bank liabilities are in foreign currency, then the government's commitments to the banks and to the fixed exchange rate become even more closely intertwined. A bank bailout draws on the same resources needed to support the fixed exchange rate. The government's commitment to the banks is only as good as its commitment to the fixed exchange rate. As the reserve backing erodes, both commitments are undermined.[17]

Second, the Dooley story shows that the private sector always has an incentive to transfer to its own balance sheet the government assets backing a nominal commitment. When a positive shock produces an increase in the government's net worth, agents may take advantage of the government's nominal commitments to increase their own net worth at the government's expense. Just as currency speculators try to purchase the remaining government reserves in the hopes of making capital gains, bank owners may steal a fraction of foreign-currency deposits, knowing that the government will draw on its reserves to bail out depositors.

Third, the Dooley model shows that an economy can experience international capital inflows and an increasing stock of international reserves up until the moment of attack. What matters is the government's *net* reserve stock. When the government's contingent foreign-currency liabilities are increasing at a faster pace than its international reserves and lines of credit, its net stock of foreign-currency reserves is deteriorating in a predictable fashion, bringing closer the time of inevitable collapse.

### *B. Unpredictable Bank Runs with Open-Economy Features*

Several papers have extended the Diamond–Dybvig (1983) model of an unpredictable bank run to an open-economy setting.[18] In these papers, the value of bank assets accessible in the short term continues to fall short of potential withdrawals, and bank runs are still generated by self-fulfilling shifts in expectations. Goldfajn and Valdés (1997) show that intermediation of foreign funds through the banking system increases the probability of currency crises and bank runs. They also show how intermediation magnifies the size of capital outflows associated with crises. Chang and Velasco (1998) explore the implications of global financial liberalization for banks' vulnerability to runs as well as the link between financial fragility and the fixed exchange-rate system. We shall focus on the Chang–Velasco open-economy extension of the Diamond–Dybvig model.

The Chang–Velasco model adds a world capital market to the three-period Diamond–Dybvig framework. One unit of a good can be invested in the world capital market at date $t_0$ to yield one unit in either time $t_1$ or $t_2$. The domestic production technology retains the same characteristic as in Diamond–Dybvig—it is quite productive if the investment is held for two periods, but it is costly to liquidate early. Suppose $R > 1$ is the return on the investment if it is held for two periods, but $L < 1$ is the return if it is liquidated after one period. Only domestic residents have access to this technology.

Demand deposit contracts require agents to surrender their endowment, $e$, and their rights to invest or borrow abroad to the bank at $t_0$. Agents have the option to withdraw $C_1^*$ units of consumption from the bank in period 1 or $C_2^*$ units of consumption in period 2, where consumption is greater if deposits are held two periods, $C_2^* > C_1^*$. The bank can borrow $b_0$ from abroad at time $t_0$ and $b_1$ at $t_1$. The bank faces an overall international credit ceiling of $\bar{b} = b_0 + b_1$. The bank invests the endowment and funds initially borrowed from abroad in the long-term illiquid technology ($I = e + b_0$).

Chang and Velasco make two assumptions about foreign debt (that are later relaxed): (1) the bank always repays its foreign debt, and (2) any foreign debt of one-period maturity acquired at time $t_0$ can be automatically renewed at $t_1$ on the same conditions as before.

The Chang–Velasco story can be illustrated in Figure 2. There are two possible equilibrium outcomes. In one equilibrium, which corresponds to the optimal allocation, only agents who find out they must consume early withdraw deposits at time $t_1$, and the bank can fully cover the withdrawals by borrowing from abroad at $t_1$. The bank does not have to liquidate its long-term asset nor hold some liquid assets between dates $t_0$ and $t_1$.

Alternatively, all domestic agents may attempt to withdraw their deposits at time $t_1$ because they believe everyone else will be doing the same. In that case, the uninsured bank will fail since its obligations to domestic depositors exceed the value of available assets.[19] As in the Diamond–Dybvig model, this open-economy version is silent on what causes the economy to jump from the no-run equilibrium to the run equilibrium.

In the Chang–Velasco model, a shift to more pessimistic expectations by foreign creditors increases the vulnerability of banks by reducing the amount of liquidity banks have available

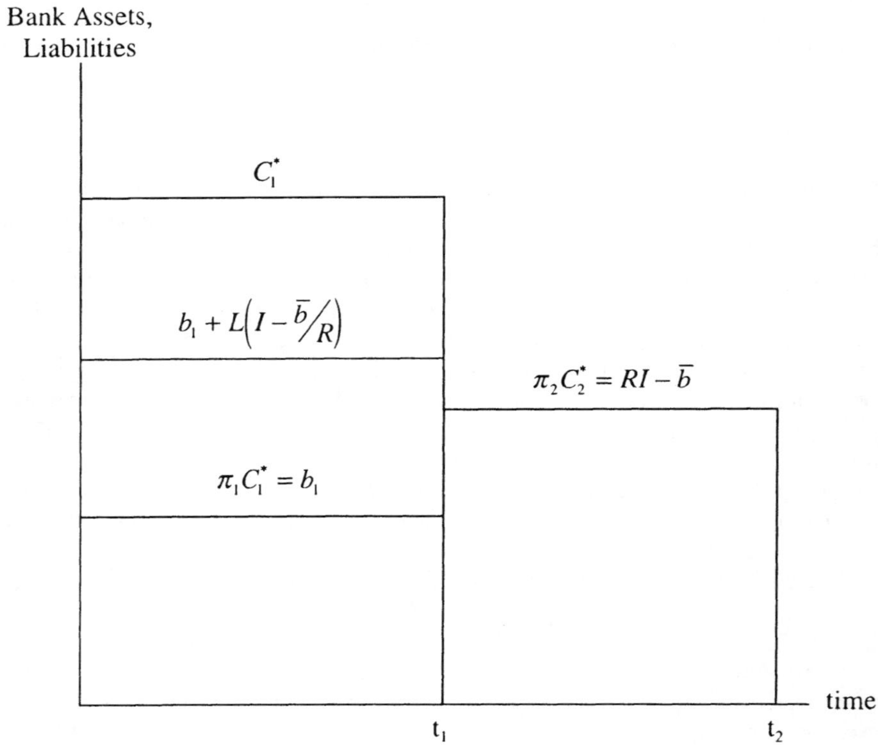


*Figure 2.* Chang–Velasco bank run.

in the short run. The expectational shift induces foreign creditors to stop lending and makes them unwilling to roll over the short-term debts banks previously incurred. As a result, the value of assets available to the bank at time $t_1$ is reduced, increasing its vulnerability to a run.[20]

Figure 3 illustrates the result of a shift to pessimism by foreign creditors. Note how banks that previously had the greatest access to the international capital markets now face the largest drop in available assets when the adverse shift in expectations occurs. The reason is that banks with greater access to external funding initially faced a higher credit ceiling and acquired more short-term debt, $b_0$. When this debt cannot be rolled over, the drop in available bank resources, $(1 - \frac{L}{R})b_0$, is greater. Without these resources, banks are more fragile. Indeed, greater fragility may increase the chance of a run.[21]

Chang and Velasco illustrate that in an open-economy version of bank runs, the central bank can try to save the banks or preserve the fixed exchange rate regime, but it cannot do both. If there is a bank run and the central bank does not supply the banks with extra liquidity (that is, act as lender of last resort), then the banks will fail. The central bank would

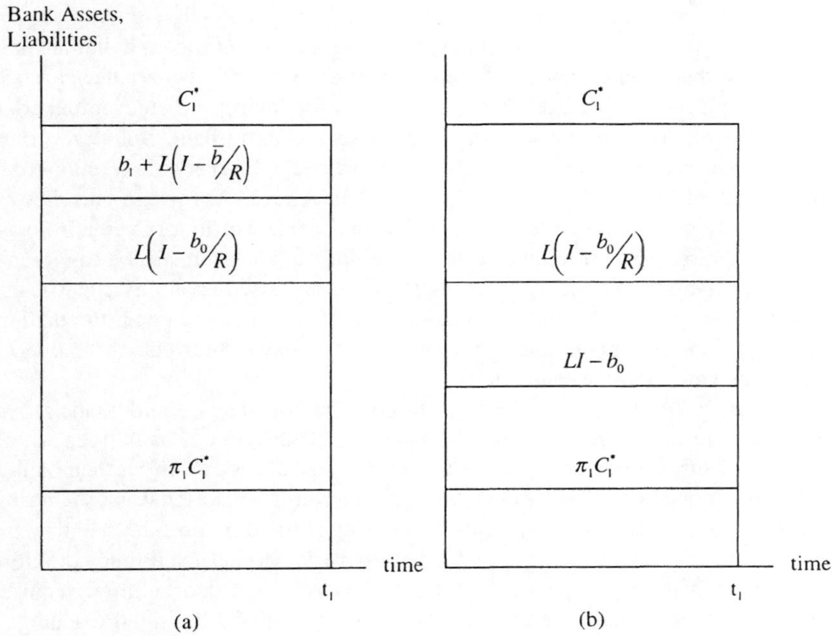


*Figure 3.* Chang–Velasco foreign creditor panic.

be constrained from supplying the extra liquidity if it operated a fixed exchange rate and a currency board, for example. In that case, it could not ensure new liquidity in the absence of an equivalent amount of new foreign-currency assets coming in. Alternatively, if the central bank did not have a currency board, it could issue the domestic liquidity to keep the banks solvent, but then depositors could attempt to trade the home currency withdrawn from the banks for foreign currency (in the amount of $C_1^*$ if the exchange rate equals one). The fixed exchange rate collapses because the foreign-currency assets available to meet this demand are only $b_1 + L(I - \frac{\bar{b}}{R})$. The central bank can borrow from abroad and it can liquidate the assets it takes over from the private banks, but the total amount of foreign-currency assets it can acquire in this manner still falls short of demand since $b_1 + L(I - \frac{\bar{b}}{R}) < C_1^*$. Unless it can acquire additional foreign assets from international lending organizations or foreign governments, the fixed exchange-rate regime will collapse.

Several important themes come out of Chang and Velasco's open-economy version of the Diamond–Dybvig bank-run model. First, newly liberalized domestic banks often borrow foreign currency from abroad and take in foreign-currency deposits but still lend mostly in domestic currency. These banks can become illiquid when their short-term liabilities in foreign currency exceed the amount of foreign currency they can get access to on short notice. This point reinforces the message by Kaminsky and Reinhart (1999), who found that 70 percent of the banking crises they studied were preceded by financial sector liberalization in the previous five years and that financial liberalizations accurately signaled 67 percent of all banking crises studied. It also corresponds to the findings of the predictable bank run models that show that deregulation combined with explicit or implicit guarantees for poorly-supervised banks can generate overlending, excessive risk taking and an eventual crisis.

Second, the open-economy version of the Diamond–Dybvig bank run shows that the accumulation of short-term external liabilities by banks can be risky. If foreign creditors should panic and refuse to roll over bank debts, the banks have less foreign-currency assets to draw on and are more vulnerable to a run. Thus the short maturity of capital inflows can contribute to bank fragility. A related point is that while a crisis can still be triggered by a shift in the expectations of domestic depositors, as in the closed economy story, a shift to pessimism by foreign creditors may also help precipitate a crisis. Indeed, the distinction between a foreign creditor panic and a domestic bank run may be blurred or both may occur at the same time and reinforce each other.

Finally, as Chang and Velasco emphasize, "the combination of an illiquid financial system and fixed exchange rates can be lethal" (1998, p. 41). If the central bank does not act as a lender of last resort (because it operates a currency board, for example), then bank runs can occur. If the monetary authority does act as a lender of last resort in domestic currency, then bank runs can be eliminated but only at the cost of undermining the fixed exchange rate, since private agents will try to convert the newly issued domestic currency into foreign exchange. If the monetary authority tries to act as a lender of last resort in foreign currency, then it is drawing on the same reserve assets needed to support the fixed exchange-rate commitment. Consequently when there is a fixed exchange rate and domestic banks are internationally illiquid, there will be either a banking crisis or a currency crisis should expectations turn pessimistic.

## V. Conclusion

In the 1990s, emerging markets have often been confronted by both currency crises and banking crises. As noted by Kaminksy and Reinhart (1999), these joint crises did not emerge in the post-war period until the 1980s, when some developing countries such as Chile liberalized financial sectors where banks played a dominant role and simultaneously dismantled controls on capital-account transactions. The linkage has become a striking aspect of the financial crises in the 1990s.

When the government fixes the price of foreign currency and stands ready to bail out banks that promise to pay depositors currency on demand, it takes on two nominal commitments. Currency and banking crises are attacks on these asset price-fixing schemes. They are attempts by the private sector to transfer the government resources backing the nominal commitments to private portfolios. They can be the predictable outcome of inconsistent policies that erode the resource backing for the fixed prices, or they can be the unpredictable outcome of a change in expectations about the credibility of the fixed-price pledges.

The literature designed to explain the causes of currency crises and the literature on the determinants of bank runs in closed economies have developed along separate but parallel lines. In response to the Asian crises, there have been attempts to develop bank-run models with open-economy features, but as yet no efforts to specify currency-crisis models with a private banking sector trading in international assets. Even though much work still needs to be done to untangle the complexity of the Asian financial crises, the new work highlights the old dilemma of having too few tools to achieve too many targets. For a number of emerging economies that have liberalized and globalized, the attempt to sustain two fixed-price schemes with the same stock of international reserves has proved to be an impossible task.

## Notes

1. The term "bank run" is often used synonymously with "bank panic" and is meant to describe an event involving a significant number of banks. It also refers to a situation where depositors *suddenly* demand conversion of their deposits into currency.
2. Robert Flood played an important role in developing these models. The seminal contributions were made by Steve Salant and Dale Henderson (1978), Paul Krugman (1979), and Bob Flood and Peter Garber (1984a).
3. For examples, see Flood and Garber (1984b), and Obstfeld (1986, 1994, 1997).
4. The escape-clause model was developed by Flood and Isard (1989) and Persson and Tabellini (1990) and applied to fixed exchange-rate regimes by Obstfeld (1997). Flood and Marion (1997) illustrate that the escape clause finds its advantage over a permanent fixed exchange-rate rule only if the economy faces very large shocks on occasion.
5. Irving Fischer (1911) was among the first economists to suggest that a bank run can occur when the bank's assets no longer cover its nominally fixed liabilities, namely its demand deposits. Note that the run is predicated on there being no lender of last resort.
6. In a later example meant to capture features of the U.S. savings and loan crisis, Garber (1981) modeled a bank run where the policy inconsistency involves thrift institutions who hold long-term, fixed-interest assets while the central bank produces accelerating inflation and offers only limited deposit guarantees.
7. Bank assets fully cover bank deposits as long as $R + P_B B = D$, where $R$ is the book value of bank reserves, $P_B B$ is the market value of long-term bonds whose price is $P_B$ and whose supply is $B$, and $D$ is the book value of deposit liabilities. (For simplicity, bank capital is zero, no interest is paid on deposits, and there are no deposit guarantees by the monetary authority.) Banks suffer capital losses on their bond holdings due to deflation. They are willing to acquire additional bonds to offset these capital losses as long as the earnings from their bonds net of capital losses exceed the costs of managing their portfolios. The condition required to maintain full asset backing is:

$$\theta P(t)\bar{Y}\frac{B(t)}{\bar{B}} + \dot{P}_B(t)B(t) > T(t)B(t) \tag{1a}$$

   where $P(t)\bar{Y}$ is nominal GDP, $\theta$ is capital's share of GDP, $B(t)/\bar{B}$ is the fraction of total bonds, $\bar{B}$, held by banks. $\dot{P}_B(t)B(t)$ is the capital loss on bonds held by banks, and $T(t)$ is the cost per bond of managing the banks' portfolio. Bond holders such as banks receive the income earnings of physical capital once deflation causes capitalists to default on their bond payments. Equation (1a) says that as long as these earnings net of capital losses exceed bank costs, banks have the incentive to maintain the market value of their assets.

   Dividing both sides of Equation (1a) by $P_B(t)B(t)$, we can restate condition (1a) as:

$$\frac{\theta P(t)\bar{Y}}{P_B(t)\bar{B}} + \frac{\dot{P}_B(t)}{P_B} > \frac{T(t)}{P_B(t)} = \bar{k} \tag{1b}$$

   The left-hand side of the inequality in (1b) is the nominal interest rate earned by banks. The right-hand side of (1b) is the lowest nominal interest rate that gives banks the incentive to maintain full backing. (This lowest rate, or floor rate, is assumed to be a constant, $k$.) A run on the bank can occur as soon as the interest rate falls to the floor.
8. For example, this early model does not consider the implications of government guarantees of bank deposits. Neither does it rationalize the special role played by private banks in transforming liquid liabilities into illiquid assets. In addition, the banks operate in a closed-economy environment.
9. Krugman (1998) has stressed this point in his description of the Asian crisis. Recall that second-generation currency crisis models are also based on an underlying conflict between economic objectives.

10. Jacklin (1987) notes that markets must also be incomplete so that agents cannot trade claims on physical assets to cover unexpected short-term consumption needs. Bryant (1980) and Waldo (1985) have developed similar models of a bank run.
11. Note that in the Diamond–Dybvig model, investment returns are certain. Thus bank runs are purely speculative in origin and, according to Diamond and Dybvig, can be triggered "by almost anything." (Diamond–Dybvig, 1983, p. 404). If we introduce the possibility that bank investments may be risky, then any information that leads individuals to alter their beliefs about the quality of bank loan portfolios might trigger a run. Gorton (1985) and others have developed models in which bank runs are motivated by shifts in beliefs about bank portfolio "fundamentals." These types of bank runs may have a predictable component.
12. See Flood and Marion (1997), p. 25.
13. Other examples of a predictable collapse of financial intermediaries in an open-economy setting are Corsetti, Pesenti and Roubini (1998) and McKinnon and Pill (1996). An important early paper that contains some of these same ideas is Diaz-Alejandro (1985). Krugman (1998) and Schneider and Tornell (1998) also develop models with explicit or implicit government guarantees to explain the Asian financial crisis but these models do not rely on open-economy features. Moreover, Krugman notes that a crisis can also be triggered by a sudden shift in expectations if the markets come to believe that government guarantees will not be forthcoming.

    Dooley's model actually applies to any domestic resident institution or individual, not just banks. Moreover, resident liabilities need not be just bank deposits but could extend to equities, corporate bonds, government securities and other instruments. In my discussion of Dooley's model, I shall focus only on banks and their financial liabilities to foreigners.
14. It is assumed it takes time to attract these deposits, so liabilities do not jump up at time $t_1$, but rather grow smoothly over time.
15. With uncertainty, doubts about the government's commitment to exhaust its reserves or confusion about the size of government assets and liabilities can also generate speculative attacks.
16. Dooley suggests it is possible for the country to continue a fixed exchange-rate regime after the bank run if a tiny positive shock turns net reserve assets positive.
17. In Corsetti, Pesenti and Roubini (1998), the government bailout of the private sector's liabilities is covered only in part by international reserves. The rest is covered by explicit taxation. Thus the contingent liabilities of the government represent a fiscal problem that is not apparent until the crisis unfolds. The expectation that tax revenue will fall short of what is required can also generate expectations of future money growth and exchange-rate depreciation that will trigger a currency crisis. The Corsetti, Pesenti, Roubini story therefore has a parallel to the first-generation currency crisis model that emphasizes fiscal deficits and their monetization as an underlying cause of crisis.
18. Some examples are Garber and Grilli (1989), Goldfajn and Valdés (1997) and Chang and Velasco (1998). It is interesting that open-economy bank run models developed to analyze the Asian crises are based on the Diamond–Dybvig approach since empirical evidence from earlier crises favors the "asymmetric information" view of bank runs over the Diamond–Dybvig "random withdrawal" story.
19. If at $t_1$ all agents try to withdraw deposits, total withdrawals will be $C_1^*$. The value of bank assets at $t_1$ is $b_1 + L(I - \frac{\bar{b}}{R})$ since the bank borrows $b_1$ from abroad and liquidates $(I - \frac{\bar{b}}{R})$ of the long-term investment at a return of $L$. Liquidation is only partial because Chang–Velasco assume the bank honors its commitment to repay all its foreign debts at $t_2$. As a result, the bank keeps a fraction $(\gamma)$ of the investment illiquid to pay off the foreign debt at $t_2$. Repayment of the foreign debt at $t_2$ requires $R\gamma I = \bar{b}$. Since only $(I - \gamma I)$ of the long-term investment is liquidated early and $\gamma I = \frac{\bar{b}}{R}$, then $L(I - \gamma I) = L(I - \frac{\bar{b}}{R})$. To show that at time $t_1$ potential bank liabilities $[C_1^*]$ exceed the liquidated value of bank assets $[b_1 + L(I - \frac{\bar{b}}{R})]$, we define $\pi_1$ as the probability of consuming early and $\pi_2$ as the probability of consuming late and use the solution for the optimal allocation $(I = e + b_0,\ \pi_1 C_1^* = b_1,\ \pi_2 C_2^* = RI - \bar{b},\ \bar{b} = b_0 + b_1)$ to write $R\pi_1 C_1^* + \pi_2 C_2^* = Rb_1 + (RI - \bar{b}) = Rb_1 + R(e + b_0) - (b_0 + b_1) = Re + (R-1)\bar{b}$. With a little bit of algebra, it can then be shown that bank assets at time $t_1$ are $b_1 + L(I - \frac{\bar{b}}{R}) = LC_1^* - L[(\bar{b} - b_0)(1 + \frac{1}{L})] < C_1^*$.
20. If foreign creditors refuse to lend more at time $t_1$, $b_1 = 0$ and the value of assets available to the bank at $t_1$ falls to $L(I - \frac{b_0}{R})$. Note that if foreign creditors also refuse to roll over the initial debt, $b_0$ must be paid back at $t_1$ and bank assets fall further, to $LI - b_0$.
21. Chang and Velasco also discuss the effect of financial liberalization, achieved through lower reserve requirements or reduced monopoly power of banks, on the availability of bank assets at time $t_1$. In addition, they analyze the effects on bank assets of asset price booms and busts, an unexpected increase in world interest

rates at $t_1$, and a government subsidy for the long-term investment project. They show that the coefficient of risk aversion for the consumer has to be greater than one to ensure the possibility of the bank-run equilibrium. The Diamond–Dybvig model assumes a risk aversion parameter greater than one.

## References


Adams, Charles, Don Mathieson, Garry Shinasi, and Bankim Chadha. (1998). *International Capital Markets: Development Prospects and Policy Issues.* Washington, D.C.: International Monetary Fund.

Bryant, John. (1980). "A Model of Reserves, Bank Runs, and Deposit Insurance." *Journal of Banking and Finance* 4, 335–344.

Calomiris, Charles, and Gary Gorton. (1991). "The Origins of Banking Panics: Models, Facts, and Bank Regulation." In R. Glenn Hubbard (ed.), *Financial Markets and Financial Crises.* Chicago: University of Chicago Press.

———, and Charles Kahn. (1991). "The Role of Demandable Debt in Structuring Optimal Banking Arrangements." *American Economic Review.*

Chang, Roberto, and Andrés Velasco. (1998). "Financial Crises in Emerging Markets: A Canonical Model." NBER Working Paper No. 6606.

Chari, V. V., and Ravi Jagannathan. (1988). "Banking Panics, Information, and Rational Expectations Equilibrium." *Journal of Finance* 43, 749–760.

Corsetti, Giancarlo, Paolo Pesenti, and Nouriel Roubini. (1998), "Paper Tigers? A Model of the Asian Crisis." Mimeo, Yale University.

Diamond, Douglas, and Phillip Dybvig. (1983). "Bank Runs, Liquidity and Deposit Insurance." *Journal of Political Economy* 91, 401–419.

Diaz-Alejandro, Carlos. (1985). "Good-Bye Financial Repression, Hello Financial Crash." *Journal of Development Economics* 19.

Dooley, Michael P. (1997). "A Model of Crises in Emerging Markets." NBER Working Paper No. 6300, December. (Revised as International Finance Discussion Paper No. 630, Board of Governors of the Federal Reserve System, November, 1998.)

Fischer, Irving. (1911). *The Purchasing Power of Money: Its Determination and Relation to Credit, Interest and Crises.* New York: Macmillan.

Flood, Robert, and Peter Garber. (1981). "A Systematic Banking Collapse in a Perfect Foresight World." NBER Working Paper No. 691.

———. (1984a). "Collapsing Exchange-Rate Regimes: Some Linear Examples." *Journal of International Economics* 17, 1–13.

———. (1984b). "Gold Monetization and Gold Discipline." *Journal of Political Economy* 92, 90–107.

———, and Peter Isard. (1989). "Monetary Policy Strategies." *International Monetary Fund Staff Papers* 36, 612–632.

———, and Nancy Marion. (1998). "Perspectives on the Recent Currency Crisis Literature." NBER Working Paper No. 6380.

Freixas, Xavier, and Jean-Charles Rochet. (1997). *Microeconomics of Banking.* Cambridge: MIT Press.

Garber, Peter. (1981). "The Lender of Last Resort and the Run on the Savings and Loans." NBER Working Paper No. 823.

———, and Vittorio Grilli. (1989). "Bank Runs in Open Economies and the International Transmission of Panics." *Journal of International Economics* 27, 165–175.

Goldfajn, Ilan, and Rodrigo Valdés. (1997). "Capital Flows and the Twin Crises: The Role of Liquidity." International Monetary Fund Working Paper Wp/97/87. (revised September, 1998).

Gorton, Gary. (1985). "Bank Suspension of Convertibility." *Journal of Monetary Economics* 15(2), 177–193.

Hausmann, Ricardo, and Liliana Rojas-Suarez (eds.). (1996). *Banking Crises in Latin America.* Washington, D.C.: Inter-American Development Bank and Johns Hopkins University Press.

Jacklin, Charles. (1987). "Demand Deposits, Trading Restrictions, and Risk Sharing." In Edward Prescott and Neil Wallace (eds.), *Contractual Arrangements for Intertemporal Trade.* Minneapolis: University of Minnesota Press.

Kaminsky, Graciela, and Carmen Reinhart. (1999). "The Twin Crises: The Causes of Banking and Balance-of-Payments Problems." *American Economic Review* 89, 473–500.

Krugman, Paul. (1998). "Will Asia Bounce Back?" Speech for Credit Suisse First Boston, Hong Kong.
———. (1998). "What Happened to Asia?" Mimeo, MIT.
———. (1979) "A Model of Balance-of-Payments Crises." *Journal of Money, Credit and Banking* 11, 311–325.
McKinnon, Ronald, and Huw Pill. (1996). "Credible Liberalization and International Capital Flows: The 'Overborrowing Syndrome.'" In T. Ito and A. O. Kruger (eds.), *Financial Deregulation and Integration in East Asia*. The University of Chicago Press.
Miller, Victoria. (1996), "Exchange Rate Crises with Domestic Bank Runs: Evidence from the 1890s." *Journal of International Money and Finance*.
Mishkin, Frederic. (1996). "Understanding Financial Crises: A Developing Country Perspective." NBER Working Paper No. 5600.
Obstfeld, Maurice. (1997). "Destabilizing Effects of Exchange Rate Escape Clauses." NBER Working Paper No. 2603, *Journal of International Economics*.
———. (1994). "The Logic of Currency Crises." *Cahiers Economiques et Monetaires* 43, 189–213.
———. (1986). "Rational and Self-fulfilling Balance of Payments Crises." *American Economic Review* 76, 72–81.
Persson, Torsten, and Guido Tabellini. (1990). *Macroeconomic Policy, Credibility and Politics*. Chur, Switzerland: Harwood Academic Publishers.
Salant, Stephen, and Dale Henderson. (1978). "Market Anticipation of Government Policy and the Price of Gold." *Journal of Political Economy* 86, 627–648.
Schneider, Martin, and Aaron Tornell. (1998). "Lending Booms and Asset Price Inflation." Mimeo, Harvard University.
Velasco, Andrés. (1987). "Financial Crises and Balance of Payments Crises." *Journal of Development Economics*, 27, 263–283.
Waldo, Douglas. (1985). "Bank Runs, the Deposit-Currency Ratio, and the Interest Rate." *Journal of Monetary Economics* 15, 269–277.

# Comment

BY CARMEN M. REINHART

Let me begin by saying that I really enjoyed reading this well written and very interesting paper. What Nancy does in this paper is to present a cohesive survey of three strands of literature: the theoretical literature on currency crises, banking crises, and the more recent papers that have attempted to link the two. It is the "twin crisis" literature, which focuses on banking crises in open economy models, that the paper devotes the most attention to. Like the literature on currency crises, very different interpretations of the causes of the twin crises have been offered and this paper lays out some of the key differences between first generation models, which stress the role of economic fundamentals, and second generation models, which highlight the role of self-fulfilling crises and multiplicity of equilibria.

I am going to divide my remarks into three parts. First, I am going to make some brief comments about the theoretical models discussed in the paper, complementing Nancy's discussion of these. Second, I am going to turn my attention to the empirical evidence on the links of currency and banking crises. Lastly, I will make some remarks about the scope and direction of future research in these areas.

## Banking Crisis Models with Open Economy Features

A predictable open-economy bank-run model, which is discussed at some length in this paper, is that by Dooley (1997). In the Dooley setting, the policy inconsistency arises because the government provides an insurance guarantee for the currency-deposit conversion rate yet allows the backing to support new guarantees to decline over time. This moral hazard story of financial crises has some appeal in explaining capital flows to emerging markets in the wake of the Mexican peso crisis of 1994 and the (then) unprecedented size of that bail out. It also may help explain why domestic-foreign interest rate spreads fail to systematically rise ahead of crises (see Kaminsky and Reinhart, 1996). However, I do have two issues as regards this story that I would like to add to Nancy's comments on this paper. The first issue has to do with the role of uncertainty. In this framework, moral hazard arises because the guarantee offered by central bank reserves is fully credible. But, of course, in reality there may be both uncertainty and information asymmetries. Surely, as was the case in Thailand, derivative positions (the central bank had borrowed dollars in the forward market) can hide what the "true" level of reserves is. Hence, an investor may not have full information on the extent to which the liabilities being issued are fully backed or not. In a similar vein, as the recent Asian crises have shown, the extent of liabilities or implicit guarantees that are outstanding is often not known until after the crisis. In either case, an investor would face the risk, with a nonzero probability, that the central bank does not actually have enough reserves (either its own or those it can borrow from international organizations) to bail out everyone. In this case, uncertainty about who gets paid and who doesn't would mitigate investors' appetite for these bank deposits.

Second, it is important to remember that these grandiose bailouts are a relatively new feature of international capital markets while booms and busts in the capital flow cycle and financial crises have been around for a long time. It must be remembered that foreign investors, harking back to the previous century and Latin American railroad bonds, have lost a lot of money during financial crises. Hence, one can only take the moral hazard argument to explain the ebb and flow of cross border capital movements so far.

Turning to second generation explanations of the twin crises, as Nancy notes, there have been two recent papers that have extended the Diamond and Dybvig (1983) framework to an open economy setting—Goldfajn and Valdés (1996) and Chang and Velasco (1998). The brief remarks that I will make here apply to both of these models. As in the original paper, the crises in these models are owing to a liquidity problem on the part of banks. The banks may be faced with runs and may not be able to borrow from abroad to satisfy deposit withdrawals. The key assumption in the models that gives rise to illiquidity is that banks borrow short (from abroad) and lend long (to domestic projects). It is worth noting, however, that this illiquidity scenario presumably rules out the existence of foreign banks, which would have recourse to liquidity in times of unexpectedly large withdrawals via the parent bank abroad. Secondly, it also rules out banks holding any liquid asset, such as an internationally traded bond, that can be liquidated if the need arises. The introduction of either of these plausible considerations into the models would considerably dampen their explosive behavior.

## Empirical Evidence on the Links of Currency and Banking Crises

Given that the theme of this paper has been the parallels and links between currency and banking crises, I feel I should discuss briefly what the empirical evidence tells us about the chronology of these events (Table 1). This part of my discussion is based on Kaminsky and Reinhart (1996), which examined the issue in some detail.

From the analysis of nearly thirty banking crises, it would appear necessary to start the discussion of these crises talking a little bit about financial liberalization. Most of the banking crises we examined in that paper shared the common feature that the financial sector had been liberalized shortly before the crisis took place. It would appear that the removal of interest rate ceilings and reductions in reserve requirements that are part of the liberalization process in an environment of lax regulation and even more lax supervision is a recipe for an indiscriminate lending boom and an eventual banking crisis. In turn, as the bad bank loans pile up and the financial sector begins to depend on central bank credit and low interest rates, the seeds are sown for a policy inconsistency between the central bank's exchange rate commitment and its endeavors to act as a lender of last resort to the banks. More often than not, this policy incompatibility ends up as a currency crisis.

However, the story does not end with the currency crisis, as the devaluation itself appears to have pernicious feedback effects on the banking sector. There are clearly balance sheet effects, among other transmission channels, that merit close scrutiny. Indeed, most often the

*Table 1.* The sequence of the twin crises.

| |
|---|
| Financial liberalization |
| ↓ |
| Banking sector problems begin |
| ↓ |
| Currency crashes |
| ↓ |
| Banking sector problems peak |
| ↓ |
| Protracted output collapse |

peak of the banking crisis (if not its beginning) occurs shortly after the currency crisis. Nor does the story end there. As the economy contracts, often severely, the domestic financial sector remains mired in serious difficulty for an extended period of time.

In that analysis, we also show that when currency crises occur alongside banking crises the crises are far more severe than when the currency crisis occurs without banking sector problems (see Table 2 and Kaminsky and Reinhart, 1998a). Also, the recessions are deeper and more protracted and the crash in asset prices far greater. Indonesia's decline in GDP of nearly 14 percent in 1998 starkly reminds us of the severity of these capital-market crises.

## Where Do We Go Next?

While the models that Nancy has reviewed in the paper capture several features of banking and currency crises, these models as well as a much broader family of first and second generation models of currency crises, are silent on several crucial dimensions. Hence, high on the list of topics for future research in the area of financial crises, I would stress three broad themes, that have received comparatively little scrutiny.

**First**, we should develop models that can explain the self reinforcing vicious circle of banking crises and currency woes. Specifically, the oft-observed pattern of banking crises leading to currency crises and the latter making the financial sector problems even worse. Pinning down the balance sheets of firms and banks and modeling the balance-sheet effects of these crises would clearly be a welcome addition to this literature.

**Second**, more research needs to be done on what Calvo (1998) has called the sudden stop problem, referring to the sudden stop or drastic reversal of capital inflows and its highly disruptive effects on economic activity. We need to gain a better understanding of the determinants of the output collapses we observe. This would be a departure from existing models. In both first generation and second generation models devaluations are expansionary. In an example of a first generation model, Gerlach and Smets (1995) explain "contagion" following a devaluation in one of two countries that are engaged in bilateral trade with one another by the recessionary effects in the second country of the real appreciation after its trading partner devalued. In that linear model the devaluation in the second country occurs because the decline in output leads to a decline in money demand and a loss

*Table 2.* The severity of the crises.

| | Banking Crises | | Balance-of-Payment Crises | |
|---|---|---|---|---|
| Severity Measure | Twin | Single | Twin | Single |
| Cost of Bailout (percent of GDP) | 13.3 | 5.1* | N.A. | N.A. |
| Loss of Reserves (percent) | N.A. | N.A. | 25.4 | 8.3* |
| Real Depreciation (percent) | N.A. | N.A. | 25.7 | 26.6 |
| Composite Index | N.A. | N.A. | 25.6 | 17.5 |

Source: Kaminsky and Reinhart (1996).
Notes: Loss of reserves is the percentage change in the level of reserves in the six months preceding the crises. Real depreciation is the percentage change in the real exchange rate (with respect to the dollar for the countries that peg to the dollar and with respect to the mark for the countries that peg to mark) in the six months following the crises. The composite index is the weighted average of the loss of reserves and real depreciation. Episodes in which the beginning of a banking crisis is followed by a balance-of-payments crisis within 48 months are classified as twin crises.
* Denotes that the measure of severity of single crisis episodes is statistically different from the twin crises severity at the 5% level. An N.A. denotes not applicable.

of international reserves. In Obstfeld (1994), for instance, the policymaker's loss function weighs the loss of credibility from devaluing from the economic loss of not doing so. In either case devaluations produce the textbook improvement in economic activity. Clearly, the aftermath of devaluations in emerging markets paint a very different picture, which we have yet fully to understand and formalize via a model. In this regard, understanding the behavior of banks following the crises is of some importance as, for a variety of reasons, bank lending dwindles and banks often hold high levels of excess reserves.

**Lastly**, the role of foreign banks in propagating disturbances—or, more broadly, the role of common lenders—as a vehicle of contagion is another area where models have been relatively scarce. Yet, some of the recent evidence on the channels of contagion, such as Frankel and Schmukler (1996) and Kaminsky and Reinhart (1998b), point to the importance of a variety of financial sector links.

## References

Calvo, Guillermo. (1998). "Capital Flows and Capital-Market Crises: The Simple Economics of Sudden Stops." *Journal of Applied Economics* 1, 35–54.

Chang, Roberto, and Andrés Velasco. (1998). "Financial Crises in Emerging Markets: A Canonical Model." NBER Working Paper No. 6606.

Diamond, Douglas, and Phillip Dybvig. (1983). "Bank Runs, Liquidity, and Deposit Insurance." *Journal of Political Economy* 91, 401–49.

Dooley, Michael P. (). "A Model of Crises in Emerging Markets." NBER Working Paper No. 6300.

Frankel, Jeffrey A., and Sergio L Schmukler. (1996). "Crisis, Contagion, and Country Funds: Effects on East Asia and Latin America." In Reuven Glick (ed.), *Managing Capital Flows and Exchange Rates: Perspectives from the Pacific Basin*. Cambridge: Cambridge University Press, pp. 232–266.

Gerlach, Stefan, and Frank Smets. (1995). "Contagious Speculative Attacks." *European Journal of Political Economy* 11, 45–63.

Goldfajn, Ilan, and Rodrigo Valdés. (1997). "Capital Flows and the Twin Crises: The Role of Liquidity." International Monetary Fund Working Paper WP/97/87.

Kaminsky, Graciela L., and Carmen M. Reinhart. (1996). "The Twin Crises: The Causes of Banking and Balance-of-Payments Problems." International Finance Discussion Paper No. 544. Washington: Board of Governors of the Federal Reserve. Forthcoming in *American Economic Review*, 1999.

Kaminsky, Graciela, and Carmen M. Reinhart. (1998a). "Financial Crises in Asia and Latin America: Then and Now." *American Economic Review* 88(2), 444–448.

Kaminsky, Graciela, and Carmen M. Reinhart. (1998b). "On Crises, Contagion, and Confusion." Unpublished paper.

Obstfeld, Maurice. (1994). "The Logic of Currency Crises." *Cahiers Economiques et Monetaires* 43, 189–213.

# Comment

BY DONALD J. MATHIESON

Nancy Marion has provided us with a very informative and readable paper. Moreover, I am in agreement with Nancy's basic conclusion that there is a fundamental conflict—embedded in both the speculative attack and banking crisis models—arising from the authorities' attempt to maintain two prices (a fixed exchange rate and the price of deposits relative to currency) with too few instruments. However, when analyzing some of the policy changes that have occurred in the emerging markets in the period since July 1997, I think that an equally useful characterization of the dilemma confronting the authorities would be a distinction between maintaining a fixed exchange rate and preserving the stability of the financial system. In most emerging markets, the latter objective is a much broader concept than just maintaining a fixed price between the currency and deposits. Indeed, in many emerging markets, the goal of stabilizing the financial system extends beyond stabilizing just the banking system and typically includes the stability of nonbank financial institutions and other asset markets. The importance of this broader objective can be illustrated by considering the policy actions that have been taken to find additional instruments to solve the Marion policy dilemma.

One policy option has been the Argentine solution—fix the exchange rate with a currency board; address the lender-of-last-resort problem by obtaining international loans (or lines of credit) that can be drawn on during crisis periods; and limit the ability of the banking system to issue insured liabilities and take excessive risks by imposing high risk-adjusted capital ratios, required reserve and liquidity ratios, and improved prudential supervision. This particular solution is not without cost, however, since it reduces the scale of financial intermediation. In Hong Kong, the authorities have sought to stabilize asset prices both by limiting the supply of land available for new housing and by intervention in the stock and stock index futures markets. Another solution, which has been utilized by Malaysia, is to use capital controls to delay and tax the exit of foreign investors. Finally, another alternative which has been utilized by Russia is to default on previously insured liabilities as well as to impose capital controls on outflows. What is not yet fully understood, however, is what the long-run effects of these policy measures are likely to be.

One aspect of the recent experience in Asia that the speculative attack and banking crisis models do not capture very well is what happened during and after the crises to the economies' institutional structures. In the speculative attack models that Nancy has surveyed, for example, the government uses up its foreign exchange reserves to defend both price commitments, and then ends its commitment to maintain one of the prices (the fixed exchange rate). The authorities typically maintain a fixed conversion price between currency and deposits because they can always print domestic high powered money whereas they cannot print foreign exchange reserves. However, even in the countries that have maintained a fixed price between currency and deposits, the speculative attacks and banking crises in the period since July 1997 have been characterized by extensive institutional changes and failures, both during and after the crises, which greatly amplified the asset price adjustments that occurred. While the collapses of the banking systems of many the Asian economies have been widely recognized, these collapses were also accompanied by sharp changes in the structures of the foreign exchange and domestic money markets, as well as the equity markets. Indeed, a key characteristic of these crises has been that the institutional structure has become endogenous during the crisis. In part, this reflects the important role that banks played in both the foreign exchange and payment systems in emerging markets. Before the crisis, the typical foreign exchange market was an interbank market, with banks willing to take on intraday foreign exchange exposures in order to provide market liquidity and to help match order flows throughout the day. Even where required by regulation to limit overnight foreign exchange exposure, these intraday exposures could be quite large. This type of interbank market totally collapsed during the crisis as banks refused to take intraday open positions (because of the fear that counterparties would not deliver). As a result, many of these foreign exchange markets became broker markets, where brokers took no intraday positions but merely quoted foreign exchange prices with large bid-ask spreads and searched for a match between buyers and sellers of foreign exchange. As a result, quoted exchange rates were often not transactions prices. Moreover, determined attempts to acquire foreign exchange by any market participant could produce large daily movements in the exchange rate due to low market liquidity. Often the central bank was the only seller of foreign exchange.

In domestic money markets, there was also a high degree of segmentation. As concerns about the solvency of domestic banks increased, many foreign banks would make domestic currency loans in the local interbank market only to other foreign banks. Moreover, some of the stronger domestic banks would only deal with the local foreign banks.

The structure of equity markets also was transformed when broker dealers that acted as market makers could no longer serve that function because of their inability to obtain bank credit. The resulting decline in market liquidity contributed to a sharp fall in equity prices. If we are going to try to limit the scope and duration of financial crises, one of the things that we need to have a better understanding of is how institutional structure changes during such crises and what factors drive these changes.

# General Discussion

**Peter Garber** agreed with Mathieson's characterization of the illiquidities that arise at the time of a crisis. Although models of speculative attacks recognize that exchange rates and other asset prices exhibit discontinuities, model builders have paid little if any attention to the illiquidities that appear at the moments of discontinuity. By contrast, considerable attention has been paid to these illiquidities in the IMF's International Capital Markets reports, most notably in the April 1993 report following the currency turmoil that shook the European Monetary System during the summer of 1992. Bob Flood had drafted material on speculative attacks for that report and had emphasized that our ability to explain the dynamics of macroeconomic behavior requires an understanding of the illiquidities that appear at times of crisis.

**Michael Mussa** noted that models of the speculative attack process were applicable to a set of phenomena that was broader than currency crises and banking crises. The same type of process occurs in many cases of ordinary businesses that are about to go bankrupt. When a company's bank creditors or suppliers of trade credit begin to suspect that the company is in trouble, they start to reduce their credit exposures, which results in fundamentally the same type of phenomenon as a bank run, though usually in slower motion. Mussa also observed that institutions that have the implicit guarantee of the government can operate fairly deeply under water for a considerable period of time before their creditors decide they have to pull the plug. As the scope of implicit guarantees has grown around the world, we've come to see very large losses associated with bankruptcies, usually because the problem banks had become deeply submerged by the time they had to be put out of their misery.

**Dale Henderson** called attention to a paper on banking crises by Douglas Waldo (Waldo, 1985). Waldo's contribution, which had been written much earlier than it was published, was overshadowed by Diamond and Dybvig (1983) but, in many ways, was more carefully developed than the latter paper, with more attention to spelling out the essentials of banking institutions.

As a comment on Reinhart's discussion, **Henderson** felt that in some cases it was misleading to place "financial liberalization" at the top of the chain. The savings and loan crisis in the United States provided an example in which financial institutions had essentially become moribund prior to financial liberalization and confronted perverse incentives once the liberalization came. Henderson thought that in analyzing cases in which financial liberalization had been followed by financial crisis, it was important to address the situation at the time of the liberalization and to try to sort out the extent to which the crisis had resulted from perverse incentives associated with the initial conditions.

In response to Henderson, **Reinhart** noted that part of the difficulties that seemed to follow financial liberalization could be attributed to the fact that in many countries, banks had little prior history of credit relationships with the private sector. Liberalization tended to induce banks to switch from lending to government to lending to private borrowers, particularly to the extent that it coincided with corrective fiscal measures that reduced the government's need for credit. In a number of countries, banks that began to lend to the private sector in significant volume following liberalization had suffered from their inexperience.

**Michael Dooley** commented on another point that Reinhart had emphasized in her discussion, namely, the failure of speculative attack models to pay much attention to the output losses that followed financial crises. In Dooley's view, this phenomenon was an endogenous and central part of the process. In particular, the prospect that large output losses would be suffered by countries that did not repay their loans, and the incentives that borrowers had to avoid such prospective losses, played a critical role in inducing lenders to extend international credits and in influencing the forms in which such credits were extended. In the absence of a clear understanding of this point, efforts to strengthen the architecture of the international monetary system could become fundamentally misguided.

In responding to the question of whether output collapses implied that IMF programs should recommend more expansionary fiscal policies, **Reinhart** observed that the output collapses were associated with a drying up of bank credit. Even banks that had liquidity didn't lend, but rather became very risk averse and held excess reserves. Regardless of fiscal positions, an understanding of this phenomenon in an open-economy setting was central to understanding the output collapses.

**Mathieson** agreed with Reinhart but emphasized that the collapse of the credit process involved nonbank credits as well as bank credit. In emerging market economies, as well as many mature market economies, credit played a key role in the production process insofar as the provision of raw materials and intermediate goods was heavily dependent on trade credits and supplier credits. In many emerging market economies, credit flows took place in an environment that lacked an effective legal system for enforcing contracts. The basis for credit flows to finance inputs to the production process in such environments—or the basis for the expectation that lenders would be repaid—was the threat that the flow of goods would stop if the credit lines dried up. In this context, Mathieson felt that the recent crisis in emerging market countries had seen the credit process between firms affected as least as dramatically as the credit process between banks and firms. In his view, the collapse of interfirm credits had had a larger and more direct impact on output than the drying up of credits from banks to the larger corporations.

In responding to the discussants, **Marion** broadly agreed with the comments that had been made. She felt that more attention should be paid to the interactions between currency crises and banking crises, to pinning down the balance sheets of firms and banks, and to modeling the balance-sheet effects of crises. Existing models of speculative attacks provided useful insights and should not be rejected too quickly, but new ways of thinking about crises were also needed.

## References

Diamond, Douglas, and Phillip Dybvig. (1983). "Bank Runs, Liquidity and Deposit Insurance." *Journal of Political Economy* 91, 401–419.

Waldo, Douglas. (1985). "Bank Runs, the Deposit-Currency Ratio, and the Interest Rate." *Journal of Monetary Economics* 15, 269–277.

# Balance Sheets, the Transfer Problem, and Financial Crises

PAUL KRUGMAN
*MIT, Department of Economics, Cambridge, MA 02139*
krugman@mit.edu

***Abstract***

In a world of high capital mobility, the threat of speculative attack becomes a central issue of macroeconomic policy. While "first-generation" and "second-generation" models of speculative attacks both have considerable relevance to particular financial crises of the 1990s, a "third-generation" model is needed to make sense of the number and nature of the emerging market crises of 1997–98. Most of the recent attempts to produce such a model have argued that the core of the problem lies in the banking system. This paper sketches another candidate for third-generation crisis modeling—one that emphasizes two facts that have been omitted from formal models to date: the role of companies' balance sheets in determining their ability to invest, and that of capital flows in affecting the real exchange rate.

For the founding fathers of currency-crisis theory—a fraternity among whom Bob Flood holds a place of high honor—the emerging market crises of 1997–8 inspire both a sense of vindication and a sense of humility. On one side, the number and severity of these crises has demonstrated in a devastatingly thorough way the importance of the subject; in a world of high capital mobility, it is now clear, the threat of speculative attack becomes a central issue—indeed, for some countries *the* central issue—of macroeconomic policy. On the other side, even a casual look at recent events reveals the inadequacy of existing crisis models. True, the Asian crisis has settled some disputes—as I will argue below, it decisively resolves the argument between "fundamentalist" and "self-fulfilling" crisis stories. (I was wrong; Maury Obstfeld was right). But it has also raised new questions.

One way to describe the problem is to think in terms of the celebrated (Eichengreen, Rose, and Wyplosz, 1995) distinction between "first-generation" and "second-generation" crisis models. First-generation models, exemplified by Krugman (1979) and the much cleaner paper by Flood and Garber (1984), in effect explain crises as the product of budget deficits: it is the ultimately uncontrollable need of the government for seignorage to cover its deficit that ensures the eventual collapse of a fixed exchange rate, and the efforts of investors to avoid suffering capital losses (or to achieve capital gains) when that collapse occurs provoke a speculative attack when foreign exchange reserves fall below a critical level. Second-generation models, exemplified by Obstfeld (1994), instead explain crises as the result of a conflict between a fixed exchange rate and the desire to pursue a more expansionary monetary policy; when investors begin to suspect that the government will choose to let the parity go, the resulting pressure on interest rates can itself push the government over the edge. Both first- and second-generation models have considerable relevance to particular crises in the 1990s—for example, the Russian crisis of 1998 was evidently driven in the first instance by the (correct) perception that the weak government was about to be forced to finance itself via the printing press, while the sterling crisis of 1992 was equally evidently driven by the perception that the UK government would under pressure choose domestic employment over exchange stability.

In the major crisis countries of Asia, however, neither of these stories seems to have much relevance. By conventional fiscal measures the governments of the afflicted economies were in quite good shape at the beginning of 1997; while growth had slowed and some signs of excess capacity appeared in 1996, none of them faced the kind of clear tradeoff between employment and exchange stability that Britain had faced 5 years earlier (and if depreciation was intended to allow expansionary policies, it rather conspicuously failed!) Clearly something else was at work; we badly need a "third-generation" crisis model both to make sense of the recent crises and to help warn of crises to come.

But what should a third-generation model look like? Most of the recent attempts to produce such a model have argued that the core of the problem lies in the banking system. McKinnon and Pill (1996) and others, myself included (Krugman, 1998), have suggested that moral-hazard-driven lending could have provided a sort of hidden subsidy to investment, which collapsed when visible losses led governments to withdraw their implicit guarantees; this line of thought has been taken to considerable lengths in the influential papers of Corsetti, Pesenti, and Roubini (1998). Meanwhile, an alternative line of work, followed in particular by Chang and Velasco (1998) attempts to explain currency crises as the byproduct of a bank run, modeled a la Diamond and Dybvig (1983) as a self-fulfilling loss of confidence that forces financial intermediaries to liquidate their investments prematurely.

But is a bank-centered view of the crisis really right? Certainly in most cases the financial crisis did involve troubles for banks as well as for currencies. But it also involved other difficulties, most notably an epidemic of financial distress that cannot be resolved simply by fixing the banks. As evidence about the Asian crisis has accumulated, I have found myself increasingly skeptical about whether either a moral-hazard or a Diamond–Dybvig story can really get at the essential nature of what went wrong.

In any case, this paper sketches out yet another candidate for third-generation crisis modeling, one that emphasizes two factors that have been omitted from formal models to date: the role of companies' balance sheets in determining their ability to invest, and that of capital flows in affecting the real exchange rate. The model is at this point quite raw, with several loose ends hanging. However, it seems to me to tell a story with a more realistic "feel" than earlier efforts, my own included. It also sheds some light on the policy dilemmas faced by the IMF and its clients in the last two years.

The remainder of this paper is in five parts. The first discusses in general terms some features of the financial crises of 1997–8, and the failure (in my view) of our models so far to reproduce some key stylized facts. The second part lays out a rough model intended to capture what I now believe to be two essential pieces of the puzzle: the role of balance sheet difficulties in constraining investment by entrepreneurs, and the impact of the real exchange rate on those balance sheets. The third part shows how these effects produce a feedback loop that can cause a potentially healthy economy to experience a self-fulfilling financial crisis. The fourth part offers a crude interpretation of the "IMF strategy" of limiting currency depreciation in order to protect against this balance-sheet effect, and shows how this strategy may simply replace one destructive feedback loop with another. A final section offers some tentative policy conclusions.

## 1. Recent Crises: Stylized Facts and Models

The Asian crisis arrived with little warning. By normal criteria, government budgets were in good shape; current account deficits were large in Thailand and Malaysia, but relatively moderate in Korea and Indonesia; despite some slowdown in growth in 1996, there was not a strong case that any of the countries needed a devaluation for competitive or macroeconomic reasons. Indeed, right up to the summer of 1997 many observers echoed the conclusion of the now-notorious World Bank report, *The East Asian Miracle* (1993), that good macroeconomic and exchange-rate management was a key ingredient in the Asian recipe for success. And as Stiglitz (1998) has emphasized, even after the fact it is very difficult to come up with any set of conventional indicators that picks out the Asian countries as particularly at risk of financial crisis, or identifies 1997–8 as a time of unusual risk.

So what went wrong? As already suggested, there are two major views in the post-crisis theoretical literature.

The first is that underneath the apparent soundness of macroeconomic policy was a large, hidden subsidy to investment via implicit government guarantees to banks, cronies of politicians, etc. The "over-borrowing syndrome" was modeled in advance of the crisis by McKinnon and Pill (1996), and for a time became the reigning orthodoxy after my own brief exposition (Krugman, 1998); Corsetti, Pesenti, and Roubini (1998a,b) have emphasized that to the extent that implicit guarantees led banks to engage in moral-hazard lending, it represented a hidden government budget deficit, and the unfunded liabilities of these banks represented a hidden government debt. According to this view, then, the apparent soundness of budgetary and macroeconomic policy was an illusion: under the surface, the governments were actually engaged in reckless and unsustainable spending.

The alternative view, strongly expressed by Radelet and Sachs (1998), is that the countries were not doing anything wrong; their investments were basically sound. At most they can be said to have suffered from some kind of "financial fragility" that made them vulnerable to self-fulfilling pessimism on the part of international lenders. Chang and Velasco (1998a,b) have made the most thoroughly worked-out attempt to model this financial fragility, relying on a version of the Diamond–Dybvig (1983) model of bank runs. In this model, investors face a choice between short-term investments with a low rate of return and long-run investments with a higher rate of return; unfortunately, the long-run investments yield relatively little if they must be liquidated prematurely, and investors are assumed to be unsure ex ante about when they will want to consume. Financial intermediaries can resolve this dilemma by pooling the resources of many investors and relying on the law of large numbers to avoid holding more short-term assets than necessary. However, such intermediaries then become vulnerable to self-fulfilling panics, in which fear of losses leads depositors to demand immediate payment, forcing destructive liquidation of long-run assets that validates these fears. In a closed economy the central bank can protect against such panics by acting as a lender of last resort; Chang and Velasco argue that in an open economy with a fixed exchange rate, the limited size of the central bank's reserves may prevent it from playing the same role.

There is no question that both of these views capture some aspects of what happened to Asia. On one side, "crony capitalism" was certainly a reality: the excesses of Thai financial companies, of members of the Suharto family, of megalomaniac *chaebol* are undeniable. On the other side, bank runs played an important role in the unfolding of the crisis, particularly in Indonesia, and a freezing up of the credit system played at least some role in deepening the recession after the crisis hit.

Yet as evidence about the crisis has accumulated, both explanations have come to seem inadequate to the task of explaining the severity of the event.

Consider first the moral hazard argument. If one really takes that argument seriously, it implies not only that there should be over-investment and excessive risk-taking by entrepreneurs with access to guaranteed finance, but also that the availability of implicit guarantees should tend to crowd out "legitimate" investment that bears the full burden of risk. Yet as Radelet and Sachs point out, in the runup to the crisis all forms of investment in the emerging Asian economies were booming, including direct foreign purchases of equity and real estate, investments that clearly were *not* protected by any form of implicit guarantee. One might point to the severity of the problem of non-performing loans after the crisis as evidence that bad banking was a key problem in the crisis economies. But as many observers have noted, and as is documented in the recent World Bank report *The Road to Recovery* (1998), the bulk of the bad loan problem is a *consequence* of the crisis—of the severe recessions and currency depreciations that followed the collapse of capital inflows. Since nobody expected a crisis of anything like this severity, the prevalence of bad loans we observe ex post does not mean that anything like the same amount of bad lending was taking place ex ante.

What about the financial fragility story? Here my main concern is not so much with Chang and Velasco as with Diamond–Dybvig—specifically, with the way that financial fragility and its real effects are modeled. In the Diamond–Dybvig model the costs of premature liquidation are *physical*—a bank run literally leads to investments being cannibalized before completion, with the output cost to the economy the result of a literal destruction of physical capital. There are a few real examples of this process in Asia—half-completed structures left to disintegrate for lack of funding, or dismantled for scrap metal. There are also some more complex stories that can be viewed metaphorically as examples of physical liquidation—for example, potentially profitable export opportunities not taken because working capital has been sold to pay off bank loans. But surely the main channels through which financial panic has turned good assets into bad involve not so much physical liquidation of unfinished projects as macroeconomic crisis: companies that looked solvent before the crisis have gone under because collapsing investment has produced a severe recession, or because capital flight has led to currency depreciation that makes their dollar debts balloon. Or to put it another way, Diamond and Dybvig used a physical metaphor for the costs of premature liquidation as a way to focus on the problem of multiple equilibria on the part of depositors; fair enough. But to make sense of the Asian crisis it is probably important to have a better metaphor, one that comes closer to matching the stylized facts of actual experience.

What are these stylized facts? Let me suggest three facts that a model should probably address—and which some or all of the existing models do not, as far as I can tell, seem to capture.

(i) *Contagion*: The most stunning aspect of the global financial crisis has been the way that events in small economies like Thailand or Russia have led more or less directly to crises in economies thousands of miles distant, with few direct trade or financial links.

From my point of view the power of contagion in the last two years settles a long-running dispute about currency crises in general: the dispute between "fundamentalists" and "self-fulfillers." In the original first-generation models, the suddenness of currency crises did not mean that their timing was arbitrary; on the contrary, such crises emerged when some set of fundamental factors (typically the level of reserves) fell below a critical level. Obstfeld (1994) argued that in second-generation models, by contrast, the timing of crisis was indeed arbitrary; in fact, a currency crisis could occur to a country whose fixed exchange rate might otherwise have survived indefinitely. I argued in reply (Krugman, 1996) that this was a misleading point: the reason that the timing of crisis seemed determinate in first-generation models was not because of the difference in the mechanism of crisis, but because in those models there was assumed to be a secular deterioration in the fundamentals—a deterioration that ensured, through backward induction, that a speculative attack would always occur as soon as it could succeed. This point was, I still think, correct. However, I then went on to argue that we should view a predictable secular deterioration in fundamentals as the normal case, whatever the specifics of the model, and that spontaneous self-fulfilling crises would therefore be rare events.

I hereby capitulate. I cannot see any way to make sense of the contagion of 1997–8 without supposing the existence of multiple equilibria, with countries vulnerable to self-validating collapses in confidence, collapses that could be set off by events in faraway economies that somehow served as a trigger for self-fulfilling pessimism. It follows that any useful model of the crisis must involve some mechanism that produces these multiple equilibria—a criterion met by the financial fragility models, but not by the moral hazard approach.

(ii) *The transfer problem*: If there is a single statistic that captures the violence of the shock to Asia most dramatically, it is the reversal in the current account: in the case of Thailand, for example, the country was forced by the reversal of capital flows to go from a deficit of some 10 percent of GDP in 1996 to a surplus of 8 percent in 1998. The need to effect such a huge change in the current account represents what may be history's most spectacular example of the classic "transfer problem" debated by Keynes and Ohlin in the 1920s. In practice this swing has been achieved partly through massive real depreciation, partly though severe recession that produces a compression of imports.

Yet despite the evident centrality of the transfer problem to what actually happened to Asia, this issue has been remarkably absent from formal models. Perhaps because the modelers have been mainly concerned with the behavior of investors rather than with the real economy per se, all of the major models so far have been one-good models in which domestic goods can be freely converted into foreign and vice versa without any movement in the terms of trade or the real exchange rate.

Is this an acceptable strategic simplification? Perhaps not: in the model I develop below, the difficulty of effecting a transfer, the need to achieve the current account counterpart of a reversal of capital flows either via real depreciation or via recession, turns out to be the heart of the story.

(iii) *Balance sheet problems*: Finally, descriptive accounts both of the problems of the crisis countries and of the policy discussions that led the crisis to be handled in the way it was place extensive emphasis on the problems of firms' balance sheets. On one side, the deterioration of these balance sheets played a key role in the crisis itself—notably, the explosion in the domestic currency value of dollar debt had a disastrous effect on Indonesian firms, and fear of corresponding balance sheet effects was a main reason why the IMF was concerned to avoid massive depreciation of its clients' currencies. On the other side, the prospects for recovery are now, by all accounts, especially difficult because of the weakened financial condition of firms, whose capital has in many cases been wiped out by the combination of declining sales, high interest rates, and a depreciated currency. Notice that while these balance sheet problems are in turn a cause of the problem of non-performing loans at the banks, they are not a banking problem per se; even a recapitalization of the banks would still leave the problem of financially weakened companies untouched.

The role of balance-sheet problems in constraining firms has been the subject of some recent work in the macroeconomics literature, notably Kiyotaki and Moore (1997) and Bernanke, Gertler, and Gilchrist (forthcoming). So far, however, despite the attention given to balance sheets in practical discussions, the issue has been neglected in the currency crisis literature.

What I will do in the remainder of this paper, then, is to try to develop a model informed by these observations. As in the Diamond–Dybvig approach, this is a model potentially characterized by multiple equilibria, in which a loss of confidence can produce a financial collapse that validates investor pessimism. However, the mechanism of that collapse is different: instead of creating losses via the premature liquidation of physical assets, a loss of confidence leads to a transfer problem. That is, in order to achieve the required reversal of its current account, the country must experience a large real depreciation; this depreciation, in turn, worsens the balance sheets of domestic firms, validating the loss of confidence. A policy that attempts to limit the real depreciation implies a decline in output instead—and this, too, can validate the collapse of confidence.

Moreover, once the crisis occurs it can have a sustained impact on the economy, because of that impact on balance sheets; as one Thai economist recently put it, the crisis leads to the "decapitation of the entrepreneurial class," and the economy cannot return to normal until it manages either to repair the balance sheets of its existing entrepreneurs or grows a new set.

It seems to me that this story—in which, incidentally, banks do not necessarily play a key role, although they could presumably also be introduced—comes closer than any of the previous models to having the right "feel" for making sense of recent events. But in any case, let us now proceed to the statement and analysis of the model.

## 2. The Model

I consider an open economy that produces a single good each period using capital and labor; for simplicity the production function is assumed Cobb–Douglas:

$$y_t = G(K_t, L_t) = K_t^{\alpha} L_t^{1-\alpha} \tag{1}$$

Capital is created through investment; I will assume, again for simplicity, that capital lasts only one period, so that this period's capital is equal to last period's investment. (This assumption also puts to one side Diamond–Dybvig-type concerns over maturity mismatch).

The residents of this economy are divided into two distinct classes. Workers play a passive role—they lack access to the capital market, and therefore must spend all their income within each period. Capital is both created and owned by a class of entrepreneurs, who are assumed to be single-mindedly engaged in accumulation at this point, saving and investing (either at home or abroad) all their income. Only these entrepreneurs have the ability to undertake domestic investment, which as we will soon see plays a crucial role in the story.

The good produced by this country is *not* a perfect substitute for traded goods produced elsewhere. Indeed, I will assume (yet another simplification) that there is a unitary elasticity of substitution, with a share $\mu$ of both consumption and investment spending on imports, $1 - \mu$ on domestic goods. The rest of the world is assumed to be much larger than the domestic economy, and to spend a negligible fraction of its income on domestic goods. (The disparity between the domestic and foreign marginal propensities to spend on domestic goods—$1 - \mu$ in the case of domestic spending, 0 for foreign spending—gives rise to the transfer problem that is crucial to this approach). If the foreign elasticity of substitution is also 1, the value of domestic exports in terms of foreign goods is fixed, say at $X$, and the value in terms of domestic goods is therefore $pX$, where $p$ is the relative price of foreign goods (a.k.a real exchange rate).

Bearing in mind that a share $1 - \alpha$ of domestic income accrues to workers who must spend it, and defining $I$ and $C$ as investment and consumption expenditures in terms of domestic goods, we can determine the real exchange rate as follows. Market clearing for domestic goods requires that

$$y = (1 - \mu)I + (1 - \mu)C + pX = (1 - \mu)I + (1 - \alpha)(1 - \mu)y + pX \tag{2}$$

which implies

$$p_t = \frac{y_t[1 - (1 - \alpha)(1 - \mu)] - (1 - \mu)I_t}{X} \tag{3}$$

We can immediately notice that the higher is investment, the lower the real exchange rate.

The next step is to describe the determination of investment. The central idea here is that the ability of entrepreneurs to invest may be limited by their wealth. Specifically, following Bernanke et al (forthcoming) I assume that lenders impose a limit on leverage: entrepreneurs can borrow at most $\lambda$ times their initial wealth.

$$I_t \leq (1 + \lambda)W_t \tag{4}$$

Underlying this limitation on borrowing, presumably, are some kind of microeconomic motives, probably involving asymmetric information. For the purposes of this paper, however, I simply assume the existence of the constraint and take $\lambda$ as a given.

This constraint need not be binding; although entrepreneurs are assumed to save all of their income, they may choose not to borrow up to the limit. In particular, they will not borrow beyond the point at which the real return on domestic investment equals that on foreign investment. One way to determine this limit is to compare the foreign real interest rate, $r^*$, with the return achieved by converting foreign goods into domestic, then converting the next-period return back into foreign goods. Because a share $\mu$ of investment falls on foreign goods, the price index for investment relative to that of domestic output is $p^{-\mu}$; the return on investment in terms of domestic goods is therefore

$$1 + r_t = G_k(I_{t-1}p^{-\mu}, L) \tag{5}$$

But a unit of foreign goods can be converted into $p_t$ units of domestic goods this period, the return converted into $1/p_{t+1}$ units next period; so the statement that the return on domestic investment must be at least as large as that on foreign bonds may be written

$$(1 + r_t)(p_t/p_{t+1}) \geq 1 + r^* \tag{6}$$

Finally, investment cannot be negative:

$$I_t \geq 0 \tag{7}$$

As we will see, depending on circumstances (4), (6), or (7) may be the binding constraint.

The last element in the statement of the model is the definition of entrepreneurs' wealth. Domestic entrepreneurs own all domestic capital; they may also own other claims on foreigners, and/or have debts to foreigners. I assume that some claims are denominated in terms of the domestic good, others in terms of the foreign good; meanwhile, since capital lasts only one period, the value of domestic capital is simply the income accruing to capital within the current period. Let $D$, $F$ be the net debts of domestic entrepreneurs indexed to domestic and foreign goods respectively; I will sloppily refer to these as "domestic currency" and "foreign currency" debt respectively, although they are really denominated in goods rather than moneys. Then the wealth of entrepreneurs in period $t$ is

$$W_t = \alpha y - D - pF \tag{8}$$

Obviously a full model should try to endogenize the "currency composition" (again, actually goods composition, since the model is not explicitly monetary) of debt; again, however, I simply take it as a given.

We now have a rough but workable model that can be used to examine one way in which a financial crisis can occur in an open economy.

## 3. The Transfer Problem and Financial Crisis

According to our model, the amount that domestic entrepreneurs can borrow from foreigners to finance investment depends on their wealth. At the same time, however, the wealth of each individual entrepreneur itself depends on the level of such borrowing in the economy as a whole, because the volume of capital inflow affects the terms of trade and hence the valuation of foreign-currency-denominated debt. We can therefore immediately see the outlines of a story about financial crisis: a decline in capital inflows can adversely affect the balance sheets of domestic entrepreneurs, reducing their ability to borrow and hence further reducing capital inflows. But we need to be a bit more precise.

Imagine a game in which lenders decide, in random order, how much credit to offer to successive domestic entrepreneurs. The offer of credit depends on what the lenders *think* will be the value of the borrower's collateral. But because some debt is denominated in foreign goods, this value depends on the real exchange rate, and hence on the actual level of borrowing that takes place. A rational-expectations equilibrium of this game will be a set of self-confirming guesses—that is, the expected level of investment implicit in the credit offers must match the actual level of investment that takes place given those offers.

As a first step, let us derive the relationship between investment and the wealth of entrepreneurs. From (8), we know that wealth depends, other things being the same, on the real exchange rate $p$; from (3) we know that $p$ depends on $I$. We therefore have that

$$\frac{dW}{dI} = \frac{(1-\mu)F}{X} \tag{9}$$

Let us define $I_f$ as the "financeable" level of investment—that is, the level of investment that would occur if the leverage constraint (4) were binding. Since the ability of entrepreneurs to borrow depends on their wealth, we have

$$\frac{dI_f}{dI} = \frac{(1+\lambda)(1-\mu)F}{X} \tag{10}$$

If $dI_f/dI$ is less than 1, the behavior of this model is relatively uninteresting: an economy with a high rate of return on investment may find that adjustment in its capital stock is delayed by financing constraints, but there will be nothing resembling an Asian-style financial crisis. But suppose that $dI_f/dI > 1$. Then there can indeed be multiple equilibria, with the possibility that a loss of lender confidence will be validated by financial collapse.

The picture would look like Figure 1.[1] On the horizontal axis is the expected level of investment, which determines via its effect on the real exchange rate, and hence on balance sheets, how much credit is extended to domestic firms. On the vertical axis is the actual level of investment that results. (The picture could alternatively be drawn in terms of the expected and actual levels of $p$). At high levels of expected $I$ the financing constraint (4) is not binding; instead, investment is determined by the rate-of-return constraint (6). At low levels of expected $I$ firms are bankrupt, and cannot invest at all—that is, they are hard against the non-negativity constraint (7). In an intermediate range $I$ is constrained by financing, and the schedule is therefore steeper than the 45-degree line.

There are clearly three equilibria in this picture. The intermediate, internal equilibrium may be dismissed as likely to be unstable under any plausible mechanism of expectation formation. This leaves us with two possible outcomes: a high-level outcome $H$ in which investment takes place up to the point where domestic and foreign rates of return are equal; and a low-level outcome $L$ in which lenders do not believe that domestic entrepreneurs have any collateral, their failure to provide funds means a depreciated real exchange rate, and that unfavorable real exchange rate means that entrepreneurs are in fact bankrupt, validating lenders' poor opinion.

And we therefore now have our extremely stylized version of the Asian financial crisis: something—it does not matter what—caused lenders to become suddenly pessimistic, and

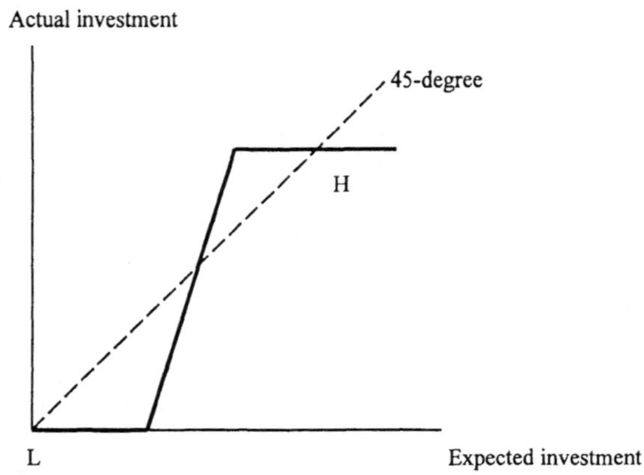


*Figure 1.*

the result was a collapse from $H$ to $L$. The collapse does not indicate that the previous investments were unsound; the problem is instead one of financial fragility.

The difference between this story of financial fragility and that told by Chang and Velasco can be highlighted by considering the conditions under which this fragility can occur—namely, when $dI_f/dI > 1$. By construction here, this criterion has nothing to do with the mismatch between short-term debt and long-term investments; nor does it appear to depend on foreign exchange reserves. Instead, as we see from (10), the factors that can make financial collapse possible are:

(i) High leverage

(ii) Low marginal propensity to import

(iii) Large foreign-currency debt relative to exports

These factors matter, of course, because they make the circular loop from investment to real exchange rate to balance sheets to investment more powerful.

We can now also offer a possible answer to the great mystery: Why Asia? Why now? If we ask what was special about Asian economies, something that may have made them peculiarly vulnerable to financial crisis, the answer is high leverage: all of the now afflicted countries had unusually high levels of $\lambda$. If we ask why now—given that high leverage, "crony capitalism," etc. have been characteristic of Asian economies for decades—the answer is that only after 1990 did these economies begin extensive borrowing denominated in foreign currencies, borrowing that placed them at risk of financial collapse if the real exchange rate depreciated.

## 4. The Dilemma of Stabilization

Although standard models of currency crisis have not to date taken account of the problems posed by foreign-currency debt, practitioners have been aware of this issue for decades. And the risks of financial trauma because of that debt were a major reason why the IMF advised its Asian clients to follow the much-criticized "IMF strategy" of defending their currencies with high interest rates rather than simply letting them decline.

This model does not allow a direct analysis of monetary policy. We can, however, take a very rough cut at the nature and consequences of the IMF strategy by imagining that the effect of that strategy is to hold the real exchange rate $p$ constant even when the willingness of foreign lenders to finance investment declines. In that case, of course, something else must give; and the natural assumption is that output declines instead.

Indeed, if we hold $p$ constant, output will be determined by a sort of quasi-Keynesian multiplier process; rearranging (2) we have

$$y = \frac{pX + (1-\mu)I}{1-(1-\alpha)(1-\mu)} \tag{11}$$

But given that a share $\alpha$ of output goes to profits, a decline in investment will reduce entrepreneurs' wealth:

$$\frac{dW}{dI} = \frac{\alpha(1-\mu)}{1-(1-\alpha)(1-\mu)} \tag{12}$$

and hence once again there will be a feedback from actual to financeable investment:

$$\frac{dI_f}{dI} = \frac{(1+\lambda)\alpha(1-\mu)}{1-(1-\alpha)(1-\mu)} \tag{13}$$

It is immediately clear that stabilizing the real exchange rate, while closing one channel for potential financial collapse, opens another: if leverage is high, the economy may stabilize its real exchange rate only at the expense of a self-reinforcing decline in output that produces an equivalent decapitation of the entrepreneurial class.

## 5. Policy Implications

One would ordinarily be somewhat diffident about drawing policy implications from so rough a framework. However, policy must be and is being made, by and large without any explicit analytical framework at all; so here are some conclusions inspired from the model. They pertain to three rather different questions. First is the question of prophylactic measures: what can we do to prevent such crises in the future? Second is the question of policy in the crisis: how can the crisis be halted or at least limited? Finally there is the question of what to do once the crisis has occurred: how does one rebuild the economy?

*Prophylactic measures*: In the aftermath of the Asian crisis, a broad consensus has emerged among responsible people that countries need to take much greater care with their banking systems—that they need "transparency," better capital standards, more careful regulation of risk-taking, an end to cronyism, etc. Underlying such recommendations is the belief that the crisis was largely due either to moral hazard, Diamond–Dybvig-type problems, or both. And it is hard to disagree that such measures are a good thing. If I am right about the mechanism of crisis, however, even a very clean and prudent banking system may not be enough to protect open economies from the risk of self-reinforcing financial collapse.

A more controversial proposal is for the widespread imposition of Chilean-type restrictions on short-term borrowing denominated in foreign currencies. The idea here is that by reducing short-term foreign-currency exposure, countries can reduce the risks of being forced into crisis by a loss of confidence.

I have been skeptical about this argument on the general grounds that as long as a country has free convertibility of capital, short-term foreign loans are only one of many different possible sources of capital flight. We cannot deal with the issue of maturity structure in this model, since such issues have been ruled out by assumption. But in the spirit of the model, consider the following situation: domestic firms are financed by a mixture of short-term debt denominated in domestic currency, and long-term debt denominated in foreign currency. Does the fact that the foreign currency debt is long-term protect the country from financial crisis? Surely not: if people expect a financial crisis, the holders of domestic short-term debt will refuse to roll it over, generating an exchange rate depreciation that bankrupts the firms even though the foreign-currency debt itself is long term.

So what is the appropriate prophylactic policy? The answer from this model, at any rate, seems to be to discourage firms from taking on foreign-currency-denominated debt of any maturity. Loosely speaking, there appears to be a sort of external diseconomy to borrowing in foreign currencies: because such borrowing magnifies the real-exchange-rate impact of adverse shocks, and because real depreciation interacts with capital-market imperfections to cause economic distress, the decision by an individual firm to borrow in dollars imposes costs on the rest of the economy.

*Dealing with crisis*: Much of the vituperative public debate over how to deal with crisis has involved the question of whether to let the exchange rate go or stabilize it. The answer suggested by this model is that this is a real choice, but that both answers may be equally bad. Is there a third way?

One possibility would be the provision of emergency lines of credit. However, in the context of this model it appears that these credit lines would have to do more than provide balance-of-payments financing, or even provide lender-of-last resort facilities to banks: they would have to make up the credit being lost by firms, so as to allow investment to continue. Thus the credit lines would have to be very large indeed, and also be accompanied by a mechanism that funnels the funds to troubled entrepreneurs. (This would be especially difficult politically, since in the midst of crisis there is widespread and often justified vilification of those same entrepreneurs, on the grounds that their excesses brought on the crisis in the first place). Of course if one takes the model seriously, a sufficiently large credit line would never actually have to be used, since its very existence would prevent the crisis from ever getting under way (but one has to be credibly willing to use it in order not to have to).

Another possibility is to rule out the possibility of a downward financial spiral by being ready to impose a curfew on capital flight. Again, there is substantial sympathy even among respectable opinion for standstill agreements on foreign-currency debt; but this may well not be sufficient, if capital-account convertibility means that other forms of capital flight are still possible. All of which raises the possibility that it might be necessary, and even in the interests of investors themselves, to impose emergency capital controls . . . enough said.

*After the fall*: Finally, what we hope is the current question: once the crisis has happened, how does one get the economy going again? To date most actual efforts have focused on bank restructuring and recapitalization; but if this model is on the right track, this will not be sufficient. The main problem at this point, the model (like many practitioners) suggests, is that the firms and entrepreneurs who drove investment and growth before the crisis are now effectively bankrupt and unable to raise capital.

If this is right, the key to resuming growth is either to rescue those entrepreneurs, through some kind of "private sector Brady Plan," or to grow a new set of entrepreneurs—or both. A likely source of new entrepreneurs is, of course, from abroad: a welcome mat for foreign direct investment might be just what the doctor ordered.

Again, all of this is based on a liberal interpretation of a very rough model. It seems to me, however, that this model does provide at least a different perspective on how to think about these issues.

As I said at the beginning of this paper, the Asian crisis inspires mixed emotions in those of us who, like Bob Flood, have shared a decades-long fascination with the issue of currency crises. Our obsession has been spectacularly and tragically vindicated; but the world seems to keep finding new ways to generate crises. Let us hope that the lessons of this "third-generation" crisis are learned, and that no future crises arise in the same way; but even if that hope is fulfilled, one can be sure that there are many more generations to come.

## Notes

1. Strictly speaking, there are two other possibilities even if $dI_f/dI > 1$. If domestic-currency debt is very high, entrepreneurs may be unable to borrow even with a favorable exchange rate; if $D$ is low, even a very unfavorable rate will not cause financial collapse. I neglect these cases for the sake of the main story.

## References

Bernanke, Ben, Mark Gertler, and Simon Gilchrist. (forthcoming). "The Financial Accelerator in a Quantitative Business Cycle Framework." In J. Taylor and M. Woodford (eds.), *Handbook of Macroeconomics*.

Chang, Roberto, and Andres Velasco. (1998). "Financial Crises in Emerging Markets: A Canonical Model." NBER Working Paper No. 6606.

Corsetti, Giancarlo, Paolo Pesenti, and Nouriel Roubini. (1998). "Paper Tigers? A Model of the Asian Crisis." Mimeo.

Diamond, Douglas, and Philip Dybvig. (1983). "Bank Runs, Deposit Insurance, and Liquidity." *Journal of Political Economy* 91 401–419.

Eichengreen, Barry, Andrew Rose, and Charles Wyplosz. (1995). "Exchange Market Mayhem: The Antecedents and Aftermath of Speculative Attacks." *Economic Policy*, 251–312.

Flood, Robert, and Peter Garber. (1984). "Collapsing Exchange Rate Regimes: Some Linear Examples." *Journal of International Economics* 17, 1–13.
Kiyotaki, Nobuhiro, and John Moore. (1997). "Credit Cycles." *Journal of Political Economy* 105, 211–248.
Krugman, Paul. (1979). "A Model of Balance-of-Payments Crises." *Journal of Money, Credit, and Banking* 11, 311–325.
Krugman, Paul. (1996). "Are Currency Crises Self-Fulfilling?" In B. Bernanke and J. Rotemberg (eds.), *NBER Macroeconomics Annual 1996*. Cambridge: MIT Press.
Krugman, Paul. (1998). "What Happened to Asia?" Mimeo, MIT.
McKinnon, Ronald, and Huw Pill. (1996). "Credible Liberalizations and International Capital Flows: The 'Overborrowing Syndrome.'" In T. Ito and A. Krueger (eds.), *Financial Deregulation and Integration in East Asia*. Chicago: University of Chicago Press.
Obstfeld, Maurice. (1994). "The Logic of Currency Crises." *Cahiers economique et monetaires* 43, 189–212.
Radelet, Steven, and Jeffrey Sachs. (1998). "The Onset of the East Asian Financial Crisis." Mimeo.

# Comment

BY PETER GARBER

As usual, there is much with which I can agree in Paul's paper.

First, and most importantly, the balance sheet problems of the corporates in Asia are currently at the heart of the problem, and this has been widely known since the Korean and Indonesian collapses. Resolving the banks through capital injections, removal of bad loans from the books, and rationalization will not solve the credit problem. Even after being written off, bad loans remain as claims against the borrowers, so they will not attract further credit—especially not from a soundly-run banking system. Eventually, new creditworthy borrowers will appear, of course, but because the bulk of corporate activity is in entities with impaired credit, recovery will take a long time.

Second, and as usual, thinking along the lines of the Diamond–Dybvig bank-run model does not take us very far and, indeed, misleads us about the basic causes of banking problems. The historical ratio of banks that failed because they were run, to banks that were run because they had failed, is near zero. Yet, every time we face a banking crisis the Diamond–Dybvig model is invoked. Rarely has the disconnect between our esthetic preference for modeling elegance and our need to understand real events been so stark. Automatically applying the concept at the country level has generated an equally unreal view. Let us remember that the chaebols were going bankrupt in Korea, and the finance companies were going bankrupt in Thailand, before the attacks on their currencies.

Third, the Asia crisis has provided one case for multiple equilibria. Malaysia has a two-state leader. In the branch of events where capital kept flowing in and stayed in, he would always be congenial to foreign capital. This equilibrium would be self-generated if capital stayed in. In the branch of events where capital flowed out, he would impose controls. This equilibrium would be self-generated if foreign investors started to pull out. Thus, we score a point for the Dellas–Stockman version of the multiple equilibrium model. Indeed, if Paul's prescription to impose capital controls as a response to an attack is ever taken seriously as a policy, we are immediately in a multiple-equilibrium world.

Fourth, it is necessary to get the Asian entrepreneurs started again, including with foreign ownership. I would say especially with foreign ownership. Indeed, this policy prescription has been at the heart of the U.S. Treasury's policy toward the crisis, which has recognized from the outset the need to restructure massively local corporates with foreign money. This is what is behind the Treasury's push to force the restructuring of the chaebols in Korea, which have valuable industrial properties. Korea is an especially important case that shows that rescuing the banks is not enough—and is in fact counterproductive. The banks' only outlet for lending is to the very chaebols that should be restructured, but that are the lowest credit risks because of likely bailouts.

There are several places where I think Paul has pulled rabbits out of hats, however.

First, he has bought into the Generation 1, 2, 3, . . . , *n* characterization of speculative attacks. The use of this characterization is a prime example of what many of us fondly call a name swindle. Generation 1 and 2 models are really twins that were born almost simultaneously. Generation 3 is still non-existent, a Madison Avenue concept like Generation X or the Pepsi Generation. Pulling out a new generation of models for each new crisis speaks more about the sociology of academic economics than it does about the usefulness of previously existing models.

Indeed, Paul and others have characterized the 1980's style speculative attack models in a most strangely narrow way—they claim that in these models crises are driven by domestic credit creation. This was true of the earliest versions of the model, which were streamlined to the maximum extent in order to make the initial intellectual sale. But it ignores the development and empirical implementation of the model throughout the 1980s, in which anything that enters the money demand function or money supply process can contribute to triggering a crisis—real exchange rate movements, money demand disturbances (both domestic and from abroad), real income movements, foreign interest rates or real income movements, and changes in the processes that generate the future realizations of these variables. In the single equilibrium models, the constellation of these forcing variables is exogenous to the exchange rate—i.e., they cause and are not caused by the movements in the exchange rate—although they may be simultaneously determined among themselves. In the multiple equilibrium models, they are endogenous to the exchange rate or exchange rate regime—i.e., they are co-determined with the exchange rate. Endogeneity vs. exogeneity of other relevant variables to the exchange rate is what distinguishes multiple (Generation 2) from single (Generation 1) equilibrium models of crisis, not a narrow vs. a broad list of forcing variables.

Second, Paul rejects the moral hazard view of the crisis that he and many others have earlier postulated. This moral hazard view is congenial to the classical crisis model's view of crises—the governments had ongoing quasi-deficits because of their implicit guarantees of the banks that would eventually become visible and could not be financed because they were backed by trash projects.

He rejects this view because all forms of foreign investment in Asian markets were underway—e.g., direct foreign purchases of equity and real estate. Unlike loans to local banks, these were not guaranteed, so moral hazard could not have been a factor for them. Also, he argues—citing the World Bank's *The Road to Recovery* (1998)—that the bulk of the bad loans that materialized resulted from the unforeseen severity of the downturn, and not from ex ante bad lending.

Here the rush to the new model has made Paul and the World Bank excessively glib. (The World Bank has its own axe to grind.) It is well-known that local government guarantees (backed in part by implicit IMF guarantees) were only one side of the moral hazard problem. There was moral hazard emanating from lender country guarantees as well. The dead banks walking of Japan and also those of Korea were major lenders directly to corporates in other Asian countries and indirectly through the securities markets. That they took losses on these activities that were not covered by local guarantees does not undermine the moral hazard story—they were covered by the Japanese taxpayers' willingness forever to be sheared.

Nobody expected a crisis of this magnitude because the bad news was obscured both by official interference with information flows—even extending to direct censorship and the use of the criminal system—and by private lender incentives to obscure the risks they were taking to their supervisors. If there is a massive amount of bad lending that is hard to observe, for a period there will be massively excessive growth, as we now see in China. When the piper has to be paid and the non-viability of the projects is revealed, the unexpected crisis will be severe, but it is a non-sequitur to conclude that the ex ante lending was not high risk or bad.

Third, throughout his various analyses of the eighteen months of world crisis, Paul has confessed to being confused and "stunned" by the way that events in Russia have been connected to other dissimilar and unrelated economies. We also would be intellectually stunned by events if the range of models that we use to give structure to events are wildly at odds with what we observe in financial markets. We have several choices at this point. We can admit that our mental model is too rigid—I would say too macro—and investigate more carefully what the connection might be. Alternatively, we can without any direct observation blame the deviation on crazed 29-year-old green screen traders, as Paul has done elsewhere, who make "countries vulnerable to self-validating collapses in confidence, collapses that could be set off by events in faraway economies that somehow served as a trigger for self-fulfilling pessimism."

Bob Flood and I have long argued that the invocation of the bubble or self-fulfilling story of asset price collapse is the easy and empty way of explaining a deviation of asset prices from one's internal model of fundamentals. It is empty because it makes our theories of asset prices tautological. It relies as the primary explanation of events on expectations and behaviors on the part of traders that we cannot observe. Imagine that we regress an asset price on the fundamentals implied by our maintained theory of asset prices. For some observations, there will be a large deviation of the realized price from the in-sample forecast. Generally, we call this deviation epsilon, the unobservable and unexplainable random disturbance. If we get enough of these big epsilons, we might reject the model of fundamentals and do the hard work of starting again to look for a new one. Alternatively, we might keep our model and say we have found a self-generating epsilon. Financial market and exchange rate work undertaken by international macroeconomists is unique in that we give names to our epsilons—bubbles, herding, contagion, self-validating multiple equilibria—all of them devoid of observable or verifiable content.

A little scratching below the surface makes clear many of the cross-country financial connections in the past two years. First, what connected Russia to Brazil in the August 1998 crisis was the new information that lenders would be subjected to much more punitive restructurings in potential IMF program countries. That is something very tangible. Automatic risk control mechanisms imposed by industrial country regulators to control moral hazard—certainly not by green-screen traders who have the opposite incentive—then acted to tighten credit generally. In earlier phases of the crisis, there was a direct financial connection across financial markets. Korean banks were notorious risk takers; they lent to other Asian countries, especially through Peregrine to Indonesia in massive amounts. They also had a taste for Brazilian and Russian risk. When the October 1997 Asian crisis hit, the Korean banks needed cash and pulled funds out of Brazil and Russia. Brazilians also love risk. They had large leveraged positions in Brazilian Bradies and large positions in Russian paper. The October 1997 Asia crisis led to a general widening of emerging market spreads and particularly hit the Brazilian speculators hard. Getting margin calls, they could get the needed dollars by going to their central bank—and this looked like a run on the real. They could also get them by selling their Russian claims. There is very little puzzle about what connected these markets once you learn that "globalization" is more than a cliché—it means the intimate cross-connection of financial markets, if it means anything at all.

# Comment

BY OLIVIER JEANNE

This paper is significant for at least two reasons. First, it is the statement of a conversion. In a 1996 Brookings paper, Paul Krugman had expressed his skepticism about the idea that we should view currency crises as self-fulfilling events. In this paper he explains why the Asian crisis has made him revise his earlier judgment. And second, the paper proposes a "third generation" model which, by its elegance and simplicity, could aspire to become a canonical model of the Asian crisis.

Paul Krugman's conversion to the self-fulfilling view will undoubtedly be noted as symbolic of a more general shift of opinion in the profession. In one decade the self-fulfilling hypothesis has gone from the status of theoretical curiosity to that of a theory accepted by many, if not a majority, of economists. It may be interesting to put Krugman in perspective by recalling briefly the main steps of this evolution.

The self-fulfilling view started to be discussed seriously following the EMS crisis of 1992–3, most notably with the work of Obstfeld. Curiously, the emergence of this particular theme at this particular time looks, in retrospect, like an accident of theory. There is not much in the EMS crisis that makes it more suggestive of self-fulfilling speculation than any other crisis. What the EMS crisis made clear was the inadequacy of models where the crisis is the mechanical consequence of excessively expansionary monetary policy, and the need to develop models based on the conflict between external and internal objectives of policymakers. A priori, this conflict can be thought of completely separately from multiple equilibria. However, it also happened that the so-called "second generation" models generically gave rise to multiple equilibria, and thus became the vehicle for a debate on self-fulfilling speculation.[1]

True, some features of the EMS crisis were suggestive of multiple equilibria, but these features were not specific to the EMS crisis. For example, it was noted that the crisis was preceded by a slow and predictable degradation of the fundamentals,[2] but erupted suddenly and unexpectedly without dramatic concomitant fundamental development. The same can be said about all currency crises, however. Moreover, as Krugman (1996) argued, the apparent disconnection between fundamental developments and the timing of crises is not irrefutable proof of self-fulfilling speculation since it can be reproduced by second generation models with learning and no multiple equilibria.

The "manifest sign" in Paul Krugman's conversion to the self-fulfilling view was contagion. Contagion, he states in the opening paragraph of the paper, "decisively resolves the argument between "fundamentalist" and "self-fulfilling" crisis stories" in favor of the latter. I am less confident that contagion will condemn the remaining skeptics to silence. More likely, the reluctant skeptics will resist the evidence by staying on Krugman's (1996) line, namely that contagion may be the result of something other than multiple equilibria.[3] First, apparent contagion could reflect learning about common hidden fundamentals. A problem in one country leads investors to revise their beliefs about other countries that share the same hidden characteristics. For example, to the extent that Thailand and other Southeast Asian countries were perceived to share the same model of bank-firm relationships and the same weakness in banking supervision, a bank failure in Thailand was bad news not only for Thailand (and its creditors) but for the whole region. True, the learning story can hardly explain contagion from, say, Russia to Brazil. But then a second explanation in terms of financial spillovers can be called upon to fill the gap. International investors liquidated their positions in Brazil to meet the margin calls resulting from their losses in Russia.[4]

I am not arguing in favor of these explanations. My point is rather to express skepticism about the possibility of an irrefutable argument that will "settle the dispute." Maybe this reflects, to some extent, a disillusion with my own attempts at finding an econometric test of the self-fulfilling hypothesis (Jeanne, 1997). The problem is a familiar one. While a lot of evidence is consistent with the hypothesis that crises are self-fulfilling, the irreducible skeptic can always put forward alternatives that are difficult and often impossible to test. I have resigned myself to the idea that, ultimately, the empirical case for the self-fulfilling hypothesis must be of the Occam razor's type. Granted, it is possible to find explanations for the stylized facts that do not rely on multiple equilibria. Taken together, however, these explanations make a somewhat disparate lot. The self-fulfilling hypothesis, instead, explains several aspects of reality at one strike and in a simple way.

In this paper Krugman proposes a self-fulfilling model of the Asian crisis, that he calls "third generation." Before proceeding with the discussion of the model, let me state briefly why I am bit uncomfortable with the label. The name "third generation" suggests that, the Asian crisis being as different from the EMS crisis as the latter was from its predecessors, it is now time to put second generation models back on the shelf and start developing a new framework. While this view contains some truth, it neglects important dimensions in which the second generation approach transcends the event in which it originated. Consider again the main message of the second generation approach: that currency crises should be analyzed in the context of a conflict between internal and external objectives. This is a good starting point for thinking not only about the EMS crisis of 1992–93, but also about older events[5] or the most recent ones. Clearly the Asian authorities were faced with a dilemma between the external objective of defending their currency, which required high interest rates, and the internal objective of preserving their banking sectors, which required low ones. In the limit, any crisis can be analyzed in a second generation perspective, the whole point being to specify well the terms of the conflict between policy objectives.[6]

Let me come to the model of this paper. All models with multiple equilibria rely on some sort of circularity. Here, the circularity may be described by the following diagram.

In the model, the dollar debt real appreciation reduces investment through a balance sheet channel. It is important to note that this channel does not involve the maturity structure of the dollar denominated debt. What constrains domestic entrepreneurs, in other words, is not that they have to repay a large short-term dollar denominated debt, but the increase in

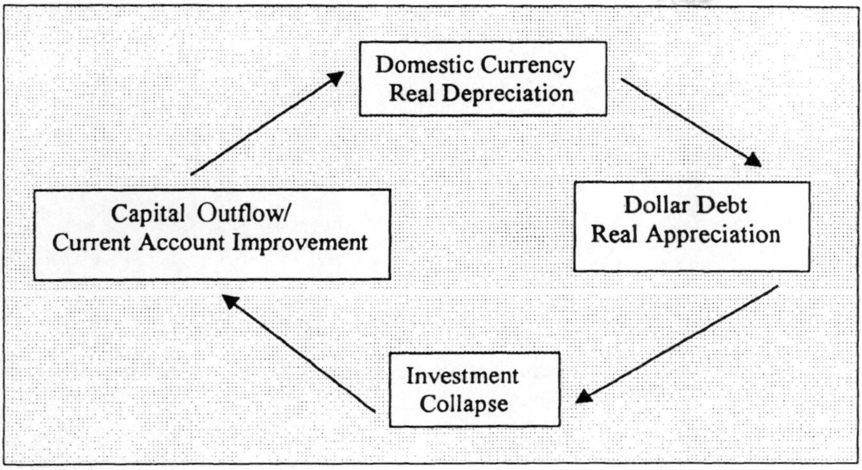


*Figure 1.*

the real value of their dollar-denominated debt in terms of domestic goods. In this sense, the underlying mechanism is quite different from the bank-run type stories that rely on a liquidity mismatch between the assets and the liabilities of the corporate sector. Krugman insists on this difference and its policy implications. For example, he argues in Section 5 that measures aimed at lengthening the maturity structure of the foreign currency debt, such as Chilean-type controls on short-term inflows, would not protect the country from a crisis.

Returning to the diagram, the fall in investment is then associated with a capital outflow—the accounting mirror image of which is a current account improvement. The reason for this, in the model, is that home output and the consumption of home good being constant,[7] the output that is no longer invested must be exported. The current account reversal is made possible, in turn, by a real depreciation of the domestic currency, which closes the circle.

The point that dollar-denominated debts create a self-reinforcing mechanism is often mentioned in informal discussions of the Asian crisis. Krugman's paper captures the point with a model that is elegant and simple-canonical, in the sense that it is difficult to imagine a model that would need less variables and equations to make the same point. That being the main quality of the model, it might be unfair or naive to go too far in confronting it with the facts. Even when confronted with facts, however, the model fares pretty well. Table 1 reports—for Indonesia, Korea, Malaysia, and Thailand—the growth rates of the main macroeconomic aggregates between 1996 and 1998. The case of Korea, for example, seems pretty close to the model, with a big fall in investment associated with a surge in exports, while output and consumption barely move.[8] Of course, the model does not exactly fit the data, in particular the large fall in output in Indonesia and Thailand. It would not be difficult, however, to make the model predict also a fall in output, for example by assuming that the financial disruption induced by the crisis reduces not only the investment flow, but

*Table 1.* Evaluation of the main macro-aggregates, 1996–98. (Growth rates, in percent.)

| | Indonesia | Korea | Malaysia | Thailand |
|---|---|---|---|---|
| GDP | −11.1 | −1.9 | 1.0 | −8.4 |
| Consumption | 7.0 | −7.2 | −3.6 | −11.6 |
| Investment | −55.2 | −55.7 | −24.6 | −46.5 |
| Exports | 6.0 | 40.0 | 7.7 | 9.1 |
| Imports | −9.0 | −15.7 | −5.6 | −31.1 |

Source: World Economic Outlook Database

also the productivity of installed capital and labor. Overall, it is remarkable how well the model fits the data, given its simplicity.

There is one respect, however, in which the extreme simplicity of the model is more costly in terms of insights. The model is static, and purely real. We don't have the combination of money and short-run nominal friction that would make it possible to distinguish between a Keynesian short-run and a Lucasian long-run. But, as I am going to argue below, such a distinction becomes important if we try to quantify the size of the debt revaluation mechanism. Moreover, distinguishing between the long run and the short run opens a back door to the idea that the maturity structure of the foreign currency debt might matter, even in Krugman's story.

Table 2 presents data on foreign currency debt and exchange rates for the same countries as in Table 1. The first line reports estimates of the pre-crisis external debt denominated in dollars as a percentage of GDP.[9] The second line reports the percentage by which currencies depreciated against the dollar in the second half of 1997. These depreciations are in nominal terms, but at the six months horizon they must be quite close to their real counterparts. The third line reports the increase in the real value of the dollar-denominated external debt in terms of percentage points of GDP, which was computed using the first two lines. To illustrate, the 45.4 percent depreciation of the Thai baht increases the dollar-denominated debt from 16.8 percent of GDP to $16.8/(1 - 0.454) = 30.8$ percent of GDP, whence the 14 percent increase reported in the third line.

This back-of-the-envelope calculation suggests that the debt appreciation shock may have been quite large, especially in Thailand and Korea, where it amounted to a transfer to the rest of the world in excess of 10 percent of GDP. On the other hand, it is important to realize that these figures relate to an immediate post-crisis situation, when the domestic price level had not yet adjusted to the change in the exchange rate. In the longer run, if the initial nominal exchange rate depreciation is not reversed, the domestic price level will go up, offsetting most of the initial real depreciation. To illustrate, if the price level completely catches up with the initial depreciation in five years, the real value of a dollar in terms of domestic good will be exactly the same five years after the crisis as before the crisis.[10]

So after all, the maturity structure of foreign currency debt does matter. The real value of a dollar, in terms of domestic goods, is likely to be much higher in the aftermath of the crisis than, say, five years later. Krugman's debt appreciation mechanism, hence, is likely to be much more potent in practice if a large share of the dollar-denominated debt is short

*Table 2.* External debt and exchange rates.

| | Indonesia | Korea | Malaysia | Thailand |
|---|---|---|---|---|
| External dollar denominated debt in percentage points of GDP 1997-Q2 1/ | 5.2 | 12.7 | 6.2 | 16.8 |
| Nominal depreciation against the dollar, June–December 97 | 47.3 | 47.6 | 35.1 | 45.4 |
| Debt appreciation, in percentage points of GDP | 4.7 | 11.5 | 3.3 | 14.0 |

1/Net Foreign Liabilities toward BIS Reporting Banks in 1997-Q2 in percentage points of the dollar PPP valuation of 1997 GDP.
Source: Author's computations based on BIS and IMF data.

term and not rolled-over at the time of the crisis. In other words, Krugman's story, to be empirically relevant, probably needs to involve also the illiquidity of borrowers.

## Notes

1. One additional reason for the popularity of these models is that they provide a compromise between the "fundamentalists" and the "self-fulfillers." The self-fulfilling view is often resisted on the grounds that it seems to absolve policymakers from the responsibility for crises. But second generation models predict that speculation can become self-fulfilling only if the fundamentals are deteriorated, so that bad policies do matter.
2. Namely, mounting unemployment (aggravated, in some countries, by an overvaluation of the currency) coupled with a high level of German interest rates.
3. This line of argument has been developed, for example, by Corsetti, Pesenti, and Roubini (1998). Drazen (1998) and Masson (1998) review different channels of contagion, including multiple equilibria.
4. Calvo (1998) outlines a model of this story.
5. Such as the 1931 sterling crisis (Eichengreen and Jeanne, 1998).
6. For this reason, I prefer to call the second generation approach "escape clause" or "policy optimizing" (Jeanne, 1999).
7. Output is constant because the stock of productive capital is predetermined.
8. Note, however, that the table compares 1996 and 1998, The fall in Korean output and consumption is much larger between 1997 and 1998. We chose 1996 as the pre-crisis benchmark to avoid mixing pre-crisis and post-crisis data.
9. Finding reliable data on foreign currency debt is notoriously difficult. The estimates reported in Table 2 are based on the *net* foreign liabilities toward BIS Reporting Banks. More than 90 percent of these liabilities were denominated in dollars. These estimates are a lower bound, of course, to the extent they do not include debts to creditors other than BIS Reporting Banks.
10. Some factors, however, may contribute to making the price level adjustment slow and incomplete. First, the financial crisis may generate deflationary forces that counter the effect on domestic prices of the nominal depreciation. Second, the intertemporal approach to the current account suggests that an output loss, even a temporary one, will result in a real depreciation of the domestic currency in the long run.

## References

Calvo, Guillermo. (1998). "Understanding the Russian Virus, with Special Reference to Latin America." Mimeo, presented at the Deutsche Bank's conference on *Emerging Markets: Can They Be Crisis Free*? Washington, D.C.

Corsetti, Giancarlo, Paolo Pesenti, and Nouriel Roubini. (1998). "What Caused the Asian Currency and Financial Crisis?" Mimeo (available on Asian Crisis Homepage).

Drazen, Allan. (1998). "Political Contagion in Currency Crises." Mimeo, presented at the NBER Conference on Currency Crises. Cambridge, MA, February 6–7.

Eichengreen, Barry, and Olivier Jeanne. (1998). "Currency Crisis and Unemployment: Sterling in 1931." NBER Working Paper No. 6563.

Jeanne, Olivier. (1997). "Are Currency Crises Self-Fulfilling? A Test." *Journal of International Economics* 43, 263–286.

———. (1999). "Currency Crises: A Perspective on Recent Theoretical Developments." Mimeo, IMF.

Krugman, Paul. (1996). "Are Currency Crises Self-Fulfilling?" *NBER Macroeconomics Annual*. Cambridge, MA: MIT Press.

Masson, Paul. (1998). "Contagion: Monsoonal Effects, Spillovers, and Jumps Between Multiple Equilibria." IMF Working Paper.

# General Discussion

**Maurice Obstfeld**, who had presented the paper in Krugman's absence, responded to the discussants by emphasizing that we have to be very careful when we disparage theories based on psychology, or when we characterize theories as being based on psychology. Fundamentals are very important in second-generation models, but the fundamentals are endogenous as a result of government policies, and that can give rise to multiple equilibria. We have many models in economics with multiple equilibria. Often people are unhappy about them or bemoan the fact that they don't make unique predictions, and there is a real philosophical question about whether we should accept multiple equilibria models or not.

In **Obstfeld's** opinion, the timing issues that Jeanne had raised are essential in judging whether models with multiple equilibria are relevant. So are counterfactual issues: Would a crisis occur in the absence of an attack? It is very hard, maybe impossible, to answer these questions on the basis of data.

The models that we are now developing in the profession seem to point to the view that the range of speculative attacks may be larger than one would have thought on the basis of first-generation models, and that vulnerabilities which might not even be expanding or on-going can give rise to attacks through self-fulfilling types of mechanisms. In **Obstfeld's** view it is really the plausibility of those mechanisms that is central in judging the relevance of a model, rather than the number of equilibria.

# Financial Crises: What Have We Learned From Theory and Experience?

CHAIR: MICHAEL MUSSA
*Economic Counsellor and Director of Research Department, International Monetary Fund*

PANELISTS: MICHAEL P. DOOLEY
*Professor of Economics, University of California at Santa Cruz*

RUDIGER DORNBUSCH
*Ford Professor of Economics and International Management, Massachusetts Institute of Technology*

DAVID FOLKERTS-LANDAU
*Managing Director, Deutsche Morgan Grenfell*

JACOB A. FRENKEL
*Governor, Bank of Israel*

## Summary of Panel Remarks

**Michael Mussa** opened the panel by recalling the occasion of the first seminar he had given as a graduate student at the University of Chicago, which was scheduled for Monday August 19, 1969. The topic was devaluation, and as events would have it, President Pompidou devalued the French franc the preceding Sunday. The Brazilian authorities, by floating the real on January 15, the day before the present panel discussion, had provided similar background for this occasion.

The panelists spoke in alphabetical order. **Michael Dooley** observed that as initial reactions to the Brazilian float, the Brazilian and U.S. stock markets had risen on January 15. Perhaps this reflected sentiment that abandoning the peg would have an expansionary effect on output in Brazil. Regardless of the ultimate outcome for Brazil, however, one thing we had learned from experience was that the bevavior of real output following financial crises had varied widely across different episodes. The United Kingdom had actually prospered following Britain's withdrawal from the ERM in September 1992, while in contrast, the output losses that followed the 1994 Mexican crisis were very large.

Dooley's remarks were focused on two related questions. Why have there been such large differences in the output costs that have followed financial crises? And where do the output costs come from? As a trivial point, we knew that cases of large output costs were cases in which exchange rate movements, along with the interest rate policies that governments had followed in response to the crises, had bankrupted a lot of firms and banks, and had even bankrupted the governments themselves. But if financial market participants knew that surges in capital flows into an emerging market economy would create an environment that was ripe for a financial crisis with large output losses, why did we see such large capital inflows in the first place?

One possible explanation was that market participants were irrational. A second line of explanation, consistent with the hypothesis of rational behavior, was that private investors regarded their claims on emerging market economies as "insured." Despite the fact that in some crisis episodes private investors had suffered large losses, Dooley was a proponent of the second view.

In particular, Dooley argued that private investors create "insurance" by structuring their claims on a country in a manner that will impose substantial costs on the country if it fails to meet its financial obligations. The success of private investors in insuring that financial obligations were met required the threat of a financial crisis that in turn would precipitate a significant downturn in economic activity. An intriguing element of the paradigm, in Dooley's view, was the idea that even a small miscalculation would trigger a crisis right away. This created a game with official creditors, in which the IMF or creditor-country governments had to decide quickly whether to bail everyone out.

In closing, Dooley conjectured that the large output losses associated with financial crises were accidents. Private lenders to an emerging market economy set up, endogenously, a structure of claims on the country's government, banks, and firms that they believed would inflict the maximum pain on that economy—and on their own economies—if the claims were not serviced and repaid. Occasionally they miscalculated. And when they did, there was no effective way to renegotiate, and we were stuck in a bad equilibrium in which the large real costs were imposed.

**Rudiger Dornbusch** addressed the question of how to model financial crises. In his view, the paradigm provided by Salant and Henderson (1978) and Flood and Garber (1984) was still valid, and a good model of a modern-day financial crisis had to include a focus on three basic elements: vulnerability, globalization, and illiquidity. Models that emphasized "special effects" without addressing these basic elements were not very useful.

Vulnerability could emerge in the corporate-sector balance sheet, the banking-sector balance sheet, or the government's balance sheet. And if vulnerability surfaced in any one of these places, it would likely end up in all three. Moreover, once a country's balance sheet became vulnerable, there was only one place people would want to hold their assets, and that was outside the country. So any balance sheet problem would inevitably become an exchange rate problem. The degree to which the exchange rate looked over-valued or under-valued according to traditional perspectives was irrelevant when the country's balance sheet was regarded as vulnerable.

Globalization was also an important part of the modern-day setting. It was silly to focus on small-country models of financial crises. The Koreans were playing in Brazil, the Brazilians were playing in Russia, and the three were holding hands. And because portfolio positions were leveraged, it didn't take very much to draw attention to the prospect that all three would go bust together.

Illiquidity was the third basic element in the story. Dornbusch recalled that the discussion of illiquidity had been very important in the 1930s and cited a paper by McKean (1949) on liquidation scrambles. McKean had emphasized the need for countries to pay careful attention to maturity structure in managing their balance sheets, recognizing that when something goes wrong, everybody wants liquidity.

Together, vulnerability, globalization, and liquidity scrambles were, in Dornbusch's view, the essence of the balance-of-payments and exchange rate crises we see today, which had become fast-action crises rather than old-style current account crises that lacked an interesting capital account story. In trying to anticipate crises, one had to ask the question: Where is the vulnerability hidden? The Brazilian crisis was no surprise. With large stocks of short-term dollar-denominated external debt, a substantial budget deficit, an overvalued exchange rate, and a banking system that couldn't stand six months of high interest rates, vulnerablity was extensive.

What should come next for Brazil? Dornbusch thought the intelligent answer was to recognize that when a country had experienced zero growth in per capita GDP over 20 years for macroeconomic reasons, it was time to try to get rid of macroeconomics. To him, a currency board was the obvious answer. There were many arguments against a currency board, the leading one being that it wasn't a perfect arrangement. But nothing perfect was about to happen in Brazil. As Dornbusch saw things, a currency board had the advantages of taking the exchange rate off the table and taking the central bank out of business. In his view, a currency board arrangement had worked spectacularly in Argentina, not only in the sense of promoting inflation stability narrowly defined, but much more so in lengthening the decision-making horizons of economic participants.

**David Folkerts-Landau** spoke from the perspective of a former staff member looking at the Fund from the outside. He regarded surveillance as the core of the Fund's responsibilities and was strongly critical of the Fund's performance in recent years. The fact that the Fund had failed to anticipate the magnitude and scope of the current financial crisis was not the central issue; nobody else had anticipated it either. The crux of Folkert-Landau's criticism, rather, reflected his view that the Fund had failed to respond adequately to changes in the global economy and the global financial environment.

Folkerts-Landau regarded the Fund's culture as still predominantly influenced by a paradigm of macroeconomic behavior that was relevant to the 1970s and 1980s, but not to the 1990s. While the resources that the Fund was devoting to financial sector surveillance had increased, thanks mainly to strong efforts by Jacob Frenkel and Michael Mussa, they remained relatively small. Resource constraints, moreover, were not the only factor that limited the effectiveness of financial sector surveillance. In addition, the effectiveness of the Fund's general surveillance efforts was hampered by the difficulties that the Fund confronted in criticising member countries and by the incentive structure that that the organization provided for its staff members. In Folkerts-Landau's view, part of the problem was that staff members who played instrumental roles in shaping the Fund's policy advice to member countries were not held adequately accountable by the Fund's senior management—that is to say, they were not appropriately rewarded or penalized for the successes or failures of the policy programs they recommended.

Folkerts-Landau was also critical of the Fund's performance in the areas of crisis management and crisis resolution. He felt that in some prominent cases, such as Brazil, the Fund had been inclined to support programs based on projections that were widely regarded as unrealistically optimistic. As a result, the Fund was now widely perceived as "talking its own book" and no longer operating on the basis of first-rate analysis. This was a serious matter for an institution as well regarded as the Fund, and for an institution that had been given the special role of promoting the stability of the international monetary system.

**Jacob Frenkel** spoke next. He subsequently submitted a written version of his remarks, which follows this summary.

**Michael Mussa** focused first on the question of what we had learned about the causes of crises. He viewed crises as very complex events with a multiplicity of causes. A good analogy was provided by the sinking of the Titanic. The simple explanation described the cause as an iceberg. But we know that the disaster should be attributed to much more than the iceberg—in particular, to how the ship was constructed and operated, to how it was managed after it hit the iceberg, to what the radio man on the California was or was not doing, and so forth.

An even more complex story needed to be told about the economic disasters that had befallen a number of countries around the world over the past few years. Certainly the fundamentals mattered. Brazil had a fiscal problem. Russia had not only a fiscal problem, but also a massive problem associated with a culture of nonpayment and a government that was incapable of carrying out some of its most basic functions. A number of the Asian economies had problems in their financial sectors, and in the financial structures of their business sectors; and they also suffered a variety of adverse external disturbances, including a sharp decline in the volume of world trade in 1996 and unfavorable movements in the dollar/yen exchange rate.

Another contributing factor that Mussa regarded as important was the nature of the policy response as the crisis developed. In Indonesia, which at the outset of its crisis had a very powerful government led by a very powerful president, it was the president's failure to act initially in a sufficiently constructive manner that helped to transform a situation of severe economic difficulties into an economic catastrophe. Disfunctional policy responses had also been important, in Mussa's view, at the initial stages of the difficulties in Korea and Thailand.

Moral hazard was an additional contributing element. Significant parts of the imbalances or disequilibria that developed in these economies, and that turned into real problems as the economies fell into difficulties, were the consequences of actual or perceived guarantees, by the national governments, of various businesses and financial institutions. Still another contributing factor was contagion—not only financial contagion, but also the real spillover effects that countries feel when trading partners experience severe economic contractions.

The second issue addressed by Mussa was the perception that the economic costs of crises have been excessive—beyond what reasonably needed to occur, given the circumstances of the economies before the crises started. The cumulative output loss for Korea, over a horizon of roughly 6 years, was projected to amount to about 50 percent of Korea's annual GDP. The projected output loss for Indonesia looked even worse. It was Mussa's perception that once we get into the crisis mode, the system disfunctions. It disfunctions at the national level because of our incapacity to resolve bankruptcy problems and the like. It also disfunctions at the international level as creditors scramble madly to pull their money out, which then pushes the economy into a situation akin to national default, which in turn creates a massive disfunction in the real economy as well as in the financial sector. Regardless of whether or not one viewed this as a situation of multiple equilibria, Mussa felt that we needed to focus considerable attention on trying to understand why the system disfunctions and what could be done to avoid the various types of disfunctional responses of a system in crisis.

Turning next to some of the issues that Folkerts-Landau had raised, Mussa argued that the most that the Fund could be expected to do in the area of predicting crises was to identify areas of vulnerability. With regard to the Fund's surveillance activities and internal dialog, considerable improvements in recognizing countries vulnerable to crises had been made in recent years. It was the Fund's job to identify vulnerabilities, to work on policy-reform efforts aimed at correcting those vulnerabilities, and to help deal with crises when they came. But in Mussa's view, it was not feasible for the Fund to identify, in any public way, the countries that it regarded as on the hit list for the next financial crisis. That was a function that needed to be performed much more by private financial markets, which did not have the type of membership responsibilities that constrained the Fund.

## References

Flood, Robert, and Peter Garber. (1984). "Collapsing Exchange Rate Regimes: Some Linear Examples." *Journal of International Economics* 17, 1–13.

McKean, Roland N. (1949). "Liquidity and a National Balance Sheet." *Journal of Political Economy* 57, 506–522. Reprinted in Friedrich A. Lutz and Lloyd W. Mints (eds.), *Readings in Monetary Theory*. Homewood, Ill.: Richard D. Irwin, 1951.

Salant, Stephen, and Dale Henderson. (1978). "Market Anticipation of Government Policy and the Price of Gold." *Journal of Political Economy* 86, 627–648.

# Remarks

BY JACOB A. FRENKEL

When we ask ourselves what we should learn from financial crises, we may first ask ourselves which crises we try to understand because, unfortunately, there have been several periods of crises over, say, the last three decades. Certainly there are important differences between the debt crisis of the late 1970s and early 1980s, the ERM crisis of the early 1990s, the Mexican crisis and its "Tequila-effect" in 1994/95, and the recent crises in South East Asia and Russia with the ensuing world financial turmoil. However, there seems to be one common factor that manifests itself in each episode in a somewhat different disguise: moral hazard.

But before we proceed with the issue of moral hazard, we may question the timing of the learning process: when should one start learning? When the horses have left the stable? This reminds me of the criminal who was heard mumbling on his way to the electric chair, saying to himself, "Well, this will teach me a lesson!" The fact is that the present situation is not so much the end of an era as it is a mid-point—each point is a mid-point. One may of course ask the Fund, "How could this organization have made so many mistakes?" But for that matter, a similar question could be put to the crisis country's authorities (today this would be the Brazilian authorities): "How could you have made so many mistakes?" This reminds me yet of another story: There was this little schoolboy, who had written an exam, and when returning the exam to him, the teacher exclaimed: "My goodness, how could one person make so many mistakes?" And the pupil answered: "I did not do it alone, my father helped me."

So, what is the solution? David Folkerts-Landau proposed a deep change within the staff, a change of the incentive structure; one could go on and on—a change of top government officials, etc. Reshuffling international organizations, governments, and other important national institutions requires a great deal of motivation and time.

## What Have We Learned?

I remember that, when I came to the University of Chicago together with Rudi Dornbusch and Michael Mussa as graduate students, I was impressed by Milton Friedman's capacity to go from one country to another, not knowing much or anything about the details of the country, but coming home with very strong recommendations. When asked about how he was so sure about the necessary steps, he used to say: "I know what data to look at"—needless to say, the relevant data were the monetary data.

When I joined the Fund, the many young and talented economists, going from one country to another (and membership has doubled since then) knew very clearly what economic prescriptions to recommend after very short missions in the country. When I asked them, how they know what to do, they told me that the key figure to look at is the country's government-budget deficit.

It turns out that, in many cases, classified as crises today, neither the money supply nor the budget deficit would have been useful indicators for predicting the crisis. So now there is a new fashion—probably the right one—emphasizing the functioning of the financial system, the soundness of the banking system, the existence of moral hazard. These concepts were not mentioned in the textbooks of the past. This suggests, that with this time perspective, when asking "What have we learned?" the question is not about what we have learned since last Friday, although we may state that quite a remarkable number of things have happened within such a short period of time. A crucial point in this respect is that we are in a new era—an era of globalization. The meaning of globalization has at least two facets:

- Geography matters much less than before. It has become less important to know where a crisis started. In this sense, the name "Asian crisis" is a misnomer, because in many respects, countries in Latin America exhibit similar characteristics to those associated with the Asian or the Russian crisis. The first element of globalization is that geography has been substituted by a more functionally-related phenomenon.
- Time is not linear any more. Not in a backward-looking sense, but in a forward-looking sense: the time available to policy makers, to surmount an economic crisis by choosing the right actions, gets shorter and rapidly so.

## The Butterfly Effect

You probably recall the book by James Gleick (1997). It starts with a butterfly that moved its wings somewhere in the Pacific, and through the laws of physics in a frictionless world, it created a typhoon and a hurricane in some faraway place. Of course, this does not really happen, because in reality there is friction. And it is precisely globalization that brings us closer to the (frictionless) chaos—we may call it the "butterfly factor." Rudi Dornbusch was perfectly right by noting that vulnerability, or the balance sheet problem, is not of a single entity. Indeed, looking at Korea, and recognizing the extraordinary cross-guaranties among firms and other institutions within the same conglomerates, helps us understand that the notion of a balance sheet has stopped being merely a notion of an enterprise, and has become a notion of the transmission mechanism of difficulties. And Rudi Dornbusch is also right in pointing at the exchange market, where turmoil manifests itself most rapidly. This is vividly illustrated in Figure 1.

Another financial market importantly sensitive to crisis is of course the stock market. Also in this market the difference between crisis countries and any other category of countries is vividly visible; see Figure 2.

## The Currency Board

We should always keep in mind one thing and try to address it up front. In a currency board system, a liquidity crisis gets easily translated into a financial crisis. And Argentina's

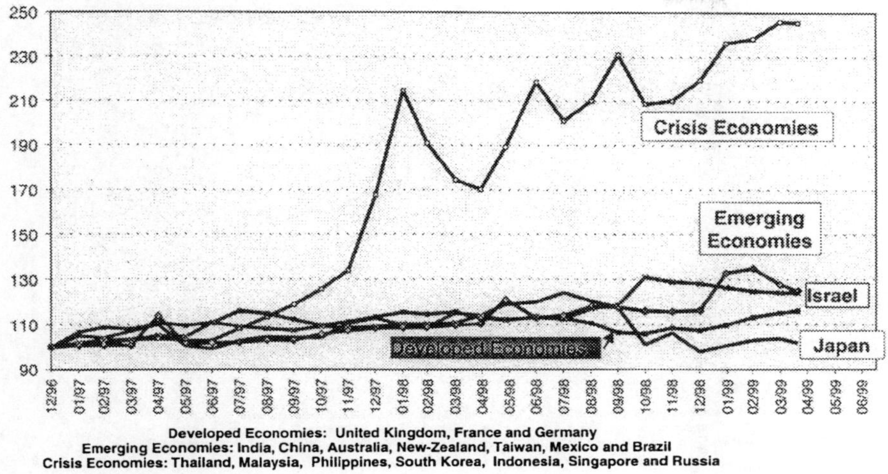


*Figure 1.* Nominal Exchange Rates Against the U.S. Dollar.

experience, i.e. the post-tequila effects, must teach us a lesson, not as a case against currency boards, but rather about what should be done in order to avoid the situation of the liquidity crisis being transformed into a full-fledged financial crisis.

## Banking Supervision, Globalization and Financial Crisis

This brings me to the concept that has recently gained a lot of attention—the soundness of the financial system. There is now greater understanding and consensus that in order to carry out a successful macroeconomic policy you must have a sound financial system, especially a strong banking system. If your banking system is not sound and there is a crisis, it may transform itself into a macroeconomic crisis. By the same token, if you have a macroeconomic system that is not stable and if your banks are not sound enough, then an unstable macroeconomic system can transform itself into a banking panic, or a banking collapse. So, we see the recent interaction between macroeconomic stability on the one hand, and soundness of the banking system on the other.

Furthermore, in order to be able to pursue an effective monetary policy, you must make sure that you are not constrained by a fragile banking system that may prevent you from imposing or adopting the appropriate policy measures because you are afraid to shatter the banking system. You'd better have a strong and sound banking system. Furthermore, since one of the important channels of transmission—the effects of monetary policy—works through the banking system, in order to ascertain the full efficacy of monetary policy, you'd better have a banking system that functions well and that is sound. All this suggests (and the lessons from Asia reveal) that in the modern era the soundness of the financial system

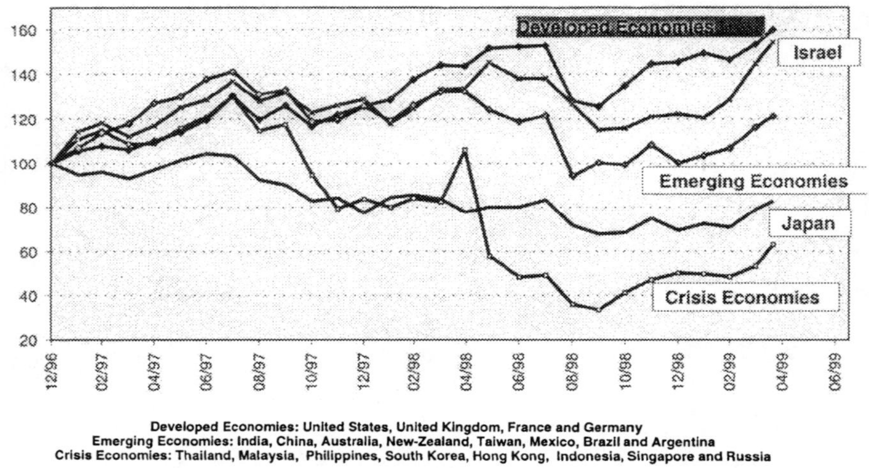


*Figure 2.* Equity Indices.

has become an extremely important element of successful policymaking. Therefore, much effort is now being put by Central Banks the IMF and the BIS (Bank for International Settelments) into strengthening bank supervision.

## How Should We Define Successful Supervision?

There are two issues that must be emphasized here. First, financial markets are very innovative. And second, because of the fact that they are so innovative, these markets are relentlessly developing financial instruments (like derivatives) and new technologies. Therefore supervisors with the institutional and technical knowledge of yesterday are not adequately equipped, to deal with financial developments of tomorrow. This situation implies that banking supervisors must improve their knowledge continually because the subject is very dynamic. It follows, therefore, that the concept of banking soundness is also a dynamic one and should not be defined in terms of a rigid set of technical conditions but rather adapt itself to the changing realities.

As we analyze developments in Asia, we realize that most of the problems there stem from moral hazard: Financial intermediaries extended loans that were very risky. Those who deposited financial resources with the financial intermediaries did so under the (implicit or explicit) assumption that the government provides a guarantee to the intermediaries. Therefore they had no incentive to monitor the quality of the loans extended by the intermediaries. They just assumed that all was safe. Managers of the intermediaries did not have the incentive to gauge carefully the riskiness of their loans because they always trusted the implicit government guarantee. They also just assumed that all was safe. In many cases these loans were extended in order to purchase assets such as real estate. The growing demand for such

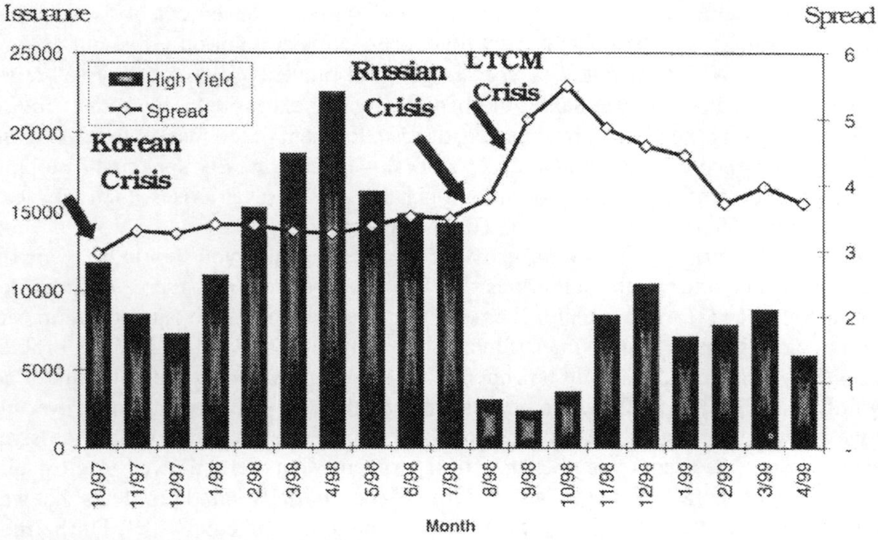


SOURCE: CREDIT SUISSE - FIRST BOSTON

*Figure 3.* High Yield Market: Issuance and Spread.

"assets," financed by the readily available credit, brought about a continuous rise in their price since the mechanism that normally puts a check on such a trend, i.e. the rise in the perceived risk associated with the growing stock of debt, was absent. The implicit assumption that all is safe since the government provides insurance without charging the appropriate premium, created the environment of a "One-way bet" and planted the seeds for a bubble—for the analysis and understanding of which the economics profession owes a large debt to Bob Flood. Depositors put their money into the financial intermediaries with the idea that it was safe and secure. The financial intermediaries, with these resources, gave the loans to risky enterprises, like real estate, thus blowing up asset prices. And basically there was a vicious circle that kept everyone happy, as long as it worked. The depositors saw their assets grow. Real estate developers got financial resources from their banks and financial intermediaries. Financial intermediaries saw the collateral on their books go up in price, and everything was all right up to the point at which the first burst in the bubble took place. At that time, when it turned out, that the government was not fully securing particular loans, suddenly the flow of resources into the intermediaries dwindled. And therefore the engine that had generated the rise in asset prices stopped working. Asset prices tumbled. The collateral on the books of the financial institutions dwindled. Loans had to be called back and soon certain institutions became insolvent and the crisis of the financial sector turned into a major economic crisis.

Two issues arise: How should supervisors deal with fragile banks? How should they deal with prospective crises? Should they deal with five of, say, seven potential crises, or should they "solve" seven of, say, five potential crises? Before the crisis sets off, nobody knows when and where the crisis will emanate. And the supervisor stands before a strategic choice. Should he act with excessive prudence and "prevent" seven out of five potential crises, or should there be less than perfect prudence—prevention of only five out of seven potential crises? Which is better? If you are going to prevent "seven of the five" crises, it means that you are over-regulating the banks; you are excessively cautious. You are therefore paralyzing the system, by deterring the development of the market for risk taking, which is the essence of entrepreneurship. You are—metaphorically speaking—stopping too much traffic. But if you are preventing only five of the seven crises, then you leave some possibility of crises in the system. That is the strategic question.

If you adopt the strategy of preventing five of seven crises, then you should be aware that crises might occur, and that the authorities should be ready to deal with them. An important lesson that has been learned is that it is essential to deal with an insolvent institution early on, and to close it rather than to inject funds into it without sense and make a big problem of an initially small one. It should be understood that a supervisor should not think of any bank failure as the end of his career, because this would imply that no bank will ever fail. And we know that a system, which does not allow any bank ever to fail, is an excessively prudent system. We must remember that most problems that were allowed to grow until they became part of the "too big to fail" syndrome, were initially small problems that were ignored for too long because they were just "too small to be bothered with." Furthermore one should make sure to avoid cross guarantees between related businesses, conflicts of interest between the public and the private sector. Corruption has to be eradicated. A very efficient way of dealing with such problems is to increase transparency and accountability. All these terms have become slogans, but that doesn't change the fact that they are relevant.

A former colleague of mine at the University of Chicago, the Nobel Laureate, Bob Lucas, once asked me how many times I had missed a plane. And when I told him that I never missed a plane, he told me "You must be wasting a lot of time at airports." He asked me how many times I had gotten a ticket for speeding. I said, "Never." "Well," he replied, "you must be driving systematically under the speed limit." Well, analogies may have their limits, but there is a point in this. The point is that if you are not going to waste too much time in airports, you must be ready, maybe once or twice, to miss a plane, but also be prepared to know what to do about it. This suggests that in spite of the desire to avoid crises, we must be aware of the fact that if we avoid all crises at all cost, we are overdoing it. It is better to design mechanisms and instruments that reduce the cost of the few crises, once they occur, than to upset the efficient mechanism of risk taking by over-regulation designed to eliminate the likelihood of crises at all cost. Experience in the past half-year or so shows that financial markets tend to be overshooting. Over the previous two years international financial investors have clearly been chasing excessively after yields, without paying due regard to the risks associated. This is common in situations of *moral hazard*, because it implies that somebody will bail you out if trouble appears. There is an implicit insurance, while the financial investor did not have to pay any insurance premium.

## Moral Hazard and the Exchange Rate System

A similar problem is encountered in relation to the exchange rate risk. If a country's authorities promise a fixed exchange rate system (this is a close relative to the currency board) it is also planting the seeds for moral hazard. The business sector will take this promise into account and assume that there is some kind of a commitment. After the collapse, especially in the aftermath of the Russian crisis—the most recent *World Economic Outlook* presents a fascinating analysis of the world financial crisis—there clearly occurred an overshooting of risk premia and an excessive drying up of institutional savings. While before the Russian crisis one could observe an excessive chase after yields and a neglect of risk, after the Russian debt default the wheel turned around and we could observe an excessive chase after liquidity, with confidence sitting on the fence, willing to forego tremendous profit opportunities. Interest spreads went up and new issuances dropped, as you may observe in Figure 3.

### World Financial Crisis and Economic Reform

One of the lessons obtained from the financial crisis in Asia, and also one of the issues the IMF and the World Bank have been working on very hard—is the need to have early identification and prompt closure of insolvent institutions. Some economies have tried to confront the financial crisis by considering a retreat from the strategy of openness regarding the capital account of the balance of payments. The approach was, in some places, "Let's close the capital account," which is similar to the reaction "let's close the window when too much wind comes in through the window," while forgetting that with the open window, you not only get wind but also oxygen. Another idea was to put "sand in the wheels"—or in our context—taxes on capital flows (as if this would make things simpler). I think that anyone who has tried to implement the idea of imposing controls on capital flows in practice rather than just preaching it, has recognized how futile and expensive such a strategy is. Any mechanic knows that if you put sand in the wheels, it's very difficult to get it out once you wish to get rid of it. The problem is that it is illusory to believe that you can prevent only the volatile capital flows, while hoping that the "good" capital flows will continue to flow into the country. Like in a diet, it is very difficult to separate the "good" from the "bad" cholesterol. Closing or hampering the functioning of the capital account is like saying that in order to prevent a car accident, you should close the road. Well, we know that's not the right way to deal with the problem of car accidents. The right way to deal with the occurrence of car accidents is—among other things—to widen the road, rather than narrow it, in order to lower the likelihood of an accident, and also to install seat belts in order to lower the cost of accidents, once they occur. In discussions on the strategy of capital market liberalization the question whether we should put "sand in the wheels" has become a major issue in the international financial system. Should we slow capital flows, or should we—metaphorically speaking—"widen the road" and install seat belts?

As a matter of fact, we have seen heated debates between the IMF and the World Bank on that issue, where the IMF is more reluctant to impose capital controls and some in the World Bank are less reluctant. The IMF is reminding everyone of what Churchill used to say that "markets are like parachutes. They work best when they are open." And there is a lot to that; in this debate my own view is closer to that of the IMF.

Another lesson that we have learned from the recent Asian financial crisis—and the IMF came out with this conclusion—is the following:

Those countries that have not yet fully opened their capital account of the balance of payments should proceed slowly, whereas those countries that have already opened it, should not retreat. Not because you should not retreat in order to "save face" but because once the market participants have learnt to function within open markets, this is irreversible, just as there is no way you can divert water in a permanent way. You can distort it's course, but the water will find its way.

Another issue that came up in the debate on financial systems, was whether reform should be slow or fast? Should it be gradual, or should it be drastic? In my own judgment, it should be implemented according to a specific order. First, we should create the preconditions. Once the preconditions are in place, the system may be changed rapidly. You know Mendes France, the Prime Minister of France long ago, wanted to convince the French to drink less alcohol. So he had signs put in the metro stations of Paris saying, "Stop drinking alcohol, because it will kill you slowly." And somebody wrote underneath this sign, "That's okay. I'm not in a hurry." The fact is that while one may not be in a hurry to create the preconditions and the capacity of supervisors, and to create the legal and the prudential system, once you are ready, you'd better do it quickly and not in stages. In the United Kingdom where cars ride on the left-hand side of the road, it was said that when they considered to adopt the American system where you drive on the right hand side of the road, there was a proposal to do it gradually. On Mondays the trucks will move, on Tuesday the bicycles, and so on .... Of course, such changes can not be implemented gradually. Such changes must be adopted at once; this is a case for a drastic move.

Capital markets are unique. They have memory, and yet one can be baffled. I remember in 1995 when there was the so-called "Tequila Crisis" in Mexico. We saw a lot of money flowing out of Mexico and Latin America into Asia, to the "tigers." If I had told you then, in 1995, that within 2 years we would see money flow out of the "tiger countries," instead of coming in, and if you had asked: "Where will the money go, that will be flowing out?" and if I had answered: "Back to Mexico, to Latin America," you would have said that I was irrational. Yet this is exactly what has happened. And the question is, why? Are the markets irrational? Don't they have memory? Somebody said once that there are two kinds of investors, those with short memory—the bankers—and those who have no memory—the institutional investors and international organizations. I think that the markets do have memory, but the fact of the matter is, that markets respond quickly to policy changes, and they are good in doing so. We have seen dramatic changes in economic policy in Latin America in general, and in Mexico in particular and, therefore, it is not by accident that we see the money that left these countries making a U-turn and coming back.

I was told that in Chinese the word "crisis" consists of two characters: one meaning danger and the other meaning opportunity. The successful handling of a crisis combines the recognition that a crisis contains both the elements of danger and of opportunity. This is another way of saying that the problem of moral hazard needs to be addressed.

Thank you.

## Reference

Gleick, J. (1997). *CHAOS—Making A New Science*. U.K.: Random House.

# On the Foreign Exchange Risk Premium in Sticky-Price General Equilibrium Models

CHARLES ENGEL cmengel@u.washington.edu
*University of Washington and NBER, Department of Economics, Seattle, WA 98195*

***Abstract***

The properties of the foreign exchange risk premium in general equilibrium models with sticky nominal prices are examined. In these models, risk premiums arise endogenously because monetary shocks lead to covariation of consumption and exchange rates. In some cases, the risk premiums are much larger than those produced in neoclassical general equilibrium models.

In general equilibrium models in which prices are perfectly flexible and output fluctuations occur solely because of supply shocks, the source of a foreign exchange risk premium is the correlation between supply shocks to output and shocks to the money supply (see Stulz (1984) and Engel (1992).) Monetary volatility or exchange rate volatility per se will not necessarily result in a risk premium. Monetary shocks that have no impact on consumption will not increase the riskiness of holding domestic or foreign nominal assets.

When nominal prices are sticky, however, monetary shocks will cause changes in output and consumption. While in sticky-price models the risk premium still arises from the covariance of exchange rates with consumption, it is inevitable that such a correlation will exist. A positive domestic monetary shock generally leads to a depreciation of the domestic currency and an increase in home consumption.

The first section of this paper briefly reviews the concept of the foreign exchange risk premium. There is a tradition in the literature of defining the risk premium as deviations from uncovered interest parity. Empirically, that is a useful approximation for a measure of the risk premium, but it can lead one astray in theoretical analyses of the determinants of the risk premium. Some of my previous papers (Engel (1984, 1992, 1996)) have discussed this issue extensively, so the discussion in section 1 will be short. Still, it is helpful to review this distinction because Obstfeld and Rogoff's (1998) analysis of the foreign exchange risk premium in their sticky-price general equilibrium model relies on the traditional (but somewhat misleading) definition of the risk premium.

Section 2 presents the sticky-price general equilibrium models. Again, this presentation is very abbreviated. That is because the models are drawn directly from Obstfeld and Rogoff (1998) and Devereux and Engel (1998). The distinction between these two models is that in the Obstfeld-Rogoff model, producers set prices in their own currency. The price paid by foreigners for home goods (and the price paid by domestic residents for foreign goods) varies instantaneously when the exchange rate changes. The law of one price holds. In the Devereux–Engel model, producers set a price in the home currency for domestic residents and in the foreign currency for foreign residents. When the exchange rate fluctuates, the law of one price does not hold. The type of price-setting behavior of producers matters for the size of the risk premium.

Another thing that matters for the size of the risk premium is the money demand function. For both models of price setting, the nature of the risk premium depends on whether money demand is derived from a real-balances-in-the-utility-function framework or a cash-in-advance framework.

Section 3 derives expressions for the foreign exchange risk premium in this matrix of models: prices set in producers' currencies versus consumers' currencies; and money demand derived from cash in advance versus real balances in the utility function.

Section 4 analyzes the findings. There are four main points:

1) While the existence of a risk premium in the flexible-price general equilibrium models depends on the correlation of exogenous monetary shocks and aggregate supply shocks, the risk premium arises endogenously in sticky-price models. Monetary variability induces correlation between consumption and exchange rates. This result is appealing in that the foreign exchange risk premium is directly related to the volatility of exchange rates, which is consistent with the finding of Flood and Rose (1996).

2) The distribution of aggregate supply shocks has no bearing on the foreign exchange risk premium in the sticky-price models we analyze.

3) Engel (1984, 1992, 1996) shows the risk premium depends on the prices faced by consumers. When the law of one price does not hold, as in the model in which producers set prices in consumers' currencies, there is no unique foreign exchange risk premium. The risk premium for home investors is different from the risk premium for foreign investors.

4) Standard general equilibrium models are incapable of producing risk premiums that are very large. One sticky-price model we examine (prices set in consumers' currencies with a cash-in-advance constraint) can generate much larger risk premiums.

## 1. The Foreign Exchange Rate Risk Premium

A useful way to analyze the risk premium implicit in the forward exchange rate (defined here as the home currency cost of buying a unit of foreign exchange one period forward) is to compare the forward rate to what it would be if investors were risk neutral. Let $F_t$ be the forward rate and $F_t^{RN}$ the risk-neutral forward rate.

If there were only a single consumption good, risk neutrality implies that utility is linear in consumption. Engel (1984) argues that the risk-neutral investor would arbitrage the market until the condition:

$$E_t\left(\frac{F_t^{RN} - S_{t+1}}{P_{t+1}}\right) = 0 \tag{1}$$

holds, where $E_t$ refers to expectations conditional on time $t$ information; $S_t$ is the spot exchange rate (domestic price of foreign currency); and $P_t$ is the nominal domestic-currency price of the consumption good. In words, expression (1) means that under risk neutrality there are no expected real profits from forward market speculation.

Engel (1992) demonstrates that when utility is time separable, and felicity (period by period utility) is a function of more than one good, equation (1) still defines the risk-neutral forward rate. It is possible to write an expression such as (1) when felicity is homothetic. In this case, $P_t$ is the exact price index associated with the felicity function. Risk-neutrality means that felicity is linear in the consumption index, where the consumption index is defined as total nominal consumption expenditure in the period divided by the price index.

Equation (1) gives an expression for the risk-neutral forward rate:

$$F_t^{RN} = \frac{E_t\left(\frac{S_{t+1}}{P_{t+1}}\right)}{E_t\left(\frac{1}{P_{t+1}}\right)}. \tag{2}$$

The risk premium is the defined by comparing $F_t$ to $F_t^{RN}$.

Hodrick (1987) and Engel (1996) show that in models where utility is time-separable with a constant rate of time preference that the actual forward rate is derived from the expression:

$$E_t\left(\frac{F_t - S_{t+1}}{P_t} \cdot \frac{\beta u'(C_{t+1})}{u'(C_t)}\right) = 0, \tag{3}$$

where $\beta$ is the discount factor in utility; $u(\cdot)$ is the felicity function; the prime (′) indicates the first derivative; so

$$A_{t+1} \equiv \frac{\beta u'(C_{t+1})}{u'(C_t)}$$

is the intertemporal marginal rate of substitution. $C_t$ is a real consumption index in the many-goods case.

If all variables are distributed log-normally, we can write equation (3) as

$$f_t = E_t(s_{t+1}) + \frac{1}{2} Var_t(s_{t+1}) - Cov_t(s_{t+1}, p_{t+1}) + Cov_t(s_{t+1}, a_{t+1}), \tag{4}$$

where lower-case letters are the natural logs of the corresponding variables in upper cases; and, $Var_t$ and $Cov_t$ refer to the variance and covariance, respectively, conditional on time $t$ information.

When felicity can be written in the constant-relative-risk-aversion form, so:

$$u(C_t) = \frac{1}{1-\rho} C_t^{1-\rho},$$

equation (4) can be further specialized to:

$$f_t = E_t(s_{t+1}) + \frac{1}{2}\,Var_t(s_{t+1}) - Cov_t(s_{t+1}, p_{t+1}) - \rho\, Cov_t(s_{t+1}, c_{t+1}). \tag{5}$$

Then, using equation (2), we can derive the expression for the risk premium as:

$$rp_t \equiv f_t - f_t^{RN} = -\rho\, Cov_t(s_{t+1}, c_{t+1}). \tag{6}$$

We can contrast this expression for the risk premium with the usual one in the literature (see most recently, Obstfeld and Rogoff (1998)), $f_t - E_t(s_{t+1})$. From equation (5), we have immediately that

$$f_t - E_t(s_{t+1}) = \frac{1}{2}\,Var_t(s_{t+1}) - Cov_t(s_{t+1}, p_{t+1}) - \rho\, Cov_t(s_{t+1}, c_{t+1}).$$

The difference between this expression and the one given in equation (6) is the term $\frac{1}{2}\,Var_t(s_{t+1}) - Cov_t(s_{t+1}, p_{t+1})$, which is usually called the "Jensen's inequality" term. It is typically argued that the Jensen's inequality term is small empirically, and so it does not matter whether it is included as part of the definition of the risk premium.

But Engel (1996) shows that in standard general equilibrium models, the Jensen's inequality term generated from the model is just about the same size as the risk premium. While it is true that the Jensen's inequality terms is not large empirically, neither is the risk premium generated from standard models. One way of stating how poorly these models do in producing large risk premiums is that the risk premium the model generates is approximately the same size as the Jensen's inequality term, the latter of which is nearly universally recognized to be small.

Moreover, from the standpoint of economic intuition, the risk premium defined in equation (6) is much more useful than the standard measure. For example, holding the covariance constant in equation (6), the risk premium goes to zero as risk aversion disappears ($\rho$ goes to zero). But, in the usual definition, there is a risk premium even when there is no risk aversion.

All of the models we will examine satisfy the conditions used in deriving expression (6): variables are distributed log-normally and utility is time-separable with constant time discounting and constant relative risk aversion.

## 2. The Sticky-Price Models

The models we consider are derived in detail in Devereux and Engel (1998). Here only the salient details of the model will be brought out.

We consider two sticky-price models:

**PCP:** In this model, there is producer-currency pricing. That is, producers set the price in their own currency. The price that foreigners pay for domestic goods and the price that home residents pay for foreign goods fluctuate when the exchange rate changes. This is the model examined by Obstfeld and Rogoff (1995, 1998).

**PTM:** In this model, there is pricing to market. That is, producers set the price in the consumers' currency. Prices consumers face do not respond at all to exchange rate changes.

The models are two-country models. In both models, the representative consumer in the home country is assumed to maximize

$$U_t = E_t\left(\sum_{s=t}^{\infty} \beta^{s-t} u_s\right), \qquad 0 < \beta < 1$$

where

$$u_s = \frac{1}{1-\rho} C_s^{1-\rho} + \frac{\chi}{1-\varepsilon}\left(\frac{M_s}{P_s}\right)^{1-\varepsilon} - \eta V(L_s), \quad \rho > 0, \varepsilon > 0, V' > 0, V'' \geq 0.$$

$C$ is a consumption index that is a geometric average of home and foreign consumption:

$$C = \frac{C_h^n C_f^{1-n}}{n^n (1-n)^{1-n}}.$$

We assume that there are $n$ identical individuals in the home country, $0 < n < 1$. $C_h$ and $C_f$ are Dixit–Stiglitz constant-elasticity-of-substitution indexes over consumption of goods produced at home and in the foreign country, respectively. (See Devereux and Engel (1998) for their exact form.) $M/P$ are domestic real balances, and $L$ is the labor supply of the representative home agent.

The price index, $P$, is defined by

$$P = P_h^n P_f^{1-n}, \tag{7}$$

where $P_h$ is a price index over prices of home goods, and $P_f$ is a price index over prices of goods produced in the foreign country.

There are $1 - n$ identical individuals in the foreign country. Their preferences are similar to home country residents' preferences. The terms in the utility function involving consumption are identical in the home and foreign countries. The functional form for real balances and labor are the same as for the home country residents, but, for foreign residents, they are functions of foreign real balances and foreign labor supply.

We assume that there are complete asset markets. Specifically, we assume that residents of each country can purchase state-contingent nominal bonds. We can write the budget constraint of the representative home agent as:

$$P_t C_t + M_t + \sum_{z^{t+1}} q(z^{t+1}, z^t) B(z^{t+1}) = W_t L_t + \pi_t + M_{t-1} + B_t + T_t.$$

Here, $B(z^{t+1})$ are contingent home-currency denominated nominal bonds whose prices at time $t$ are $q(z^{t+1}, z^t)$, where $z^t$ represents the state at time t. $\pi_t$ is the representative agent's share of profits from home firms. $T_t$ are monetary transfers from the government. $W_t$ is the wage rate.

The money demand equation for the representative home-country resident:

$$\frac{M_t}{P_t} = \frac{\chi^{1/\varepsilon} C_t^{\rho/\varepsilon}}{(1-d_t)^{1/\varepsilon}}, \tag{8}$$

where $d_t$ is the inverse of the gross nominal interest rate, given by

$$d_t = E_t\left(\beta \frac{C_{t+1}^{-\rho} P_t}{C_t^{-\rho} P_{t+1}}\right). \tag{9}$$

Consumers equate the marginal rate of substitution between leisure and consumption to the real wage:

$$\frac{W_t}{P_t} = \frac{\eta V'(L_t)}{C_t^{-\rho}},$$

where $W_t$ is the wage rate.

Optimal risk sharing implies

$$\frac{S_t P_t^*}{P_t} = \left(\frac{C_t}{C_t^*}\right)^{\rho} \tag{10}$$

in equilibrium. Consumption will differ across the two countries only to the extent that there are changes in the real exchange rate. In the PCP model, since purchasing power parity holds, we have, as Obstfeld and Rogoff (1998) derive, $C_t = C_t^*$.

Government increases the money supply with direct transfers. The government budget constraint (in per capita terms) is simply

$$M_t = M_{t-1} + T_t.$$

The firms are monopolistic competitors. The production function for firm $i$ is given by:

$$Y(i) = L(i).$$

Devereux and Engel (1998) derive the price-setting behavior of firms. Here we note only that the objective of the domestic firms is to set prices to maximize the expected utility of the owners, who are the domestic residents. Firms must set prices before information about the random domestic and foreign money supplies is known. No state-contingent pricing is allowed in any of the models. Wages are perfectly flexible ex post, and firms hire as many workers as needed to produce output demanded at ex post prices. Wages adjust to insure supply of labor equals demand.

In the PCP model, $P_{ht}$ and $P_{ft}^*$ (the foreign-currency price of foreign goods) are predetermined at time t. Since the law of one price holds, so $P_{ft} = S_t P_{ft}^*$ and $P_{ht}^* = P_{ht}/S_t$, the prices $P_{ft}$ and $P_{ht}^*$ vary concurrently with the exchange rate. In the PTM model, all four nominal prices are predetermined.

We will specialize the term in the utility function to have real balances enter logarithmically ($\varepsilon \to 1$). We will also assume that the money supply follows a random walk of sorts. Specifically:

$$E_t\left(\frac{M_t}{M_{t+1}}\right) = 1.$$

These two assumptions together imply nominal interest rates are constant. We can derive from equations (8) and (9):

$$C_t^\rho = \left(\frac{1-\beta}{\chi}\right)\frac{M_t}{P_t}. \tag{11}$$

Intuitively, a monetary expansion leads to a decline in real interest rates (current consumption rises while next period's consumption is expected to be unaffected by a monetary shock) but an increase in expected inflation. When money follows a random walk and real balances enter utility logarithmically, movements in real interest rates and expected inflation rates always exactly offset each other. Nominal interest rates are constant.

Equations (10) and (11) together give us a very simple expression for the exchange rate:

$$S_t = \frac{M_t}{M_t^*}. \tag{12}$$

Now assume that money supplies are distributed logarithmically. So,

$$m_{t+1} - m_t = \frac{1}{2}\sigma_m^2 + \nu_{t+1}. \tag{13}$$

Here, $\sigma_m^2$ is the variance of the money supply, which is assumed to be constant over time.

It is useful to collect equations (10), (11) and (12) in log form:

$$s_t = p_t - p_t^* + \rho c_t - \rho c_t^* \tag{14}$$

$$\rho c_t = m_t - p_t + \ln\left(\frac{1-\beta}{\chi}\right) \tag{15}$$

$$s_t = m_t - m_t^* \tag{16}$$

As an alternative to the money demand relationship derived from assuming real balances are in the utility function, let us consider a cash-in-advance constraint. We will assume that home residents must buy all goods with home currency, and foreign residents must buy all goods with foreign currency. This gives us:

$$m_t - p_t = c_t \tag{17}$$

$$m_t^* - p_t^* = c_t^* \tag{18}$$

The risk-sharing condition (14) still holds in this model. Together with equations (17) and (18) we arrive at this expression for the exchange rate:

$$s_t = (1-\rho)(p_t - p_t^*) + \rho(m_t - m_t^*). \tag{19}$$

## 3. Expressions for the Risk Premium

In this section, we derive expressions for the risk premium in our various models. Discussion of the expressions is postponed until section 4. We shall consider the model with real balances in the utility function first, and then proceed to the cash-in-advance model. In all cases, we shall use equation (6) for the risk premium.

***Real Balances in the Utility Function***

In the PTM model, all good prices are predetermined. So, using equations (6), (15), and (16), the risk premium in the PTM model given by:

$$\begin{aligned} rp_t^{PTM} &= -\rho\, Cov_t(s_t, c_t) \\ &= -\rho\, Cov_t\left(m_t - m_t^*, \frac{1}{\rho}m_t - \frac{1}{\rho}p_t\right) \\ &= -\rho\, Cov_t\left(m_t, \frac{1}{\rho}m_t\right) \\ &= -\sigma_m^2 \end{aligned} \tag{20}$$

In the PCP model, the domestic price of foreign goods fluctuates with the exchange rate. So, we have:

$$p_t = np_{ht} + (1-n)s_t + (1-n)p_{ft}^*. \tag{21}$$

We can then derive the risk premium in the PCP model from equations (6), (15), (16) and (21):

$$\begin{aligned} rp_t^{PCP} &= -\rho\, Cov_t(s_t, c_t) \\ &= -\rho\, Cov_t\left(m_t - m_t^*, \frac{1}{\rho}m_t - \frac{1}{\rho}(np_{ht} + (1-n)s_t + (1-n)p_{ft}^*)\right) \\ &= -\rho\, Cov_t\left(m_t - m_t^*, \frac{1}{\rho}(nm_t + (1-n)m_t^*)\right. \\ &= -n\sigma_m^2 + (1-n)\sigma_m^2. \end{aligned} \tag{22}$$

It is easy to find the risk premium in the more general utility specification for real balances in which $\varepsilon \neq 1$ by examining the solutions for consumption and exchange rates in Devereux and Engel (1998). The risk premiums in the more general specifications are simply a multiple of the expressions given in equations (20) and (22). The factor multiplying these expressions is $\frac{1+i\varepsilon}{1+i}$, where $i$ is the steady-state nominal interest rate.

***Cash-in-Advance***

In the cash-in-advance model, equations (6), (17) and (19) give us the expression for the risk premium in the PTM model, recalling that goods prices are predetermined in that model:

$$\begin{aligned} rp_t^{PTM} &= -\rho\, Cov_t(s_t, c_t) \\ &= -\rho\, Cov_t(\rho(c_t - c_t^*) + p_t - p_t^*, c_t) \\ &= -\rho^2\, Var_t(c_t) \\ &= -\rho^2\sigma_m^2 \end{aligned} \tag{23}$$

In the PCP model, we need to derive the solution for the exchange rate:

$$
\begin{aligned}
s_t &= (1-\rho)(p_t - p_t^*) + \rho(m_t - m_t^*) \\
&= (1-\rho)s_t + \rho(m_t - m_t^*) \\
&= m_t - m_t^* \qquad (24)
\end{aligned}
$$

where we have used in the derivation that purchasing power parity holds in the PCP model.

Then we can derive from equation (6), (17) and (24):

$$
\begin{aligned}
rp_t^{PCP} &= -\rho\, Cov(s_t, c_t) \\
&= -\rho\, Cov_t(m_t - m_t^*, m_t - np_{ht} - (1-n)s_t - (1-n)p_{ft}^*) \\
&= -\rho\, Cov_t(m_t - m_t^*, nm_t + (1-n)m_t^* \\
&= -\rho n\sigma_m^2 + \rho(1-n)\sigma_m^2. \qquad (25)
\end{aligned}
$$

## 4. Interpretation

To understand the nature of the risk premium in the sticky-price models, it is helpful to compare expressions (20), (22), (23) and (25) to the expression for the risk premium in Lucas's (1984) two-country asset-pricing model. In Lucas's model, prices are perfectly flexible. There effectively are complete asset markets. Output is determined exogenously, and varies over time due to random supply shocks. Money demand arises from cash-in-advance constraints.

While Lucas assumes that domestic agents need domestic money to buy home goods and foreign money to buy foreign goods, we will assume the cash-in-advance constraints given in equations (17) and (18). This will make no difference ultimately, because the expressions we derive for the risk premium is exactly that derived by Engel (1992), which assumes the Lucas cash-in-advance constraint.

Since purchasing power parity holds in this model, and since the complete asset markets equalize home and foreign consumption, equations (17) and (18) give us

$$s_t = m_t - m_t^*.$$

Output at home and abroad, $y_t$ and $y_t^*$ are exogenously given. In equilibrium, each agent consumes exactly the same amount of each good, and all of output is consumed. So:

$$
\begin{aligned}
rp_t^{FLEX} &= -\rho\, Cov_t(s_t, c_t) \\
&= -\rho\, Cov_t(m_t - m_t^*, ny_t + (1-n)y_t^*) \\
&= -\rho n\, Cov_t(m_t, y_t) + \rho n\, Cov_t(m_t^*, y_t) - \rho(1-n)\, Cov_t(m_t, y_t^*) \\
&\quad + \rho(1-n)\, Cov_t(m_t^*, y_t^*) \qquad (26)
\end{aligned}
$$

*Endogeneity of Risk Premium in Sticky-Price Models*

It is clear from equation (26) that the risk premium in the Lucas model arises out of correlations between exogenous money supplies and exogenous supply shocks. If those correlations were zero, the risk premium would be zero. Engel (1992) emphasizes this fact, and points out that much of the literature is misleading on the source of the risk premium in the Lucas model. Because that literature incorrectly focuses on $f_t - E_t(s_{t+1})$ as the measure of the risk premium, it misses the importance of the covariance between monetary and real shocks. Engel (1992) cites several papers which assume the covariance of monetary and real shocks are zero in the Lucas model. The risk premium ought to be zero, but those papers add in the Jensen's inequality terms as part of the risk premium. The Jensen's inequality terms are non-zero even when real and monetary shocks are uncorrelated. Hence, the literature mistakenly derives expressions for the risk premium that are functions of the variances of monetary and real shocks, because the Jensen's inequality terms are functions of the variances. As equation (26) shows, only the covariances of monetary and real shocks matter for the risk premium in the Lucas model.

But, all of the expressions for the risk premium in the sticky-price models ((20), (22), (23) and (25)) involve only the variance of home and foreign money supplies. The reason is that shocks to money generate changes in exchange rates and consumption. So, exchange rates and consumption can covary even when there are only monetary shocks. While ultimately the foreign exchange risk premium depends on there being a correlation between monetary and real variables, in sticky-price models that correlation arises endogenously.

One appealing feature of the risk premiums generated in the sticky-price models is that the size of the risk premium is directly related to the volatility of the nominal exchange rate. In the Lucas model, by contrast, when exchange rate volatility is reduced, the risk premium is only reduced if there is a parallel reduction in the covariance of real and monetary shocks. Flood and Rose (1996) find that deviations from uncovered interest parity are lower in the EMU, where exchange rates are less volatile.

*Productivity Shocks Do Not Matter for the Risk Premium in Sticky-Price Models*

Not only can we generate a foreign exchange risk premium in sticky-price models with monetary variance alone, but also productivity shocks do not affect the risk premium in the models we have examined. We did not introduce productivity shocks into the sticky-price model, but we can do that by adding a multiplicative aggregate productivity shock for each industry, so that output is given by:

$$Y_t(i) = \theta_t L_t(i).$$

But the output equation plays no role in determining either consumption or the exchange rate in the models we have examined. Equations (14), (15) and (16) completely determine the covariance of the exchange rate with consumption in the real-balances-in-the-utility-function model. Equations (14), (17), (18) and (19) determine that covariance in the cash-in-advance model.

If we allowed real balances to enter utility in a form more general than logarithmic (so $\varepsilon \neq 1$), there is a channel through which productivity shocks could affect the risk premium. The productivity shocks could affect the nominal interest rate, which in turn could influence consumption.

Interestingly, that channel is not open in the cash-in-advance formulation of the sticky-price model. So, while the stochastic properties of productivity shocks are key to determining the risk premium in the cash-in-advance Lucas model, they play no role in the cash-in-advance sticky-price models.

### *There Is No Unique Risk Premium in PTM Models*

As Engel (1984) emphasizes, the measure of the risk premium requires a measure of the price index of consumption goods. When individuals consume different baskets, or when they face different prices, the price indexes will be different. Then, the risk premium will not be the same for all individuals.

In the PTM models we have presented, the law of one price does not hold. So, individuals in each country face different price indexes. It is easy to see in our general equilibrium models how failure of purchasing power parity affects the risk premium. In the class of models we examine, the risk premium is given by $-\rho\, Cov_t(s_t, c_t)$ for home residents and $-\rho\, Cov_t(s_t, c_t^*)$ for foreign residents. From equation (10) we find that if purchasing power parity holds, then $c_t = c_t^*$ and the two measures of the risk premium are the same.

In the PTM model, where consumption is not equal across countries, the risk premium for foreign residents is not the same as the expressions given in equations (20) and (23). Those equations show that for the home resident, the risk premium is a function only of home country monetary variance. The analogous expressions for the foreign resident are functions of foreign monetary variance. In the real-balances-in-the-utility-function model, the risk premium is $-\sigma_{m^*}^2$ for foreigners. In the cash-in-advance framework, the risk premium for foreign residents is $-\rho^2\sigma_{m^*}^2$.

Engel suggests testing the null hypothesis of no risk premium and efficient markets by testing the hypothesis that $\frac{F_t - S_{t+1}}{P_{t+1}}$ has a conditional mean of zero. But that test depends on the choice of price index. As stated, the null is that there is no risk premium for domestic residents. The analog for no foreign risk premium is to put the foreign price level in the denominator (converted into domestic currency units). That is, $\frac{F_t - S_{t+1}}{S_{t+1}P_{t+1}^*}$ should have a conditional mean of zero. This is equivalent to $\frac{F_t^* - S_{t+1}^*}{P_{t+1}^*}$ having a conditional mean of zero, where $F_t^* \equiv 1/F_t$ and $S_t^* \equiv 1/S_t$.

### *The Size of the Risk Premium*

In the PCP and PTM models in which money demand arises from the assumption that real balances are in the utility function, the risk premium is independent of the degree of risk aversion. (See equations (20) and (22). Obstfeld and Rogoff (1998) make this point for the PCP model.) That might initially seem puzzling since $rp_t \equiv -\rho\, Cov_t(s_{t+1}, c_{t+1})$. But the covariance term declines as $\rho$ rises. This occurs because the variance of consumption is inversely related to $\rho$.[1] So, large values of $\rho$ are associated both with more risk aversion and less risk. As $\rho$ goes to zero, the variance of consumption goes to infinity, so even when individuals are nearly risk neutral the size of the risk premium does not decline.

These models are incapable of generating large risk premiums. We can make an argument similar to those in Engel (1992, 1996), which pertained to the Lucas model. For example, suppose that a 95% confidence interval for the money growth rate was $\pm 7$ percent per year. This is surely a generously wide confidence interval. It implies a standard deviation of money growth of about 4 percent at annualized rates, or 0.04. The variance of money growth, then, is 0.0016. So, the PTM model with money in the utility function can only generate a risk premium of much less than one percentage point, since it has a value of the risk premium of $-\sigma_m^2$. In the PCP model, the risk premium would be even smaller in the symmetric case of equal domestic and foreign monetary variances. There the risk premium is (from equation (22)) $(1 - 2n)\sigma_m^2$.

(The risk premium in the more general specification in which $\varepsilon \neq 1$ could be larger, since the value of the risk premium more generally is $\frac{1+i\varepsilon}{1+i}$ times the values taken from equations (20) and (22). But, unless $\varepsilon$ is extremely large, implying both low income and interest elasticities of money demand, the risk premium would still be small.)

In the PCP model with the cash-in-advance constraint the risk premium could be larger, depending on the value of $\rho$. In the symmetric case, the risk premium is $\rho(1 - 2n)\sigma_m^2$. Still, with a plausible value for $\rho$ of 5, and with $n = 1$, the risk premium is less than one percentage point. Note, however, that the Lucas model could only generate risk premiums this high if the covariance of real productivity shocks and money growth shocks were as high as the variance of money supply shocks.

The interesting case is the PTM model with the cash-in-advance constraint. In this case, the risk premium is $-\rho^2\sigma_m^2$. Here with a value of $\rho$ equal to 5, and a variance of money growth equal to 0.0016, we get a risk premium of 0.04, or 4 percentage points. This is very close to the size of the conditional risk premiums that many studies on U.S. data have found (see Engel (1996) for a survey of the empirical literature.)

To generate risk premiums even close to this size in neoclassical models, researchers have had to resort to models where some of the axioms of expected utility are not satisfied. These models of "first-order" risk aversion generate risk premiums that are not of the form of $\rho$ times a variance (or covariance), but rather $\rho$ times a standard deviation. (See, for example, Bekaert, Hodrick and Marshall (1997).)

Intuitively, why does the risk premium in this model depend on the square of $\rho$? The log of the exchange rate is linearly related to the log of consumption with a factor of $\rho$ on the log of consumption. Hence, the covariance of the log of the exchange rate with the log of consumption rises with $\rho$. Since the amount of risk aversion increases linearly with $\rho$ as well, the risk premium is proportional to the square of $\rho$.

A case can be made that this is a plausible formulation. First, empirical evidence suggests that almost all of the short-term volatility in real exchange rates comes from volatility in nominal exchange rates (see, for example, Engel (1999).) This is consistent with the PTM model. If the risk-sharing condition (14) is true, the covariance of the exchange rate with consumption must be $\rho$ times the variance of consumption. Even if one were not willing to accept the assumption that asset markets are complete, it is plausible that equation (14) is the right order of magnitude. When purchasing power parity fails, even complete asset markets do not eliminate country-specific risk. But, the more risk averse individuals are, the more risk sharing is likely to occur. So, equation (14)'s implication that the standard deviation of relative consumption is equal to $1/\rho$ times the standard deviation of the exchange rate is natural.

No matter how money demand is modeled, the PTM set-up along with the risk-sharing equation (10) gives us that $Cov_t(s_t, c_t) = \rho\, Var_t(c_t) - \rho\, Cov_t(c_t, c_t^*)$. In the models we have examined, $Cov_t(c_t, c_t^*) = 0$ so $Cov_t(s_t, c_t) = \rho\, Var_t(c_t)$. Since we have the risk premium given by $rp_t \equiv -\rho\, Cov_t(s_{t+1}, c_{t+1})$, the risk premium must be $rp_t \equiv -\rho^2\, Var_t(c_{t+1})$. Thus, sticky-price models of the PTM variety, with a risk-sharing condition that implies there is more consumption smoothing as the degree of risk aversion increases, naturally give rise to a risk premium equal to the square of the risk aversion coefficient times the variance of consumption.

This result is not dependent on the cash-in-advance formulation. Indeed, this result holds even in our real-balances-in-the-utility-function model. But that model has the unfortunate property that the variance of consumption is $1/\rho^2$ times the variance of the money supply, so the coefficient of risk aversion drops completely out of the expression for the risk premium. But if the link between consumption variance and the variance of money growth does not depend on $\rho$, then the PTM model will produce much larger risk premiums than models that assume purchasing power parity (either with sticky prices or without).

## 5. Conclusions

While the PTM model is capable of producing large enough risk premiums to match the data, there is another empirically puzzling aspect to the foreign exchange risk premium that has not yet been addressed here. As Engel (1996) emphasizes, models of the risk premium also need to generate correlations between the risk premium and the forward premium in order to explain the uncovered interest parity puzzle. In the data $\frac{F_t - S_{t+1}}{P_{t+1}}$ is positively correlated with $F_t - S_t$. In log terms, the risk premium as we have defined it, $rp_t$ must be positively correlated with the interest differential, $i_t - i_t^*$ to be able to explain that empirical regularity.

The models presented in this paper have assumed a constant variance of the money supply, which implies constant risk premiums. To generate this correlation, time-varying variances need to be introduced.

Consider the PTM model with the cash-in-advance constraint. Since the risk premium is given by $-\rho^2\sigma_m^2$, we need a negative correlation between monetary variance and $i_t - i_t^*$ to get the desired correlation between the risk premium and the interest differential. Such a model is beyond the scope of this paper. But, if an increase in the money supply lowers nominal interest rates (as it would in the constant-variance version of this model), then we need that the variance of money growth rates increases with the level of the money supply.

Bekaert, Hodrick and Marshall (1997) show that the nominal interest rate volatility predicted in flexible-price general equilibrium models is far too great relative to the size and variance of the risk premium. It seems that the sticky-price models have some potential of resolving this issue. We have seen that when the money supply follows a random walk and real balances enter the utility function logarithmically, nominal interest rates are constant. That property holds whether the second moments of money are constant or not. In that case we can build a model with a time-varying risk premium with completely stable nominal interest rates. However, it was the cash-in-advance formulation, not the money-in-the-utility model, that held the greatest promise for generating large risk premiums. In the cash-in-advance model with random-walk money, nominal interest rates are no longer constant.

It is an open question whether one could build a PTM model with an empirically plausible money demand and money supply specification that could explain the uncovered interest parity puzzle. But, this appears to be a promising avenue for future research.

### Acknowledgments

I have borrowed heavily from joint work with Mick Devereux for this paper. I thank the discussants Jim Boughton and Dick Meese for helpful comments. Some of the work on this paper was done while I was a Visiting Scholar at the Federal Reserve Bank of San Francisco. The views expressed in this paper do not necessarily represent those of the FRB-SF or the Federal Reserve System. This research was supported in part by a National Science Foundation grant to the NBER.

### Notes

1. The correlation between $s$ and $c$ is independent of $\rho$.

### References

Bekaert, Geert, Robert J. Hodrick, and David A. Marshall. (1997). "The Implications of First-Order Risk Aversion for Asset Market Risk Premiums." *Journal of Monetary Economics* 40, 3–39.

Devereux, Michael B., and Charles Engel. (1998). "Fixed vs. Floating Exchange Rates: How Price Setting Affects the Optimal Choice of Exchange-Rate Regime." *National Bureau of Economic Research*, working paper no. 6867.

Engel, Charles. (1984). "Testing for the Absence of Expected Real Profits from Forward Market Speculation." *Journal of International Economics* 17, 299–308.

Engel, Charles. (1992). "On the Foreign Exchange Risk Premium in a General Equilibrium Model." *Journal of International Economics* 32, 305–319.

Engel, Charles. (1996). "The Forward Discount Anomaly and the Risk Premium: A Survey of Recent Evidence." *Journal of Empirical Finance* 3, 123–192.

Engel, Charles. (1999). "Accounting for U.S. Real Exchange Rate Changes." *Journal of Political Economy* 107, 507–553.

Flood, Robert P., and Andrew K. Rose. (1996). "Fixes: Of the Forward Discount Puzzle." *Review of Economics and Statistics* 78, 748–752.

Hodrick, Robert. (1987). *The Empirical Evidence on the Efficiency of Forward and Futures Foreign Exchange Markets*. Chur: Harwood.

Obstfeld, Maurice, and Kenneth Rogoff. (1995). "Exchange Rate Dynamics Redux." *Journal of Political Economy* 103, 624–660.

Obstfeld, Maurice, and Kenneth Rogoff. (1998). "Risk and Exchange Rates." *National Bureau of Economic Research*, working paper no. 6694.

Stulz, Rene. (1984). "Currency Preferences, Purchasing Power Risks, and the Determination of Exchange Rates in an Optimizing Model." *Journal of Money, Credit and Banking* 16, 302–316.

# Comment

BY JAMES M. BOUGHTON

Charles Engel's paper is a highly appropriate choice for opening a conference in honor of Bob Flood. First, the subject is appropriate, because some of Bob's best work has analyzed the theory and estimation of exchange rate behavior and policy. Working with Bob Hodrick on speculative bubbles and regime switching, with Peter Garber on collapsing regimes, and with Nancy Marion on dual exchange markets and other regime choices, Bob Flood has helped us break through the fog and see more clearly how exchange markets work. Second, Engel's treatment of the subject is appropriate, because—like so many of Bob's papers—it finds an elegant way to model the theory so as to make empiricists question conventional interpretations.

This paper looks closely at one of the standard building blocks of exchange rate models: the time-variant risk premium ($rp_t$). This term has long been used as a short-hand expression for any departure from uncovered interest parity. It began life in the1970s as a reduced-form variable that harbored a host of omitted variables and concepts. Since then, as Engel has reviewed in this and earlier papers, he and other theoreticians have developed an underlying structure and have provided several competing explanations for the existence and properties of the risk premium. The fact remains that $rp_t$ is not a structural or "deep" parameter, and the empirical requirements for it to have stable properties are daunting. For a long time, modelers have been troubled by the apparently small risk premia implied by theoretical models of risk aversion: much too small to explain observed departures from uncovered interest parity. In the models analyzed here, risk aversion is only part of the explanation for the risk premium, and the puzzle is at least reduced. An interesting feature of these models is that $rp_t$ can be different in each country; there is no unique premium that clears the market. This makes great sense, but it does not instill a great deal of confidence in those seeking stable results from empirical estimation of exchange rate models.

Looking further into the determinants of the risk premium, one sees immediately that the most basic building block of the whole class of models examined in this paper is the demand for money in each country. In spite of its importance and the many thousands of articles (including several of my own) devoted to its study, the demand for money is not a very well-established concept in macroeconomics. In a modern economy with a continuum of financial assets (basic and derivative) across a broad maturity spectrum, the division of all such assets into one aggregate called "money" and another called "bonds" (or into two others called short- and long-term bonds) is quite arbitrary. The assumptions that a stable market exists for this weakly defined aggregate and that this market regularly clears within a reasonable period of time are not well supported by empirical estimates for the largest industrial countries. What is well established (see Boughton, 1991) is that certain empirical regularities hold in the long run, linking some (but not all) monetary aggregates to aggregate national economic activity and to risk-free rates of return. What behavioral or causal relationships underpin those regularities is still in dispute.

In the final paragraph of his paper, Engel suggests that we might get a better understanding of the risk premium if we could work with models that incorporate "empirically plausible" money demand equations. Unfortunately, those equations would bear little resemblance to the sweetly innocent equations in this and every other paper on exchange rates. The standard theoretical equation, in logs, is:

$$m_t - p_t = \beta y_t - \gamma i_t \tag{1}$$

which Charles simplifies further to:

$$m_t - p_t = \beta c_t - \gamma \tag{2}$$

Consumption ($c$) replaces output ($y$) because of the assumed nature of the utility function, and the last variable drops out because the supply of money is assumed to be determined by a stable process that makes the nominal interest rate ($i$) constant over time.

In contrast, one widely cited empirical model of the demand for $M1$ in the United States (Baba, Hendry, and Starr, 1985) has the following form:[1]

$$\begin{aligned}\Delta(m-p) = \; & \underset{(0.02)}{0.352} - \underset{(0.10)}{0.334}\Delta_4(m-p)_{-1} - \underset{(0.02)}{0.249}(m-p-0.5y)_{-2} - \underset{(0.10)}{1.409}AS \\ & - \underset{(0.06)}{0.973}Ai - \underset{(0.05)}{0.255}\Delta R_{ma} - \underset{(0.13)}{1.097}\Delta_4 p_{-1} - \underset{(0.05)}{0.330}\Omega + \underset{(0.07)}{0.395}\Delta AY \\ & + \underset{(0.08)}{0.859}V + \underset{(1.49)}{11.680}\Delta SV_{-1} + \underset{(0.06)}{0.435}R^2_{nsa} - \underset{(0.04)}{0.156}\Delta(m-p)_{-4} + \underset{(0.003)}{0.013}D\end{aligned}$$

where

$m$, $p$, and $y$ are logs of $M1$, the GNP deflator, and real GNP;

$i$ is the short-term interest rate;

$S$ is the long-term interest rate minus $i$ (the term structure);

$Ai$, $AS$, and $Ay$ are two-period averages [$Ax = 0.5(x + x_{-1})$, for $x = i, S, y$];

$R_{ma}$ is a learning-adjusted maximum yield on assets in $M2$ but not in $M1$;

$R_{nsa}$ is a learning-adjusted yield on "other checkable" deposits in $M1$;

$\Delta_i x \equiv (x - x_{-i})/i$

$\Delta^2 x \equiv \Delta x - \Delta x_{-1}$

$\Omega = \Delta p + \Delta^2 p$;

$V$ is a measure of volatility in bond yields;

$SV = \max(0, S)V$; and

$D$ is a dummy variable for the temporary imposition of credit controls in 1980.

Some, but by no means all, of this jungle of terms has been introduced to account for the extraordinarily complex dynamics in the relationship. Even in equilibrium, the cointegrating form of this equation includes five substitution effects in addition to the activity variable.

Needless to say, equation (2) is much more suitable for Engel's purposes. Moreover, to avoid unnecessary cluttering, Charles makes the usual simplification that money demand functions are similar between countries. That is, the parameters $\beta$ and $\gamma$ in equation (2) are the same in each country. This assumption seems out of place here: differences in consumption baskets play a large role in helping to explain the risk premium, and it is not clear why asset preferences should be identical when consumption preferences are not. In any event, the assumption does not hold even approximately in empirical tests. As shown in my 1991 paper cited above, income, interest rate, and even steady-state price elasticities differ substantially across major industrial economies.

These two facts—that money demand differs significantly and substantially between countries and that parameter estimates only weakly reflect theoretical expectations—are consistent with the hypothesis that financial markets are segmented both geographically and temporally. Currency substitution in these economies is very weak, and bond substitution is not enough stronger to warrant anything like a perfect-market approach to modeling international financial linkages.

The bottom line, empirically, is that Engel's paper illustrates once again the need for both perseverance and humility. We need, as he says, more detailed empirical research on the risk premium, based on empirically plausible behavioral equations. But no matter how we try, our success will be limited because of temporal instabilities and shifts in the most basic building blocks. In the late 1970s, Mike Mussa suggested that an exchange rate model that could explain 10 percent of the quarterly variance of key-currency exchange rates should be judged a success. (So far as I know, this was not a scientifically derived estimate, but it has the ring of truth.) Twenty years later, careful researchers still feel heartened if they can cross that low threshold.

## Notes

1. The numbers in parentheses are standard errors.

## References

Baba, Yoshihisa, David F. Hendry, and Ross M. Starr. (1992). "The Demand for M1 in the U.S.A., 1960–1988." *Review of Economic Studies* 59, 25–61.

Boughton, James M. (1991). "Long-Run Money Demand in Large Industrial Countries." International Monetary Fund, *Staff Papers* 38, 1–32.

Mussa, Michael. (1979). "Empirical Regularities in the Behavior of Exchange Rates and Theories of the Foreign Exchange Market." In Karl Brunner and Allan H. Meltzer (eds.), *Policies for Employment, Prices, and Exchange Rates*. Amsterdam: North-Holland. Vol. 11 of the Carnegie-Rochester Conference Series on Public Policy, pp. 9–57.

# Comment

BY RICHARD A. MEESE

Charles Engel has done much to improve our understanding of the elusive foreign exchange risk premium, including his campaign to get us to define the risk premium so that it is equal to zero when agents are risk neutral. Charles has expanded our understanding of the likely magnitude of the risk premium and its source, in the context of current generation asset pricing models. While this is not an active area of inquiry in international finance these days, it remains an interesting and important topic.

The first part of this paper builds on Charles' earlier work on the exchange rate risk premium that he published in a series of articles in the *Journal of International Economics*. The newer material in the second part of this paper builds on his more recent research with Michael Devereux; NBER Working Paper No. 6867. The value added in this line of research is to explore the likely size of the risk premium and its source, in sticky price general equilibrium models with two different specifications of money demand (cash in advance, money in utility), and two different models of price setting behavior (one pricing model where purchasing power parity holds, and one where it does not).

For this Festschrift it is important to find an appropriate Bob Flood paper to cite. While Bob has made numerous contributions to international economics, he has tended to steer clear of the well-worked risk premium area. A notable exception is the Flood paper entitled, "Fixes: Of the Forward Discount Puzzle," published in the *Review of Economic Statistics*, co-authored with Andrew Rose. This empirical paper is only tangentially related to the topic here, although it does provide limited support for some of the theoretical results presented by Charles.

More specifically Bob Flood and Andrew Rose find less forward rate bias, or deviations from uncovered interest parity, in data from the European Monetary System (EMS) than for countries that exercise less government control over their exchange rates. The forward rate is still a biased predictor of the future spot rate using daily EMS exchange rate observations, although the slope coefficient is more often of the right sign (positive). So what's the connection between the Flood-Rose paper and Charles' current effort to quantify the risk premium? For most of the paper there is none. Engel derives the risk premium in a number of theoretical models and talks about its magnitude. He finds that a cash in advance specification for money demand coupled with a pricing to market specification (price setting where PPP does not hold) is capable of producing large enough risk premiums to match the data. Charles then draws on the biased forward rate hypothesis literature. In sticky price models the size of the risk premium is proportional to the volatility of the nominal exchange rate, and Flood-Rose find that deviations from uncovered interest parity are lower in the EMU where exchange rates are less variable.

Charles also reminds us that any general equilibrium risk premium model should endeavor to explain both empirical puzzles. The first is the size of the risk premium required to match the data, and the second is the correlation between the risk premium and the forward premium required to explain the aforementioned uncovered interest rate puzzle. I look forward to a model that can resolve both issues.

There are several possible sources of additional model complexity that may help in this endeavor. The first is the consideration of a more realistic money supply specification, such as a money supply reaction function. The second would be more detailed modeling of the real side of the economy such as the labor market. A more careful examination of these markets has the potential to expand both the magnitude and the components of the exchange rate risk premium.

# General Discussion

Several conference participants felt that while Engel had taken a number of nice steps in getting more insights out of sticky-price general equilibrium models, an important next step would be to replace his random-walk money-supply process with a more realistic monetary policy reaction function. **Bennett McCallum** argued that the main empirical puzzle was not so much the size of the exchange risk premium, but rather the apparent failure of uncovered interest rate parity, which was a puzzle about covariances. In his view, the observed covariances resulted from monetary policy behavior that mixed together elements of interest rate smoothing and leaning against exchange rate movements. **Robert Hodrick** noted that the challenge was not simply to find a model that could generate the observed variability of the risk premium, but to find a model that could explain the risk premium without simultaneously generating puzzles about the variability of interest rates or the behavior of other variables. **Dale Henderson** focused on the fact that in all four of Engel's sticky-price model variants, the only shock terms that entered the reduced-form expressions for the risk premium were the money supply variances. He wondered if this reflected an assumption that wages were perfectly flexible and conjectured that other shocks would show up in the risk premium expressions in models in which households were not able to optimally adjust their labor/leisure choices.

# An Information-Based Model of Foreign Direct Investment: The Gains from Trade Revisited

ASSAF RAZIN razin@post.tau.ac.il
*Eitan Berglas School of Economics, Tel Aviv University, Tel Aviv 69978, Israel*

EFRAIM SADKA sadka@post.tau.ac.il
*Eitan Berglas School of Economics, Tel Aviv University, Tel Aviv 69978, Israel*

CHI-WA YUEN cwyuen@hkusub.hku.hk
*School of Economics and Finance, University of Hong Kong, Pokfulam Road, Hong Kong*

***Abstract***

The financial aspects of foreign direct investment (FDI) are the focus of this paper. The gains from trade argument (applied to intertemporal trade) is re-examined in this case of informational-asymmetry-driven FDI. FDI is observed to be a predominant form of capital flows to emerging economies, especially when they are liquidity-constrained internationally during a global financial crisis. We analyze the problem of channeling domestic savings into productive investment in the presence of asymmetric information between the managing owners of firms and portfolio stakeholders. We explore the role played by FDI in reviving equity-financed capital investment for economies plagued by such information problems. In the presence of information asymmetry, the paper identifies how FDI gives rise to foreign overinvestment as well as domestic undersaving. We show that the gains from trade could be sizable when the domestic credit market is either under-developed or failing as a result of a financial crisis. But with a well-functioning domestic credit market, the gains turn into losses. Surprisingly, capital may flow into the country even when the autarkic marginal productivity of capital in the domestic economy falls short of the world rate of interest. In such a situation, capital should have efficiently flown out rather than in, and FDI becomes a social loss-generating phenomenon.

## 1. Introduction

The financial turmoil in East Asia was both a consequence of, and a trigger for, severe international illiquidity.[1] Despite their being liquidity-constrained internationally when foreign bank lending and foreign portfolio equity flows dry up, the Asian crisis economies continue to be recipients of large foreign direct investment (FDI) flows, which remarkably have not declined at all (see Figure 1). Similarly, the liquidity problems associated with the debt crisis in the early 1980s and with the currency collapse in Mexico in the mid-1990s demonstrate also the resilience of FDI to financial crises. These striking episodes underscores an essential role of FDI: it serves as a major link between the domestic capital market and the world capital market when other types of international financial investment become deficient. This paper develops a model aimed at highlighting this important role of FDI, and addresses the issue of whether this type of international capital market link through FDI is in general also beneficial from the social welfare perspective.

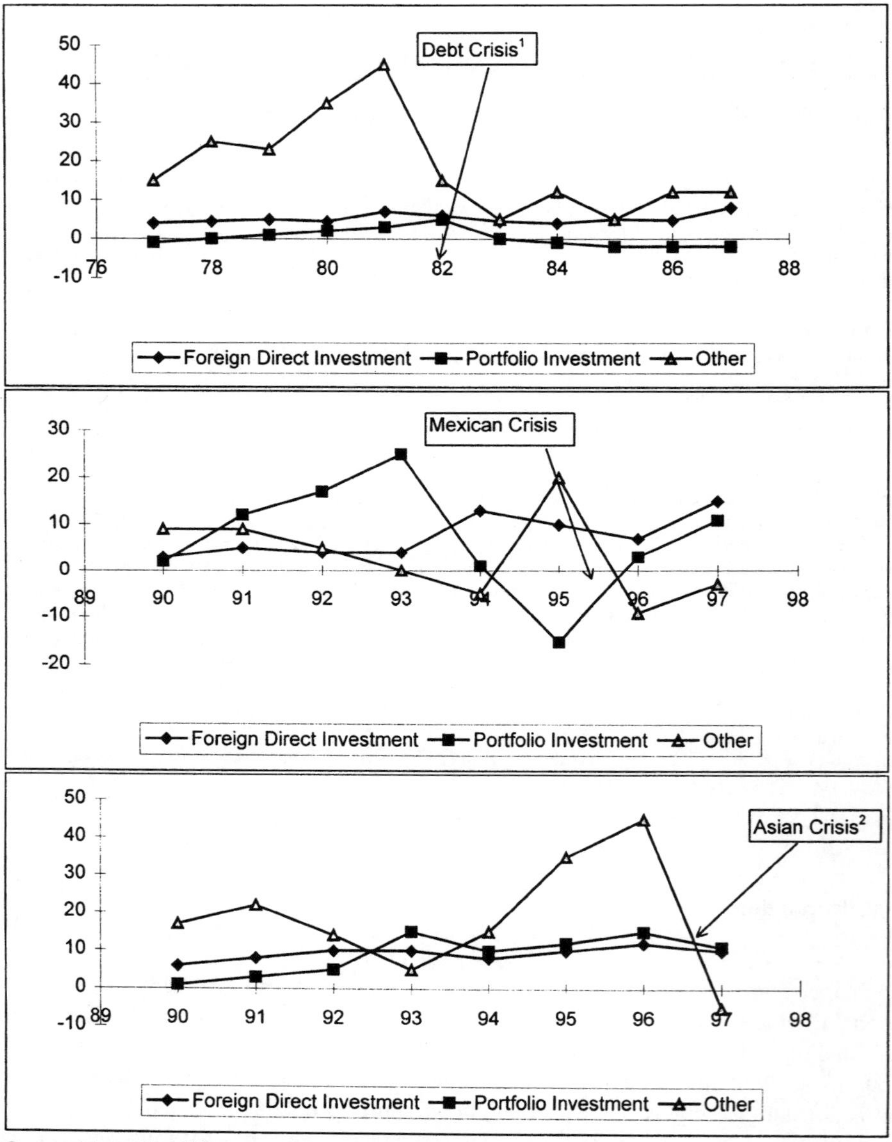


Source: International Monetary Fund, World Econmic Outlook Database

[1] Aggregate Flows to Argentina, Bolivia, Brazil, Chile, Columbia, Cote d'Ivoire, Ecuador, Mexico, Morocco, Nigeria, Peru, the Philippines, Uruguay, and Venezuela

[2] Aggregate Flows to Indonesia, Korea, Malaysia, the Philippines, and Thailand

*Figure 1.* FDI flows, foreign portfolio flows, and other flows to developing countries.

In a formal sense, foreign acquisition of shares in domestic firms is classified as FDI when the acquired shares exceed a certain fraction of ownership (usually, 10–20%). From an economic point of view, however, FDI is not just a purchase of a sizable share in a company but, more importantly, is an actual exercise of control and management. The exercise of control enables the foreign direct investors better access to hard-to-get *information* about the acquired firm's current and potential performance than what is generally available to a minority shareholder.

Frequently, there is a significant asymmetry in information between the managing stockholders (owner-managers) and other portfolio stakeholders (such as the debt and small equity holders) . In the absence of FDI, this informational asymmetry causes a market failure which can be quite severe in the case of equity-financed capital investment. In such case, the equity market shrinks to a "lemons" market *á la* Akerlof (1970), implying a severe shortage of financing for capital investment. We show here that FDI has an essential role to play in restoring the proper functioning of the domestic equity market for capital investment. As indicated, though, such a market will not be fully efficient because it leads to foreign over-investment and domestic under-saving.[2]

The inefficiencies associated with FDI finance may sometimes dominate the traditional gains from trade emanating from directing capital from the world market (where the rate of interest is relatively low) to the domestic capital market (where the return to capital is relatively high). Furthermore, the inefficient domestic capital market may attract FDI even when the domestic social rate of return to capital is below the world rate of interest. In such a case, financial liberalization may even misdirect the world capital flows. Accordingly, we demonstrate how the existence of informational-asymmetry-driven FDI can actually turn the gains from international (intertemporal) trade into strict losses.

Our focus on the welfare consequences of FDI from a finance-based perspective is different from most of the existing literature, which focuses on the various explanations for the widespread flows of FDI in the world economy. The international trade literature has examined closely the interactions between FDI and international trade, highlighting the role of multinationals and of FDI in explaining intra-industry trade (see Helpman (1984) and an empirical analysis by Wickham and Thompson (1989)). Brainard (1993a, 1993b) provides a useful empirical assessment of the tradeoff between the proximity to the market and the advantages of concentration in production. FDI is the main instrument that affects this tradeoff. Goldberg and Klein (1997) investigate the relation among trade, FDI, and the real exchange rate. As an extension to this literature, we identify in this paper a distinct mechanism associated with the financial aspects of FDI that turns out to be important in determining its welfare consequences as well.

The organization of the paper is as follows. Section 2 develops an FDI-equity model without a domestic credit market and examines the welfare gains (losses) from FDI. Section 3 introduces a well-functioning domestic credit market and reexamines the gains (losses) from FDI. Concluding remarks are provided in Section 4.

## 2. Foreign Direct Investment and Equity Finance

In this section and the next, we assume a two-period model of a small, capital-importing country, referred to as the home country. It is assumed that capital imports are channelled solely through foreign direct investment (FDI), due to home-bias in portfolio flows as in Gordon and Bovenberg (1996) and Razin, Sadka, and Yuen (1998a, 1999a). The economy is small enough so that, in the absence of any government intervention, it faces a perfectly elastic supply of external funds at a given risk-free world rate of interest, $r^*$.

Suppose there is a very large number ($N$) of *ex ante* identical domestic firms. Each firm employs capital input ($K$) in the first period in order to produce a single composite good in the second period. We assume that capital depreciates at the rate $\delta$. Output in the second period is equal to $F(K)(1+\varepsilon)$, where $F(\cdot)$ is a production function exhibiting diminishing marginal productivity of capital and $\varepsilon$ is a random productivity factor. The latter has zero mean and is independent across all firms. ($\varepsilon$ is bounded from below by $-1$, so that output is always nonnegative.) We assume that $\varepsilon$ is purely idiosyncratic, so that there is no aggregate uncertainty. Through optimal portfolio decisions, consumer-investors will thus behave in a risk-neutral way.

Investment decisions are made by the firms before the state of the world (i.e., $\varepsilon$) is known.[3] Since all firms face the same probability distribution of $\varepsilon$, they all choose the same level of investment. They then seek funds to finance the investment. At this stage, the owner-managers of the firms are better informed than the outside fund-suppliers. There are many ways to specify the degree of this asymmetry in information. In order to facilitate the analysis, however, we simply assume that the owner-managers, being "close to the action," observe $\varepsilon$ before they make their financing decisions; but the fund-providers, being "far away from the action," do not.

In this section where investment is equity-financed, the original owner-managers observe $\varepsilon$ while the new potential shareholders of the firm do not. The market will be trapped in the "lemons" situation described by Akerlof (1970). At the price offered by the new (uninformed) potential equity buyers, which reflects the average productivity of all firms (i.e., the average level of $\varepsilon$) in the market, the owner-manager of a firm experiencing a higher-than-average value of $\varepsilon$ will not be willing to sell its shares and will pull out of the market completely. The equity market will fail to serve its investment financing functions efficiently. We therefore turn to consider another source of equity finance—viz. international capital flows in the form of FDI.

### 2.1. *The FDI-Equity Market Equilibrium*

In a formal sense, foreign acquisition of shares in domestic firms is classified as FDI when the shares acquired exceed a certain fraction of ownership (say, 10–20%). From an economic point of view, we look at FDI not just as ownership of a sizable share in a company but, more importantly, as an actual exercise of control management and acquisition of inside information (the value of $\varepsilon$ in our model).

Suppose that foreign direct investors purchase domestic companies from scratch, at the "greenfield" stage, i.e., before any capital investment is made.[4] For the sake of simplicity and in order to focus on FDI, we ignore, with no loss of generality, all other sectors of the economy in which information is symmetric, and assume that foreign direct investors acquire all the greenfield investment sites. Any single home investor who lacks access to foreign capital markets cannot challenge the foreign direct investors for these sites.[5] Note that if a home investor uses only her own fund, she can purchase only a tiny fraction of a greenfield investment site. In such a case, she cannot gain control of the site and the informational advantage entailed by such control.

Upon acquisition and before $\varepsilon$ is known, these foreign investors make their capital investment decisions. The realized value of $\varepsilon$ is then revealed to them, but not to the potential new equity holders who are solicited to finance the capital investment. Being unable to observe $\varepsilon$, domestic investors will offer the same price for all firms, reflecting the average productivity for the group of low productivity firms they purchase. On the other hand, the foreign direct investors who do observe $\varepsilon$ will not be willing to sell at this price the firms which experience high values of $\varepsilon$. Therefore, there will be a cutoff level of $\varepsilon$, say $\varepsilon^o$, such that all firms which experience a lower value of $\varepsilon$ than the cutoff level will be purchased by domestic investors. All other firms will be retained by the foreign direct investors.

Define $e^-$ as the mean value of $\varepsilon$ realized by the low productivity firms:

$$e^-(\varepsilon^o) \equiv E(\varepsilon/\varepsilon \leq \varepsilon^o), \tag{1}$$

i.e., $e^-$ is the conditional expectation of $\varepsilon$, given that $\varepsilon \leq \varepsilon^o$. For later use, we also denote by $e^+(\varepsilon^o)$ the conditional expectation of $\varepsilon$, given that $\varepsilon \geq \varepsilon^o$:

$$e^+(\varepsilon^o) \equiv E(\varepsilon/\varepsilon \geq \varepsilon^o) \tag{2}$$

Note that the weighted average of $e^-(\varepsilon^o)$ and $e^+(\varepsilon^o)$ must yield the average value of $\varepsilon$, that is:

$$\Phi(\varepsilon^o)e^-(\varepsilon^o) + \left[1 - \Phi(\varepsilon^o)\right] e^+(\varepsilon^o) = E(\varepsilon) = 0, \tag{3}$$

where $\Phi(\cdot)$ is the cumulative probability distribution of $\varepsilon$, i.e., $\Phi(\varepsilon^o) = prob(\varepsilon \leq \varepsilon^o)$. Equation (3) also implies that $e^-(\varepsilon^o) < 0$ while $e^+(\varepsilon^o) > 0$, i.e., the expected value of $\varepsilon$ for the "bad" ("good") firm is negative (positive).

The cutoff level of $\varepsilon$ is then defined by:

$$\begin{aligned} &\left\{F(K)\left[1 + e^-(\varepsilon^o)\right] + (1 - \delta)K\right\} / (1 + \bar{r}) \\ &\qquad = \left[F(K)(1 + \varepsilon^o) + (1 - \delta)K\right] / (1 + r^*), \end{aligned} \tag{4}$$

where $\bar{r}$ is the domestic consumer rate of interest (return). The value of a typical domestic firm in the second period is equal to its output, plus the undepreciated capital, i.e., $F(K)(1+\varepsilon) + (1 - \delta)K$. Since domestic equity investors will buy only those firms with $\varepsilon \leq \varepsilon^o$, the expected second-period value of a firm they buy is $F(K)\left[1 + e^-(\varepsilon^o)\right] + (1 - \delta)K$, which they then discount by the factor $1 + \bar{r}$ to determine the price they are willing to pay in the first period. At equilibrium, this price is equal to the price that a foreign direct investor is willing to accept for the firm which experiences a productivity value of $\varepsilon^o$. The cutoff price is equal to the expected value of the marginal $\varepsilon^o$-firm, $F(K)(1 + \varepsilon^o) + (1 - \delta)K$, discounted by a factor $1 + r^*$. Firms that experience a value of $\varepsilon$ higher than $\varepsilon^o$ are retained by the foreign direct investors. This explains the equilibrium condition (4).

As $e^-(\varepsilon^o) < \varepsilon^o$, an interior equilibrium (i.e., $-1 < \varepsilon^o < 1$) requires that the foreigners' rate of return ($r^*$) be higher than the residents' rate of return ($\bar{r}$). In some sense, this means that domestic investors are "over-charged" by foreign direct investors for their purchases of domestic firms. These foreign investors will not accept a price below $\{F(K)(1+\varepsilon^o) + (1-\delta)K\}/(1+r^*)$ for the low productivity firms. Note the crucial role of FDI in allowing for an international rate-of-return differential (viz., $r^* > \bar{r}$). This differential is essential for the existence of an equity market. In an autarkic situation without FDI, there is no rate-of-return differential between the original owner-managers and potential equity buyers. Without this differential, the market will collapse to one of "lemons" and it will be difficult to equity-finance capital investment.

Consider the capital investment decision of the firm that is made before $\varepsilon$ becomes known, while it is still owned by foreign direct investors. The firm seeks to maximize its market value, net of the original investment. With a probability $\Phi(\varepsilon^o)$, it will be sold to domestic investors, who pay $\{F(K)[1+e^-(\varepsilon^o)] + (1-\delta)K\}/(1+\bar{r})$. With a probability $[1-\Phi(\varepsilon^o)]$, it will be retained by the foreign investors, for whom it is worth on average $\{F(K)\left[1+e^+(\varepsilon^o)\right] + (1-\delta)K\}/(1+r^*)$. Hence, the firm's expected market value, net of the original capital investment, is:

$$\begin{aligned} V &= \Phi(\varepsilon^o)\left(\left\{F(K)\left[1+e^-(\varepsilon^o)\right] + (1-\delta)K\right\}/(1+\bar{r}) - [K-(1-\delta)K_o]\right) \\ &\quad + \left[1-\Phi(\varepsilon^o)\right]\left(\left\{F(K)\left[1+e^+(\varepsilon^o)\right] + (1-\delta)K\right\}/(1+r^*) \right. \\ &\quad \left. - [K-(1-\delta)K_o]\right), \end{aligned} \tag{5}$$

where $K-(1-\delta)K_o$ is gross investment and $K_o$ is the initial stock of capital. Maximizing this expression with respect to $K$ yields the following first-order condition:

$$\begin{aligned} &\Phi(\varepsilon^o)\left\{F'(K)\left[1+e^-(\varepsilon^o)\right] + (1-\delta)\right\}/(1+\bar{r}) \\ &\quad + \left[1-\Phi(\varepsilon^o)\right]F'(K)\left[1+e^+(\varepsilon^o)\right] + (1-\delta)\}/(1+r^*) = 1. \end{aligned} \tag{6}$$

Equation (6) implies that:

$$\bar{r} < F'(K) - \delta < r^*. \tag{7}$$

A formal proof of these inequalities is provided in Appendix A.

Notice that the "textbook presumption" is that in the absence of capital flows (i.e., in a financial autarky) the domestic net-of-depreciation marginal productivity of capital (i.e., $F'(K_o) - \delta$) exceeds the world rate of interest $r^*$. We have shown that the flows of FDI bring down the net-of-depreciation marginal productivity of capital (i.e. $F'(K) - \delta$) below the world rate of interest. Thus, FDI transforms the initial shortage of domestic capital into an overly abundant stock of domestic capital; that is, we have foreign over-investment. Furthermore, the more surprising effect of FDI occurs when the "textbook presumption" of an initial shortage of capital does not hold (i.e., when $F'(K_o) - \delta < r^*$). In this case, capital inflows are not fundamentally needed. Nevertheless, the odd nature of incentives which emanate from the domestic equity market, plagued by asymmetric information, elicits capital inflows. These misdirected flows of capital widen the gap between the relatively high world rate of interest and the relatively low net-of-depreciation marginal productivity of capital.

The (maximized) value of $V$ in (5) is the price paid by the foreign direct investors at the greenfield stage of investment. Since the value of $\varepsilon$ is not known at this point, the same price is paid for all firms. Note, however, that some of the firms are then resold to domestic savers, so that net foreign direct investment (FDI) is equal to:

$$FDI = N[1 - \Phi(\varepsilon^o)]\{[K - (1-\delta)K_o] + \hat{V}\}, \tag{8'}$$

where

$$\hat{V} = \{F(K)[1 + e^+(\varepsilon^o)] + (1-\delta)K\} \;/\; (1 + r^*) - [K - (1-\delta)K_o]. \tag{9}$$

(Recall that {V-[1-$\Phi(\varepsilon^o)$]$\hat{V}$} / $\Phi(\varepsilon^o)$ is the price at which the low-productivity firms are resold to domestic savers. It is assumed that the foreign direct investors import capital to finance investment in the high-productivity firms which they retain.

Employing (9), equation (8′) reduces to:

$$FDI = N[1 - \Phi(\varepsilon^o)]\{F(K)[1 + e^+(\varepsilon^o)] + (1-\delta)K\} \;/\; (1 + r^*). \tag{8}$$

The remaining equilibrium conditions are standard. In the first period, the economy faces a resource constraint stating that FDI must suffice to cover the difference between domestic investment (viz. $N[K - (1-\delta)K_o]$) and national savings (viz., the difference between the first period output and saving, $NF(K_o) - c_1$:

$$FDI = N[K - (1-\delta)K_o] - [NF(K_o) - c_1]. \tag{10}$$

Since foreigners will be able to extract from the home country an amount of $1 + r^*$ units of output in the second period for each unit that they invest in the first period, the home country faces the following second-period budget constraint:[6]

$$NF(K) + (1-\delta)NK - FDI(1 + r^*) = c_2. \tag{11}$$

That is, the second period gross *national* output (namely, $NF(K) - FDI(1+r^*)$), plus the undepreciated capital, (namely, $(1-\delta)NK$), must suffice to support private consumption ($c_2$). Employing (10), one can rewrite (11) in present value terms as:

$$\begin{aligned} NF(K_o) + N[F(K) + (1-\delta)K]/(1 + r^*) &= c_1 + c_2/(1 + r^*) \\ &\quad + N[K - (1-\delta)K_o]. \end{aligned} \tag{12}$$

Naturally, $c_1$ and $c_2$ are determined by the utility-maximizing consumer-saver. But since they do not have access to the world capital market and can only borrow/lend from the domestic market, these consumer-savers will choose $c_1$ and $c_2$ by equating their intertemporal marginal rate of substitution to the domestic default-risk-free (rather than the world) rate of return:

$$\frac{\partial u}{\partial c_1}(c_1, c_2) \;/\; \frac{\partial u}{\partial c_2}(c_1, c_2) = 1 + \bar{r}, \tag{13}$$

where $u$ is the consumer's utility function.

In this model the six equations—(4), (6), (8), (10), (11) and (13)—determine the six endogenous variables—$\varepsilon^o$, $r$, $K$, $FDI$, $c_1$, and $c_2$.

### 2.2. *Gains from Trade*

We have demonstrated the crucial role of FDI in sustaining a non-"lemon"-type domestic equity market, albeit not a fully efficient one. There is also a second role, the traditional "gains from trade" role of directing foreign savings into domestic investment. To flash out in a simplified manner the kind of gains or losses brought about by FDI, we compare the laissez-faire allocation in the presence of FDI with the closed economy laissez-faire allocation.

The laissez-faire allocation in the presence of FDI is characterized by:

$$\bar{r} < F'(K) - \delta < r^*.$$

(see equation (7)). The first inequality states that the return accruing to domestic savers (i.e., $\bar{r}$) is below the return to the economy (i.e., $F'(K) - \delta$). This indicates that domestic households under-save. The second inequality states that the return accruing to the economy from the inflow of foreign capital (i.e., $F'(K) - \delta$) is below its cost to the economy (i.e., $r^*$), indicating excessive capital inflows. Therefore, the laissez-faire allocation with FDI is characterized by domestic under-saving and foreign over-investment.[7]

In a closed economy, the original owner of a greenfield investment site cannot finance capital outlays on her own. She has to appeal instead to the domestic equity market. In this case the economy will be trapped in a "lemons"-type equilibrium. Any owner-manager of a firm realizing a higher-than-average productivity factor ($\varepsilon$) will pull out of the market which prices all firms according to their average productivity. The market thus shrinks to "lemons," the shares of the firms with the lowest productivity. Strictly speaking, no new investment can be financed through the equity market and all firms will simply produce with their initial stock of capital which is $K_o$.[8] In this autarkic economy there is no capital market and there is neither saving nor investment.

In this case with no domestic credit, FDI has conflicting effects on welfare. Its first crucial (and unique to this model) role discussed above is to facilitate the channelling of domestic saving into domestic investment. This, by itself, is welfare-enhancing. But, as we have already indicated, FDI is driven also by distorted incentives and its traditional role of directing foreign savings into domestic investment generates an excessive stock of domestic capital. (Either when capital inflows were not all needed or when they were needed to start with, too much of them took place). This foreign over-investment (coupled with domestic under-saving) tends to reduce welfare.

We use numerical examples to illustrate the total effect of FDI on welfare. In these examples, we employ a logarithmic utility function ($u(c_1, c_2) = \ln(c_1) + \gamma \ln(c_2)$), with a subjective discount factor $\gamma$, a Cobb–Douglas production function ($F(K) = AK^{\alpha}$), and a uniform distribution of $\varepsilon$ defined over the interval $[-a, a]$.[9] The welfare gain (loss) is measured by the uniform percentage change (in $c_1$ and $c_2$) which is needed in order to lift the autarkic utility level to the FDI utility level. These welfare gains (losses) are calculated for various levels of the world rate of interest $r^*$, ranging from 0 to 0.45. (These rates correspond to real annual rates of interest, ranging from 0% to 1.25% on a 30-year period interval.) As shown in Figure 2, the welfare gain numbers are reasonably large. At levels of $r^*$ lower than the autarkic net-of-depreciation marginal productivity of capital ($F'(K_o) - \delta = 0.06$),

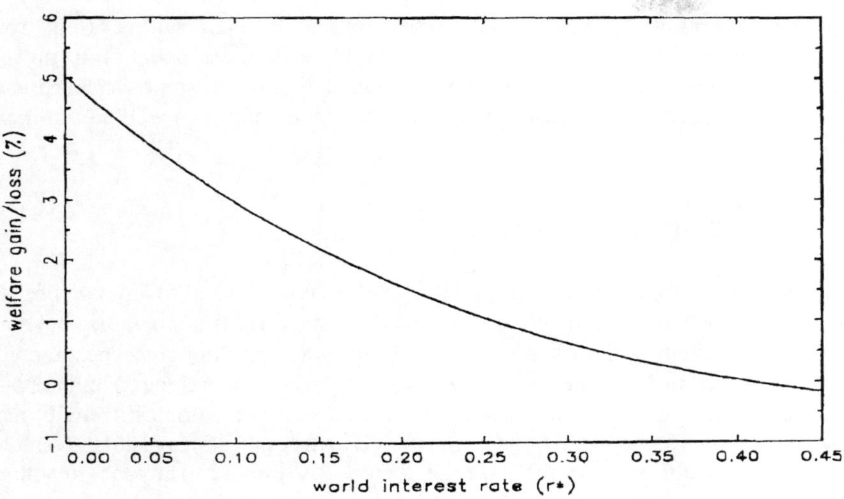


*Figure 2.* Welfare gain/loss from FDI without domestic credit

these numbers reflect a combination of the traditional gains (i.e., capital cost saving) and the two conflicting welfare effects of FDI mentioned in the preceding paragraph. The latter is still strongly positive, equal to almost a 3.7% increase in lifetime consumption, even when the former is absent, i.e., when $r^* = 0.06$. These huge gains are due to the large inflow of capital, amounting to about 60% of GDP, that finances about 50% of the firms with FDI-equity and indirectly the consumption loans made by the domestic households (at a saving rate of −43%). Naturally, the gains come down as the gap between the autarky interest rate and the world interest rate widens. Observe, though, that even when the gap is negative so that there is no economic need for capital inflows to start with, there may still exist welfare gains.[10]

## 3. FDI with Domestic Equity and Credit Markets

In the preceding section, we have demonstrated that the gains from trade brought about by FDI can be quite sizable. In fact, FDI may fulfill several roles. It may create an active (albeit distorted) domestic stock market that facilitates the channelling of domestic savings to finance new domestic investment. It may also facilitate the channelling of foreign savings to the domestic stock market to help finance part of the new investment. This is why the gains from trade through FDI can be rather substantial.

However, when a domestic credit market is doing most of the job of channelling domestic savings into domestic investment, the role of FDI diminishes. In fact, it is often observed that FDI is highly leveraged domestically. After gaining control of the domestic firm, a foreign direct investor usually resorts to the domestic credit market to finance new investment and possibly trade shares of the firm in the domestic equity market later on after profits from its original investment are realized. We thus extend in this section the model of the preceding section to include a domestic credit market. We then demonstrate, somewhat surprisingly, that not only the gains from trade through FDI diminish, but they can well be significantly negative.

### 3.1. *The FDI-Equity-Credit Equilibrium*

The sequencing of firm decisions is as follows. Before $\varepsilon$ is revealed to anyone (i.e., under symmetric information), foreign investors bid up domestic firms from their original domestic owners, investment decisions are made, and full financing through domestic credit is secured. Then, $\varepsilon$ is revealed to the owner-managers (who are all foreigners), but not also to domestic equity investors. At this stage, shares are offered in the domestic equity market and the ownership in some of the firms is transferred to the domestic investors. The foreign direct investors are able in the initial stage (i.e., before $\varepsilon$ is revealed to anyone) to outbid the domestic savers because the latter lack access to large amounts of funds necessary in order to seize control of the firms while the former, by assumption, are not liquidity constrained.

Since credit is extended *ex ante*, before $\varepsilon$ is revealed, firms cannot sign default-free loan contracts with the lenders. We therefore consider loan contracts which allow for the possibility of default. We adopt the "costly state verification" framework *á la* Townsend (1979) in assuming that lenders make firm-specific loans, charging an interest rate of $r^j$ to firm $j$ $(0 \leq j \leq N)$.[11] The interest and principal payment commitment will be honored when the firms encounter relatively good shocks, and defaulted when they encounter relatively bad shocks. The loan contract is characterized by a loan rate $(r^j)$, with possible default, and a threshold value $(\bar{\varepsilon}^j)$ of the productivity parameter as follows:

$$F(K^j)(1+\bar{\varepsilon}^j) + (1-\delta)K^j = [K^j - (1-\delta)K_o^j](1+r^j). \tag{14}$$

When the realized value of $\varepsilon^j$ is larger than $\bar{\varepsilon}^j$, the firm is solvent and will thus pay the lenders the promised amount, consisting of the principal $K^j - (1-\delta)K_0^j$ plus the interest $r^j[K^j - (1-\delta)K_o^j]$ as given by the right-hand-side of (14). If, however, $\varepsilon^j < \bar{\varepsilon}^j$, the firm will default. In the case of default, the lenders can incur a cost in order to verify the true value of $\varepsilon^j$ and to seize the residual value of the firm. This cost, interpretable as the cost of bankruptcy, is assumed to be proportional to the firm's realized gross return, $\mu[F(K^j)(1+\varepsilon^j) + (1-\delta)K^j]$, where $\mu \leq 1$ is the factor of proportionality. Net of this cost, the lenders will receive $(1-\mu)[F(K^j)(1+\varepsilon^j) + (1-\delta)K^j]$.

Since there is no aggregate risk, the expected rate of return required by domestic consumer-savers, denoted by $\bar{r}$, can be secured by sufficient diversification,. Therefore, the "default" rate of interest, $r^j$, must offer a premium over and above the default-free rate, $\bar{r}$, according to:

$$\begin{aligned}&\left[1-\Phi(\bar{\varepsilon}^j)\right][K^j-(1-\delta)K_0^j](1+r^j)\\&\quad+\Phi(\bar{\varepsilon}^j)(1-\mu)\left\{F(K^j)\left[1+e^-\left(\bar{\varepsilon}^j\right)\right]+(1-\delta)K^j\right\}\\&\quad=\left[K^j-(1-\delta)\,K_0^j\right](1+\bar{r})\,.\end{aligned} \tag{15'}$$

The first term on the left-hand-side of (15′) is the contracted principal and interest payment, weighted by the no-default probability. The second term measures the net residual value of the firm, weighted by the default probability. The right-hand-side is the no-default return required by the domestic lender. Observe that (14) and (15′) together imply that:

$$\left[1-\Phi(\bar{\varepsilon}^j)\right]+\frac{\Phi(\bar{\varepsilon}^j)(1-\mu)\{F(K^j)\left[1+e^-\left(\bar{\varepsilon}^j\right)\right]+(1-\delta)K^j\}}{F(K^j)(1+\bar{\varepsilon}^j)+(1-\delta)K^j}=\frac{1+\bar{r}}{1+r^j}.$$

Since $e^-(\bar{\varepsilon}^j) < \bar{\varepsilon}^j$ and $\mu \geq 0$, it follows that $r^j > \bar{r}$, the difference being a risk-premium (which depends, among other things, on $K^j$, $\bar{\varepsilon}^j$, and $\mu$).

The firm in this setup is competitive (price-taker) only with respect to $\bar{r}$, the market default-free rate of return. This $\bar{r}$ cannot be influenced by the firm's actions. However, $r^j$, $K^j$, and $\bar{\varepsilon}^j$ are firm-specific and must satisfy equations (14) and (15′). In making its investment, $K^j-(1-\delta)K_o^j$, and its financing (loan contract) decisions, the firm takes these constraints into account. Since these decisions are made before $\varepsilon$ is known, i.e., when all firms are (ex-ante) identical, they all make the same decision. We henceforth drop the superscript $j$.

The remainder of this section proceeds along similar lines as the preceding section. In the equity market which opens after $\varepsilon$ is revealed to the (foreign) owner-managers, there is a cutoff level of $\varepsilon$, denoted by $\varepsilon^o$ (generally different than the corresponding $\varepsilon^o$ of the preceding section), such that all firms experiencing a value of $\varepsilon$ above $\varepsilon^o$ will be retained by the foreign direct investors and all other firms (with $\varepsilon$ below $\varepsilon^o$) will be sold to domestic savers. This cutoff level of $\varepsilon$ is given by:

$$\begin{aligned}&\frac{[F(K)(1+\varepsilon^o)+(1-\delta)K]-(1+r)[K-(1-\delta)K_o]}{1+r^*}\\&\quad=\frac{\Phi(\varepsilon^o)-\Phi(\bar{\varepsilon})}{\Phi(\varepsilon^o)}\cdot\frac{\{F(K)\left[1+\hat{e}\left(\bar{\varepsilon},\varepsilon^o\right)\right]+(1-\delta)K\}-(1+r)[K-(1-\delta)K_o]}{1+\bar{r}}\\&\qquad+\frac{\Phi(\bar{\varepsilon})}{\Phi(\varepsilon^o)}\cdot 0,\end{aligned}\tag{16′}$$

where

$$\hat{e}(\bar{\varepsilon},\varepsilon^o)\equiv E\{\varepsilon/\bar{\varepsilon}\leq\varepsilon\leq\varepsilon^o\}\tag{17}$$

is the conditional expectation of the $\varepsilon's$ between $\bar{\varepsilon}$ and $\varepsilon^o$.

Notice that firms that experience a value of $\varepsilon$ below $\bar{\varepsilon}$ default and have zero value. These firms are not retained by the foreign direct investors; hence $\varepsilon^o \geq \bar{\varepsilon}$. All other firms generate in the second period a *net* cash flow of $[F(K)(1+\varepsilon)+(1-\delta)K]-(1+r)[K-(1-\delta)K_o]$. The left-hand-side of (16′) represents the marginal (from the bottom of the distribution) firm retained by foreign investors. The right-hand-side of (16′) is the expected value of the firms that are purchased by domestic savers. With a conditional probability of $[\Phi(\varepsilon^o)-\Phi(\bar{\varepsilon})]\ /\ \Phi(\varepsilon^o)$, they generate a net expected cash flow of $F(K)[1+\hat{e}(\bar{\varepsilon},\varepsilon^o)]+(1-\delta)K\}-(1+r)[K-(1-\delta)K_o]$; with a probability of $\Phi(\bar{\varepsilon})\ /\ \Phi(\varepsilon^o)$ they generate a zero net cash flow. This explains equation (16′).

We can substitute equation (14) into (15′) and (16′) in order to eliminate $r$ and then rearrange terms to obtain:

$$[1-\Phi(\bar{\varepsilon})]\,F(K)(1+\bar{\varepsilon})+\Phi(\bar{\varepsilon})(1-\mu)F(K)\left[1+e^{-}(\bar{\varepsilon})\right]+[1-\Phi(\bar{\varepsilon})\mu]\,(1-\delta)K$$
$$=[K-(1-\delta)K_o]\,(1+\bar{r}), \tag{15}$$

and

$$\frac{\varepsilon^o-\bar{\varepsilon}}{1+r^*}=\frac{\hat{e}(\bar{\varepsilon},\varepsilon^o)-\bar{\varepsilon}}{1+\bar{r}}\left[\Phi(\varepsilon^o)-\Phi(\bar{\varepsilon})\right]\;/\;\Phi(\varepsilon^o). \tag{16}$$

Consider now the capital investment decision of the firm that is made before $\varepsilon$ becomes known, while it is still owned by foreign direct investors. With a probability of $\Phi(\varepsilon^o)-\Phi(\bar{\varepsilon})$, it will be sold to domestic savers who pay a positive price equalling

$$\left\{F(K)\left[1+\hat{e}(\bar{\varepsilon},\varepsilon^o)\right]+(1-\delta)K-(1+r)[K-(1-\delta)K_0]\right\}/(1+\bar{r}),$$

which reduces to $F(K)\left[\hat{e}(\bar{\varepsilon},\varepsilon^o)-\bar{\varepsilon}\right]/(1+\bar{r})$, where use is made of (14). With a probability of $1-\Phi(\varepsilon^o)$, it will be retained by the foreign investors for whom it is worth

$$\left\{F(K)[1+e^{+}(\varepsilon^o)]+(1-\delta)K-(1+r)[K-(1-\delta)K_o]\right\}/(1+r^*)$$
$$=F(K)[e^{+}(\varepsilon^o)-\bar{\varepsilon}]/(1+r^*),$$

where use is made of (14). Hence, the firm seeks to maximize

$$V=\frac{[1-\Phi(\varepsilon^o)]F(K)[e^{+}(\varepsilon^o)-\bar{\varepsilon}]}{1+r^*}+0\cdot\Phi(\bar{\varepsilon})$$
$$+\frac{[\Phi(\varepsilon^o)-\Phi(\bar{\varepsilon})]F(K)[\hat{e}(\bar{\varepsilon},\varepsilon^o)-\bar{\varepsilon}]}{1+\bar{r}} \tag{18}$$

subject to constraint (15), by choice of $K$ and $\bar{\varepsilon}$,. given $\varepsilon_0$.[12] This maximization yields the following first-order conditions:

$$\left\{\frac{[1-\Phi(\varepsilon^o)][e^{+}(\varepsilon^o)-\bar{\varepsilon}]}{1+r^*}+\frac{[\Phi(\varepsilon^o)-\Phi(\bar{\varepsilon})][\hat{e}(\bar{\varepsilon},\varepsilon^o)-\bar{\varepsilon}]}{1+\bar{r}}\right\}F'(K)$$
$$+\lambda\left\{[1-\Phi(\bar{\varepsilon})]\,(1+\bar{\varepsilon})+\Phi(\bar{\varepsilon})(1-\mu)[1+e^{-}(\bar{\varepsilon})]\right\}F'(K)$$
$$-\lambda(\bar{r}+\delta)-\lambda\Phi(\bar{\varepsilon})\mu(1-\delta)=0, \tag{19}$$

and

$$\left\{-\frac{1-\Phi(\varepsilon^o)}{1+r^*}-\frac{\Phi'(\bar{\varepsilon})\left[\hat{e}(\bar{\varepsilon},\varepsilon^o)-\bar{\varepsilon}\right]}{1+\bar{r}}+\frac{[\Phi(\varepsilon^o)-\Phi(\bar{\varepsilon})][\frac{\partial\hat{e}}{\partial\bar{e}}(\bar{\varepsilon},\varepsilon^o)-1]}{1+\bar{r}}\right.$$
$$-\lambda\Phi'(\bar{\varepsilon})(1+\bar{\varepsilon})+\lambda[1-\Phi(\bar{\varepsilon})]+\lambda\Phi'(\bar{\varepsilon})(1-\mu)[1+e^{-}(\bar{\varepsilon})]$$
$$\left.+\lambda\Phi(\bar{\varepsilon})(1-\mu)\frac{de^{-}(\bar{\varepsilon})}{d\bar{\varepsilon}}\right\}F(K)-\lambda\mu\Phi'(\bar{\varepsilon})(1-\delta)K=0, \tag{20}$$

where $\lambda$ is a Lagrange multiplier. Our numerical simulations reported below suggest that in this case too there will be domestic undersaving and foreign overinvestment: $\bar{r} < F'(K) - \delta < r^*$.

The (maximized) value of $V$ in (18) is the price paid by the foreign direct investors at the greenfield stage of investment. Since the value of $\varepsilon$ is not known at this point, the same price is paid for all firms. As in the preceding section, the low-$\varepsilon$ firms are then (after $\varepsilon$ is revealed to the foreign direct investors) resold to domestic savers, all at the same price, because $\varepsilon$ is not observed by these savers. Net capital inflows through FDI are given by:

$$FDI = N[1 - \Phi(\varepsilon^o)]F(K)[e^+(\varepsilon^o) - \bar{\varepsilon}]/(1 + r^*) \tag{21}$$

(see equation (18)). Unlike the preceding section (with no domestic credit), in this section all capital outlays are financed domestically and FDI consists only of the price paid for the ownership and control of the high-$\varepsilon$ firms.

The remainder of the equilibrium conditions is standard. The first-period resource constraint is given by:

$$FDI = N[K - (1 - \delta)K_o] - [NF(K_o) - c_1]. \tag{22}$$

The second-period resource constraint is

$$\begin{aligned} &NF(K) + (1 - \delta)NK - FDI(1 + r^*) \\ &\qquad -N\mu\Phi(\bar{\varepsilon})\left\{F(K)\left[1 + e^-(\bar{\varepsilon})\right] + (1 - \delta)K\right\} = c_2. \end{aligned} \tag{23}$$

Note that the last term on the left-hand-side of (23) reflects the existence of real default costs. Finally, utility maximization implies that

$$\frac{\partial u}{\partial c_1}(c_1, c_2) \Big/ \frac{\partial u}{\partial c_2}(c_1, c_2) = 1 + \bar{r}. \tag{24}$$

In this model the eight equations ((15), (16), (19)–(24)) determine the eight endogenous variables ($K$, $\bar{\varepsilon}$, $\varepsilon^o$, $c_1$, $c_2$, $\bar{r}$, $FDI$, $\lambda$).

### 3.2. *Gains from Trade*

Unlike the preceding case of no domestic credit, an autarkic economy in this case can utilize domestic savings to debt-finance domestic investment. The crucial role of FDI as a vehicle for sustaining a domestic equity market through which domestic savings are channelled into domestic investment is thus substantially diminished. Consequently, the negative effect of FDI associated with the distorted incentives emanating from the domestic equity market dominates, and altogether there may exist a net welfare loss from trade. Figure 3 illustrates the welfare gains and losses occurring at various levels of the world rate of interest, $r^*$, for the same set of parameter values as in Figure 2.[13] Except for levels of $r^*$ ranging from 4.1 to 4.7 (equivalent to an annual real rate of 5.58% to 5.97%) where some minimal welfare gains of 0.04% to 0.55% are recorded, welfare losses are prominant (about −2% at lower levels of $r^*$ and increasing to more than −20% when $r^*$ exceeds 4.7) Compared with the

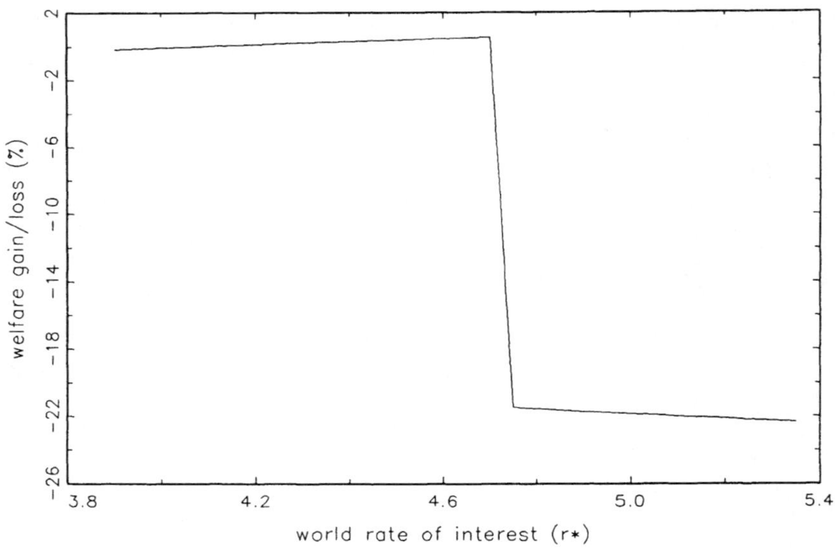


*Figure 3.* Welfare gain/loss from FDI with domestic credit

case of no domestic credit, the role of FDI in financing domestic investment is much less important. At $r^* \leq 4.7$, the FDI-GDP ratio is about 6–8% whereas the fraction of firms financed by FDI-equity is less than 40% (and domestic savings are positive, i.e., no FDI-funded consumption loans). Note that the autarkic risk-free interest rate of 2.9 falls short of all the values of $r^*$ considered here. So here again, we have the possibility that although the FDI flows are not fundamentally needed, they do nevertheless flow in.

## 4. Concluding Remarks

International capital markets are notoriously imperfect. Indeed, under asymmetric information, the equity market may be plagued by the Akerlof-type lemons problem. In the absence of a well-developed domestic credit market, in which case domestic savings cannot be efficiently channelled into domestic investment, FDI can play a double role. First, it provides a vehicle for reviving the domestic equity market as a channel to direct domestic savings into domestic investment. Second, it supplies foreign savings on top of domestic savings to finance domestic investment in a capital-hungry economy.

The second role of FDI generates the traditional gains from trade to the domestic country. However, its first role, though crucial to the financing of investment projects in the domestic country, is not costless. As the equity market is characterized by asymmetric information, it does not always transmit the "correct" signals about the social rates of return to domestic capital. As a result, there are some welfare losses that may offset some or all of the gains stemming from the mere channelling of domestic savings into domestic investment.

When a well-developed domestic credit market exists, through which domestic savings can be channelled into domestic investment even in the absence of an equity market, the first role played by FDI will no longer generate any gain. On the contrary, the "incorrect" signalling effect entails a strict welfare loss. When FDI can be leveraged domestically (through the domestic credit market), the traditional gains from trade associated with the second role of FDI will be severely curtailed. As a result, the total net effect of FDI on the welfare of the domestic economy could well be negative. As usual in normative economics, social losses are not inconsistent with individual maximization. In particular, although there are possibly losses for the society as a whole due to the information-based distortions, each individual domestic saver is utility-maximizing and the individual foreign direct investors all gain from their investment in the domestic economy.

The recent debate over international capital market liberalization generally focuses on the possible negative effects of short-term capital flows. Some economists even advocate a levy on short-term capital inflows in order to reduce the magnitude of these inflows on the ground that such large inflows could turn around abruptly into uncontrollable capital outflows during financial crises. Although unrelated to financial crises, we have seen here that at least one type of long-term capital inflows—namely, FDI—may also entail some welfare losses.[14]

Evidently, the gains from trade discussion in this paper has focused entirely on the financial aspects of inward FDI. In the absence of a well-developed credit market, our theory shows that FDI helps revive the domestic equity market and, in so doing, creates incentives for expansion in domestic investment. Interestingly, there is some evidence that shows that FDI in developing countries does tend to "crowd in" domestic investment (see Borensztein, De Gregorio, and Lee (1998)). However, the reader should not lose sight of the potential gains from FDI even when its contribution to the total size of capital inflows is not all that big, as when FDI is heavily domestically leveraged. The potential gains stem from the additional role of FDI as a vehicle for technology transfer from the industrial countries to the emerging market economies. In addition, some recent evidence suggests that FDI may promote competition. The large size of and the advanced technology possessed by multinationals often enable them to compete in industries in which barriers to entry, such as large capital requirements, limit the access of potential firms. Well-known also is the hypothesis that, as a vehicle for technology transfer, FDI contributes to productivity growth. (See World Bank (1999).) In a companion paper (Razin, Sadka, and Yuen (1999b)), we extend the model of this paper to provide a theoretical framework under which gains from FDI can be based not only on the inside information argument, but also on its role in the promotion of competition and growth of productivity in the domestic economy. In many cases, the losses from the former may well be outweighed by the gains from the latter.

Furthermore, if the government applies corrective taxes to counteract the information-based distortions associated with FDI, then the otherwise closed economy will be distortion-free and introducing capital flows through FDI will restore the usual gains from trade. These corrective taxes, which take the form of an ex ante corporate subsidy (to stimulate savings in domestic equity), coupled with a tax on FDI (to discourage excessive foreign investment), can be implemented without endowing the government with information about the productivity levels of the firms.[15] This underscores the importance of intervention through the imposition of taxes/subsidies in the capital market also in the presence of FDI.

**Appendix A: Proof of Inequality (7)**

Substituting for $1/(1+\bar{r})$ from (4) into (6) and rearranging terms we get:

$$\Phi(\varepsilon^o)[F'(K)(1+\varepsilon^o)+(1-\delta)]x+[1-\Phi(\varepsilon^o)]\{F'(K)[1+e^+(\varepsilon^o)]+(1-\delta)\}$$
$$=1+r^*, \qquad \text{(A1)}$$

where $x = [F(K)(1+\varepsilon^o)+(1-\delta)K] \;/\; \{F(K)[1+e^-(\varepsilon^o)]+(1-\delta)K\} > 1$, since $\varepsilon^o > e^-(\varepsilon^o)$. It follows from (A1) that:

$$1+r^* \;>\; [F'(K)+(1-\delta)]\{\Phi(\varepsilon^o)[1+e^-(\varepsilon^o)]+[1-\Phi(\varepsilon^o)][1+e^+(\varepsilon^o)]\}$$
$$=\; F'(K)+1-\delta$$

because the term in the curly brackets is equal to one (see equation (3)). This proves the inequality at the right end of (7).

Substitute for $1+r^*$ from (4) into (6) and rearrange terms to get:

$$\Phi(\varepsilon^o)\{F'(K)[1+e^-(\varepsilon^o)]+(1-\delta)\}$$
$$+[1-\Phi(\varepsilon^o)]\{F'(K)[1+e^+(\varepsilon^o)]+(1-\delta)\} \;/\; x = 1+\bar{r}. \qquad \text{(A2)}$$

Since $x > 1$, it follows from (A2) that

$$1+\bar{r} \;<\; [F'(K)+(1-\delta)]\{\Phi(\varepsilon^o)[1+e^-(\varepsilon^o)]+[1-\Phi(\varepsilon^o)][1+e^+(\varepsilon^o)]\}$$
$$=\; F'(K)+(1-\delta),$$

which completes the proof of (7).

**Appendix B: An Alternative Autarkic Model of Domestic Equity Market with No Domestic Credit**

One can restore some investment in our closed economy by modifying the decision-making process of the firm. We can envisage a two-stage decision rule imposed by firm owners on the managers. In the first period, firms determine their investment rules in the planning stage while the actual investment and its funding are delayed to the implementation stage. These investment rules are approved by the owners of the firms before $\varepsilon$ is known. The management then implements these rules by seeking funds from the domestic equity market to finance the investment, after $\varepsilon$ is known. They are also empowered by the owners not to invest at all when their $\varepsilon$ is higher than some threshold level. For further discussion of the rationale behind this sequence of firm decisions, the reader is referred to Razin, Sadka, and Yuen (1998b).

When the value of $\varepsilon$ that is revealed to the manager is high enough, she would prefer to employ just the existing capital (i.e., $K_o$) rather than to raise equity in a market that will not pay a premium for a high value of $\varepsilon$. Thus, there exists a cutoff level of $\varepsilon$, denoted by $\varepsilon^o$ (generally different from the $\varepsilon^o$ in the FDI case), such that all firms which experience a value of $\varepsilon$ above $\varepsilon^o$ will not make any new investment, while all other firms (i.e., the low-$\varepsilon$

firms) will equity-finance their new investments at a price reflecting the average value of the "lemons." This cutoff level of $\varepsilon$ is defined by:

$$-[K^{-} - (1-\delta)K_o] + \{F(K^{-})[1 + e^{-}(\varepsilon^{o})] + (1-\delta)K^{-}\} \,/\, (1+\bar{r})$$
$$= \{F[(1-\delta)K_o](1+\varepsilon^{o}) + (1-\delta)^2 K_o\}/(1+\bar{r}),$$

where $K^{-}$ is the stock of capital of the low-$\varepsilon$ firms that do make new investments, and $(1-\delta)K_o$ is the stock of capital for the high-$\varepsilon$ firms that do not make any new investment. Thus, in contrast with the autarkic equilibrium of section 2.2, we have here a positive level of new investment.

## Acknowledgments

Research on this paper was conducted while the authors were visiting the IMF, Razin and Yuen at the Research Department and Sadka at the Fiscal Affairs Department. We wish to thank Evgeny Agronin for very competent research assistance, and Joshua Aizenman and other conference participants for useful comments. Financial support from the RGC through a HKU-CRCG grant and an earmarked grant is gratefully acknowledged.

## Notes

1. See, for example, Chang and Velasco (1998), who trace the emergence of international illiquidity to the shortening of the foreign debt structure, the mismatch in currency denomination between assets and liabilities, and a vulnerability triggered by financial liberalization.
2. See Frenkel, Razin and Sadka (1991) for a discussion of these two wedges of inefficiency associated with capital flows and their corrective tax implications.
3. For a principal-agent foundations for such an economic structure in which investment is precommitted before the realization of the productivity parameter, see Sosner (1998).
4. For instance, Barry and Bradley (1997) report that "... most of the FDI into Irish manufacturing entails the construction of entirely new state-of-the-art factories on green-field sites..." (p. 1809). This is not the case in Central and Eastern Europe where most of the FDI flows to "brown-field" sites.
5. The existence of wealthy individuals or families in the home country may possibly limit the scope of our analysis to the extent that they can compete with the foreign direct investors on control over these greenfield investment sites. Our analysis will carry over, however, if they form joint ventures with the foreign direct investors. On the other hand, the foreign direct investors need not be excessively resourceful. Even a small technological advantage they may enjoy over and above the domestic investors will enable them to bid up all these investment sites from the domestic investors and to gain control of these industries.
6. Note that aggregate output is $NF(K)$, since $E(\varepsilon) = 0$.
7. One can show that it is possible to partially restore a first-best efficiency (i.e., $\bar{r} = F'(K) - \delta = r^*$) by employing a Pigouvian corrective policy which consists of a corporate income subsidy and a tax on capital income of non-residents.
8. One can restore some investment into this closed economy by modifying the decision-making process of the firm; see Appendix B.
9. We set the parameter values as follows: $\gamma = 0.295$, $\alpha = 0.333$, $\delta = 0.723$, $N = 1$, $A = 1$, $K_0 = 1$, and $a = 0.99$. Since we think of each period as constituting half of the lifetime of a generation (i.e., about 25 years), the values of $\gamma$ and $\delta$ are chosen to reflect this assumption.
10. For another example of misdirected capital flows in the context of international trade with differentiated products, see Helpman and Razin (1983).

11. See also Stiglitz and Weiss (1981).
12. The $\varepsilon^0$-condition, as given by equation (16), is determined by equilibrium in the equity market. As such, it will not be taken into account by the price-taking firms when choosing their investment levels.
13. Here, in order to obtain sensible solutions, we vary $r^*$ from 3.85 to 5.35 (equivalent to an annual real interest rate of 5.4% to 6.36%). In addition, we assume that the bankruptcy cost parameter has a value $\mu = 0.05$. Note that there could be two equilibria for levels of $r^*$ between 4.6 and 5.0. For a more detailed explanation of this probability of multiple equilibria, see Razin, Sadka, Yuen (1999c).
14. See also Aizenman (1998) for an alternative modelling of financial intermediation based on moral hazard that generates losses from capital inflows.
15. Similar analysis of an optimal tax design has been carried out in Razin, Sadka, and Yuen (1998a).

## References


Aizenman, Joshua. (1998). "Capital Mobility in a Second-Best World—Moral Hazard with Costly Financial Intermediation." Dartmouth College, mimeo.

Akerlof, George. (1970). "The Market for 'Lemons': Qualitative Uncertainty and the Market Mechanism." *Quarterly Journal of Economics* 89, 488–500.

Barry, Frank, and John Bradley. (1997). "FDI and Trade: The Irish Host-Country Experience." *Economic Journal* 107, 1798–1811.

Brainard, S. L. (1993a). "An Empirical Assessment of Factor Proportions Explanation of Multinationals Sales." NBER Working Paper No. 4580.

———. (1993b). "An Empirical Assessment of the Proximity-Concentration Tradeoffs Between Multinational Sales and Trade." NBER Working Paper No. 4269.

Borensztein, Eduardo, Jose De Gregorio, and Jong-wha Lee. (1998). "How Does Foreign Direct Investment Affect Economic Growth?" *Journal of International Economics* 45, 115–135.

Chang, Roberto, and Andres Velasco. (1998). "The Asian Liquidity Crisis." NBER Working Paper No. 6796.

Frenkel, Jacob A., Assaf Razin, and Efraim Sadka. (1991). *International Taxation in an Integrated World Economy.* Cambridge, MA: MIT Press.

Goldberg, Linda S., and Michael W. Klein. (1997). "Foreign Direct Investment, Trade and Real Exchange Rate Linkages in Southeast Asia and Latin America." NBER Working Paper 4344.

Gordon, Roger H., and A. Lans Bovenberg. (1996). "Why is Capital So Immobile Internationally?: Possible Explanations and Implications for Capital Income Taxation." *American Economic Review* 86, 1057–1075.

Helpman, Elhanan, and Assaf Razin. (1983). "Increasing Returns, Monopolistic Competition and Factor Movements: A Welfare Analysis." *Journal of International Economics* 14, 263–276.

Helpman, Elhanan. (1984). "A Simple Theory of International Trade with Multinational Corporations." *Journal of Political Economy.*

Razin, Assaf, Efraim Sadka, and Chi-Wa Yuen. (1999a). "Implications of Home Bias: A Pecking Order of Capital Inflows and Corrective Taxation." In Assaf Razin and Efraim Sadka (eds.), *The Economics of Globalization: Policy Perspectives from Public Economics.* Cambridge University Press.

———. (1999b). "Host Country Benefits from FDI: Two Non-traditional Views on Gains from Trade." Paper prepared for an NBER EASE conference in Hawaii, June 12–14, 1999.

———. (1999c). "Excessive FDI Flows Under Asymmetric Information." Paper prepared for a Federal Reserve Bank of San Francisco conference.

———. (1998a). "A Pecking Order of Capital Inflows and International Tax Principles." *Journal of International Economics* 44, 45–68.

———. (1998b). "Capital Flows with Debt- and Equity-Financed Investment: Equilibrium Structure and Efficiency Implications." IMF Working Paper, WP/98/159.

Sosner, Nathan. (1998). "The Sequence of Investment Decisions as a Solution of an Agency Problem." The Eitan Berglas School of Economics, Tel-Aviv University, mimeo.

Stiglitz, Joseph E., and Andrew Weiss. (1981). "Credit Rationing in Markets with Imperfect Information." *American Economic Review* 71, 393–410.

Townsend, Robert M. (1979). "Optimal Contracts and Competitive Markets with Costly State Verification." *Journal of Economic Theory* 21, 265–293.

United Nations. (1998). *World Investment Report 1998: Trends and Determinant.* New York and Geneva.

Wickham, E., and H. Thompson. (1989). "An Empirical Analysis of Intra-Industry Trade and Multinational Firms." In P. K. M. Tharakan and J. Cole (eds.), *Intra-Industry Trade: Theory, Evidence and Extensions.* London: Macmillan.

World Bank. (1999). *Global Development Finance.*

# Comments

BY JOSHUA AIZENMAN

This interesting paper has two main contributions. First, it models FDI in the presence of asymmetric information, where being "close to the action" leads to information advantages. Second, it identifies conditions under which FDI may be welfare reducing, questioning the presumption that long term investment is welfare improving.

The first part of my comments will provide a diagrammatic interpretation of the paper, using a demand/supply, consumer/producer surplus welfare analysis. The second part will put the present paper in the context of the second best literature, and will discuss possible policy interpretations.

## Supply/Demand Interpretation of the Model

The insight of the paper may be traced with the help of the familiar diagrammatic analysis of saving and investment decisions. To simplify, let the depreciation rate be zero. A useful benchmark is the full information case, with unfettered access to the capital market, summarized in Figure 1. Output is produced by a large number of small firms. The production of firm $i$ is

$$F(K_i)(1+\varepsilon_i); \quad F' > 0, \ F'' < 0 \tag{1}$$

where $\varepsilon_i$ is i.i.d. shock, with zero mean. Curve $MP_K$ plots the expected marginal productivity of capital as a function of the stock of capital; the latter is measured horizontally from point $O$. Let the initial stock of capital in the emerging market economy be $K_o$. We plot domestic saving (curve $S$) using $K_o$ as the modified origin. With risk neutrality, the equilibrium investment is characterized by equating the expected marginal productivity of capital with the interest rate. Hence, the autarky interest rate is $\bar{r}_A$, and the autarky investment is $I^o$. Suppose that this interest rate exceeds the global rate ($r^*$), as is frequently the case in emerging markets. The open economy equilibrium is obtained in panel II of Figure 1. The inflow of capital increases the stock of capital to $K^*$. The drop in the interest rate reduces domestic saving, and the gap between the higher investment and the lower saving is met by the inflow of foreign capital, depicted by $I^*$. The welfare gain from capital inflows is provided by the dotted triangle.

Figure 1 provides us with the benchmark for the more complex case investigated in the present paper. Suppose that domestic agents lack access to the foreign saving market—they can not save at the global interest rate, apparently due to financial repression. In financial autarky, all domestic agents face the same interest rate. The authors show that the

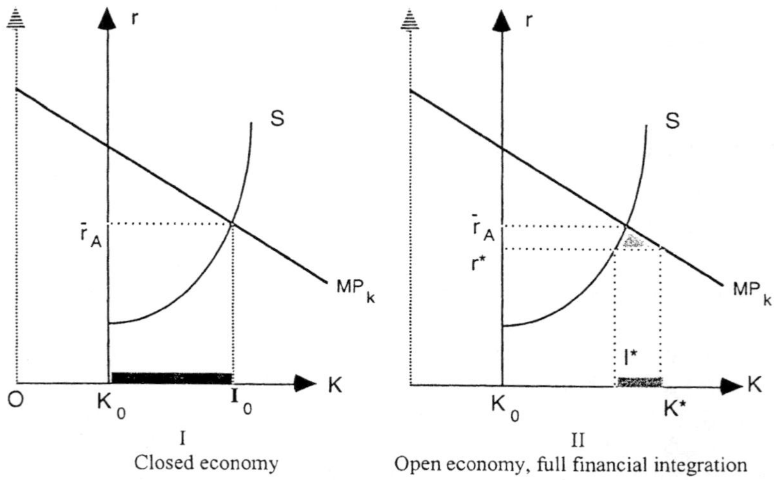


*Figure 1.* Complete information.

information advantage of the owner-manager leads to a lemon equilibrium—the collapse of the market for new capital, akin to Akerlof's (1970) seminal paper. More precisely, an agent who purchases a firm has an information advantage, being "close to the action," observing the realized i.i.d. shock. His attempt to sell the firm would signal the inferiority of his firm. As all agents face the same interest rate, no buyer would be interested in buying such a firm, leading to a zero investment equilibrium.

Suppose now that we allow multinationals to invest in the economy. Foreign agents have access to the "deep pocket" of global capital, and they can purchase the stock of capital prior to the realization of productivity shocks. In contrast, domestic agents are too small to bid for the exclusive control of production sites at the green field level. As before, the advantage of gaining such control is being "close to the action." Inflows of capital introduce a new dimension of heterogeneity, as foreign agents face an interest rate that may differ from the domestic one. The key condition characterizing the resultant equilibrium is equation (4). The inflow of capital leads to a domestic interest rate that is below the foreign one. Foreign agents will retain the control of the superior production sites—firms the realized productivity of which is above a cutoff level of $\varepsilon_0$. They will sell the inferior sites—firms the productivity of which is below that cutoff level. Domestic agents are willing to buy these firms, because they discount future income using a lower interest rate. The asymmetric information implies that the expected productivity of the firms sold corresponds to the expected productivity of firms below the cutoff rate, $\varepsilon_0$, denoted by $e^-(\varepsilon_0)$. As the expected productivity of all firms is zero, it follows that $e^-(\varepsilon_0) < 0$. The gains from trade stem from the differences in firms' valuation—domestic agents facing a lower interest rate are valuing more a given future income stream than the corresponding valuation of the same income stream by the foreign owners. The cutoff productivity rate is determined by equating the value of the average firm bought by domestic agents [the LHS of (4)] to

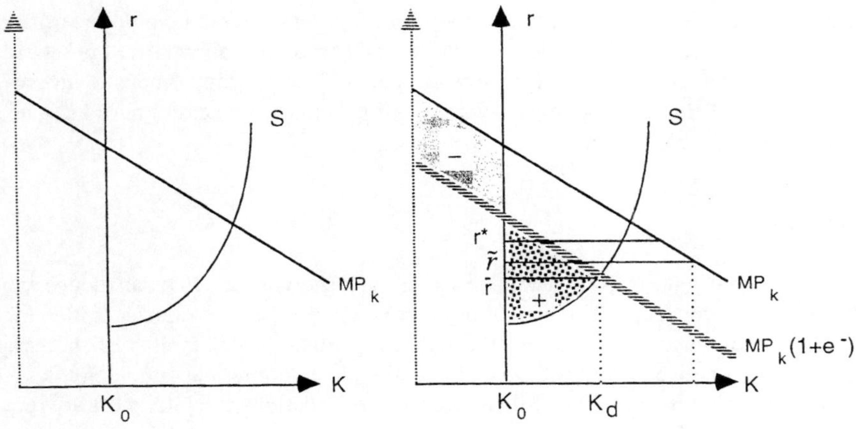


I
Closed economy

II
FDI and welfare

*Figure 2.* Asymmetric information.

the value of the marginal firm sold by the multinationals, i.e., the value of the firm the productivity of which is $\varepsilon_0$ [the RHS of (4)].

The resultant equilibrium can be traced with the help of Figure 2. In the absence of FDI, the lemon equilibrium would prevail, and the stock of capital would be $K_o$. With multinationals, the expected marginal productivity of the firms bought by domestic agents is $MP_K(1 + e^-(\varepsilon_0))$, where $MP_K(1 + e^-(\varepsilon_0)) < MP_K$. The modified expected marginal productivity curve is depicted in Figure 2, panel II by the dashed curve to the left of the original curve. The resultant equilibrium is characterized by relatively large FDI. The inflow of foreign capital depresses the expected marginal productivity of domestic capital to $\tilde{r}$, below the international interest rate $r^*$ but above the domestic one, $\bar{r}$. An interesting feature of this equilibrium is that the marginal productivity of capital is below the level observed with full financial integration and complete information equilibrium (see Figure 1, panel II), manifesting excessive investment even relative to the complete information benchmark.

Figure 2, panel II also identifies the welfare effects of FDI from the vantage point of domestic agents, using the autarky, zero investment as the benchmark. FDI has 2 fundamental welfare effects. First, it leads to the 'export' of rents, an effect that may be referred to as "cherry picking" by multinationals. Having access to the "deep pocket" enables multinationals to buy firms at the green field stage, to retain the control of the superior firms, and to sell the inferior firms to domestic agents. This is equivalent to an adverse productivity shock from the point of view of domestic agents, reducing welfare by the dotted trapezoid in Figure 2, panel II (denoted by −). Second, FDI enables the formation of capital, increasing the domestic ownership of capital to $K_d$. This increases the domestic surplus by the dotted triangle (denoted by +). Hence, FDI is a mixed blessing in such an economy, and the simulation in the paper shows that the ultimate welfare effect is ambiguous. Figure 2, panel II suggests that the balance between 'rent export' and capital formation would determine the ultimate welfare effects of FDI. Indeed, in the second part of the paper the authors show that if the domestic financial market is functioning in autarky, supporting domestic investment, then the "capital formation" gain associated with the inflow of capital shrinks, and FDI unambiguously reduces welfare.

## Interpretations

This paper is a contribution to the second best literature, showing that FDI can reduce welfare due to existing distortions. The interest in these issues has been revitalized following the financial crises of the nineties, opening the debate regarding the desirability of encouraging free capital flows between the OECD countries and the emerging market economies. This remains a disputable issue, as the ultimate welfare contribution of capital mobility remains elusive [see Rodrik (1998)].

A selective tour of the second best literature in international economics should start with the 'founding fathers'—Bhagwati and Johnson. Their seminal papers on tariffs and immiserizing growth focused attention on the impact of distortions on growth. They showed that growth magnifies the welfare costs of existing distortions, leading to ambiguous net welfare effects. Brecher and Diaz Alejandro (1977) were among the first to focus on capital mobility in a second best world. The events in Chile in the eighties triggered a lively discussion about the desirable order of reforms. Contributions by McKinnon (1982) and Edwards and van-Wijnbergen (1986) showed that the sequencing of reforms in a second best universe is not obvious, and deserves further attention. More recently, Kohn and Marion (1992) showed in the context of a knowledge-based endogenous growth framework, that opening capital markets does not necessarily improve welfare for the nation or for the world as a whole. In the context of costly risk monitoring by banks, Aizenman (1998) showed that excessive risk undertaken in the presence of moral hazard leads to a distortion, implying that unrestricted capital mobility tends to reduce (increase) welfare if banks are relatively inefficient (efficient).

The novel aspect of the present paper is the focus on FDI, the inflow of which frequently has been viewed more favorably than short term capital inflows. The authors are identifying conditions under which even FDI may be welfare worsening. As is the case with all the above literature, the peril of dealing with second best is that there is no unique policy prescription that follows from the second best equilibrium. Specifically, the policy implications are conditional on the initial distortions, and on the degrees of freedom available to the policy maker.

In the context of the present paper, it is not obvious whether this paper calls for restrictions on FDI. The adverse welfare effects of FDI in the present paper are due to the combination of asymmetric information and implicit financial repression, where domestic agents are not allowed to save at the world interest rate. This separation of markets is needed to support an equilibrium where the domestic interest rate is below the international one. Hence, one may argue that the present paper calls either for limiting FDI in the presence of financial repression, or for removing financial repression in the first place, prior to FDI.[1] Obviously, which of these options is more feasible will be determined by both efficiency and political economy considerations, and may vary from country to country.

## Notes

1. As is shown by the experience of various countries (including Korea), financial repression may be sustained for long periods, despite the presence of various 'leaks' that may mitigate its effects.

## References

Aizenman, J. (1998). "Capital Mobility in a Second Best World—Moral Hazard With Costly Financial Intermediation." NBER Working paper no. 6703.

Akerlof, G. (1970). "The Market for Lemons: Quality Uncertainty and the Market Mechanism." *Quarterly Journal of Economics* 89, 488–500.

Bhagwati, J. N. (1956). "Immiserizing Growth: A Geometrical Note." *Review of Economic Studies*, June.

Brecher, A. R., and C. F. Diaz Alejandro. (1977). "Tariff, Foreign Capital and Immiserizing Growth." *Journal of International Economics* 7, 317–322.

Edwards, S., and van-Wijnbergen, S. (1986), "The Welfare Effects of Trade and Capital Market Liberalization." *International Economic Review* 27(1), February, 141–148.

Johnson, G. H. "The Possibility of Income Losses from Increased Efficiency or Factor Accumulation in the Presence of Tariffs." *The Economic Journal*, March, 151–154.

Kohn, M., and Marion, N. (1992). "The Implications of Knowledge-Based Growth for the Optimality of Open Capital Markets." *Canadian Journal of Economics* 25(4), November, 865–883.

McKinnon, R. I. (1982). "The Order of Economic Liberalization: Lessons from Chile and Argentina." *Carnegie Rochester Conference Series on Public Policy* 17(0), Autumn, 159–186.

Rodrik, D. (1998). "Who Needs Capital Account Convertibility?" Manuscript, Harvard University.

# General Discussion

**Tamim Bayoumi** noted that most of the existing literature on FDI had focused on attempting to explain its causes. By contrast, Razin, Sadka, and Yuen (RSY) had focused on the welfare consequences of FDI, which was praiseworthy. In Bayoumi's view, the limited attention that the profession had paid to the welfare consequences of FDI reflected a tendency of macroeconomists to ignore the distinction between GDP and GNP. In this context, it would be very interesting to analyze the welfare consequences of the heavy subsidization of inward FDI by Ireland during the 1980s. It is generally assumed that the subsidies resulted in significant welfare gains for Ireland. But Bayoumi noted that part of Ireland's economic growth over the past decade could be attributed to the process of European integration (as was also the case, for example, in Portugal), and that a careful study that isolated the effects of the subsidization policy might well conclude that Ireland's GNP had been negatively affected, ceteris paribus.

**James Boughton** asked how the analysis might be affected by the addition of mutual funds to the set of investors that RSY had considered. **Razin** answered that without positions of control over firms, mutual funds could not exploit the inside information that the paper had highlighted as a source of distortion. Subsequent discussion involving Razin, **Sadka**, and **Aizenman** clarified that the adverse welfare effects of FDI in the RSY model were not entirely attributable to asymmetric information, and that these adverse effects could be mitigated through mutual funds or other means to address what Aizenman had referred to as "financial repression."

**Razin** emphasized that the authors did not want their analysis to be interpreted as a negative verdict on FDI. In seeking to flesh out the financial aspects, the RSY model had abstracted from some widely-recognized gains from FDI.

# An International Dynamic Asset Pricing Model

ROBERT J. HODRICK rh169@columbia.edu
*Graduate School of Business, Columbia University, NY, NY 10027, and the National Bureau of Economic Research*

DAVID TAT-CHEE NG tdn@columbia.edu
*Department of Economics, Columbia University, NY, NY 10027*

PAUL SENGMUELLER pfs11@columbia.edu
*Department of Economics, Columbia University, NY, NY 10027*

***Abstract***

We examine the ability of a dynamic asset-pricing model to explain the returns on G7-country stock market indices. We extend Campbell's (1996) asset-pricing model to investigate international equity returns. We also utilize and evaluate recent evidence on the predictability of stock returns. We find some evidence for the role of hedging demands in explaining stock returns and compare the predictions of the dynamic model to those from the static CAPM. Both models fail in their predictions of average returns on portfolios of high book-to-market stocks across countries.

## I. Introduction

The starting point of this paper is the observation of Flood, Hodrick, and Kaplan (1986) that stock returns are predictable. Flood, Hodrick, and Kaplan (1986) argued that one could not test for bubbles in stock prices without controlling for the rational movements in stock prices that are caused by fluctuations in expected rates of return. They used annual data and demonstrated that dividend yields, the ratio of the annual dividend to the current stock price, provided statistically significant forecasts of future stock returns, especially at the two-year horizon. Subsequent research by Campbell (1991) and Hodrick (1992) demonstrates that a vector autoregressive approach with monthly data generates significant time-varying forecasts of stock returns at any future horizon and has better small-sample properties than the direct long-horizon approach.

While theories of stock return predictability have been available since Merton (1973), the links between the theories of stock return predictability and the empirical analysis of this issue have been weak.[1] The intuition of Merton's model is that risk-averse consumer-investors want to hedge against adverse changes in their consumption and investment opportunity sets. Thus, the cross-section and time-series patterns of expected asset returns are determined by more than just the covariances of the returns on the assets with the return on the market portfolio, as in the static capital asset pricing model (CAPM). Expected returns also depend on the covariances of the returns on the assets with the state variables that describe the consumption and investment opportunity sets. The generality of this specification provided little basis for a tight econometric test of Merton's theory.

Predictability of international equity returns is inconsistent with the static CAPM. Some researchers, Harvey (1991), Bekaert and Hodrick (1992), and Ferson and Harvey (1993) for example, have characterized the predictability of country returns and developed tests of conditional CAPM's in which the conditional expected return on an asset is related to the conditional expected return on the market portfolio with a conditional, time-varying beta. The main problem with this approach is that it lacks a sound theoretical foundation. Once the conditional distributions are allowed to vary, Merton's (1973) logic indicates that additional hedge portfolios, other than the market, may be priced. This paper develops a formal test of an international, intertemporal, asset-pricing model in which state variables may be priced.

Our analysis builds on the work of Campbell (1993, 1996). The failure of the consumption-based, asset-pricing literature of the 1980's motivated Campbell (1993) to develop a theoretical model that avoids direct measurements of consumption. Campbell (1996) extended this theoretical model and generated empirically testable specifications directly linking the cross-section of expected stock returns to time variation in expected returns on the market portfolio. Campbell (1996) applied his model to a cross-section of returns on 25 portfolios of U.S. stocks taking the value-weighted U.S. market return as the market portfolio.[2] While the theory was marginally rejected, the pricing errors of the model were small on most portfolios. Most of the explanatory power of the model was in the market portfolio, as is predicted by the CAPM.

The purpose of this paper is to determine whether variation in expected returns on the world market portfolio induces significant hedging motives, which are reflected in average returns across countries. We extend Campbell's (1996) model to an international environment, and we utilize recent evidence of Lamont (1998) to specify the state variables in the forecasting equation.

Our analysis is effectively a constrained arbitrage-pricing model. Korajczyk and Viallet (1989) and Ferson and Harvey (1993) have tested multi-factor, international, arbitrage-pricing models. The problem with these specifications is that one must pre-specify the identity and number of factors with little theoretical guidance. Our framework imposes the restriction that the factors affecting the cross-sectional asset pricing must be those that forecast market returns.

As with many studies of international asset pricing, we assume that national equity markets are integrated, with no barriers to investment, transaction costs or differential taxes. We will also assume a representative agent framework, which raises the issue of aggregation across countries and the failure of purchasing power parity, see Adler and Dumas (1983).

Section II provides a review of Campbell's (1996) model. Section III describes the data. Section IV discusses forecasting of real and excess nominal stock returns and compares the results of our analysis with Lamont's (1998) analysis. Section V discusses the econometric aspects of the asset-pricing model, while section VI provides the estimation and testing of the model. Section VII contains concluding remarks.

## II. A Review of Campbell's (1996) Model

Campbell's (1996) model uses a representative agent framework, and hence, it shares the weaknesses of the consumption CAPM and Euler equation methods that were developed in the 1980's to test intertemporal asset-pricing models.[3] Nevertheless, there is an advantage to the approach because Campbell uses log-linearization to eliminate observations on consumption from the asset-pricing model. Ultimately, the model relates expected returns on assets to covariances of returns with the market portfolio, as in the traditional static CAPM, and to covariances of returns with changes in the expected future returns on the market portfolio.[4]

The representative agent's budget constraint is written in real terms as

$$W_{t+1} = R_{m,t+1}(W_t - C_t), \tag{1}$$

where $W_t$ is real wealth, $C_t$ is real consumption, and $R_{m,t+1}$ is the gross return on aggregate wealth, which is the return on the market portfolio.

Campbell (1996) divides equation (1) by $W_t$ and log-linearizes the resulting expression in a first-order Taylor approximation around the mean log consumption-wealth ratio, $c - w$. The result is

$$\Delta w_{t+1} = r_{m,t+1} + k_w + (1 - (1/\rho))(c_t - w_t), \tag{2}$$

where lower case letters are natural logarithms of upper case counterparts, $\rho \equiv 1 - \exp(c - w)$, and $k_w$ is a constant.

When the log consumption-wealth ratio is stationary, equation (2) implies that the innovation in logarithm of consumption can be written as the innovation in the discounted present value of the return on the market minus the innovation in the discounted present value of consumption growth:

$$\begin{aligned} c_{t+1} - E_t c_{t+1} &= (E_{t+1} - E_t) \sum_{j=0}^{\infty} \rho^j r_{m,t+1+j} \\ &\quad - (E_{t+1} - E_t) \sum_{j=1}^{\infty} \rho^j \Delta c_{t+1+j} \end{aligned} \tag{3}$$

Equation (3) indicates that an unanticipated increase in consumption today must be due to an innovation in the return on wealth, either today or an expected increase in the future, or it must coincide with a planned reduction in the growth rate of consumption in the future.

Campbell (1993, 1996) next uses a log-linear Euler equation to eliminate expected future consumption growth from the right-hand side of equation (3). The consumer's preferences are modeled as in Epstein and Zin (1989) and Weil (1989) with separate parameters for the coefficient of relative risk aversion, $\gamma$, and for the elasticity of intertemporal substitution, $\sigma$. The objective function is defined recursively by

$$U_t = \left[ (1-\beta) C_t^{(1-\gamma)/\theta} + \beta \left( E_t U_{t+1}^{(1-\gamma)} \right)^{1/\theta} \right]^{\theta/(1-\gamma)}, \tag{4}$$

where $\theta \equiv (1-\gamma)/[1-(1/\sigma)]$. Campbell (1996) notes that $\theta$ can have either sign, $\theta \to 0$ as $\gamma \to 1$, $\theta \to \infty$ as $\sigma \to 1$, and $\theta \to 1$ as $\gamma \to 1/\sigma$.

Epstein and Zin (1989) solve for the Euler equations associated with maximizing equation (4) subject to the budget constraint given in (1). When asset returns are conditionally homoskedastic and log-normally distributed, the Euler equations may be written in log-linear form as

$$E_t \Delta c_{t+1} = \mu_m + \sigma E_t r_{m,t+1} \tag{5}$$

and

$$E_t r_{i,t+1} - r_{f,t+1} + \frac{V_{ii}}{2} = \theta \frac{V_{ic}}{\sigma} + (1-\theta) V_{im}. \tag{6}$$

In equation (6), $r_{f,t+1}$ is the riskless real interest rate, $V_{ii} = \text{var}(r_{i,t+1} - E_t r_{i,t+1})$, $V_{ic} = \text{cov}(r_{i,t+1} - E_t r_{i,t+1}, c_{t+1} - E_t c_{t+1})$, and $V_{im} = \text{cov}(r_{i,t+1} - E_t r_{i,t+1}, r_{m,t+1} - E_t r_{m,t+1})$.

Equation (5) indicates that consumption growth is linearly related to the expected return on the market portfolio, and this fact is used in conjunction with the linearized budget constraint to eliminate consumption from the asset-pricing model. Equation (6) indicates that the continuously compounded risk premium on an asset plus one-half of the asset's variance is determined by the covariances of the asset's return with consumption and with the return on the market.

By substituting equation (5) into equation (3), Campbell (1996) derives

$$c_{t+1} - E_t c_{t+1} = r_{m,t+1} - E_t r_{m,t+1} + (1-\sigma)(E_{t+1} - E_t) \sum_{j=1}^{\infty} \rho^j r_{m,t+1+j}. \tag{7}$$

Equation (7) indicates that the innovation in consumption, which enters the asset-pricing equation (6), can be eliminated by focusing on the innovations in the return on the market portfolio and in the discounted expected future returns. Intuitively, consumption responds one-for-one to the current return on the market portfolio because the objective function is homogeneous of degree one. The response of an innovation in consumption to an innovation in expected future returns depends on income and substitution effects. When the elasticity of substitution, $\sigma$, is less than one, the income effect dominates causing current consumption to rise. When $\sigma$ is greater than one, the substitution effect dominates; and current consumption falls.

By substituting from equation (7) into the asset-pricing equation (6), we find

$$\text{cov}\left(r_{i,t+1} - E_t r_{i,t+1}, c_{t+1} - E_t c_{t+1}\right) \equiv V_{ic} = V_{im} + (1-\sigma) V_{ih}, \tag{8}$$

where $V_{ih} \equiv \text{cov}[r_{i,t+1} - E_t r_{i,t+1}, (E_{t+1} - E_t) \sum_{j=1}^{\infty} \rho^j r_{m,t+1+j}]$, which is the covariance of the return on an asset with the revision in expectations about discounted future market returns.

After substituting equation (8) into equation (6) and using the definition of $\theta$, the asset-pricing equation becomes

$$E_t r_{i,t+1} - r_{f,t+1} + \frac{V_{ii}}{2} = \gamma V_{im} + (\gamma - 1) V_{ih}. \tag{9}$$

Equation (9) demonstrates that an asset's risk premium (adjusted for one-half its own variance) depends on the asset's covariance with the market portfolio, with weight $\gamma$, and on its covariance with the innovation in discounted expected future market returns, with weight $(\gamma - 1)$.

The coefficient of relative risk aversion determines the compensation that investors demand for covariance risks. When $\gamma = 1$, the model's predictions coincide with those of the static CAPM. When $\gamma > (<)1$, investors require higher (lower) expected returns on assets that covary positively with innovations in discounted expected future returns. Campbell (1996) notes that a positive covariance carries a mixed blessing. On the one hand, investors like assets that have good payoffs when expected future returns are high. But, on the other hand, investors dislike the fact that such assets provide poor hedging against deterioration in future investment opportunities. When $\gamma$ is greater than one, the latter effect dominates the former.

While the derivation of equation (9) follows Campbell (1996) in assuming conditional homoskedasticity, Campbell (1993) discusses several conditions under which such an equation can be derived in a more realistic environment of conditional heteroskedasticity.[5] The most straightforward approach is to assume that the elasticity of substitution, $\sigma$, equals one. In this case, equation (9) holds in terms of conditional expected returns with all second moments replaced by conditional second moments. Below, we derive and test the unconditional implications of such a specification.[6]

## III. The Data

Table 1 presents some summary statistics for the primary data set that will be used in our study. We use monthly data from 1970:1 to 1998:4. The first variable is the real return on the MSCI world market portfolio (RRET). The units are percent per month, so the mean return of 0.546% corresponds to an annualized value of 6.55%. The next four variables are the additional state variables that are the predictors of real returns. The first is the logarithm of the annualized payout-ratio of world dividends relative to world earnings (LOGDE). The second is the logarithm of the annualized world dividend-price ratio (LOGDP). The third is the relative bill rate (RREL), which is the one-month U.S. interest rate minus its previous twelve-month moving average, in percent per month. The fourth variable is the Treasury bond term spread (TSPD) between the 30-year U.S. interest rate and the one-year U.S. interest rate, in percent per month.

The next seven variables in Table 1 are the dollar rates of return on the MSCI G7 country portfolios in excess of the one-month U.S. Treasury bill rate of return. The countries are the United States (US), Japan (JP), Germany (GE), the United Kingdom (UK), France (FR), Canada (CA), and Italy (IT). These variables are also measured as percent per month. The mean excess rates of return range from Italy's 1.056% per annum to the U.K.'s 6.732% per annum. The U.S. has the lowest standard deviation, and Italy has the highest.

## IV. The Forecasting Model

The first task in developing testable restrictions from equation (9) is to determine that the real return on the world equity market portfolio is forecastable. Since the theoretical

*Table 1.* Summary statistics. The sample period is 1970:01 to 1998:04. The variables are the monthly real return on the MSCI world market portfolio (RRET), the logarithm of world dividends relative to world earnings (LOGDE), the logarithm of the world dividend-price ratio (LOGDP), the one-month U.S. Treasury bill interest rate minus its twelve-month moving average (RREL), the 30-year minus one-year U.S. Treasury bond term spread (TSPD), and the dollar rates of return on the G7 countries' equities in excess of the U.S. Treasury bill rate.

| | Mean | Std.Dev. | Minimum | Maximum |
|---|---|---|---|---|
| RRET | 0.546 | 4.166 | −18.849 | 13.342 |
| LOGDE | −0.744 | 0.118 | −0.965 | −0.483 |
| LOGDP | −5.946 | 0.343 | −6.641 | −5.348 |
| RREL | −0.003 | 0.117 | −0.489 | 0.440 |
| TSPD | 0.087 | 0.113 | −0.281 | 0.359 |
| EXRET-US | 0.464 | 4.363 | −24.306 | 15.570 |
| EXRET-JP | 0.488 | 6.529 | −21.788 | 21.162 |
| EXRET-GE | 0.485 | 5.854 | −20.080 | 17.337 |
| EXRET-UK | 0.561 | 6.845 | −24.701 | 44.048 |
| EXRET-FR | 0.447 | 6.723 | −28.154 | 23.622 |
| EXRET-CA | 0.290 | 5.366 | −25.776 | 15.487 |
| EXRET-IT | 0.088 | 7.578 | −24.613 | 26.441 |

model requires multi-period forecasts of the equity return, it is useful to stack the equity return as the first element of a $k$-dimensional vector of state variables, $z_t$, and use a vector autoregression (VAR) as in the following:

$$z_{t+1} = Az_t + \varepsilon_{t+1}. \tag{10}$$

The representation of the VAR as a first-order system is not restrictive, as the variables can always be stacked into a first-order companion form. We report the results of the first-order specification as this is the order chosen by the Schwarz (1978) criterion.

Panel A of Table 2 presents a five-variable, first-order vector autoregression. The first variable is the real return on the MSCI world market portfolio (RRET). The other four variables are the payout ratio, LOGDE; the dividend yield, LOGDP; the relative bill rate, RREL; and the term spread, TSPD. We use RREL and TSPD of the U.S. because we are pricing the excess dollar returns on the G7 equities.

Lamont (1998) finds that the payout ratio is an important predictor of the U.S. S&P 500 excess return. Rozeff (1984), Campbell and Shiller (1988), Fama and French (1988), and Flood, Hodrick and Kaplan (1986) emphasize the importance of the dividend yield in forecasting stock returns at short and long horizons. Campbell (1991) and Hodrick (1992) use the relative bill rate. Fama and French (1989) find that the term structure of interest rates predicts stock and bond returns.

For the return forecasting equation, the value of the chi-square statistic with five degrees of freedom is 15.56, which indicates that real equity returns are predictable at standard levels of statistical significance. Nevertheless, the adjusted $R^2$ for the real return equation is only 3.3%. This pattern of strong statistical significance with low percentage predictability is

*Table 2.* Fundamental VAR and forecasting equations. Panel A contains a five variable VAR in the real return on the MSCI world market portfolio (RRET), the logarithm of dividends relative to earnings (LOGDE), the logarithm of the dividend-price ratio (LOGDP), the one-month Treasury bill interest rate minus its twelve-month moving average (RREL), and the 30-year minus one-year Treasury bond term spread (TSPD). The sample period is 1970:01 to 1998:04. Regressions in Panel B project excess dollar returns on the G7 countries onto the same information set as the VAR. The joint predictability test examines the predictive power of the five lagged variables. The Cumby–Huizinga (1992) L-test is a joint test that the first eight autocorrelations of the residuals are all zero.

| | Coefficients on Regressors | | | | | | | Joint predictability | L-test |
|---|---|---|---|---|---|---|---|---|---|
| Dependent Variable | RRET (std.err.) | LOGDE (std.err.) | LOGDP (std.err.) | RREL (std.err.) | TSPD (std.err.) | CONST (std.err.) | $R^2$ | $\chi^2(5)$ $p$-value | $\chi^2(8)$ $p$-value |
| | | | | Panel A: Fundamental VAR | | | | | |
| RRET | 0.058 | −3.998 | 1.073 | 0.892 | 9.577 | 3.110 | 0.033 | 15.56 | 13.08 |
| | (0.063) | (2.134) | (0.751) | (2.190) | (3.052) | (4.234) | | 0.01 | 0.11 |
| LOGDE | −0.0001 | 0.963 | 0.005 | −0.038 | 0.011 | 0.0002 | 0.949 | 8847 | 14.80 |
| | (0.0003) | (0.017) | (0.004) | (0.015) | (0.019) | (0.022) | | 0.00 | 0.06 |
| LOGDP | −0.0010 | 0.015 | 0.986 | −0.001 | −0.081 | −0.067 | 0.985 | 19698 | 11.56 |
| | (0.0006) | (0.022) | (0.008) | (0.021) | (0.030) | (0.045) | | 0.00 | 0.17 |
| RREL | −0.0023 | 0.111 | −0.057 | 0.580 | −0.353 | −0.223 | 0.621 | 360.4 | 49.14 |
| | (0.0013) | (0.039) | (0.016) | (0.061) | (0.071) | (0.082) | | 0.00 | 0.00 |
| TSPD | −0.0011 | 0.017 | 0.001 | 0.016 | 0.951 | 0.022 | 0.894 | 2139 | 8.69 |
| | (0.0007) | (0.017) | (0.007) | (0.031) | (0.030) | (0.036) | | 0.00 | 0.37 |
| | | | | Panel B: Forecasting Equations | | | | | |
| EXRET-US | 0.0043 | −4.446 | 0.532 | −0.588 | 7.322 | −0.293 | 0.015 | 10.65 | 9.40 |
| | (0.0726) | (2.251) | (0.853) | (2.598) | (3.433) | (4.716) | | 0.06 | 0.31 |
| EXRET-JP | 0.1846 | 1.450 | 2.643 | 2.652 | 10.303 | 16.294 | 0.033 | 16.16 | 6.11 |
| | (0.1056) | (3.328) | (1.075) | (3.402) | (4.085) | (6.200) | | 0.01 | 0.63 |
| EXRET-GE | 0.0252 | −5.413 | 0.659 | −0.248 | 9.781 | −0.493 | 0.013 | 8.99 | 11.59 |
| | (0.0995) | (2.897) | (0.981) | (2.986) | (4.045) | (5.795) | | 0.11 | 0.17 |
| EXRET-UK | 0.0331 | −7.339 | 1.943 | 1.149 | 13.971 | 5.432 | 0.019 | 8.42 | 4.95 |
| | (0.1000) | (3.970) | (1.507) | (3.368) | (5.681) | (7.295) | | 0.13 | 0.76 |
| EXRET-FR | 0.0187 | −5.009 | 0.930 | 1.288 | 11.221 | 1.297 | 0.007 | 6.67 | 7.06 |
| | (0.0879) | (3.102) | (1.245) | (3.539) | (4.825) | (6.778) | | 0.25 | 0.53 |
| EXRET-CA | 0.1521 | −1.505 | 0.685 | 3.025 | 5.018 | 2.726 | 0.006 | 7.28 | 11.58 |
| | (0.0656) | (2.676) | (1.050) | (3.330) | (4.915) | (5.740) | | 0.20 | 0.17 |
| EXRET-IT | 0.1121 | −6.785 | 0.223 | 2.422 | 8.790 | −4.457 | 0.004 | 8.96 | 13.63 |
| | (0.0914) | (3.568) | (1.294) | (3.812) | (4.694) | (7.179) | | 0.11 | 0.09 |

to be expected in monthly data. In efficient markets, most of the observed return will be unexpected, unless economic agents are extremely risk averse.

The most important features of the other forecasting equations are the coefficients on the own lags, which indicate that there is strong positive serial correlation in the log payout ratio, the log dividend-price ratio, and the term premium. There are also important off-diagonal terms indicating significant dynamics between the dividend yield, the payout ratio, the relative bill rate, and the term spread.

*Table 3.* Covariances and correlations of VAR residuals. This table reports the covariances and correlations of the VAR residuals from Table 2. The correlations are in bold above the diagonal. The variables are the real return on the MSCI world market portfolio (RRET), the logarithm of dividends relative to earnings (LOGDE), the logarithm of the dividend-price ratio (LOGDP), the one-month Treasury bill interest rate minus its twelve-month moving average (RREL), and the 30-year minus one-year Treasury bond term spread (TSPD). The sample period is 1970:01 to 1998:04.

| | RRET | LOGDE | LOGDP | RREL | TSPD |
|---|---|---|---|---|---|
| RRET | 16.4194 | **0.0628** | **−0.8629** | **−0.1007** | **0.1246** |
| LOGDE | 0.0067 | 0.0007 | **0.2144** | **0.0481** | **0.0851** |
| LOGDP | −0.1474 | 0.0002 | 0.0018 | **0.1502** | **−0.0612** |
| RREL | −0.0292 | 0.0001 | 0.0005 | 0.0051 | **−0.0490** |
| TSPD | 0.0183 | 0.0001 | 0.0001 | 0.0001 | 0.0013 |

Panel A of Table 2 also reports the Cumby–Huizinga (1992) L-tests for residual serial correlation of the first eight lags in each equation. Except for the relative bill rate equation, a first-order VAR appears to be a good approximation to the data-generating process.

Panel B of Table 2 reports unconstrained excess return forecasting equations for the G7 countries. Here again, the evidence for predictability of the excess returns is not overwhelmingly strong. These equations are provided as a comparison to the constrained equations that will enter the asset-pricing model.

Table 3 reports the covariances and correlations of the innovations in the VAR. The correlations are in bold above the diagonal. The innovation variance of the real stock return is much larger than the other innovation variances, and the innovation in the real stock return is highly negatively correlated with the innovation in the log dividend yield. The log dividend yield is positively correlated with the log payout ratio and the relative bill rate.

Our results on the predictability of returns present a striking contrast to those of Lamont (1998). We explore these differences in Table 4, which adopts a quarterly measurement interval for comparison purposes.[7] Lamont (1998) forecasts the excess nominal return on the S&P 500 and reports a significantly higher $R^2$ for the sample period 1947:Q1 to 1994:Q4. We use Lamont's (1998) data and our programs to produce the first line of Table 4, which coincides with the first line of Lamont's (1998) Table VI. Aside from the higher $R^2$ in the return equation, Lamont (1998) also reports that the dividend-payout ratio positively forecasts returns, which he interprets as a business-cycle effect. The argument is that the payout ratio is countercyclical as earnings fluctuate more than dividends across business cycles. Since expected returns are thought to be countercyclical, being higher in recessions than in booms, the coefficient linking the payout ratio to returns should be positive. Line 2 of Table 4 demonstrates that this effect persists in Lamont's data for the sample period 1970:Q2 to 1994:Q4, which is the part that overlaps most with our sample. Line 3 of Table 4 demonstrates that the effects are not diminished by the inclusion of the term spread in the regression. Line 4 of Table 4 presents an analogous regression to line 3, but the data are changed. Line 4 uses the excess nominal return on the MSCI-US portfolio, which has a correlation of .997 with the S&P 500 return, and employs the associated MSCI-US div-

*Table 4.* Quarterly return forecasting equations. This table compares equity return forecasting equations using quarterly data. The first three rows use data from Lamont (1998), and the dependent variable is the excess return on the S&P 500. The last three rows use excess return data from the MSCI-US or the MSCI-World indexes. For Lamont's data, the regressors are the lagged excess return (RET), the logarithm of S&P dividends relative to S&P earnings (LOGDE), the logarithm of the S&P dividend-price ratio (LOGDP), the one-month Treasury bill interest rate minus its twelve-month moving average sampled at the end of the quarter (RREL), and the long-term government bond yield minus the T-bill yield (TSPD). For the MSCI regressions, the regressors are the lagged MSCI return (RET), the logarithm of MSCI dividends relative to MSCI earnings (LOGDE), the logarithm of the MSCI dividend-price ratio (LOGDP), the three-month Treasury bill interest rate minus its four-quarter moving average (RREL), and the 30-year minus one-year Treasury bond term spread (TSPD).

| Data | Constant (std.err.) | RET (std.err.) | LOGDP (std.err.) | LOGDE (std.err.) | RREL (std.err.) | TSPD (std.err.) | $R^2$ | Sample |
|---|---|---|---|---|---|---|---|---|
| Lamont (S&P) | 0.209 | 0.066 | 0.078 | 0.086 | −0.892 | | 0.13 | 47:Q1 – |
| | (0.062) | (0.069) | (0.020) | (0.030) | (0.465) | | | 94:Q4 |
| Lamont (S&P) | 0.284 | 0.037 | 0.105 | 0.103 | −0.777 | | 0.12 | 70:Q2 – |
| | (0.118) | (0.099) | (0.039) | (0.046) | (0.604) | | | 94:Q4 |
| Lamont (S&P) | 0.352 | 0.034 | 0.126 | 0.093 | −0.433 | 3.712 | 0.12 | 70:Q2 – |
| | (0.131) | (0.099) | (0.043) | (0.047) | (0.668) | (3.096) | | 94:Q4 |
| MSCI – US | 0.275 | 0.015 | 0.076 | −0.033 | −3.669 | 5.104 | 0.06 | 70:Q2 – |
| | (0.316) | (0.103) | (0.044) | (0.083) | (2.935) | (3.655) | | 94:Q4 |
| MSCI – US | −0.238 | 0.035 | 0.010 | −0.137 | −4.032 | 5.190 | 0.06 | 70:Q2 – |
| | (0.162) | (0.098) | (0.027) | (0.061) | (2.751) | (3.512) | | 98:Q2 |
| MSCI – World | −0.058 | −0.024 | 0.022 | −0.075 | −1.834 | 6.310 | 0.03 | 70:Q2 – |
| | (0.168) | (0.099) | (0.026) | (0.072) | (2.781) | (3.543) | | 98:Q2 |

idend and earning series. LOGDE loses significance, and its sign changes from positive to negative. The $R^2$ for the return equation also falls from .12 to .06. Line 5 of Table 4 demonstrates that extending the sample to 1998:2 causes the dividend yield to lose significance. The last line of Table 4 presents the forecasting regression for the MSCI-World excess nominal return, which is similar to the forecasting equation for the real return in Table 1.

### *Innovations in Forecasts of Future Stock Returns*

The next step in the analysis is to calculate the innovation in the discounted expected future stock returns, since this is the other factor in the asset-pricing framework. To generate the innovation in the discounted present value of the market equity returns from the VAR, define the $k$-dimensional indicator vector $e1$, whose first element is one and whose other elements are zero. Because $E_t z_{t+j} = A^j z_t$, the innovation in the discounted expected future value of the stock market returns is

$$\begin{aligned}(E_{t+1} - E_t)\sum_{j=1}^{\infty} \rho^j r_{m,t+1+j} &= e1'\sum_{j=1}^{\infty} \rho^j A^j \varepsilon_{t+1} \\ &= e1'\rho A(I - \rho A)^{-1}\varepsilon_{t+1} \\ &= \lambda_h' \varepsilon_{t+1}. \end{aligned} \tag{11}$$

The last line of equation (11) defines the vector $\lambda_h$ to be a nonlinear function of the VAR coefficients equal to $e1'\rho A(I-\rho A)^{-1}$. The subscript $h$ is used to identify this coefficient with the hedging demands of investors.

The differences in the variances of the innovations and the correlations between innovations make it hard to interpret the estimation results for a VAR factor model unless the factors are orthogonalized and scaled in some way. To deal with this problem, Campbell (1996) employs Sims's (1980) triangular orthogonalization of the innovations. He also scales the innovations such that they have the same variance as the innovation to the real return. We adopt a similar procedure. Thus, the orthogonalized innovation in the real return is unaffected, and the orthogonalized innovation in the payout ratio is the component of the payout ratio that is orthogonal to the real return. The orthogonalized innovation in the dividend yield is the component of the dividend yield that is orthogonal to the real return and the payout ratio, etc. Since fluctuations in the payout ratio are dominated by fluctuations in earnings, the orthogonalized innovation is essentially an earnings shock that is uncorrelated with returns. The orthogonalized innovation in the dividend yield becomes a dividend shock, and the innovations in the relative bill rate and the term premium become shocks to short-term and long-term interest rates that are orthogonal to returns, earnings and dividends.

Table 5 reports the coefficients of $\lambda_h$ for the raw innovations and for the orthogonalized innovations using a $\rho = 0.9949$. Asymptotic standard errors are reported in parentheses under the coefficients. We find that shocks to the dividend yield, the relative bill rate, and the term premium have positive influences on the innovation in discounted expected future returns, while the innovation in the stock return and the payout ratio have a negative effect. Although none of the coefficients is particularly large relative to its standard error, the $\chi^2(5)$ statistic that tests whether all five coefficients are zero is 10.940, which has a $p$-value of .053. Hence, the group of variables as a whole does have some predictive power.

Campbell (1996) notes that the coefficient on the orthogonalized innovation to the real return in the $\lambda_h$ vector represents the percent of an innovation in returns that is expected to be reversed over the long run. Our point estimate implies considerably less reversion in international stock returns than Campbell finds in post-war U.S. data. Our coefficient is $-0.23$, whereas Campbell reports a coefficient of $-0.92$. We also find somewhat different results on the importance of the term premium. Here, we find a coefficient on the orthogonalized term premium of 0.65 while Campbell reports 0.21. Since the scale of the orthogonalized variables is quite similar because our variance is 16.42 versus Campbell's 17.04, fluctuations in the term premium are much more important for the international equity markets than for the U.S. domestic market.

Panel B of Table 5 reports the covariances and correlations of the two sources of risk in the asset-pricing model, $e1'\varepsilon_{t+1}$ and $\lambda_h'\varepsilon_{t+1}$. We find that innovations to discounted expected future real returns are slightly more than half as variable as innovations to current returns, whereas Campbell (1996) finds them to be approximately equal, and we find a correlation between the two factors of $-.324$, whereas Campbell's is $-.915$. The decline in the correlation between $e1'\varepsilon_{t+1}$ and $\lambda_h'\varepsilon_{t+1}$ may be due to the decline in the importance of the dividend yield in predicting future stock returns.

*Table 5.* Innovations to the long-run stock return. Panel A reports the coefficients of the vector defining the innovation in the discounted present value of the future world stock market returns in equation (11). The variables of the VAR are the real return on the MSCI world market portfolio (RRET), the logarithm of dividends relative to earnings (LOGDE), the logarithm of the dividend-price ratio (LOGDP), the one-month Treasury bill interest rate minus its twelve-month moving average (RREL), and the 30-year minus one-year Treasury bond term spread (TSPD). The sample period is 1970:01 to 1998:04. The $\chi^2(5)$ test examines whether the five coefficients are jointly equal to zero. The second set of coefficients is orthogonalized by triangularizing the innovations and scaling them to have the same variance as the innovation in the real return. Panel B reports the covariances and correlation (in bold) of the innovation in the real return and the innovation in the discounted expected future returns.

Panel A: Coefficients of $\lambda_h$

| | Shocks to | | | | |
|---|---|---|---|---|---|
| Orthogonalized | RRET (std.err.) | LOGDE (std.err.) | LOGDP (std.err.) | RREL (std.err.) | TSPD (std.err.) |
| No | −0.064 | −30.576 | 25.043 | 7.431 | 73.547 |
| | (0.079) | (43.078) | (35.378) | (7.692) | (60.299) |
| Yes | −0.233 | −0.070 | 0.165 | 0.098 | 0.649 |
| | (0.342) | (0.305) | (0.135) | (0.137) | (0.532) |
| $\chi^2(5)$ | 10.940 | | | | |
| $p$-value | 0.053 | | | | |

Panel B: Covariance and Correlation of News Variable

| | $e1'\varepsilon_{t+1}$ | $\lambda_h'\varepsilon_{t+1}$ |
|---|---|---|
| $e1'\varepsilon_{t+1}$ | 16.419 | **−0.324** |
| $\lambda_h'\varepsilon_{t+1}$ | −3.819 | 8.485 |

## V. The Econometric Asset-Pricing Model

The next task is to develop the econometric specification to test the asset-pricing model. We use Hansen's (1982) generalized method of moments (GMM), which requires that the econometrician define a set of orthogonality conditions specified by the theoretical model.

Three basic sets of orthogonality conditions are used. The first set is derived from the requirements that the errors in the VAR equations are required to be orthogonal to the right-hand-side forecasting variables:

$$E_t\left[\varepsilon_{t+1} \otimes (1, z_t')'\right] = 0. \tag{12}$$

The second set of orthogonality conditions involves the equations that define the innovations in the excess country returns. Here, as in Panel B of Table 1, the excess rate of return for country $i$ at time $t+1$ is projected onto the same information set, $(1, z_t')$, that is used to forecast the real return on the world market portfolio:

$$r_{i,t+1} - r_{f,t+1} = \mu_i + \delta_i' z_t + \eta_{i,t+1}. \tag{13}$$

Thus, the orthogonality conditions for the $i$-th country excess rate of return are

$$E_t\left[\eta_{i,t+1} \otimes (1, z_t')'\right] = 0. \tag{14}$$

The third set of orthogonality conditions involves the asset-pricing equations. Since the asset-pricing equations are written in terms of conditional expectations at time $t$, and the innovations to the first two sets of orthogonality conditions are defined above, the asset-pricing equations (9) can be written as

$$E_t r_{i,t+1} - r_{f,t+1} + \frac{E_t \eta_{i,t+1}^2}{2} = \gamma E_t(\eta_{i,t+1} e1'\varepsilon_{t+1}) + (\gamma - 1) E_t(\eta_{i,t+1} \lambda_h' \varepsilon_{t+1}). \tag{15}$$

By substituting for the expected return and using realizations for conditional expectations, we can define the innovation in the $i$-th asset-pricing equation relative to the time $t$ information set as

$$u_{i,t+1} = \mu_i + \delta_i' z_t + \frac{\eta_{i,t+1}^2}{2} - \gamma\left(\eta_{i,t+1} e1'\varepsilon_{t+1}\right) - (\gamma - 1)\left(\eta_{i,t+1} \lambda_h' \varepsilon_{t+1}\right). \tag{16}$$

In the first set of empirical results, we only impose the orthogonality conditions

$$E\left(u_{t+1}\right) = 0, \tag{17}$$

where $u_{t+1}$ is the vector of the $u_{i,t+1}$'s. We do not impose additional restrictions because all of the orthogonality conditions of the model must be estimated simultaneously.

With seven country returns and five forecasting variables, there are thirty orthogonality conditions in the first set, forty-two in the second set, and seven in the third for a total of seventy-nine. There are also thirty parameters in the first set, forty-two in the second, and one in the third for a total of seventy-three parameters. Thus, the entire system of equations has six more orthogonality conditions than parameters, and the test of the overidentifying restrictions of the model is a $\chi^2(6)$.

## VI. Estimation of the Model

Table 6 reports the seventy-three parameter estimates of the model associated with the VAR forecasting equations, the G7 excess-return forecasting equations, and the asset-pricing equations, as well as the constrained prices of risks. As might be expected, there is little change in the parameters of the VAR forecasting equations or the excess return forecasting equations relative to their respective unconstrained estimates that are reported in Table 1. The key parameter of the model is the coefficient of relative risk aversion, $\gamma$. Its estimated value is 5.06, with a standard error of 2.54. Often, in the consumption-based asset-pricing literature and in Campbell (1996), the estimated coefficients of relative risk aversion are implausibly large, but our value is quite reasonable.

The overidentifying restrictions of our model are not rejected, since the $\chi^2(6)$ statistic has a value of 1.23, which corresponds to a $p$-value of 0.975. Thus, Campbell's dynamic asset-pricing model explains the cross-section of the G7 country equity returns. When we

*Table 6.* GMM estimates of the constrained model.

| | Coefficients on Regressors | | | | | |
|---|---|---|---|---|---|---|
| Dependent Variable | RRET (std.err.) | LOGDE (std.err.) | LOGDP (std.err.) | RREL (std.err.) | TSPD (std.err.) | CONST (std.err.) |
| | | | Panel A: VAR | | | |
| RRET | 0.0666 | −3.751 | 1.082 | 0.715 | 9.022 | 3.385 |
| | (0.0620) | (2.071) | (0.713) | (2.159) | (2.960) | (4.064) |
| LOGDE | 0.0000 | 0.964 | 0.004 | −0.038 | 0.010 | −0.003 |
| | (0.0003) | (0.017) | (0.004) | (0.015) | (0.019) | (0.022) |
| LOGDP | −0.0010 | 0.012 | 0.986 | 0.0002 | −0.076 | −0.071 |
| | (0.0006) | (0.022) | (0.008) | (0.021) | (0.030) | (0.043) |
| RREL | −0.0023 | 0.112 | −0.057 | 0.570 | −0.359 | −0.227 |
| | (0.0013) | (0.038) | (0.016) | (0.060) | (0.069) | (0.081) |
| TSPD | −0.0011 | 0.017 | 0.0004 | 0.017 | 0.950 | 0.021 |
| | (0.0007) | (0.017) | (0.007) | (0.031) | (0.029) | (0.035) |
| | | | Panel B: Forecasting equations | | | |
| EXRET-US | 0.0136 | −4.201 | 0.533 | −0.871 | 6.721 | −0.093 |
| | (0.0700) | (2.166) | (0.831) | (2.552) | (3.352) | (4.616) |
| EXRET-JP | 0.190 | 1.735 | 2.634 | 2.728 | 10.194 | 16.492 |
| | (0.104) | (3.286) | (1.036) | (3.315) | (4.017) | (6.050) |
| EXRET-GE | 0.039 | -4.917 | 0.631 | −0.677 | 8.791 | −0.269 |
| | (0.097) | (2.848) | (0.962) | (2.934) | (3.867) | (5.685) |
| EXRET-UK | 0.0453 | −6.909 | 1.940 | 1.101 | 12.762 | 5.798 |
| | (0.099) | (3.753) | (1.357) | (3.361) | (5.432) | (6.547) |
| EXRET-FR | 0.025 | −4.927 | 1.005 | 0.725 | 10.621 | 1.841 |
| | (0.087) | (3.037) | (1.151) | (3.441) | (4.683) | (6.249) |
| EXRET-CA | 0.154 | −1.300 | 0.896 | 2.766 | 4.156 | 4.359 |
| | (0.065) | (2.566) | (0.990) | (3.320) | (4.768) | (5.362) |
| EXRET-IT | 0.117 | −6.359 | 0.370 | 2.810 | 8.547 | −3.093 |
| | (0.090) | (3.498) | (1.248) | (3.700) | (4.635) | (6.885) |
| | | | Panel C: Constrained Prices of Risks and Estimate of $\gamma$ | | | |
| Prices of Risks | 4.065 | −0.308 | 0.689 | 0.370 | 2.411 | |
| | (1.541) | (1.187) | (0.809) | (0.550) | (1.834) | |
| $\gamma$ | 5.058 | | $\chi^2(6)$ | 1.234 | | |
| | (2.539) | | $p$-value | 0.975 | | |

Note to Table 6: This table contains the 73 constrained parameter estimates from the dynamic pricing model. Panel A reports the forecasting equations from the VAR. Panel B reports the forecasting equations from the G7 excess equity returns. Panel C reports the constrained prices of risks, the estimate of the coefficient of relative risk aversion, $\gamma$, and the test of the model's six overidentifying conditions. The forecasting variables are the real return on the MSCI world market portfolio (RRET), the logarithm of dividends relative to earnings (LOGDE), the logarithm of the dividend-price ratio (LOGDP), the one-month Treasury bill interest rate minus its twelve-month moving average (RREL), and the 30-year minus one-year Treasury bond term spread (TSPD). The assets are the excess dollar equity returns on the G7 countries. The sample period is 1970:01 to 1998:04.

estimate the model without imposing the constraint that the coefficient on $V_{ih}$ is $(\gamma - 1)$, the estimated value of the coefficient is 3.056 with a standard error of 12.330. The resulting chi-squared test that the coefficient on $V_{ih}$ equals the coefficient on $V_{im}$ minus one has a value of 0.004. The fact that the coefficient on $V_{ih}$ is insignificantly different from zero suggests that more restricted models may adequately represent the data.

### *Tests of CAPM Restrictions*

There are several conditions that allow the predictions of the dynamic model to collapse to the predictions of the CAPM. This section investigates whether we can reject these conditions or not.

The first way that the dynamic model reduces to the CAPM is if $\gamma = 1$, since then expected returns are determined only by the covariance of an asset with the market portfolio. A GMM likelihood ratio test of the hypothesis that $\gamma = 1$ involves estimation of the model under this restriction with the same GMM weighting matrix as is used without the restriction. The difference in the values of the criterion functions is a $\chi^2(1) = 4.512$, which coincides with a $p$-value of .033 indicating that it is unlikely that $\gamma = 1$.

The second way that the model reduces to the CAPM is if the covariances of the asset returns with the hedge portfolio are all zero. The test of these restrictions is a $\chi^2(7) = 54.035$ with a $p$-value less than .0001 indicating very strong evidence that the covariances with the hedge portfolios are important in pricing the cross-section of asset returns.

The third way that the dynamic model can be reduced to the CAPM is if each $V_{ih}$ is proportional to its $V_{im}$ with the same factor of proportionality. The test of these restrictions is a $\chi^2(6) = 4.512$. Hence, we are unable to reject that the dynamic model collapses to the CAPM for this set of assets. The importance of the hedge portfolios in the pricing of the assets indicates that the hedge portfolios might be important in pricing other assets in which the proportionality does not hold.

### *Estimated Prices of Risks*

The asset-pricing model implies that expected returns on assets adjust to reflect the covariances of asset returns with the return on the market portfolio and with the other underlying factors that forecast the market portfolio. These covariances are the asset's risk characteristics, and the compensations or prices of the risks are constrained by the model. The price of risk that arises from the traditional covariance of an asset's return with the market return is $\gamma + (\gamma - 1)\lambda_{h1}$, where $\lambda_{hk}$ represents the $k$-th element of $\lambda_h$. The price of the $k$-th risk that arises from the covariance of an asset's return with the innovation in a variable that forecasts the market return is $(\gamma - 1)\lambda_{hk}$. Thus, this model provides a clear link between the coefficient of relative risk aversion, $\gamma$, and the prices of risks that arise from covariances between asset returns and various factors.

The prices of risks are given in Panel C of Table 6 for the orthogonalized innovations. The covariance of a return with the return on the market portfolio indeed commands the largest price of risk, which justifies the important role of this variable in the traditional CAPM.

The estimated price the risk caused by covariance of the return with the market return is 4.065 with a standard error of 1.541. The covariance of a return with the term premium also incurs a large price of risk, a value of 2.411 with a standard error of 1.834. The prices of other covariance risks are an order of magnitude smaller than these coefficients and have standard errors larger than the coefficients. The results for the prices of risks for the market return and the term premium are comparable to those estimated by Campbell (1996), but he finds much larger prices of risks for the dividend yield and the relative bill rate. These findings are consistent with Korajczyk and Viallet (1989) and Ferson and Harvey (1993) who also find significant risk prices for factors other than the risk generated by covariance with the return on the international market portfolio.

It is also possible to estimate unconstrained prices of risks. That is, the asset-pricing model is simply postulated to be

$$E_t r_{i,t+1} - r_{f,t+1} + \frac{E_t \eta_{i,t+1}^2}{2} = \sum_{k=1}^{5} \pi_k E_t \left(\eta_{i,t+1}\varepsilon_{k,t+1}\right), \tag{18}$$

where the $\pi_k$ parameters represent the five unconstrained prices of risks associated with covariances between the asset returns and the innovations in the factors that forecast the market return. This specification is essentially a five-factor asset-pricing model as in Ross's (1976) arbitrage pricing theory (APT). Table 7 presents the estimated parameters of this model, and the unconstrained prices of risk are given at the bottom. Compared to the results of the constrained model, there is a slight reduction in the price of risk associated with the covariance of an asset's return with the real return on the world market portfolio. There are large changes in the prices of the other covariance risks, which are also very imprecisely estimated. Because this model uses the same orthogonality conditions as the constrained model and estimates four additional parameters, the overidentifying restrictions of this unconstrained model also are not rejected. The $\chi^2(2)$ statistic has a value of 0.133, which corresponds to a $P$-value of 0.936.

### *Pricing Errors from the Dynamic Model*

Table 8 provides the average adjusted excess rates of return for the seven country portfolios for two samples, which have units of percent per month. The first is our base sample of 1970:01 to 1998:04. The second is a sub-sample from 1975:01 to 1995:12, which corresponds to the Fama–French (1998) sample. The average adjusted return corresponds to

$$\text{Ave. Adj. return } i = \frac{1}{T-1}\sum_{t=1}^{T-1}\left(r_{i,t+1} - r_{f,t+1} + \frac{\eta_{i,t+1}^2}{2}\right), \tag{19}$$

where the estimated residuals are used. This is simply the average risk premium, which is adjusted for the Jensen's inequality effect that arises because we are using log returns instead of gross returns. The dynamic pricing model predicts that the average adjusted return contains two parts: a part corresponding to risk induced by covariance with the

*Table 7.* GMM estimates jointly with unconstrained risk prices.

| | Coefficients on Regressors | | | | | |
|---|---|---|---|---|---|---|
| Dependent Variable | RRET (std.err.) | LOGDE (std.err.) | LOGDP (std.err.) | RREL (std.err.) | TSPD (std.err.) | CONST (std.err.) |
| | | | Panel A: VAR | | | |
| RRET | 0.057 | −3.974 | 1.097 | 0.900 | 9.546 | 3.275 |
| | (0.063) | (2.128) | (0.744) | (2.177) | (3.044) | (4.198) |
| LOGDE | −0.0001 | 0.963 | 0.005 | −0.038 | 0.012 | −0.001 |
| | (0.0003) | (0.017) | (0.004) | (0.015) | (0.019) | (0.022) |
| LOGDP | −0.001 | 0.015 | 0.986 | −0.001 | −0.081 | −0.069 |
| | (0.001) | (0.022) | (0.008) | (0.021) | (0.030) | (0.044) |
| RREL | −0.002 | 0.113 | −0.057 | 0.575 | −0.359 | −0.224 |
| | (0.001) | (0.039) | (0.016) | (0.059) | (0.068) | (0.082) |
| TSPD | −0.001 | 0.017 | 0.001 | 0.017 | 0.951 | 0.023 |
| | (0.001) | (0.017) | (0.007) | (0.031) | (0.029) | (0.036) |
| | | | Panel B: Forecasting equations | | | |
| EXRET-US | 0.004 | −4.427 | 0.570 | −0.588 | 7.292 | −0.045 |
| | (0.072) | (2.247) | (0.846) | (2.572) | (3.423) | (4.664) |
| EXRET-JP | 0.184 | 1.527 | 2.628 | 2.543 | 10.159 | 16.284 |
| | (0.106) | (3.310) | (1.067) | (3.391) | (4.064) | (6.177) |
| EXRET-GE | 0.026 | −5.351 | 0.684 | −0.289 | 9.644 | −0.285 |
| | (0.099) | (2.892) | (0.979) | (2.984) | (4.029) | (5.767) |
| EXRET-UK | 0.033 | −7.256 | 1.919 | 1.234 | 13.842 | 5.326 |
| | (0.100) | (3.967) | (1.505) | (3.352) | (5.671) | (7.274) |
| EXRET-FR | 0.019 | −5.058 | 1.001 | 1.390 | 11.285 | 1.682 |
| | (0.088) | (3.092) | (1.215) | (3.515) | (4.803) | (6.610) |
| EXRET-CA | 0.151 | −1.567 | 0.762 | 2.994 | 5.096 | 3.164 |
| | (0.066) | (2.649) | (1.019) | (3.311) | (4.901) | (5.584) |
| EXRET-IT | 0.111 | −6.765 | 0.249 | 2.326 | 8.787 | −4.303 |
| | (0.091) | (3.554) | (1.288) | (3.799) | (4.691) | (7.158) |
| | | | Panel C: Unconstrained Prices of Risks | | | |
| Prices of Risks | 3.589 | −1.751 | −13.337 | 18.714 | 22.946 | |
| | (2.948) | (19.247) | (39.381) | (46.744) | (66.272) | |
| | | | $\chi^2(2)$ | 0.133 | | |
| | | | $p$-value | 0.975 | | |

Notes to Table 7: This table contains the 77 parameter estimates from the APT version of the dynamic pricing model. Panel A reports the forecasting equations from the VAR. Panel B reports the forecasting equations from the G7 excess returns. Panel C reports the unconstrained prices of risks and the test of the model's two overidentifying conditions. The forecasting variables are the real return on the MSCI world market portfolio (RRET), the logarithm of dividends relative to earnings (LOGDE), the logarithm of the dividend-price ratio (LOGDP), the one-month Treasury bill interest rate minus its twelve-month moving average (RREL), and the 30-year minus one-year Treasury bond term spread (TSPD). The assets are the excess dollar equity returns on the G7 countries. The sample period is 1970:01 to 1998:04.

*Table 8.* Pricing components and errors from the dynamic asset pricing model. This table reports the average adjusted percentage monthly excess rates of return, defined in equation (19), for the seven countries for two samples. The first is our base sample of 1970:01 to 1998:04, and the second is a sub-sample from 1975:01 to 1995:12, which is used by Fama and French (1998). The pricing model predicts that the average adjusted return contains two parts: a part corresponding to covariance with the market portfolio, $\gamma V_{i,m}$, and a part corresponding to covariance with the innovation in discounted expected future returns, $(\gamma - 1) V_{i,h}$. The pricing error is the difference between the data and the model's prediction.

| | Ave. Adj. | $\gamma V_{i,m}$ | $(\gamma - 1) V_{i,h}$ | Pricing Error |
|---|---|---|---|---|
| Sample: 1970:01–1998:04 | | | | |
| EXRET-US | 0.545 | 0.724 | −0.184 | 0.005 |
| EXRET-JP | 0.730 | 0.866 | −0.132 | −0.005 |
| EXRET-GE | 0.587 | 0.661 | −0.076 | 0.002 |
| EXRET-UK | 0.757 | 0.936 | −0.181 | 0.002 |
| EXRET-FR | 0.686 | 0.839 | −0.152 | −0.001 |
| EXRET-CA | 0.582 | 0.771 | −0.171 | −0.019 |
| EXRET-IT | 0.515 | 0.661 | −0.133 | −0.014 |
| Sample: 1975:01–1995:12 | | | | |
| | Ave. Adj. | $\gamma V_{i,m}$ | $(\gamma - 1) V_{i,h}$ | Pricing Error |
| EXRET-US | 0.569 | 0.795 | −0.226 | 0.001 |
| EXRET-JP | 0.930 | 1.146 | −0.202 | −0.014 |
| EXRET-GE | 0.679 | 0.805 | −0.115 | −0.011 |
| EXRET-UK | 0.828 | 1.066 | −0.231 | −0.007 |
| EXRET-FR | 0.797 | 1.012 | −0.197 | −0.018 |
| EXRET-CA | 0.599 | 0.877 | −0.233 | −0.045 |
| EXRET-IT | 0.660 | 0.834 | −0.149 | −0.024 |

world market portfolio, $\gamma V_{i,m}$, and a part corresponding to risk induced by covariance with the innovation in discounted expected future returns, $(\gamma - 1) V_{i,h}$. The model does very well at pricing the average adjusted returns. The pricing error for the U.S. is only 0.001 percent per month or 0.012 percent per annum. The Canadian pricing error is the largest at −0.045 percent per month for the basic sample or −0.54 percent per annum. The pricing errors are even smaller, in general, for the Fama–French (1998) sub-sample.

Since the estimates of $V_{i,h}$ are uniformly negative, each equity return covaries negatively with the innovation in discounted expected future market returns. As we noted above, when $\gamma > 1$, investors view such negative covariation as desirable for hedging purposes. Hence, these terms contribute negatively to the assets' required rates of return.

### *CAPM Specification Tests*

Our inability to reject the restrictions of the CAPM and the imprecision in the estimates of the unconstrained prices of risks, for the factors other than the market portfolio, suggest that the traditional CAPM may be an adequate representation of the expected returns on the seven country portfolios in the sense of having comparable pricing errors. To investigate this conjecture, we set up the following system of equations:

$$
\begin{aligned}
r_{m,t+1} &= \mu_m + \varepsilon_{m,t+1} \\
r_{i,t+1} - r_{f,t+1} &= \mu_i + \eta_{i,t+1} \\
u_{i,t+1} &= \mu_i + \frac{\eta_{i,t+1}^2}{2} - \gamma\left(\eta_{i,t+1}\varepsilon_{m,t+1}\right),
\end{aligned}
\tag{20}
$$

for $i = 1, \ldots, 7$. The system is estimated by making each of the error terms orthogonal to a constant. Since there are nine parameters in the system of equations and fifteen orthogonality conditions, the test of the overidentifying restrictions is a $\chi^2(6)$.

This version of the CAPM is estimated in Panel A of Table 9. For the full sample, the estimated value of $\gamma$ for is 3.776, with a standard error of 1.478. The $\chi^2(6)$ statistic that tests the overidentifying restrictions of the model is 1.079, which corresponds to a $p$-value of 0.982. Hence, the CAPM is not rejected by the data. The average returns are larger in the sub-sample, but inference about the validity of the CAPM is similar.

The pricing errors of the CAPM for the two samples are given in Panel B of Table 9. The largest pricing error is again smaller than 0.05 percent per month.

Predictability of returns is generally inconsistent with the CAPM. Only if $\gamma = 1$, or if $V_{ih}$ is proportional to $V_{im}$, does Campbell's (1996) theory collapse to a conditional CAPM. If the static CAPM is true, the pricing errors should not be predictable with conditioning information. We test this predictability restriction by examining the additional orthogonality conditions that the asset-pricing errors from the CAPM model should be orthogonal to $z_t$. Since there are seven assets, five elements in $z_t$, and no additional parameters to estimate, we can calculate a $\chi^2(35)$ statistic directly from the value of the GMM objective function for these thirty-five orthogonality conditions. The value of this statistic is 69.553, with a $p$-value of 0.0005. This indicates considerable evidence against the static CAPM.

Of course, we also did not require the pricing errors of the dynamic model to be orthogonal to the $z_t$ information set. When we calculate the analogous $\chi^2(35)$ statistic for these restrictions on the dynamic model, we find a test statistic of 178.87, with a $p$-value smaller than .00001. Thus, the dynamic model also fails this test of dynamic asset pricing.

### *High Book-to-Market Returns*

Fama and French (1998) further demonstrate the inadequacy of the static international CAPM by constructing portfolios of stocks for each country based on book-to-market ratios.[8] They find that portfolios with high book-to-market (HBM) ratios are particularly troublesome for the CAPM to price. The average returns on high book-to-market firms are significantly higher than those predicted by the CAPM. Our version of these results is presented in Table 10, which excludes Canada because of data availability. Notice that the average adjusted returns on the HBM portfolios are considerably higher than the returns on the value-weighted MSCI market portfolios, except in the case of Italy. For example, the average adjusted return for the German HBM portfolio is 0.213 percent per month higher

*Table 9.* Estimation, pricing components and pricing errors from the static CAPM. This table contains the parameter estimates from the static CAPM pricing model. Panel A reports the parameters from equation (20) and the test of the model's six overidentifying conditions. Panel B reports the average adjusted percentage monthly excess rates of return, defined in equation (19), for the seven countries for two samples. The first is our base sample of 1970:01 to 1998:04, and the second is a sub-sample from 1975:01 to 1995:12, which is used by Fama and French (1998). The pricing model predicts that the average adjusted return is explained by covariance of a return with the return on market portfolio, $\gamma V_{i,m}$. The pricing error is the difference between the data and the model's prediction.

Panel A: Parameter Estimates

| | Sample: 1970:01–1998:04 | Sample: 1975:1–1995:12 |
|---|---|---|
| | Coefficient (std. err.) | Coefficient (std. err.) |
| RRET | 0.554 | 0.761 |
| | (0.225) | (0.259) |
| EXRET-US | 0.473 | 0.583 |
| | (0.199) | (0.212) |
| EXRET-JP | 0.471 | 0.744 |
| | (0.249) | (0.321) |
| EXRET-GE | 0.350 | 0.500 |
| | (0.180) | (0.215) |
| EXRET-UK | 0.504 | 0.723 |
| | (0.267) | (0.325) |
| EXRET-FR | 0.437 | 0.627 |
| | (0.237) | (0.290) |
| EXRET-CA | 0.443 | 0.566 |
| | (0.207) | (0.233) |
| EXRET-IT | 0.227 | 0.399 |
| | (0.189) | (0.212) |
| $\gamma$ | 3.776 | 5.001 |
| (std.err.) | (1.478) | (1.757) |
| $\chi^2(6)$ | 1.080 | 2.712 |
| $p$-value | 0.982 | 0.844 |

Panel B: Pricing Components and Errors

| | Sample: 1970:01–1998:04 | | | Sample: 1975:1–1995:12 | | |
|---|---|---|---|---|---|---|
| | Ave. Adj. | $\gamma V_{i,m}$ | Pricing Error | Ave. Adj. | $\gamma V_{i,m}$ | Pricing Error |
| EXRET-US | 0.568 | 0.568 | −0.0001 | 0.673 | 0.694 | −0.021 |
| EXRET-JP | 0.683 | 0.682 | 0.001 | 0.962 | 0.978 | −0.015 |
| EXRET-GE | 0.521 | 0.522 | −0.001 | 0.682 | 0.712 | −0.030 |
| EXRET-UK | 0.737 | 0.739 | −0.002 | 0.971 | 1.007 | −0.036 |
| EXRET-FR | 0.663 | 0.664 | −0.001 | 0.870 | 0.903 | −0.033 |
| EXRET-CA | 0.586 | 0.591 | −0.005 | 0.717 | 0.761 | −0.044 |
| EXRET-IT | 0.513 | 0.519 | −0.006 | 0.695 | 0.7730 | −0.035 |

*Table 10.* Pricing components and errors from the static CAPM Fama–French (1997) high book-to-market portfolios sample: 1975:01–1995:12. This table investigates the ability of the static CAPM to price assets with high book-to-market ratios. It reports the average adjusted percentage monthly excess rates of return for these assets, defined in equation (19), for six countries. The sample is 1975:01 to 1995:12, which is used by Fama and French (1998). The pricing model predicts that the average adjusted return is explained by covariance of a return with the return on market portfolio, $\gamma V_{i,m}$. The pricing error is the difference between the data and the model's prediction.

| | Ave. Adj. | $\gamma V_{i,m}$ | Pricing Error |
|---|---|---|---|
| EXRET-US | 0.946 | 0.644 | 0.301 |
| EXRET-JP | 1.207 | 0.890 | 0.317 |
| EXRET-GE | 0.895 | 0.680 | 0.215 |
| EXRET-UK | 1.340 | 1.024 | 0.317 |
| EXRET-FR | 1.181 | 0.893 | 0.287 |
| EXRET-IT | 0.373 | 0.705 | −0.331 |

than the German market portfolio. For the U.K. the incremental value is 0.369. Table 9 indicates that this range is also the magnitude of the pricing errors from the CAPM, as well. The estimation uses the estimated value of $\gamma$ from the analogous sample for the CAPM estimation with the country market portfolios, and the mean parameters for the HBM return equations are estimated prior to examining the pricing equations.

Table 11 examines whether the dynamic model can successfully price the HBM country portfolios. The answer here, too, is negative. The pricing errors from the dynamic model are comparable to the pricing errors from the CAPM.

## VII. Conclusions

This paper develops the implications of stock-return predictability for cross-sectional international asset pricing using the framework developed by Campbell (1996). The dynamic model explains the average returns on the dollar-denominated excess returns on the market portfolios of the G7 countries quite well, but the static CAPM does also. The hedging terms of the dynamic model are non-zero, yet we are unable to reject that they are proportional to covariances with the market portfolio, in which case they have no direct role in the cross-sectional international asset pricing. Because the static CAPM is inconsistent with return predictability, which exists in the data, our specification tests demonstrate that instrumental variables can predict the asset-pricing errors from the static CAPM. Unfortunately, these same specification tests reveal that the dynamic model fails along the same dimensions. Neither model can price the high book-to-market country portfolios that Fama and French (1998) construct.

*Table 11.* Pricing components and errors from the dynamic asset pricing model Fama–French (1997) high book-to-market portfolios sample: 1975:01–1995:12. This table investigates the ability of the dynamic asset pricing model to price assets with high book-to-market ratios. It reports the average adjusted percentage monthly excess rates of return for these assets, defined in equation (19), for six countries. The sample is 1975:01 to 1995:12, which is used by Fama and French (1998). The pricing model predicts that the average adjusted return contains two parts: a part corresponding to covariance with the market portfolio, $\gamma V_{i,m}$, and a part corresponding to covariance with the innovation in discounted expected future returns, $(\gamma - 1)V_{i,h}$. The pricing error is the difference between the data and the model's prediction.

| | Ave. Adj. | $\gamma V_{i,m}$ | $(\gamma - 1)V_{i,h}$ | Pricing Error |
|---|---|---|---|---|
| EXRET-US | 0.870 | 0.710 | −0.189 | 0.349 |
| EXRET-JP | 1.192 | 1.041 | −0.182 | 0.332 |
| EXRET-GE | 0.840 | 0.761 | −0.095 | 0.174 |
| EXRET-UK | 1.142 | 1.096 | −0.221 | 0.267 |
| EXRET-FR | 1.080 | 0.999 | −0.190 | 0.271 |
| EXRET-IT | 0.336 | 0.795 | −0.135 | −0.324 |

A rational explanation of the data requires a bridge between the intertemporal predictability of international equity returns and the cross-section of asset returns. Harvey (1991) and Ferson and Harvey (1993) develop an eclectic, empirical approach. Harvey (1991) postulates a conditional CAPM, and Ferson and Harvey (1993) develop conditional beta-pricing models in which expected returns equal the sum of several betas times their associated prices of risks. They allow the betas to vary over time depending on local information, but they require the prices of risks to vary only with global information. The problem with such approaches is that they are not tightly linked to theory.

Fama and French (1996) argue that the static CAPM is flawed, but they develop multi-factor explanations of the data. In domestic U.S. asset pricing, they allow expected returns to depend on sensitivities of returns to three factors. The first is the excess return on a broad market portfolio. The second is the difference between the return on a portfolio of small-capitalization stocks and the return on a portfolio of large-capitalization stocks. The third is the difference between the return on a portfolio of high book-to-market stocks and the return on a portfolio of low book-to-market stocks. For international asset pricing, Fama and French (1998) use two factors: the excess return on the world market portfolio, and the difference in returns between the world high and low book-to-market portfolios. Since the Fama–French (1998) model successfully prices the problematic returns on high book-to-market country portfolios, a risk-based theoretical explanation for the presence of the second risk factor seems plausible. But, Fama and French (1998) note that their tests do not cleanly identify the consumption-investment state variables that would link their analysis to intertemporal asset-pricing theories.

The Campbell (1996) model provides a tight theoretical framework that allows us to test the implications of a truly dynamic asset-pricing model of international equity returns. We demonstrate that this particular dynamic model provides only a marginal improvement over the static CAPM. Our extension of the model to price international assets involves some strong assumptions. Perhaps the strongest is the assumption of a representative international investor. Adler and Dumas (1983) note that failure of purchasing power parity implies that an international representative investor does not exist. They demonstrate that in such a world expected equity returns depend on hedging terms involving foreign exchange rates. Vassalou (1997) provides some tests of unconditional restrictions implied by this approach by developing indexes of exchange rates and inflation rates. She finds support for the pricing of foreign exchange risk in equity returns. Dumas and Solnik (1995) postulate a version of the Adler–Dumas model that allows time-varying world prices of foreign-exchange risk that are postulated to depend on the conditioning information of the econometrician. They, too, find that conditioning information is important and that foreign-exchange risk is priced. De Santis and Gerard (1998) develop tests of the Adler–Dumas model using a conditional approach that estimates parametric conditional means and covariances. Since there is strong evidence against purchasing power parity, modifying the model to allow for different real returns in different countries is an extension that is pursued in Ng (1999).

Another weakness of our approach is its assumption that the value-weighted real stock return correctly measures the return on real wealth. Both Jagannathan and Wang (1996) and Campbell (1996) stress the importance of labor income and human capital in asset pricing. While Jagannathan and Wang (1996) and Campbell (1996) treat labor income as tradeable in a domestic asset-pricing context, such an assumption appears untenable in a multicountry model. Unfortunately, the required extension of the Campbell (1996) model to allow non-traded human wealth in different countries appears non-trivial.

As Flood, Hodrick, and Kaplan (1986) note, asset return predictability is not inconsistent with rational, maximizing behavior. Indeed, modern asset-pricing theories link this return predictability to hedging motives of investors. Different sensitivities of asset returns to the underlying state variables that generate time-varying market returns cause risk premiums on the assets to differ. This paper investigates the links between return predictability and the cross-section of country returns. Hedging demands may play a role in cross-sectional asset pricing, but there are still many puzzles that remain to be investigated.

## Acknowledgments

We thank the participants at the conference, especially Marjorie Flavin, Paul Kaplan, and Louis Scott, for their comments. We also thank Geert Bekaert, John Campbell, Ken Froot, Laurie Hodrick, and Owen Lamont for their comments, as well as the participants in seminars at Columbia University, Georgetown University, Stanford University, the NBER International Finance Group, and the Federal Reserve Bank of New York. We are very grateful that Owen Lamont and Kenneth French each provided us with part of the data.

## Notes

1. Hodrick (1981) and Stulz (1981) extended the Merton (1973) analysis to develop international, intertemporal asset pricing models.

2. The model also incorporates human capital as an additional asset.
3. The Euler equation approach of Hansen and Singleton (1982) provides researchers with econometric tools that allow tests of models in which expected returns on stocks were allowed to fluctuate, but the approach requires correct specification of a representative agent's utility function and direct observations on the consumption of this agent. Both aspects are problematic.
4. Campbell (1996) also allows for an additional factor in the asset-pricing model related to human wealth. He argues that the return on the real wealth portfolio is appropriately measured as the value-weighted sum of the return on assets and the return on human wealth. Jagannathan and Wang (1996) also include labor income in their analysis. While there may be an asset-pricing role for labor income, in a global economy the variable would have to be some measure of the world's labor income. We have made no attempt to measure such a variable.
5. Chang and Hung (1999) independently develop an international version of Campbell's (1996) model allowing for time-varying conditional second moments.
6. While it is tempting to substitute $\sigma = 1$ in equation (7) and conclude that intertemporal considerations are not important in this case, which would imply that equation (9) is wrong, the correct derivation follows Giovannini and Weil (1989) who note that L'Hopital's rule must be applied because $\theta \to \infty$ as $\sigma \to 1$.
7. We thank Owen Lamont for providing the data used in the comparisons to his article in Table 4.
8. We thank Kenneth French for providing the data on the HBM portfolios used in this part of our paper.

## References


Adler, Michael, and Bernard Dumas. (1983). "International Portfolio Choice and Corporation Finance: A Synthesis." *Journal of Finance* 38, 925–984.

Bekaert, Geert, and Robert J. Hodrick. (1992). "Characterizing Predictable Components in Excess Returns on Equity and Foreign Exchange Markets." *Journal of Finance* 47, 467–510.

Campbell, John Y. (1991). "A Variance Decomposition for Stock Returns." *Economic Journal* 101, 157–179.

Campbell, John Y. (1993). "Intertemporal Asset Pricing Without Consumption." *American Economic Review* 83, 487–512.

Campbell, John Y. (1996). "Understanding Risk and Return." *Journal of Political Economy* 104, 298–345.

Campbell, John Y., and Robert J. Shiller. (1988). "The Dividend-Price Ratio and Expectations of Future Dividends and Discount Factors." *Review of Financial Studies* 1, 195–228.

Chang, Jow-ran, and Mao-wei Hung. (1999). "An International Asset Pricing Model With Time-varying Hedging Risk." Manuscript, National Taiwan University.

Cumby, Robert E., and John Huizinga. (1992). "Testing the Autocorrelation Structure of Disturbances in Ordinary Least Squares and Instrumental Variables Regressions." *Econometrica* 60, 185–196.

De Santis, Giorgio, and Bruno Gerard. (1998). "How Big Is the Premium for Currency Risk." *Journal of Financial Economics* 49, 375–412.

Dumas, Bernard, and Bruno Solnik. (1995). "The World Price of Foreign Exchange Risk." *Journal of Finance* 50, 445–479.

Epstein, Larry G., and Stanley E. Zin. (1989). "Substitution, Risk Aversion, and the Temporal Behavior of Consumption and Asset Returns." *Econometrica* 57, 937–969.

Fama, Eugene F., and Kenneth R. French. (1988). "Dividend Yields and Expected Stock Returns." *Journal of Financial Economics* 22, 3–26.

Fama, Eugene F., and Kenneth R. French. (1989). "Business Conditions and Expected Returns on Stocks and Bonds." *Journal of Financial Economics* 25, 23–50.

Fama, Eugene F., and Kenneth R. French. (1996). "Multifactor Explanations of Asset Pricing Anomalies." *Journal of Finance* 51, 55–84.

Fama, Eugene F., and Kenneth R. French. (1998). "Value versus Growth: The International Evidence." *Journal of Finance* 53, 1975–1999.

Ferson, Wayne E., and Campbell R. Harvey. (1993). "The Risk and Predictability of International Equity Returns." *Review of Financial Studies* 6, 527–566.

Flood, Robert P., Robert J. Hodrick, and Paul Kaplan. (1986). "An Evaluation of Recent Evidence on Stock Market Bubbles." Northwestern University Working Paper. Reprinted in Peter M. Garber and Robert P. Flood (eds.). (1994). *Speculative Bubbles, Speculative Attacks, and Policy Switching* (pp. 105–133). Cambridge: MIT Press.

Giovannini, Alberto, and Philippe Weil. (1989). "Risk Aversion and Intertemporal Substitution in the Capital Asset Pricing Model." NBER Working Paper No. 2824.
Hansen, Lars Peter. (1982). "Large Sample Properties of Generalized Method of Moments Estimators." *Econometrica* 50, 1029–1054.
Hansen, Lars Peter, and Kenneth J. Singleton. (1982). "Generalized Instrumental Variables Estimation of Nonlinear Rational Expectation Models." *Econometrica* 50, 1269–1286.
Harvey, Campbell. (1991). "The World Price of Covariance Risk." *Journal of Finance* 46, 111–157.
Hodrick, Robert J. (1981). "International Asset Pricing with Time-Varying Risk Premia." *Journal of International Economics* 11, 573–587.
Hodrick, Robert J. (1992). "Dividend Yields and Expected Stock Returns: Alternative Procedures for Inference and Measurement." *Review of Financial Studies* 5, 357–386.
Jagannathan, Ravi, and Zhenyu Wang. (1996). "The Conditional CAPM and the Cross-Section of Expected Returns." *Journal of Finance* 51, 3–53.
Korajczyk, Robert A., and Claude J. Viallet. (1989). "An Empirical Investigation of International Asset Pricing." *Review of Financial Studies* 2, 553–586.
Lamont, Owen. (1998). "Earnings and Expected Returns." *Journal of Finance* 53, 1563–1587.
Merton, Robert C. (1973). "An Intertemporal Capital Asset Pricing Model." *Econometrica* 41, 867–887.
Ng, David Tat-Chee. (1999). "Foreign Exchange Risk and Intertemporal Hedging in International Asset Pricing," manuscript, Columbia University.
Ross, Stephen A. (1976). "The Arbitrage Theory of Capital Asset Pricing." *Journal of Economic Theory* 13, 341–360.
Rozeff, Michael. (1984). "Dividend Yields Are Equity Risk Premiums." *Journal of Portfolio Management* 11, 68–75.
Schwarz, Gideon. (1978). "Estimating the Dimension of a Model." *Annals of Statistics* 6, 461–464.
Sims, Christopher A. (1980). "Macroeconomics and Reality." *Econometrica* 48, 1–48.
Vassalou, Maria. (1997). "Exchange Rate and Foreign Inflation Risk Premiums in Global Equity Returns." Columbia University Working Paper.
Weil, Philippe. (1989). "The Equity Premium Puzzle and the Risk-Free Rate Puzzle." *Journal of Monetary Economics* 24, 401–421.

# Comment

BY LOUIS SCOTT

In this paper, Hodrick, Ng, and Sengmueller use cross section and time series data to test the implications of a dynamic asset pricing model. The objective of the paper is to develop a model that explains both the predictability of stock returns over time and one of the anomalies in the finance literature, the empirical observation that portfolios of stocks with high book to market ratios have higher average returns. Much of the empirical asset pricing research on stock returns relies on ad hoc empirical models or extensions of the single period Sharpe–Lintner capital asset pricing model (CAPM). Hodrick, Ng, and Sengmueller work with an empirical model that is derived within the framework of an intertemporal CAPM. Merton (1973), in the development of the intertemporal CAPM, showed that expected returns are influenced by desires to hedge unfavorable changes in the investment opportunity set. In this paper, the changes in the investment opportunity set are changes in future expected returns. The intertemporal CAPM is the appropriate framework for modeling and explaining the predictability of returns over time, and this approach is superior to the frequently encountered ad hoc approach of specifying a Sharpe–Lintner CAPM with dynamic changes in expected returns and risk premia.

The model is successful empirically at explaining the predictability of international stock returns, but it is not able to explain the higher average returns on portfolios with high book-to-market ratios. Hodrick, Ng, and Sengmueller use a vector autoregression to identify changes in expected returns; the four variables that are useful for predicting stock returns are the dividends to earnings ratio, the dividend yield, the one month Treasury-bill rate relative to a moving average, and the slope of the term structure. The $R^2$ for the stock return regression is only 3 percent, which is statistically significant, but the predictable variation of stock returns is small relative to its total variation. The slope of the term structure variable appears to be the most important variable for predicting stock returns. In most of the previous work on stock return predictability, dividend yields have been useful as predictors of stock returns, but not in this study in which the sample is extended to 1998.

The empirical result that dividends yields have not predicted subsequent stock returns is new. In numerous studies using stock return data back to the 1920's, researchers have found that dividend yields predict subsequent stock returns. In regressions of future stock returns on the dividend yield, the coefficient on the dividend yield is typically positive and statistically significant, and the $R^2$ is small, but statistically significant. Dividend series are relatively smooth over time so that most of the variation in dividend yields is due to the stock price in the denominator. When stock prices rise relative to dividends, the dividend yield drops, and subsequent stock returns tend to be lower. Conversely, when stock prices fall relative to dividends, the dividend yield increases, and subsequent stock returns tend to

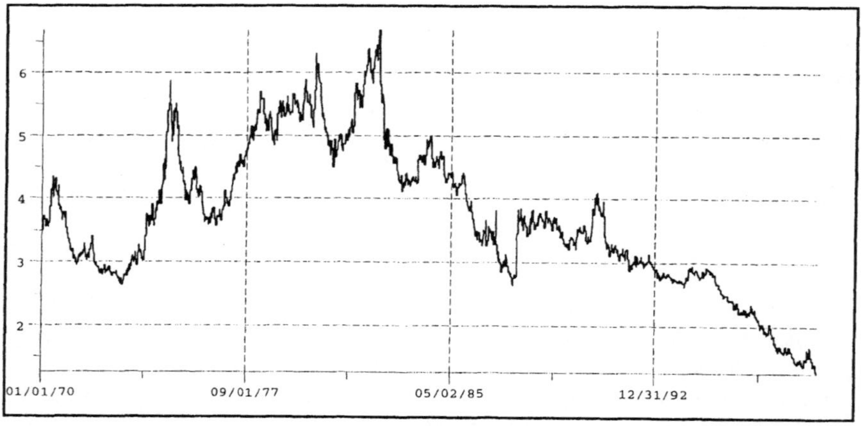


*Figure 1.* Dividend yield for the S&P 500.

be higher. In Figure 1, I have reproduced the dividend yield for the S&P 500 from 1970 to the beginning of 1999. Dividend yields have fluctuated between 3 percent and 6 percent over most of this period, but since 1992, there has been a steady decrease and the S&P 500 dividend yield is now (January 1999) below 2 percent. Since 1992, stock prices have generally risen and stock returns have been strongly positive, which is a departure from the previous relationship. What happens next? There are, of course, several explanations for the recent behavior of dividend yields. One is that the stock market is overvalued and dividend yields will return to historical norms when there is a major correction. The alternative explanation is that firms have been paying out less of their earnings in the form of cash dividends and have been using the extra cash to buy back shares of stock and invest. Earnings will grow at a faster rate in the future and dividends will eventually catch up so that dividend yields will gradually increase and return to historical averages. This issue will, of course, be settled by future research.

In Figure 2, I have reproduced the price-earnings ratio for the S&P 500 because it is a widely followed indicator of the stock market. This P/E ratio has varied between 10 and 20, but in recent months it has surpassed a level of 30, which is a record high. The challenge is to build a model of rational, optimizing agents that explains the observed variability of P/E ratios. One explanation is variability in the market risk premium, but one must use some extreme variability in this risk premium to explain the variability observed in Figures 1 and 2. One possibility is to work with a dynamic asset pricing model, similar to the model used by Hodrick, Ng, and Sengmueller, and have factors driving earnings, dividends, and the marginal utility of wealth, and solve the model for equilibrium stock prices. Models of this form are difficult to solve, but are necessary in order to understand the behavior of dividend yields and P/E ratios. A framework for analyzing this issue is the Euler equation from which dynamic asset pricing models are derived:

$$P(t)U'(W_t) = E_t\{\beta U'(W_{t+1})[D_{t+1} + P_{t+1}]\}$$

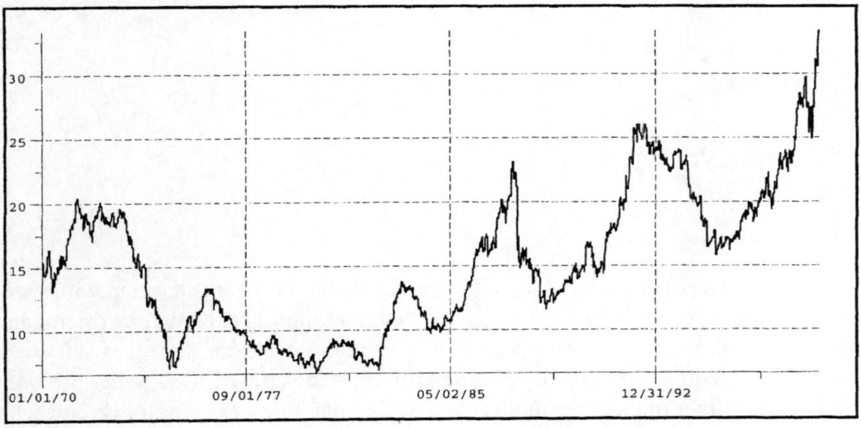


*Figure 2.* Price-earnings ratio for the S&P 500.

In this model, the stock price is a solution to a first order difference equation, and a solution with a Flood–Garber bubble is

$$P(t) = E_t\left\{\sum_{j=1}^{\infty} \beta^j \frac{U'(W_{t+j})}{U'(W_t)} D_{t+j}\right\} + \frac{A_t}{\beta^t U'(W_t)}$$

where $A_t$ is a martingale, $E_t(A_{t+j}) = A_t$. The last term is the Flood–Garber bubble and there are many possible solutions or models for its behavior. One example is a bubble that grows exponentially and every period there is a small probability that it will collapse. The bubble solution can generate the observed variability in dividend yields and P/E ratios. The open issue is whether one can generate this variability with the fundamental part of the solution.

## Reference

Merton, Robert C. (1973). "An Intertemporal Capital Asset Pricing Model." *Econometrica* 41.

# Comment

BY PAUL D. KAPLAN

The premise of this paper is that asset return predictability is not inconsistent with rational, maximizing behavior. Campbell's versions of the intertemporal capital asset pricing model seem to be the most promising approach to producing a model derived from rational, maximizing behavior in which asset returns exhibit predictability. This paper provides an elegant framework for tracing the implications of Campbell's models for the cross-sectional variation of expected returns.

The merit of this paper is that it tries to tightly tie a multivariate model of time-varying expected returns with asset pricing theory. In contrast, the multivariate models of Fama and French (1996, 1998) are not tied to any specific theory.

The weakness of this paper is that it tries to impose too much structure on the data. The failure to reject the model of average expected returns is likely due to a lack of statistical power. The failure to also reject the static CAPM confirms this view. Furthermore, when all of the instrumental variables are included in the asset pricing restrictions, both the dynamic model and the static CAPM are rejected. This is because including all of the instrumental variables raises the power of the test. The failure of the model to explain the average returns of the high book-to-market portfolios also shows that the data do not conform to the restrictions imposed by the model.

One suggestion that I have for refining the empirical model is to let $\rho$ be a free parameter rather than a predetermined value. It would be interesting to see if the point estimate comes out plausible.

This paper provides an excellent example of what it means to say that predicable asset returns can be the outcome of rational, maximizing behavior. However, most of the money management industry is based on the premise that returns are predicable because of market inefficiencies and irrational behavior. Empirical refutation of that view continues to elude us, even with models such as this one.

## References

Fama, Eugene F., and Kenneth R. French. (1996). "Multifactor Explanations of Asset Pricing Anomalies." *Journal of Finance* 51, 55–84.

———. (1998). "Value versus Growth: The International Evidence." *Journal of Finance* 53, 1975–1999.

# General Discussion

**Alessandro Prati** noted that the sample periods used in estimating the model parameters—from 1970 to 1998 or 1975 to 1995—included changes in capital mobility and exchange rate regimes that were particularly important for the European members of the G-7 countries. Such changes presumably influenced the covariances of returns, certainly the cross-section covariances, so one would expect that the parameters that were estimated would not have been stable over time. **Richard Meese** wondered why the authors had not drawn more on the work of Michael Adler and Bernard Dumas in considering the types of factors that one might expect to be priced in an international setting.

**Marjorie Flavin** pointed out that there were several ways to interpret the empirical findings. The authors had assumed that the consumption CAPM model was true, had built on the work of John Campbell in deriving an asset-pricing model that could be estimated without using data on consumption, and had then used that model to test the hypothesis that the coefficient of relative risk aversion ($\gamma$) was equal to unity. Testing $\gamma = 1$ was equivalent to testing the validity of the traditional static CAPM model, given the assumptions that had been made in deriving the asset-pricing model, but Flavin argued that the authors' rejection of the hypothesis $\gamma = 1$ should not be interpreted as a rejection of static CAPM. An alternative possibility was that the consumption CAPM model should be rejected, and that the static CAPM model with $\gamma > 1$ provided a perfectly reasonable view of the world.

**Ng** thought that the comments by Prati, Meese, and Flavin were well taken and indicated that he and his co-authors were intending to address them in their future work. He would be looking at the Adler–Dumas model in his doctoral dissertation. **Hodrick** added that the problem with the Adler–Dumas framework was that covariances of asset returns with every exchange rate in the world had to be priced. One of his colleagues, Maria Vassalou, had tried to estimate the Adler–Dumas model by developing indexes of exchange rates, which was an ad hoc modification of the Adler–Dumas model but might be a promising direction for investigation. With regard to the point that Flavin had made, Hodrick noted a subtlety that he hadn't brought up in his presentation—namely, that the exercise of moving from the conceptual framework to testing the model involved changing the weighting matrix on the rates of return.

**Flood** wondered how to think about the substitutions that Campbell and Hodrick, Ng, and Sengmueller had made to derive specifications that did not involve consumption terms. These substitutions were motivated by the results of previous studies that had found that consumption correlations don't work very well. Was there some "terrible error" with the earlier consumption equations, and if so, how should one view where that error had gone?

**Flavin** responded that Campbell's rationalization for substituting out the consumption terms was based on discrepancies between measured consumption and the concept of consumption that was envisioned in the theoretical framework. In an idealized world, measured consumption might be a good proxy for the marginal utility of wealth, but Campbell and others had taken the view that it was not a good proxy in reality. Flavin herself felt that the lack of empirical support for consumption CAPM frameworks based on measured consumption might reflect more than measurement problems and called into question the consumption CAPM model. Grossman and Laroque (1990), for example, had made some allowances for the adjustment costs associated with durables consumption, and had found that during periods in which consumers do not adjust the sizes of their houses, the consumption CAPM model fails while the traditional CAPM model holds.

**Hodrick** recalled a seminar at Carnegie-Mellon in the early 1980s, when Lars Hansen and Kenneth Singleton presented the results of their first attempts to estimate the consumption CAPM model and were confronted with the objection that such attempts were hopeless owing to problems associated with durables consumption, aggregation issues, and so forth. He nevertheless thought that the framework provided a useful parable. The intuition really came from Robert Merton's model: when there is time variation in rates of return, investors will want to hedge against it. That's a general principle. But in Merton's general framework, the coefficients of the model are functions of the state, and the model is too complex to be estimable. It was nice to have a more simplified conceptual framework in which hypotheses could be tested.

The fact that the tests did not find dividend yields to be important was a problem in **Hodrick's** view. There had been a large move toward repurchases in the stock market, as opposed to dividends, for reasons on which Hodrick did not want to elaborate. It was also the case that calculations of the ex ante expected rates of returns on the market, conditional on forecasts of future earnings, had been suggesting that equity premiums were very low. This was true not only in the United States, but also around the world; and it had been true for the past five or ten years. There are two schools of thought on this. One is that it reflects irrational exuberance. The other is that a structural change has occurred and we are now in a world in which risks are being shared differently and more internationally. According to the latter view, although we may not yet have a good understanding of the structural change that has taken place, increases in volatility associated with events like the Russian crisis wind up affecting all assets around the world, which is very different than the effects that such events might have had in the 1970s.

**Dale Henderson** wondered how much credence could be attached to the view that a structural break had been brought about by the widening of access to mutual funds. What was the order of magnitude of the change that had occurred in the amount of wealth that can be easily invested in equities? **Flavin** thought that the proportion of people who have easy access to equity investments had increased considerably, but because the distribution of wealth is skewed, the proportion of wealth that had easy access to equity investments might not have increased dramatically.

## References

Grossman, Sanford J., and Guy Laroque. (1990). "Asset Pricing and Optimal Portfolio Choice in the Presence of Illiquid Durable Consumption Goods." *Econometrica* 58, 25–51.

# Role of the Minimal State Variable Criterion in Rational Expectations Models

BENNETT T. MCCALLUM bm05@andrew.cmu.edu
*Carnegie Mellon University and National Bureau of Economic Research, Pittsburgh, PA 15213*

***Abstract***

This paper concerns the minimal-state-variable (MSV) criterion for selection among solutions in rational expectations models that feature a multiplicity of paths that satisfy all of the model's conditions. It compares the MSV criterion with others, including the widely used saddle-path (dynamic stability) criterion. It is emphasized that the MSV criterion can be viewed as a scientifically useful classification scheme that delineates the unique solution that is free of bubble components. In the process of demonstrating uniqueness for a broad class of linear models, the paper exposits a convenient computational procedure. Applications to current issues are outlined.

## I. Introduction

It is well known that Bob Flood's second paper with Peter Garber (Flood and Garber, 1980b) was an influential pioneering work in empirical testing for the existence of bubble phenomena in rational expectations macroeconomics. It is not so well known, by contrast, that his paper with Burmeister and Garber (Burmeister, Flood, and Garber, 1983) provided one of the earliest steps toward a useful and general classification of rational expectations solutions, theirs focussing on the distinction between bubble and bubble-free (or fundamentals) solutions.[1] The present paper amounts to an extension of this type of classificational analysis, together with an attempt to establish the scientific merits of one particular scheme.

For many years now it has been commonplace knowledge that many dynamic models with rational expectations (RE) feature a multiplicity of paths that satisfy all of the conditions for intertemporal equilibrium. Indeed, most dynamic RE models that are not based on explicit optimization analysis of individuals' behavior fall into that category and so do some that involve full-fledged general equilibrium analysis with optimizing agents.[2] But in many applications the analyst is not specifically concerned with this multiplicity—often interpreted as the possible existence of "bubbles"—and wishes to focus attention on one particular path that is presumed to be of economic relevance, e.g., if bubbles were absent.[3] Consequently, several alternative criteria have been proposed for selection of the path on which to focus. Among these are Taylor's (1977) "minimum-variance" criterion, the "expectational-stability" criterion of Evans (1985, 1986), the "minimal-state variable" criterion made explicit in McCallum (1983), and the popular "saddle path" or "stability" criterion. The latter is favored by Sargent (1987), Whiteman (1983), Blanchard and Kahn (1980), Blanchard and Fischer (1989), and many others, and is often used in computation algorithms such as King and Watson (1995) or Klein (1997).

In practice, analysts are often unclear as to which of the criteria is being utilized, when attention is focused on a single solution, because in many cases the last three of the four above-listed criteria all point to the same solution. Some analysts are explicit, however, and a sampling of the literature suggests that the most frequently adopted of the criteria, in these cases of explicit justification, is that of stability or non-explosiveness. The stability criterion has been recommended, moreover, in the influential textbooks of Sargent (1987, pp. 197–9, 306–7) and Blanchard and Fischer (1989, pp. 225, 260).

One purpose of the present paper is to consider the strengths and weaknesses for scientific research of these alternative criteria. In particular, it will be argued that the stability and minimum-variance criteria are inherently unsatisfactory. By contrast, the minimal-state-variable (MSV) criterion is scientifically attractive, according to our argument, for it provides a classificational scheme that is designed to be useful in terms of positive analysis. The criterion of expectational stability, finally, will be characterized as reflecting a substantive behavioral hypothesis rather than a classification scheme, so its attractiveness is an empirical issue rather than a question of constructive scientific practice.

A second purpose of the paper is to emphasize that the minimal-state-variable (MSV) criterion generally identifies a single solution that can reasonably be interpreted as the unique solution that is free of bubble components, i.e., the fundamentals solution. It can accordingly be used as the basis for tests of a substantive hypothesis to the effect that bubble solutions are not of empirical relevance. This hypothesis would remain of interest, moreover, even if the association of the MSV criterion with the bubble-free property were not accepted.

In conducting this argument, it will be expositionally useful to provide illustrations in the context of a particular example. Consequently, one will be developed in Section II. The unsatisfactory nature of the minimum variance and stability criteria will then be argued in Section III. Section IV will make the case for the MSV criterion, with attention being devoted to a critical argument of Froot and Obstfeld (1991), and Section V will consider the "expectational stability" criterion of Evans (1985, 1988). Next, Section VI will demonstrate how unique MSV solutions can be defined and calculated in a very wide class of linear rational expectations models, after which Section VII will describe the relevance of the foregoing analysis for some prominent recent research. Finally, Section VIII will provide a brief summary.

## II. An Illustrative Model

As a vehicle for illustrating several of the points to be made below, consider the familiar Cagan money demand function

$$m_t - p_t = \gamma + \alpha E_t \Delta p_{t+1} + \xi_t, \qquad \alpha < 0 \tag{1}$$

where $m_t$ and $p_t$ are logs of an economy's nominal money stock and its price level. Also, $E_t(\cdot)$ is defined as $E(\cdot|\Omega_t)$, where $\Omega_t$ includes $m_t, m_{t-1}, \ldots, p_t, p_{t-1}, \ldots$, and $\xi_t, \xi_{t-1}, \ldots$. The disturbance $\xi_t$, which reflects random behavioral demand shifts, will be assumed to be a random walk variate so that $\Delta\xi_t = u_t$ is white noise. For our purposes it is of no consequence whether or not one conceives of (1) as resulting from an explicit maximization problem, since there are such models that give rise to multiple solutions and our points are designed to be relevant for any model with multiple solutions—with correct account being taken of all non-negativity requirements, transversality conditions, and anything else that might eliminate some paths from contention as solutions.

To represent policy behavior that generates the money supply, we will adopt a rule of the following form:

$$\Delta m_t = \mu_0 + \mu_1 \Delta p_{t-1}. \tag{2}$$

Thus the money stock growth rate in each period is related to inflation in the previous period. One would expect sensible policy behavior to involve a negative value of $\mu_1$, so that money creation is slowed when recent inflation has been rapid, and a value that is not too large (so as to avoid instrument instability). But for the present we shall adopt only the restriction $\mu_1 \leq (\alpha - 1)^2/(-4\alpha)$, which is necessary (as we shall see) for the $\Delta p_t$ solution values to involve real (i.e., non-complex) numbers. It would of course be possible to include a random disturbance term in (2) as well as (1), but nothing would be gained and clutter would be added. To complete the model, it needs to be specified that it pertains to all periods $t = 1, 2, \ldots$ with $m_0$ and $\Delta p_0$ given. The specified type of policy behavior can therefore only be adopted after an economy is already in existence so that $\Delta p_0$ and $m_0$ will be well defined. Inserting (2) into the first difference of (1) yields

$$\mu_0 + \mu_1 \Delta p_{t-1} = \Delta p_t + \alpha E_t \Delta p_{t+1} - \alpha E_{t-1} \Delta p_t + u_t, \tag{3}$$

and for present purposes it will suffice to consider solutions of the form[4]

$$\Delta p_t = \pi_0 + \pi_1 \Delta p_{t-1} + \pi_2 u_t. \tag{4}$$

The latter implies $E_t \Delta p_{t+1} = \pi_0 + \pi_1(\pi_0 + \pi_1 \Delta p_{t-1} + \pi_2 u_t)$ so substitution into (3) yields

$$\begin{aligned} \mu_0 + \mu_1 \Delta p_{t-1} &= \pi_0 + \pi_1 \Delta p_{t-1} + \pi_2 u_t + \alpha\pi_0 + \alpha\pi_1(\pi_0 + \pi_1 \Delta p_{t-1} + \pi_2 u_t) \\ &\quad - \alpha(\pi_0 + \pi_1 \Delta p_{t-1}) + u_t. \end{aligned} \tag{5}$$

Thus for (4) to be a solution it must be true that

$$\mu_0 = \pi_0 + \alpha\pi_1\pi_0 \tag{6a}$$

$$\mu_1 = \pi_1 + \alpha\pi_1^2 - \alpha\pi_1 \tag{6b}$$

$$0 = \pi_2 + \alpha\pi_1\pi_2 + 1. \tag{6c}$$

The second of these clearly implies that[5]

$$\pi_1 = \frac{(\alpha - 1) \pm [(\alpha - 1)^2 + 4\alpha\mu_1]^{1/2}}{2\alpha} \tag{7}$$

Once it is decided whether to add or subtract the positive term $d \equiv [(\alpha - 1)^2 + 4\alpha\mu_1]^{1/2}$, the values of $\pi_0$ and $\pi_2$ will be defined uniquely. But that decision is crucial for determining the model's implied behavior of $\Delta p_t$. That fact is illustrated in Figure 1, where $\pi_1^+ = (\alpha - 1 + d)/2\alpha$ and $\pi_1^- = (\alpha - 1 - d)/2\alpha$ are plotted for $\alpha = -4$ (representative for all $\alpha < -1$) against $\mu_1$. Clearly, values of $\pi_1^+$ (the lower branch) and $\pi_1^-$ (the upper branch) lie both within and outside of the range $-1 < \pi_1 < 1$ that is necessary for dynamic stability. (In the somewhat unrealistic case with $-1 < \alpha < 0$, not illustrated in Figure 1, $\pi_1^-$ exceeds 1.0 for all $\mu_1$ that give real roots.)

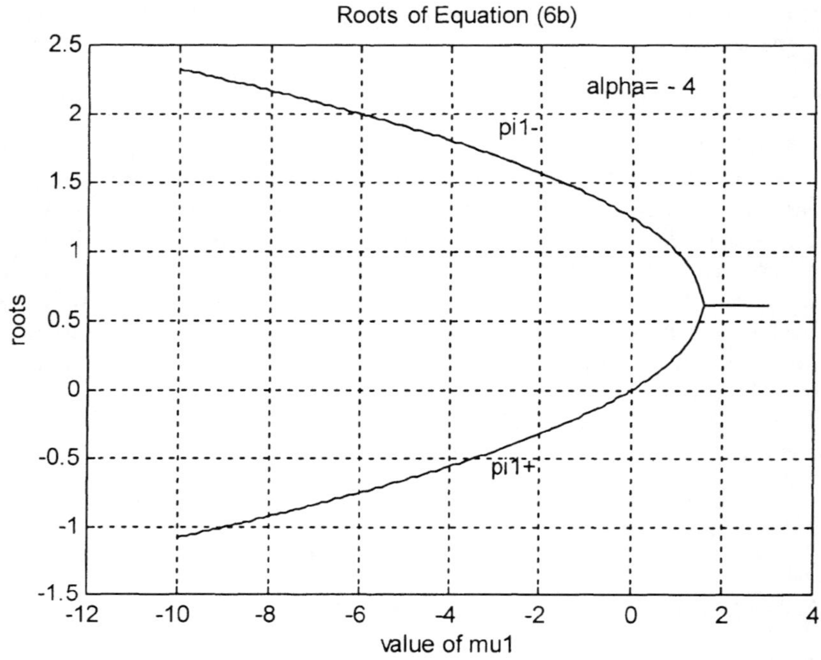


*Figure 1.*

A particularly simple and transparent special case of this example occurs when $\mu_1 = 0$ in (2), so that the money stock growth rate is constant. In that case one might expect $\Delta p_{t-1}$ to be absent from (4), since it does not appear in the model and can affect the value of $\Delta p_t$ only if it is (arbitrarily) expected by the economy's participants to affect $\Delta p_t$. Thus we are led to look for solutions of the form $\Delta p_t = \pi_0 + \pi_2 u_t$ in this case, and we find that $\Delta p_t = \mu_0 - u_t$. This result is of course consistent with our more general example. Indeed, the solutions in (7) for $\pi_1$ are $\pi_1^+ = 0$ and $\pi_1^- = (\alpha - 1)/\alpha$ when $\mu_1 = 0$, the first of which implies the absence of $\Delta p_{t-1}$ from (4) and duplicates the solution just found.[6] The second value, $\pi_1^- = (\alpha - 1)/\alpha$, is with $\alpha < 0$ unambiguously greater than 1.0, so it implies an explosive, dynamically unstable path. Furthermore, this value $\pi_1^-$ will support an infinity of unstable paths. This may be seen by supposing that $\pi_3 u_{t-1}$ is added to the conjectured solution in (4) and then verifying that this expression is consistent with all of the model's equations for any value of $\pi_3$ (upon which $\pi_2$ depends).[7] If $\pi_1^+ = 0$ is taken as the relevant value for $\pi_1$, however, it is implied that $\pi_3 = 0$ and $\pi_2 = -1$.

Note that in the special case in which $\mu_1 = 0$, the solution involving $\pi_1^+$ (i.e., $\Delta p_t = \mu_0 - u_t$) is clearly the one that would be regarded as the bubble-free or fundamentals solution by Burmeister, Flood, and Garber (1983).[8] Indeed, analogous solutions are so regarded quite generally in the literature in examples similar to our special case. By contrast, the solutions involving $\pi_1^-$ would generally be regarded, in this special case, as bubble solutions—i.e., solutions that add bubble components to the fundamentals solution. McCallum (1983, pp. 147, 161) proposed a general extension of the bubble vs. bubble-free terminology to cases analogous to those in which $\mu_1 \neq 0$ in the example at hand; that extension will be utilized below.

## III. The Stability and Minimum Variance Criteria

As it happens, extensive utilization of the foregoing example will be briefly delayed, for our argument concerning the stability and minimum-variance criteria can be developed without reference to any particular model. Let us begin with Taylor's (1977) minimum-variance criterion. According to the latter, the choice among multiple solutions should be dictated by the unconditional variance of a variable analogous to $\Delta p_t$ in the foregoing example. But there are two serious flaws with this proposal, the first of which is its ambiguity. Specifically, in many models there will be more than one endogenous variable of interest. (In fact, even in the example of Section II—despite the appearance of equation (3)—there are two endogenous variables, $\Delta p_t$ and $\Delta m_t$.) But in such cases the minimum variance criterion will not be well specified, because the various endogenous variables may indicate different solutions. Indeed, in some cases there may even exist some ambiguity as to whether the (possibly detrended) level or first difference of a given variable is relevant. Second, the minimum-variance criterion is presumably intended to pertain to the solution path that would be empirically relevant. But that would of course suggest that the modeled economy's agents are motivated to choose the minimum-variance solution over others, and it is not the case that agents will typically be so motivated. Indeed, the minimum-variance criterion evidently pertains to some social desideratum, not anything that could be affected by any single agent's choice. Consequently, the model's agents will have no incentive to select this solution path, so there is no particular reason to believe that it would in fact be empirically relevant.

Turning now to the case of the stability criterion, our argument is quite different. Here the problem is that the criterion is, to a significant extent, self-defeating. For the criterion is precisely that the selected solution path must be non-explosive—dynamically stable—under the natural presumption that exogenous driving variables (such as shocks and policy instruments) are non-explosive. Yet one important objective of dynamic economic analysis is to determine whether particular hypothetical policy rules—or institutional arrangements—would lead to desirable economic performance, which will usually require stability. Or, to express the point somewhat differently, the purpose of a theoretical analysis will often be to determine the conditions under which a system will be dynamically stable and unstable. But, obviously, the adoption of the stability criterion for selection among solutions would be logically incompatible with use of the models' solution to determine if (or under what conditions) instability would be forthcoming. To the extent, then, that this objective of analysis is important, the stability criterion is inherently unsuitable. One cannot use a model to determine whether property "A" would be forthcoming, if the model includes a requirement that "A" must not obtain.

In addition, there are a substantial number of cases in which there exists an infinity of solution paths all of which are stable. In such cases, then, the stability criterion fails to select a single path on which to focus as the bubble-free or fundamentals path.[9] That failure would be defensible if it were true that no single path has special characteristics that justify labeling it as bubble-free, but it is not. Even in these cases the MSV criterion provides a clear demarcation between one path and the others. To develop that argument is the purpose of the next section.

## IV. The MSV Criterion

The MSV criterion is designed to yield a single bubble-free solution *by construction.* Its definition begins by limiting solutions to those that are linear[10] functions—analogous to (4) in the example of Section II—of a minimal set of "state variables," i.e., predetermined or exogenous determinants of current endogenous variables. For a set of state variables to be minimal, it must be "one from which it is impossible to delete ... any single variable, or group of variables, while continuing to obtain a solution valid for all admissible parameter values" (McCallum, 1983, p. 145). Here the language is somewhat convoluted because there is not in general a unique minimal set of state variables, even though there is a unique MSV solution. Two or more different sets of variables may span the same space, of course, with neither being a proper subset of the other.

But relying upon a minimal set of state variables is not the only requirement (in addition to linearity) for a MSV solution. In cases in which the minimal set includes a lagged value of an endogenous variable there will typically be more than one solution to the undetermined-coefficient identities analogous to equations (6) above. So one part of the definition of the MSV solution is a rule for selection of the appropriate solution. That rule is that the solution continues to be based on a minimal set of state variables for all special cases of the parameter values. Typically, some admissible sets of parameter values will include zero coefficients in all structural equations for a lagged endogenous variable. But in any such case, this lagged value will not be part of a minimal set, so its solution-equation coefficient analogous to $\pi_1$ will be zero for the MSV solution in that special case. Thus the MSV solution must be, to pertain for all admissible parameter values, the one that is the MSV solution in that special case.

To illustrate this determination, consider the choice between $\pi_1^+$ and $\pi_1^-$ in the example of Section II. In the special case in which $\mu_1 = 0$ in (2), the variable $\Delta p_{t-1}$ does not appear in model (and in fact appears to be an irrelevant bygone). Thus $\Delta p_{t-1}$ can in this case affect the value of $\Delta p_t$ only if it is—arbitrarily—expected by the economy's participants to affect $\Delta p_t$. Thus it does not appear in the minimal set of state variables in this special case with $\mu_1 = 0$, so $\pi_1 = 0$ is implied. But from the perspective of the general case, it is $\pi_1^+$ that yields the value 0 in this special case, $\pi_1^-$ instead being equal to $(\alpha - 1)/\alpha$. Consequently, it is the solution to equations (6) with $\pi_1 = \pi_1^+$ that makes (4) the MSV solution expression for $\Delta p_t$ in this model.

It is important to recognize that this definition for the MSV solution involves a procedure that makes it unique by construction. It is logically possible to dispute whether this solution warrants being termed the bubble-free or fundamentals solution, although the answer seems to the present writer to be a clear "yes."[11] But it makes no logical sense to argue that the MSV solution is not unique.[12]

In that regard, Froot and Obstfeld (1991) have suggested that the MSV solution is not unique by demonstrating an example in which there is a non-linear function of the single state variable that constitutes a minimal set. That demonstration does not provide a valid counterexample to the claim of the last paragraph above, however, because linearity of the solution expressions such as (4) is required for the MSV solution. It is not surprising, it should be said, that Froot and Obstfeld would have misinterpreted the definition given in McCallum (1983), because the latter mistakenly took it for granted that only linear expressions would provide solutions in the class of linear models considered. But the outlined procedure, which defines the MSV solution, was expressly designed to yield a unique solution. So the restriction of linearity would have been explicitly included if the author had realized that it was needed.

The example presented in Section II was chosen, as one would expect, to illustrate points concerning the contrast between MSV and other solution criteria. In particular, for values of $\mu_1 < 2\alpha - 1$, the MSV solution features dynamic instability since $\pi_1^+ < -1$. Thus this case demonstrates that the set of solutions selected by the MSV criterion, but ruled out by the stability criterion, is not empty. It is, moreover, intuitively plausible that instability would obtain in this case, as it reflects a very strong application of policy feedback response—which when excessive induces "instrument instability." Indeed, this is an example of the type of determination that a dynamic model should be able to provide—i.e., the conditions under which feedback is destabilizing. Alternatively, the example of Section II also illustrates the possibility of non-exploding bubble solutions, which occur when $1 < \mu_1 < (\alpha-1)^2/(-4\alpha)$.

At this point in the discussion it should be clear that the MSV criterion may be regarded as a classification scheme, i.e., a technique for delineating the solution that is of a bubble-free or fundamental nature from those that include bubble components. This scheme is intended to be scientifically useful, by providing a single solution that the researcher may focus upon if he/she is engaged in an investigation such that the possibility of bubbles is deliberately excluded at the outset. In addition, the classification scheme serves a second scientific purpose by providing the basis for a substantive hypothesis to the effect that market outcomes in actual economies are generally of the bubble-free variety. Even though RE general equilibrium analysis provides no general theoretical basis for ruling out bubble solutions, it is a coherent plausible substantive hypothesis that such solutions do not occur in practice.

The plausibility of that hypothesis is emphasized by the undetermined-coefficient method of deriving the MSV solution. The relevant point is that, in the space of $\pi_1$ values, the bubble-free value $\pi_1^+$ is of measure 1/2. And this continues to be true in the special case with $\mu_1 = 0$ in which there is an infinity of non-MSV bubble paths. In that case, the MSV solution features $\pi_1^+ = 0$, yielding $\Delta p_t = \mu_0 - u_t$. Use of the value $\pi_1^- = (\alpha - 1)/\alpha$, however, gives rise in this case to an infinity of solutions of the form

$$\Delta p_t = \pi_0 + \pi_1 \Delta p_{t-1} + \pi_2 u_t + \pi_3 u_{t-1}, \tag{8}$$

where the multiplicity arises because any value of $\pi_3$ will satisfy the model when $\pi_1$ equals $(\alpha - 1)/\alpha$ (given that $\mu_1 = 0$). For some researchers, it is a common practice in such cases to presume that the outcome—the particular path realized in the market—is determined by an "initial condition" $\Delta p_0$ that serves to pin down $\pi_2$. From that perspective there is only a single value of $\Delta p_0$ that will imply $\pi_2 = -1$, and also that $\pi_1 = \pi_3 = 0$, thereby yielding the bubble-free solution.[13] In the space of initial conditions, then, the bubble-free outcome is of measure zero. But is entirely unclear which of these spaces is relevant to the market's solution outcome. It is thus a plausible hypothesis that bubble-free solutions will obtain generally.[14] The generation of that hypothesis is the second scientific contribution of the MSV solution criterion.

## V. The Expectational Stability Criterion

The last alternative criterion to be explicitly discussed is that of "expectational stability" as developed by Evans (1985, 1986).[15] The basic idea is to determine whether there is convergence of an iterative procedure toward a RE solution; if there is such convergence the RE solution approached is the one selected by this criterion. It is not entirely clear whether the steps in the iterative process are supposed to reflect sequential positions in calendar time or in some type of conceptual meta-time, but to this reader the latter seems more appropriate. In any event, the sequence of calculations begins with a function, analogous to the expression just below (4), that determines expectations—but with coefficients that differ somewhat from those implied by RE in the model at hand. Then the model and this expectation function imply a "law of motion" for the model's endogenous variables. This law of motion, which may not be fully consistent with the expectation function used in its derivation, is then adopted as the basis for a revised expectation function to be used (in the same way) in the next round of the iterative process. Expectational stability obtains when this process converges to the RE solution under consideration.[16] In fact there are two variants: weak expectational stability obtains if the original expectation function is specified so as to include the same determining "state variables" as the RE solution under consideration, whereas strong expectational stability obtains when additional variables are permitted in the expectations function.

The process can be illustrated with the model of Section II. With a RE solution of form (4), whether or not it is the MSV solution, expectations will conform to $E_t \Delta p_{t+1} = \pi_0 + \pi_1 \Delta p_t$ so the iterative procedure assumes that expectations at $t$ of $\Delta p_{t+1}$ satisfy

$$\Delta p_{t+1}^{e,n} = \phi_0^n + \phi_1^n \Delta p_t, \tag{9}$$

where $n$ indexes the iterations. Now with (9) prevailing, $\Delta p_t$ will be determined by the analog of (3), namely, $\mu_0 + \mu_1 \Delta p_{t-1} = \Delta p_t + \alpha(\phi_0^n + \phi_1^n \Delta p_t) - \alpha \Delta p_t^e + u_t$, where $\Delta p_t^e$ is given from the past.[17] The last equation can be written as

$$\Delta p_t = (1 + \alpha\phi_1^n)^{-1}[\mu_0 - \alpha\phi_0^n + \mu_1 \Delta p_{t-1} + \alpha \Delta p_t^e - u_t] \tag{10}$$

and it suggests that expectations for $\Delta p_{t+1}$ should satisfy

$$\Delta p_{t+1}^{e,n+1} = (1 - \alpha + \alpha\phi_1^n)^{-1}[\mu_0 - \alpha\phi_0^n + \mu_1 \Delta p_t] \tag{11}$$

since $u_t$ is white noise. Then writing the right-hand side of the latter in form (9) gives

$$\phi_0^{n+1} = (1 - \alpha + \alpha\phi_1^n)^{-1}(\mu_0 - \alpha\phi_0^n) \qquad \phi_1^{n+1} = (1 - \alpha + \alpha\phi_1^n)^{-1}\mu_1, \tag{12}$$

which defines an iterative process for the values.

From the second of expressions (12), we see that the stationary values for $\phi_1$ are the same as the two roots in (7). The expectational stability analysis selects the one—if there is one—for which the difference equation in $\phi_1^n$ is dynamically stable, i.e., the one that would be approached by the iterative process. From plots of $\phi_1^{n+1}$ vs. $\phi_1^n$ such as those in Figure 2, we can see that the root $\phi_1^+$ is (locally) stable, since the slope is less than 1.0 in absolute value for all $\mu_1 < (\alpha - 1)^2/(-4\alpha)$. At the root $\phi_1^-$, by contrast, the slope will exceed 1.0 in absolute value so the iterative process will not be convergent. With $\phi_1 = \phi_1^+$, moreover, the behavior of $\phi_0^n$ is stable for all parameter values yielding real roots in (6b). In this example, then, the expectational stability criterion points to the same solution as does the MSV criterion as long as $\mu_1 < 1$.

It is not entirely clear, however, just how much emphasis should be placed on that agreement. One reason is that Evans and Honkapohja (1992) argue that there are some cases in which expectational stability does not point to the MSV solution. I am not entirely persuaded that these cases include any well-motivated economic models, but in any event that is not the main point. The point, instead, is that if the analysis calls for focus on the bubble-free solution, then that would still be accomplished by means of the MSV criterion. If expectational stability provides an accurate guide to the behavior in actual economies, then a non-MSV bubble solution would prevail in such cases. But that would provide no reason for changing the classification of bubble vs. non-bubble solutions. And it is far from certain that expectational stability does provide a guide for actual economic behavior, for that hypothesis requires that this particular iterative process, among all those that could be conjectured, is empirically relevant. Nevertheless, while the amount of warranted emphasis is unclear, it is the case that in most—if not all—sensible models the expectational stability criterion does point to the MSV solution.[18]

## VI. General Derivation in Linear Models

The argument above has relied on the proposition that there is a unique MSV solution in a wide class of linear models; the main purpose of this section is to demonstrate the validity of that claim. In addition, a second purpose is to present a compact and easily understood exposition of a convenient and practical computational procedure for solving linear rational expectations models. This procedure, which is applicable to a class of models that is broad enough to include most cases of practical interest, can be implemented by means of a MATLAB routine provided by Paul Klein (1997).[19] The present exposition departs from Klein's, however, by relying upon the elementary undetermined-coefficients (UC) approach used throughout the present paper. In a sense, the current exposition could be viewed as merely an extension to the appendix of McCallum (1983). It is an extension that is nontrivial, however, and essential for practical (i.e., computational) purposes. Here it is accomplished by use of the generalized Schur decomposition theorem discussed by Klein. The UC reasoning utilized here is, however, much more elementary mathematically than Klein's.[20]

Let $y_t$ be a $M \times 1$ vector of non-predetermined endogenous variables, $k_t$ be a $K \times 1$ vector of predetermined endogenous variables, and $u_t$ be a $N \times 1$ vector of exogenous variables.

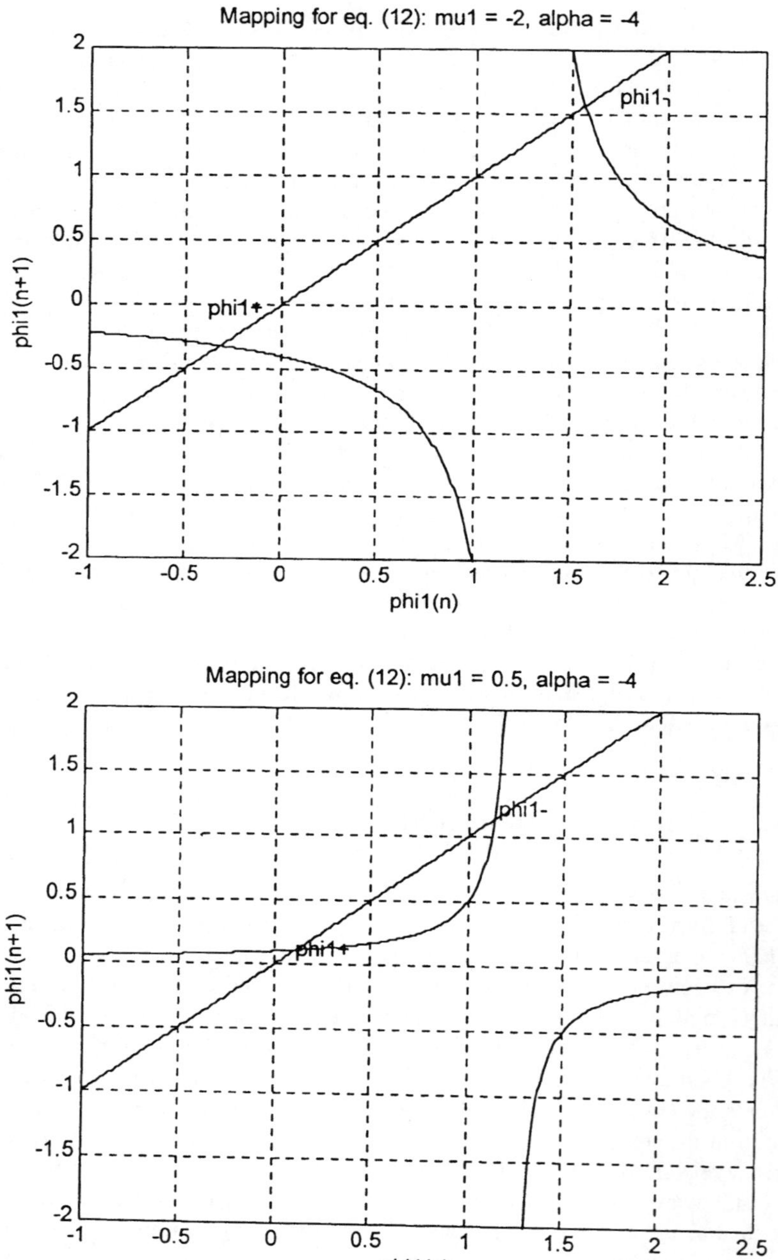
Mapping for eq. (12): mu1 = -2, alpha = -4
phi1(n+1)
phi1(n)
phi1+
phi1-
2
1.5
1
0.5
0
-0.5
-1
-1.5
-2
-1
-0.5
0
0.5
1
1.5
2
2.5
Mapping for eq. (12): mu1 = 0.5, alpha = -4
phi1(n+1)
phi1(n)
phi1+
phi1-

*Figure 2.*

The model can then be written as

$$A_{11} E_t y_{t+1} = B_{11} y_t + B_{12} k_t + C_1 u_t \tag{14}$$

$$u_t = R u_{t-1} + \varepsilon_t \tag{15}$$

where $A_{11}$ and $B_{11}$ are square matrices while $\varepsilon_t$ is a $N \times 1$ white noise vector.[21] Thus $u_t$ is formally a first-order autoregressive process, which can of course be defined so as to represent AR processes of higher orders for the basic exogenous variables. Also, for the predetermined variables we assume

$$k_{t+1} = B_{21} y_t + B_{22} k_t + C_2 u_t. \tag{16}$$

If only once-lagged values of $y_t$ were included in $k_t$, then we would have $B_{21} = I$, $B_{22} = 0$, and $C_2 = 0$, but the present setup is much more general. Crucially, the matrices $A_{11}$, $B_{21}$, and $B_{22}$ may be singular; that is what makes the setup convenient in practice.

In this setting a UC solution will be of the form

$$y_t = \Omega k_t + \Gamma u_t \tag{17}$$

$$k_{t+1} = \Pi_1 k_t + \Pi_2 u_t, \tag{18}$$

where the $\Omega$, $\Gamma$, $\Pi_1$, and $\Pi_2$ matrices are real. Therefore, $E_t y_{t+1} = \Omega E_t k_{t+1} + \Gamma E_t u_{t+1} = \Omega(\Pi_1 k_t + \Pi_2 u_t) + \Gamma R u_t$. Substitution into (14) and (16) then yields

$$A_{11}[\Omega(\Pi_1 k_t + \Pi_2 u_t) + \Gamma R u_t] = B_{11}[\Omega k_t + \Gamma u_t] + B_{12} k_t + C_1 u_t \tag{19}$$

and

$$(\Pi_1 k_t + \Pi_2 u_t) = B_{21}(\Omega k_t + \Gamma u_t) + B_{22} k_t + C_2 u_t. \tag{20}$$

Collecting terms in $k_t$, it is implied by UC reasoning that

$$\begin{bmatrix} A_{11} & 0 \\ 0 & I \end{bmatrix} \begin{bmatrix} \Omega \Pi_1 \\ \Pi_1 \end{bmatrix} = \begin{bmatrix} B_{11} & B_{12} \\ B_{21} & B_{22} \end{bmatrix} \begin{bmatrix} \Omega \\ I \end{bmatrix} \tag{21}$$

whereas the terms in $u_t$ imply

$$A_{11} \Omega \Pi_2 + A_{11} \Gamma R = B_{11} \Gamma + C_1 \tag{22}$$

$$\Pi_2 = B_{21} \Gamma + C_2. \tag{23}$$

Let $A$ and $B$ denote the two square matrices in (21), and assume that $|B - \lambda A|$ is nonzero for some complex number $\lambda$. This last condition will not hold if the model is poorly formulated (i.e., fails to place any restriction on some endogenous variable); otherwise it will be satisfied even with singular $A_{11}$, $B_{21}$, $B_{22}$.[22] Then the generalized Schur decomposition theorem guarantees the existence of unitary (therefore invertible) matrices $Q$ and $Z$ such that $QAZ = S$ and $QBZ = T$, where $S$ and $T$ are triangular.[23] The ratios $t_{ii}/s_{ii}$ are generalized eigenvalues of the matrix pencil $B - \lambda A$;[24] they can be rearranged without contradicting the foregoing theorem. Such rearrangements correspond to selection of different UC solutions as discussed in McCallum (1983, pp. 145–147 and 165–166). We shall return to this topic below; for the moment let us assume that the eigenvalues $t_{ii}/s_{ii}$ (and associated columns of $Q$ and $Z$) are arranged in order of their moduli with the largest values first.

Now premultiply (21) by $Q$ and define $H \equiv Z^{-1}$. Then since $QA = SH$ and $QB = TH$, the resulting equation is

$$\begin{bmatrix} S_{11} & 0 \\ S_{21} & S_{22} \end{bmatrix} \begin{bmatrix} H_{11} & H_{12} \\ H_{21} & H_{22} \end{bmatrix} \begin{bmatrix} \Omega\Pi_1 \\ \Pi_1 \end{bmatrix} = \begin{bmatrix} T_{11} & 0 \\ T_{21} & T_{22} \end{bmatrix} \begin{bmatrix} H_{11} & H_{12} \\ H_{21} & H_{22} \end{bmatrix} \begin{bmatrix} \Omega \\ I \end{bmatrix} \tag{24}$$

and its first row can be written as

$$S_{11}(H_{11}\Omega + H_{12})\Pi_1 = T_{11}(H_{11}\Omega + H_{12}). \tag{25}$$

The latter will be satisfied for $\Omega$ such that

$$\Omega = -H_{11}^{-1}H_{12} = -H_{11}^{-1}\left(-H_{11}Z_{12}Z_{22}^{-1}\right) = Z_{12}Z_{22}^{-1}, \tag{26}$$

where the second equality results because $HZ = I$. Thus we have a solution for $\Omega$, provided that $Z_{22}^{-1}$ exists.[25]

Next, writing out the second row of (24) we get

$$\begin{aligned} &S_{21}(H_{11}\Omega + H_{12})\Pi_1 + S_{22}(H_{21}\Omega + H_{22})\Pi_1 \\ &\qquad = T_{21}(H_{11}\Omega + H_{12}) + T_{22}(H_{21}\Omega + H_{22}). \end{aligned} \tag{27}$$

Then using (26) and $HZ = I$ we can simplify this to

$$S_{22}Z_{22}^{-1}\Pi_1 = T_{22}Z_{22}^{-1} \tag{28}$$

so since $S_{22}^{-1}$ exists by construction[26] we have

$$\Pi_1 = Z_{22}S_{22}^{-1}T_{22}Z_{22}^{-1}. \tag{29}$$

To find $\Gamma$ and $\Pi_2$ we return to (22) and (23). Combining them we have

$$G\Gamma + A_{11}\Gamma R = F \tag{30}$$

where $G \equiv A_{11}\Omega B_{21} - B_{11}$ and $F \equiv C_1 - A_{11}\Omega C_2$. If $G^{-1}$ exists, which it typically will with nonsingular $B_{11}$, the latter becomes

$$\Gamma + G^{-1}A_{11}\Gamma R = G^{-1}F. \tag{31}$$

This can be solved for $\Gamma$ by the steps given in McCallum (1983, p. 163) or can be obtained as

$$\text{vec}(\Gamma) = [I + R' \otimes G^{-1}A_{11}]^{-1}\,\text{vec}(G^{-1}F), \tag{32}$$

as in Klein (1997, p. 28).[27] Finally, $\Pi_2$ is obtained from (23). In sum, the UC solution for a given ordering of the eigenvalues is given sequentially by equations (26), (29), (32), and (23).

Different values of $\Omega$, and thus different solutions, will be obtained for different orderings of the generalized eigenvalues $t_{ii}/s_{ii}$. What ordering should be used to obtain the economically relevant solution? Many writers, following Blanchard and Kahn (1980), arrange them in order of decreasing modulus and conclude that a unique solution obtains if and only if the number with modulus less than 1.0 ("stable roots") equals $K$, the number of predetermined variables. The minimal-state-variable (MSV) procedure, by contrast, is to choose the arrangement that would yield $\Omega = 0$ if it were the case that $B_{12} = 0$—this step relying upon the continuity of eigenvalues with respect to parameters.[28] Uhlig (1997, p. 17) correctly notes that this procedure is difficult to implement and also that in many cases it will lead to the same solution as the Blanchard–Kahn stability criterion. Adoption of the decreasing-value arrangement will therefore often be attractive, even for MSV adherents. In such cases it seems unnecessary, however, to limit one's attention to problems in which there are exactly $K$ stable roots. If there are fewer than $K$ stable roots, the MSV criterion will produce a single explosive solution whereas if there are more than $K$ stable roots, it will yield the single stable solution that is bubble-free—both of these being solutions that may be of particular scientific interest. In those exceptional cases in which an MSV analyst suspects that the Blanchard–Kahn and MSV criteria would call for different solutions, he/she could replace $B_{12}$ with $\alpha B_{12}$, plot eigenvalues for various values of $\alpha$ between 1 and 0, and then adjust the ordering if necessary.

## VII. Relevance for Recent Issues

The example of Section II is simple and clearly related to much of the existing bubble literature, but may seem remote from most monetary policy discussions of the late 1990s. To show that such is not the case—that the example is in fact highly relevant—is the purpose of the present section.

Let us begin by considering the following model, in which $y_t$ denotes the log of output relative to capacity, $R_t$ is a nominal interest rate, and $v_t$ is a white-noise disturbance:

$$y_t = b_0 + b_1(R_t - E_t\Delta p_{t+1}) + v_t \qquad b_1 < 0 \tag{33}$$

$$\Delta p_t = (1-\theta)E_t\Delta p_{t+1} + \theta\Delta p_{t-1} + \alpha y_t \qquad \alpha > 0 \tag{34}$$

$$R_t = \mu_0 + \mu_1(E_t\Delta p_{t+1} - \Delta p^*) + \mu_2 y_t \qquad \mu_1, \mu_2 > 0 \tag{35}$$

Here (33) is a textbook-style IS function,[29] (34) is a price-adjustment relation that with $0 \leq \theta < 1$ can represent either the specification of Calvo (1983) and Rotemberg (1982) or the Fuhrer-Moore (1995) setup, and (35) is an interest-rate policy rule that can reflect pure inflation targeting (with $\mu_2 = 0$) or a rule of the more general Taylor (1993) variety.

Substitution of (35) into (33) and elimination of $y_t$ then yields a linear equation that includes the variables $\Delta p_t$, $E_t\Delta p_{t+1}$, $\Delta p_{t-1}$, and $v_t$. That list differs from the one pertaining to equation (5) by not including $E_{t-1}\Delta p_{t+1}$, but that difference is of no consequence for the issues at hand because the distinction between $E_t\Delta p_{t+1}$ and $E_{t-1}\Delta p_{t+1}$ is irrelevant for the condition analogous to (6b) that determines the value of the crucial coefficient on $\Delta p_{t-1}$ in the RE solution expression. Indeed, it can be verified that for some admissible parameter values the system has two stable solutions.[30] Interestingly, large values of $\mu_1$

do not generate explosive MSV solutions with the policy rule (35), but if $\Delta p_{t-1}$ is entered in place of $E_t \Delta p_{t+1}$ then large $\mu_1$ values will induce instability, just as in the example of Section II.

An issue that has attracted considerable attention recently is the so-called "Woodford warning" of possible solution "indeterminacy" when policy feedback rules relate to market expectations of inflation or some other target variable, a problem emphasized by Woodford (1994), Kerr and King (1996), Bernanke and Woodford (1997), Clarida, Gali, and Gertler (1997), and Svensson (1998). An example can be presented in the following system, which is adapted from Clarida, Gali, and Gertler (1997, p. 16):

$$y_t = E_t y_{t+1} + b_1(R_t - E_t \Delta p_{t+1}) + v_t \qquad b_1 < 0 \tag{36}$$

$$\Delta p_t = \beta E_t \Delta p_{t+1} + \alpha E_t y_t \qquad \alpha > 0, 0 < \beta < 1 \tag{37}$$

$$R_t = \mu_1 E_t \Delta p_{t+1} \qquad \mu_1 > 0 \tag{38}$$

Here we have an expectational IS function, a Calvo-Rotemberg price adjustment specification, and a pure inflation-forecast targeting rule.[31] For simplicity, constants are eliminated by normalization and $v_t$ is again taken to be white noise. In this system there are no predetermined variables so the MSV solution is of the form $y_t = \phi_1 v_t$, $\Delta p_t = \phi_2 v_t$. Trivial calculations show that $\phi_1 = 1$, $\phi_2 = \alpha$ so the solution is $y_t = v_t$, $\Delta p_t = \alpha v_t$. The policy coefficient $\mu_1$ does not appear in the solution equations because policy is responding to the expected future inflation rate, which is a constant (normalized to zero). A caveat must be applied to the foregoing, however: the MSV solution is defined only for $\mu_1 > 1.0$. Values of $\mu_1 < 1.0$ are inadmissible for "process consistency" reasons, introduced by Flood and Garber (1980a) and discussed in McCallum (1983, pp. 159–160).

But suppose that the researcher looks for solutions of the form

$$y_t = \phi_{11} \Delta p_{t-1} + \phi_{12} v_t \tag{39}$$

$$\Delta p_t = \phi_{21} \Delta p_{t-1} + \phi_{22} v_t. \tag{40}$$

Then $E_t y_{t+1} = \phi_{11}(\phi_{21} \Delta p_{t-1} \phi_{22} v_t)$, $E_t \Delta p_{t+1} = \phi_{21}(\phi_{21} \Delta p_{t-1} + \phi_{22} v_t)$, and the undetermined-coefficient conditions analogous to (6) are

$$\phi_{11} = \phi_{11}\phi_{21} + b_1(\mu_1 - 1)\phi_{21}^2 \tag{41a}$$

$$\phi_{12} = \phi_{11}\phi_{22} + b_1(\mu_1 - 1)\phi_{21}\phi_{22} + 1 \tag{41b}$$

$$\phi_{21} = \beta\phi_{21}^2 + \alpha\phi_{11} \tag{41c}$$

$$\phi_{22} = \beta\phi_{21}\phi_{22} + \alpha\phi_{12}. \tag{41d}$$

From the first and third of these we obtain the crucial requirement

$$\phi_{21} = \beta\phi_{21}^2 + \alpha b_1(\mu_1 - 1)\phi_{21}^2/(1 - \phi_{21}). \tag{42}$$

Clearly, one root of the foregoing is $\phi_{21} = 0$, which implies $\phi_{11} = 0$ and consequently gives the MSV solution. But (42) is also satisfied by values of $\phi_{21}$ such that

$$\phi_{21} = \frac{\delta \pm [\delta^2 - 4\beta]^{1/2}}{2\beta}, \qquad \delta = 1 + \beta + \alpha b_1(\mu_1 - 1). \tag{43}$$

Here $\delta^2 - 4\beta$ is positive for $\mu_1 < 1$ and $\mu_1 > 1 + [2\beta^{1/2} - (1 + \beta)]/(-b_1\alpha)$.[32] So for those values, there are non-zero real roots for $\phi_{21}$ and thus solutions in addition to the MSV solution. That this possibility obtains for large values of $\mu_1$ represents a problem for monetary policy, according to the non-MSV analysis of the authors mentioned above. But under the hypothesis that the MSV solution prevails, large values of $\mu_1$ pose no problem: the solution remains $y_t = v_t$, $\Delta p_t = \alpha v_t$. Since $\mu_1 \to \infty$ is conceptually akin to setting Rt such that $E_t \Delta p_{t+1} = 0$, where 0 is the implicit target rate of inflation, the MSV hypothesis seems more consistent with the inflation forecast targeting prescription of Svensson (1998) than does the non-MSV analysis of Bernanke and Woodford (1997) or Clarida, Gali, and Gertler (1997). This conclusion pertains, I conjecture, to this entire body of analysis, not just the single (and extreme) case considered above. In any event, it should be emphasized that if a multiplicity of solutions is found by considering non-MSV procedures, it has nothing to do with the phenomenon of "nominal indeterminacy"—i.e., cases in which a model determines values of real variables but not nominal variables. For a recent discussion of this distinction, see McCallum (1997).

Finally, we might also mention the "fiscal theory of price level determination," due principally to Woodford (1995) and Sims (1994), which has been attracting a good bit of attention. In this regard, the argument presented in Section 7 of McCallum (1997) indicates that adoption of the fiscal theory of price level determination, in contrast to the more traditional "monetarist" approach, amounts to acceptance of the hypothesis that a non-MSV or bubble solution is empirically relevant. The MSV solution is also available,[33] however, and implies fully traditional price level-money stock relationships and behavior.

## VIII. Conclusions

Let us conclude with a brief summary. This paper has been concerned with the minimal-state-variable (MSV) criterion for selection among solutions in linear rational expectations models that feature a multiplicity of paths that satisfy all conditions for equilibrium. The paper compares the MSV criterion with others that have been proposed, including Taylor's (1977) minimum-variance criterion, the expectational stability criterion of Evans (1985, 1986), and the saddle-path or non-explosiveness (i.e., dynamic stability) criterion favored by Blanchard and Kahn (1980), Blanchard and Fischer (1989), Sargent (1987), and Whiteman (1983) and utilized in practice by a large number of researchers. It is emphasized that the MSV criterion can be viewed as a classification scheme, one that delineates the unique solution that is of a bubble-free nature—i.e., reflecting only market fundamentals—from those that include bubble or bootstrap components.

It is argued that the MSV classification scheme is of scientific value in two ways. First, it provides a unique solution upon which a researcher may focus attention if the project at hand suggests or permits the a priori exclusion of bubble solutions. Second, it provides the basis for a substantive hypothesis to the effect that market outcomes in actual economies are generally of a bubble-free nature. In describing the latter role, the paper argues that the possibility that bubble-free solutions dominate empirically is much more plausible than is suggested by solution approaches that parameterize different solutions by (possibly irrelevant) initial conditions rather than by undetermined-coefficient parameter values. It also explains the basis of McCallum's (1983) "subsidiary principle" that is used to make the MSV solution unique by construction.

In the process of demonstrating the uniqueness of the MSV solution, the paper presents a convenient and practical computational procedure for solving linear rational expectations models of a very broad class. This exposition, which utilizes the generalized Schur decomposition theorem, is developed by means of the mathematically simple undetermined-coefficients approach. In addition, examples are provided that illustrate the applicability and importance of the MSV criterion to issues of current concern in the analysis of monetary policy rules.

Finally, it should be recognized that some readers may be unwilling to accept the paper's interpretation of the MSV solution as the bubble-free or fundamentals solution. In that case, it remains true that the MSV approach provides a unique solution upon which a researcher may focus attention, if desired, and provides the basis for a substantive hypothesis to the effect that actual outcomes generally conform to the MSV solution. If this hypothesis is in fact true, then several classes of problems discussed in the literature are empirically irrelevant.

### Acknowledgments

I am indebted to Edwin Burmeister, Bob Flood, Robert King, and Edward Nelson for comments on previous drafts.

### Notes

1. What, it might be asked, is the definition of a bubble in a rational expectations model? The basic idea of Burmeister, Flood, and Garber (1983) is that a bubble is an extra component that arises in addition to the component that reflects "market fundamentals," an important implication of which is that bubble components are not necessarily explosive. Unfortunately, the identification of market fundamentals has to be made on a model-specific basis, although there is rarely any disagreement. Below it will be argued that the MSV solution procedure is constructed so as to yield the market fundamentals solution, thereby providing a method for defining bubbles in particular cases.
2. Leading examples of the latter type include real asset price bubbles in overlapping-generations models, as demonstrated by Calvo (1978) and Woodford (1984), and price level bubbles in infinite-horizon monetary models, as in Brock (1975), Flood and Garber (1980b), Gray (1986), and Obstfeld and Rogoff (1983).
3. Although empirical testing is attractive in principle, this practice is in fact extremely common. This seems to be recognized by Blanchard and Fischer (1989, p. 260).
4. This point will be explained below, in Section IV.
5. From (7) we see that $\mu_1 > (\alpha - 1)^2/(-4\alpha)$ would give complex roots.
6. Note that $\pi_1^+ = 0$ because $(\alpha - 1) + [(\alpha - 1)^2]^{1/2} = (\alpha - 1) - (\alpha - 1)$ since $[(\alpha - 1)^2]^{1/2}$ is by convention a positive number and $\alpha - 1$ is in the present case negative.
7. The undetermined-coefficient conditions are (6a), (6b), $0 = \pi_2 + \alpha\pi_1\pi_2 + \alpha\pi_3 + 1$, and $0 = \pi_3 + \alpha\pi_1\pi_3 - \alpha\pi_3$. With $\pi_1 = (\alpha - 1)/\alpha$, the last of these is satisfied for any $\pi_3$ and the next to last relates $\pi_2$ to $\pi_3$.
8. Burmeister, Flood, and Garber (1983) work in the context of a Cagan-style model similar to (1), except with a white-noise rather than a random-walk disturbance, and define the bubble-free or fundamentals solution as the one that depends only upon "current and expected future values of money and the disturbance" (1983, p. 312).
9. Because of their use of the stability criterion, Blanchard and Fischer (p. 260) suggest that if bubble paths are explosive then "unless the focus is specifically on bubbles, assume that the economy chooses the [stable]

path, which is the fundamental [bubble-free] solution"—and do so even if there is no aspect of the model that explicitly disqualifies the explosive paths. But then in cases in which the bubble paths are not explosive, they are unable to recommend among various courses of action. Instead, they retreat to a hope—a "working assumption"—that "the conditions needed to generate stable multiplicities of equilibria are not met in practice" (p. 261). But we know that in various cases this hope is not justified.

10. In linear models, that is.
11. The reason, of course, is that all other solutions involve—at least in special case—"extraneous" state variables, ones not in a minimal set. Thus the solution values involve variables that do not appear in the model's structural equations and therefore affect the endogenous variables only because they are (arbitrarily) expected to do so. I would also claim that the MSV solution corresponds to the bubble-free or fundamental values in all the standard, non-contentious examples in the literature. This claim cannot be proved correct, of course, but I am happy to put it forth as a refutable conjecture.
12. Recall that our argument is presuming a linear model. It is possible to distinguish MSV solutions in some nonlinear models, but no general analysis has yet been developed.
13. Recall that we are discussing the case with $\pi_1 = 0$. The solution value for $\pi_3$ when $\pi_1 = (\alpha - 1)/\alpha$ is undetermined.
14. Application to the striking argument of Woodford (1994, pp. 105–111), Bernanke and Woodford (1997, pp. 669–675), and Clarida, Gali, and Gertler (1997, pp. 20–23), is considered below in Section VII.
15. For more recent developments see Evans (1989) and Evans and Honkapohja (1992, 1997).
16. Actually, it is shown by Evans (1989) and Evans and Honkapohja (1997) that expectational stability obtains when the differential equation analog of this difference equation converges. This will be the case under a somewhat broader set of conditions, so convergence of the iterative procedure is sufficient but not necessary for expectational stability. This result draws on Marcet and Sargent (1989).
17. It is not entirely clear whether Evans and Honkapohja (1992, 1997) would agree with this derivation, as their examples do not include expectations formed at different times. But in the present model, $\Delta p_t^e$ is clearly meant to represent the expectation of $\Delta p_t$ formed in period $t - 1$. So it is not what the iterative procedure at $t$ is concerned with! Thus it would seem incorrect to write $\phi_0^{n-1} + \phi_1^{n-1}\Delta p_{t-1}$ in place of $\Delta p_t^e$ in (10).
18. The example in Evans and Honkapohja (1992) is an exception but is not, I would suggest, as well motivated as the model in the present paper, which differs in its assumptions regarding the times (actually, information sets) relevant for forming expectations of $\Delta p_t$ and $\Delta p_{t+1}$.
19. Klein's (1997) approach builds upon earlier contributions of King and Watson (1995) and Sims (1996). Other significant recent contributions are Uhlig (1997) and Binder and Pesaran (1995), which use UC analysis. The Uhlig paper also features a useful procedure for linearizing models that include nonlinear relationships.
20. An earlier draft of this paper included a demonstration that closed-form representations of MSV solutions can be obtained by means of formulae developed by Whiteman (1983). This demonstration was illustrated in the context of the simple example of Section II, in line with the much more extensive analysis in McCallum (1985). That analysis was more tedious and less useful that that of the present section, however, since the latter is based on a convenient computational algorithm. The present discussion is taken in large part from McCallum (1998).
21. Here, as above, $E_t y_{t+1}$ is the expectation of $y_{t+1}$ conditional upon an information set that includes all of the model's variables dated $t$ and earlier.
22. See King and Watson (1995) or Klein (1997).
23. See Golub and Van Loan (1996, p. 377).
24. Or, in the terminology used by Uhlig (1997), are eigenvalues of $B$ with respect to $A$.
25. This is the same condition as that required by Klein (1997, p. 13) and King and Watson (1995, pp. 9–11). It appears to provide no difficulties in practice. The King and Watson example of a system in which the condition does not hold is one in which $B_{12} = 0$ in my notation so the MSV solution has $\Omega = 0$ and the other solution matrices follow easily.
26. By the arrangement of generalized eigenvalues, $S_{22}$ has no zero elements on the diagonal (and is triangular).
27. This uses the identity that if $A, B, C$ are real conformable matrices, $\text{vec}(ABC) = (C' \otimes A)\,\text{vec}(B)$. See Golub and Van Loan (1996, p. 180).
28. With $B_{12} = 0$, $k_t$ does not appear in the system (14) (19), in this case so $k_t$ represents extraneous variables of a bootstrap, bubble, or sunspot nature.
29. It would be more desirable theoretically to use an expectational IS relation, as argued in McCallum and Nelson (1997) and elsewhere, but that would lead to a cubic equation for the coefficient on $\Delta p_{t-1}$ in the MSV solution

without altering the basic message.

30. Two stable solutions exist if the parameters are $\alpha = 0.2$, $b_1 = 0.5$, $\theta = 0.2$, and $\mu_1 = 0.5$.
31. Clarida, Gali, and Gertler (1997) also include terms involving $y_t$ and $R_{t-1}$ on the right-hand side of (38). They are omitted here only to keep the example as simple and transparent as possible.
32. Note that with the values $\beta = .99$, $\alpha = .3$, $b_1 = -1$ used by Clarida, Gali, and Gertler (1997), this last expression equals $1 + [1.96 + 1.99]/0.3 = 14.2$, precisely as reported in their Table 4 for this special case.
33. The example cited is one in which the model is not linear, so the MSV concept has to be extended and the generality of Section VI cannot be claimed.

## References


Bernanke, B. S., and M. Woodford. (1997). "Inflation Forecasts and Monetary Policy." *Journal of Money, Credit, and Banking* 29, 653–684.

Binder, M., and M. H. Pesaran. (1995). "Multivariate Rational Expectations Models: A Review and Some New Results." In M. H. Pesaran and M. Wickens (eds.), *Handbook of Applied Econometrics*. Oxford: Basil Blackwell.

Blanchard, O. J., and C. M. Kahn. (1980). "The Solution of Linear Difference Models Under Rational Expectations." *Econometrica* 48, 1305–1311.

Blanchard, O. J., and S. Fischer. (1980). *Lectures on Macroeconomics*. Cambridge, MA: MIT Press.



Blanchard, O. J., and C. M. Kahn. (1980). "The Solution of Linear Difference Models Under Rational Expectations." *Econometrica* 48, 1305–1311.



Brock, W. A. (1975). "A Simple Perfect Foresight Monetary Model." *Journal of Monetary Economics* 1, 133–150.

Burmeister, E., R. P. Flood, and P. M. Garber. (1983). "On the Equivalence of Solutions in Rational Expectations Models." *Journal of Economic Dynamics and Control* 5, 311–321.

Calvo, G. A. (1978). "On the Indeterminacy of Interest Rates and Wages with Perfect Foresight." *Journal of Economic Theory* 19, 321–337.

———. (1983). "Staggered Prices in a Utility-Maximizing Framework." *Journal of Monetary Economics* 12, 383–398.

Clarida, R., J. Gali, and M. Gertler. (1997). "Monetary Policy Rules and Macroeconomic Stability: Evidence and Some Theory." NBER Working Paper 6442.

Evans, G. W. (1985). "Expectational Stability and the Multiple Equilibria Problem in Linear Rational Expectations Models." *Quarterly Journal of Economics* 100, 1217–1233.

———. (1986). "Selection Criteria for Models with Non-Uniqueness." *Journal of Monetary Economics* 18, 147–157.

———. (1989). "The Fragility of Sunspots and Bubbles." *Journal of Monetary Economics* 23, 297–317.

Evans, G. W., and S. Honkapohja. (1992). "On the Robustness of Bubbles in Linear RE Models." *International Economic Review* 33, 1–14.

———. (1997). "Learning Dynamics." Working Paper.

Flood, R. P., and P. M. Garber. (1980a). "An Economic Theory of Monetary Reform." *Journal of Political Economy* 88, 24–58.

———. (1980b). "Market Fundamentals vs. Price Level Bubbles: The First Tests." *Journal of Political Economy* 88, 745–770.

Froot, K. A., and M. Obstfeld. (1991). "Intrinsic Bubbles: The Case of Stock Prices." *American Economic Review* 81, 1189–1214.

Fuhrer, J. C., and G. R. Moore. (1995). "Inflation Persistence." *Quarterly Journal of Economics* 109, 127–159.

Golub, G. H., and C. F. Van Loan. (1996). *Matrix Computations* (3rd ed.). Baltimore: Johns Hopkins.

Gray, J. A. (1984). "Dynamic Instability in Rational Expectations Models: An Attempt to Clarify." *International Economic Review* 25, 93–122.

Kerr, W., and R. G. King. (1996). "Limits on Interest Rate Rules in the IS Model." *Federal Reserve Bank of Richmond Economic Quarterly* 82(2), 47–76.

King, R. G., and M. W. Watson. (1995). "The Solution of Singular Linear Difference Systems Under Rational Expectations." Working paper, University of Virginia.

Klein, P. (1997). "Using the Generalized Schur Form to Solve a System of Linear Expectational Difference Equations." Working paper, Stockholm University (IIES).

Marcet, A., and T. J. Sargent. "Convergence of Least Squares Learning Mechanisms in Self Referential Linear Stochastic Models." *Journal of Economic Theory* 48, 337–368.

McCallum, B. T. (1983). "On Non-Uniqueness in Rational Expectations Models: An Attempt at Perspective." *Journal of Monetary Economics* 11, 139–168.

———. (1985). "On z-Transform and Minimal State Variable Solutions to Linear Rational Expectations Models." Working Paper, Carnegie Mellon University.

———. (1997). "Issues in the Design of Monetary Policy Rules." NBER Working paper 6016. Also forthcoming in J. B. Taylor and M. Woodford (eds.), *Handbook of Macroeconomics*.

McCallum, B. T., and E. Nelson. (1997). "An Optimizing IS-LM Specification for Monetary Policy and Business Cycle Analysis." NBER Working Paper 5875. Also forthcoming in *Journal of Money, Credit, and Banking*.

McCallum, B. T. (1998) "Solutions to Linear Rational Expectations Models: A Compact Exposition." *Economics Letters* 61, 143–147.

Obstfeld, M., and K. Rogoff. (1983). "Speculative Hyperinflations in Maximizing Models: Can We Rule Them Out?" *Journal of Political Economy* 91, 675–687.

Rotemberg, J. J. (1982). "Sticky Prices in the United States." *Journal of Political Economy* 60, 1187–1211.

Sargent, T. J. (1987). *Macroeconomic Theory* (2nd ed.). New York: Academic Press.

Sims, C. A. (1994). "A Simple Model for Study of the Determination of the Price Level and the Interaction of Monetary and Fiscal Policy." *Economic Theory* 4, 381–399.

———. (1996). "Solving Linear Rational Expectations Models." Working paper, Yale University.

Svensson, L. E. O. (1998). "Inflation Targeting as a Monetary Policy Rule." NBER Working Paper 6790.

Taylor, J. B. (1977). "Conditions for Unique Solutions in Stochastic Macroeconomic Models with Rational Expectations." *Econometrica* 45, 1377–1385.

———. (1993) "Discretion versus Policy Rules in Practice." *Carnegie-Rochester Conference Series on Public Policy* 39, 195–214.

Uhlig, H. (1997). "A Toolkit for Analyzing Nonlinear Dynamic Stochastic Models Easily." Working paper, University of Tilburg.

Whiteman, C. H. (1983). *Linear Rational Expectations Models: A User's Guide*. Minneapolis: University of Minnesota Press.

Woodford, M. (1984). "Indeterminacy of Equilibrium in the Overlapping Generations Model: A Survey." Working Paper, Columbia University.

———. (1994). "Nonstandard Indicators for Monetary Policy: Can Their Usefulness Be Judged from Forecasting Regressions?" In N. G. Mankiw (ed.), *Monetary Policy*. Chicago: University of Chicago Press.

———. (1995). "Price-Level Determinacy without Control of a Monetary Aggregate." *Carnegie-Rochester Conference Series on Public Policy* 43, 1–46.

# Comment

BY EDWIN BURMEISTER

## Preliminaries

When someone expressed amazement to me that Tiger Woods was able to hit an eight iron 175 yards, I replied that I had seen Bob Flood hit an eight iron that far, or almost that far, many times. Unfortunately, on some of these occasions Bob's target was only 140 yards away.

His work in economics, however, has always been right on target, and it is a great pleasure for me to participate in this conference honoring him. This occasion has also brought back many, many fond memories of my days at the University of Virginia where both Bob and Ben McCallum were my colleagues and friends.

The general subject addressed by Ben McCallum's paper has been of interest to me since about 1964 when I was a graduate student at M.I.T. This general subject is the dual instability of dynamic economic models in which there is more than one way to hold wealth. The specific class of linear rational expectations models addressed by Ben may be viewed as one very important example.

## Agreements

First I want to list points about which I believe Ben and I are in complete agreement.

- Ben's problem is very important.
- His Minimal State Variable Criterion provides an elegant and computationally efficient algorithm for finding the solution to linear rational expectations models. As a bonus, Ben has convincingly argued that his approach is economically useful for other reasons as well.
- Taylor's Minimum Variance Criterion seems economically flawed.

## Potential Agreements

My second list covers points about which I believe Ben and I could be in complete agreement, especially if he has become more mellow with age.

- The general problem arises in both discrete time and continuous time formulations. Discrete time is the obvious choice for empirical applications, but the fundamental problem arises in continuous time formulations as well.

- Ben states clearly that his procedure is only for linear models. While this is true, he gives away too much. The standard approach to studying the dynamics of a nonlinear system is to first linearize it around the dynamic rest point. Provided the relevant Jacobian matrix is nonsingular (and there are no purely imaginary characteristic roots), the resulting linear system will correctly describe the nonlinear behavior in a neighborhood of the rest point. Thus, Ben's Minimum State Variable Criterion is quite relevant for studying the local behavior of nonlinear models. Often one can find some additional argument to show that the local behavior obtains globally as well.

- The general problem has nothing to do with uncertainty. In rational expectations models, once expectations are taken we are left with a set of deterministic (nonstochastic) dynamic equations. Ben's Minimum State Variable Criterion is applied to these deterministic equations and the stochastic solution follows. In perfect foresight models, we simply have a set of deterministic equations to begin with to which Ben's Minimum State Variable Criterion can be applied.

- It is economically interesting to build and analyze ***descriptive*** economic models. This is an important point; with sufficient optimizing behavior on the part of economic agents, generally (though not always) the stable path will be the only admissible solution, and in this way the dual instability problem "is solved." However, these optimizing models are of dubious value for the type of macroeconomic policy questions that Ben and others are interested in studying.

**Brief History of the General Dual Instability Property**

The general problem is very old. Perhaps the first references are Solow (1959) and Jorgenson (1960). The fact that the same problem arose in models with neoclassical production functions was demonstrated by Hahn (1966). It was also known early on that optimizing behavior would pick out the stable path. One classic example is Samuelson's (1959) Turnpike Theorem.

The identical dual instability problem then surfaced in monetary growth models, with numerous contributions by Frank Hahn, Karl Shell, M. Sidrauski, T. Sargent, N. Wallace, D. Foley, J. Stiglitz, W. Brock, and many others.

It was once conjectured that all of these descriptive models could be reduced in an "as if" manner to an optimizing model, and that this would provide a way to determine the correct stable solution. But this conjecture was proved false by Burmeister and others (1973). We showed that a growth model with $n$ capital goods could have a convergent manifold of dimension $(n + 1)$. This means that one can take as given the $n$ capital stocks (state variables) and any one of the capital good prices (costate variables) and then uniquely determine the remaining $(n - 1)$ prices such that the system will converge to its unique dynamic rest point. This is inconsistent with optimizing behavior.

Professional attention soon shifted to new rational expectations models, displacing the monetary growth models of the late 1960's and early 1970's. Now at last we had genuine stochastic models. And essentially the identical dual instability (saddlepoint) property emerged as a characteristic of the dynamic equilibria paths, though the recognition of this fact was slow to arrive. Numerous papers were published touting "new" solutions, many of them misleading at best. In view of the fact that the dynamic difference equations arising from these rational expectations models shared much of the same mathematical structure with the Solow and Jorgenson models studied some 20 years earlier, it is surprising how much effort was spent proving "new" results.

The moral for Bob Flood on this occasion is that getting old has some advantages. You do not need to search the literature when you have lived through its development.

## What Behavior Do We Want to Model?

The rational expectations models to which Ben has so elegantly applied his Minimal State Variable Criterion are well suited for addressing certain questions, certainly for the questions studied by Ben and others.

However, I am more convinced than ever that eventually we will need to do more. My fear is that actual economies may spend part of their time on paths that are not stable. If this is the case, sometimes we may be providing inaccurate or even misleading policy advice. And perhaps this happens precisely when good advice is most needed.

We might prefer models with heterogeneous agents having different information sets, different individual models, and different expectations. In particular, different agents have different time horizons (and probably none of them is infinity). Aggregation of each of these individual models (one for each heterogeneous economic agent) would give rise to the macro model. In particular, note that even when each heterogeneous agent exhibits maximizing behavior, the aggregate macro model probably could not be explained in terms of the maximizing behavior of a "representative agent." I conjecture that such an aggregated macro model would not resemble any of the current linear macroeconomic models, except perhaps under certain idealistic circumstances.

One key to how such a model might work could involve a subset of agents with unrealistic expectations, say overly optimistic earnings forecasts for firms. Eventually earnings disappointments would reveal the false expectations, they would be revised, and the economy might then return to a stable Minimum State Variable solution. The modeling of how such heterogeneous expectations get revised as new information is processed will probably be a key ingredient for any such story.

The Expectational Stability Criterion seems to me to represent one small step in this direction. Accordingly, I would view it with somewhat more promise than does Ben. I recognize, however, that the issue here really involves what economic questions we wish to address, and Ben's approach is perfectly appropriate for the specific questions he has singled out.

## Concluding Remark

It is not by accident that you have not seen the B word in any of the above. To me, the B word prejudges important economic phenomena as frivolous. I much prefer the bull and bear Wall Street terminology, or, if we must be pretentious, we could talk about "dynamic equilibria paths that lie off the convergent manifold."

Of course, we must recognize that science advances by attacking the easier problems first. It is therefore perfectly appropriate that we begin with linear rational expectations models, and Ben's Minimum State Variable Criterion is an extraordinarily valuable tool for helping us to understand them. But I am afraid that much work lies ahead if we are ever to obtain a deeper understanding of how economies actually behave, especially in times when things may have wandered off track.

## References

Burmeister, Edwin, Christopher Caton, A. Rodney Dobell, and Stephen A. Ross. (1973) "The 'Saddlepoint Property' and the Structure of Dynamic Heterogeneous Capital Good Models." *Econometrica*, January.

Hahn, Frank H. (1966). "Equilibrium Dynamics with Heterogeneous Capital Goods." *The Quarterly Journal of Economics*, November, 633–646.

Jorgenson, Dale W. (1960). "A Dual Stability Theorem." *Econometrica*, October, 892–899.

Samuelson, Paul A. (1959). "Efficient Paths of Capital Accumulation in Terms of the Calculus of Variations." In K. Arrow, S. Karlin, and P. Suppes (eds.), *Mathematical Methods in the Social Sciences*. Stanford: Stanford University Press, 1960, pp. 77–78

Solow, Robert M. (1959). "Competitive Valuation in a Dynamic Input-Output System." *Econometrica*, January, 30–53.

# General Discussion

**Jinill Kim** commented on the solution methodology, suggesting that the reshuffling of eigenvalues could be embedded automatically into the procedure. **Lars Svensson** added that, indeed, Paul Klein's algorithm, which was based on the Schur decomposition theorem, included the sorting of eigenvalues. **McCallum** responded that the difficulty was to arrange the eigenvalues in the order that his method requires. Although this was usually the same as ordering them by decreasing modulus, the orderings are different for cases in which the minimal state variable and saddle point stability conditions differ. Klein's algorithm yields the Blanchard–Kahn solution. But an algorithm that gave the minimal state variable solution had not yet been written because it was too hard for McCallum to do (although he could describe how to do so in words) and nobody else had been interested in doing so.

**Michael Mussa** expressed a general concern about procedures that picked out a solution automatically on the basis of a purely technical exercise. To illustrate his concerns, he presented phase diagrams for several variants of a modified Dornbusch overshooting model. This was a two-equation reduced-form system in which there were two key parameters: the semi-elasticity of money demand and a price adjustment parameter. For the case in which the two key parameters had "normal" signs, the system had one positive characteristic root and one negative characteristic root, and the standard criteria (whether McCallum's minimal state variable criterion or the nonexplosiveness or saddle path criterion associated with Blanchard–Kahn) picked out a unique stable solution. However, the standard criteria also picked out a unique stable solution when both of the key parameters had the "wrong" signs; this was a case in which both the model and the solution were nonsense. Moreover, for a third case in which the semi-elasticity parameter had the "wrong" sign while the price adjustment parameter had the "normal" sign, the system had an infinity of stable solutions; but once again, the model was complete nonsense, so the multiplicity of stable solutions was not reassuring. Mussa shared McCallum's view that we needed to apply economic good sense in choosing an economically-relevant solution to such models. While that, unfortunately, could be quite difficult in a highly complicated model, we needed to be very careful about just automatically applying a mathematical routine, since that could generate solutions that were just garbage.

**Flood** noted that Burmeister's aversion to the B-word evoked memories of many harangues on the golf course when they had been colleagues at the University of Virginia. On dealing with the multiplicity problem, he and Peter Garber had come up with what they thought was a pretty simple procedure—namely, to estimate the model and then look at the reduced form equations to see which solution they reflected. He still didn't see what was wrong with that approach. All of the models contain behavioral equations. These can be estimated, the reduced forms can be estimated separately, and one can then look at whether or not certain cross equation restrictions hold. McCallum was focusing on the issue of what kind of null hypothesis one wanted to test with respect to the reduced form, and that was fine. But the key point, in Flood's view, was that one should test that null hypothesis, or see what the reduced form looked like, in the context of actual empirical models.

In responding to the various comments, **McCallum** indicted that he thought he agreed with what Mussa had said and felt that the type of procedure to which Mussa had objected was associated with the Blanchard–Kahn criterion, not his. Mussa's second example was similar to one that McCallum had considered in his 1983 paper, where he had reached the conclusion that the model was economic nonsense on grounds that Flood and Garber had discussed in one of their papers. In light of such examples, McCallum had described the minimal state variable criterion as a rule for obtaining a solution valid for all "admissible parameter values." For a given model specification, there could be some parameter values that resulted in what Flood and Garber had referred to as "process inconsistency," and such parameter values were simply not admissible.

Burmeister had listed four points of potential agreement. **McCallum** was happy to note that he and Burmeister were actually in full agreement on the first three and in partial agreement on the fourth. His only disagreement with Burmeister's comments was with statements in which Burmeister seemed to imply that the minimal state variable criterion always finds stable linear solutions. This was a slight misstatement about the objective of the criterion, or about how it works. As McCallum had argued in his paper, there may be cases in which the system is not going to be dynamically stable, and he did not want to restrict himself to stable solutions.

# Exact Utilities under Alternative Monetary Rules in a Simple Macro Model with Optimizing Agents

DALE W. HENDERSON dale.henderson@frb.gov
*Federal Reserve Board*

JINILL KIM jk9n@virginia.edu
*University of Virginia*

***Abstract***

We construct an optimizing-agent model of a closed economy which is simple enough that we can use it to make exact utility calculations. There is a stabilization problem because there are one-period nominal contracts for wages, or prices, or both and shocks that are unknown at the time when contracts are signed. We evaluate alternative monetary policy rules using the utility function of the representative agent. Fully optimal policy can attain the Pareto-optimal equilibrium. Fully optimal policy is contrasted with both 'naive' and 'sophisticated' simple rules that involve, respectively, complete stabilization and optimal stabilization of one variable or a combination of two variables. With wage contracts, outcomes depend crucially on whether there are also price contracts. For example, if labor supply is relatively inelastic, for productivity shocks, nominal income stabilization yields higher welfare when there are no price contracts. However, with price contracts, outcomes are independent of whether there are wage contracts, except, of course, for nominal wage outcomes.

## 1. Introduction

Interest in improving the analytical foundations of monetary stabilization policy is at a cyclical peak. This paper is a contribution to that endeavor. We construct an optimizing-agent model of a closed economy which is simple enough that we can make exact utility calculations. In this model, there is a stabilization problem because there are one-period nominal contracts for wages, or prices, or both and shocks that are unknown at the time when contracts are signed. We evaluate alternative monetary policy rules using as a criterion the utility function of the representative agent.

One well known advantage of using exact utility calculations is that it makes it possible to analyze shocks with large as well as small variances. An unexpected advantage is that it actually simplifies the algebraic derivations in our model. However, when shocks have small variances, it yields no advantage for welfare analysis in our model; welfare rankings are the same with exact and approximate utility calculations.[1]

We focus on two cases, (1) wage contracts and flexible prices and (2) wage and price contracts. If wages are fixed by contracts, for some shocks the attractiveness of some simple rules depends crucially on whether prices are also fixed by contracts. We can limit our focus to two cases because, as we show, the outcomes in the third case, price contracts and flexible wages, are the same as the outcomes in the case of wage and price contracts for all variables except, of course, for the nominal wage.[2]

We calculate the fully optimal rule under complete information for each of our two cases of interest. This rule can attain the Pareto-optimal equilibrium because we assume one-period nominal contracts, so the policymaker does not face a tradeoff.[3] Then we contrast the performance of the fully optimal policy with both 'naive' and 'sophisticated' versions of some simple rules. Naive simple rules involve complete stabilization of one variable or a combination of two variables. Sophisticated simple rules involve optimal stabilization of one variable or a combination of two variables. We consider sophisticated versions of simple rules in an attempt to put these rules in the best possible light.

Our paper is closely related to two sets of recent studies. The studies in one set contain evaluations of alternative monetary policies using approximate solutions of models with optimizing-agents.[4] Of course, the authors of these studies have used approximate solutions because their models are complex enough that obtaining exact solutions would be relatively difficult and costly if it were even feasible. It seems useful to supplement their analysis with analysis of models that are simple enough that obtaining exact solutions is relatively easy.

The studies in the other set are based on two-country models in which exact utility calculations are possible.[5] Our emphasis differs from the emphasis in these studies. We focus on the welfare effects of alternative monetary stabilization rules in a stochastic model. In contrast, the other studies focus either on the welfare effects of a one-time increase in the money supply in a perfect foresight model, on the implications of alternative money supply processes for asset returns in a stochastic model, or on a welfare comparison of fixed and flexible exchange rates in a stochastic model. Another notable difference between our paper and the other studies is that for us the interest rate, not the money supply, is the instrument of monetary policy.

The rest of this paper is organized into five more sections. Section 2 is a description of our model. We devote section 3 to the benchmark version with flexible wages and prices. In sections 4 and 5, we analyze alternative monetary policy rules in versions with wage contracts and flexible prices and with both wage and price contracts, respectively. Section 6 contains our conclusions. The demonstration that the version with price contracts and flexible wages yields the same outcomes as the version with both wage and price contracts (except for nominal wages) is in the Appendix.

## 2. The Model

In this section we describe our model. We discuss the behavior of firms, households, and the government in successive subsections.

### *2.1. Firms*

A continuum of 'identical' monopolistically competitive firms is distributed on the unit interval, $f \in [0, 1]$. With no price contracts, firms set their prices for period $t$ based on period $t$ information. With one-period price contracts, firms set prices for period $t+1$ based on period $t$ information and agree to supply whatever their customers demand at those prices. In either case, the problem of firm $f$ in period $t$ is to find the

$$\max_{\{P_{f,t+j}\}} \mathcal{E}_t \tilde{\delta}_{t,t+j} \left( s_P \mathsf{P}_{f,t+j} \mathsf{Y}_{f,t+j} - W_{t+j} L_{f,t+j} \right) \tag{1}$$

where capital letters without serifs represent choice variables of individual firms or households and capital letters with serifs represent indexes that include all firms or households. The subscript $j$ takes on the value 0 if there are no price contracts and the value 1 if there are price contracts. In period $t+j$, firm $f$ sets the price $\mathsf{P}_{f,t+j}$, produces output $\mathsf{Y}_{f,t+j}$, and employs the amount $L_{f,t+j}$ of a labor index $L_{t+j}$ for which it pays the wage index $W_{t+j}$ per unit:

$$L_{t+j} = \int_0^1 L_{f,t+j} df = \left( \int_0^1 \mathsf{L}_{h,t+j}^{\frac{1}{\theta_W}} dh \right)^{\theta_W} \qquad W_{t+j} = \left( \int_0^1 \mathsf{W}_{h,t+j}^{\frac{1}{1-\theta_W}} dh \right)^{1-\theta_W} \tag{2}$$

where $\mathsf{L}_{h,t+j}$ is the amount of labor supplied by household $h$ in period $t+j$, $\mathsf{W}_{h,t+j}$ is the wage charged by household $h$ in period $t+j$, and $\theta_W > 1$. Firm $f$ chooses quantities of $\mathsf{L}_{h,t+j}$ to minimize the cost of producing a unit of $L_{f,t+j}$ given the $\mathsf{W}_{h,t+j}$, and $W_{t+j}$ is the minimum cost. All firms receive an *ad valorem* output subsidy, $s_P$. Each element of the infinite dimensional vector $\tilde{\delta}_{t,t+j}$ is a stochastic discount factor, the price of a claim to one dollar delivered in a particular state in period $t+j$ divided by the probability of that state. We use $\mathcal{E}_t$ to indicate an expectation taken over the states in period $t+j$ based on period $t$ information. The production function of firm $f$ is[6]

$$\mathsf{Y}_{f,t+j} = \frac{L_{f,t+j}^{(1-\alpha)} X_{t+j}}{1-\alpha} \tag{3}$$

where $X_{t+j}$ is a productivity shock that hits all firms, and $x_{t+j} = \ln X_{t+j} \backsim N(0, 2\sigma_x^2)$. An expression for $L_{f,t+j}$ is obtained by inverting this production function.

Relative demand for output of firm $f$ is a decreasing function of its relative price:

$$\frac{\mathsf{Y}_{f,t+j}}{Y_{t+j}} = \left( \frac{\mathsf{P}_{f,t+j}}{P_{t+j}} \right)^{-\frac{\theta_P}{\theta_P - 1}} \tag{4}$$

where $\theta_P > 1$. In equation (4), $Y_{t+j}$ is an index made up of the output of all firms and $P_{t+j}$ is a price index which is the price of a unit of the output index:

$$Y_{t+j} = \int_0^1 Y_{h,t+j} dh = \left( \int_0^1 \mathsf{Y}_{f,t+j}^{\frac{1}{\theta_P}} \right)^{\theta_P} \qquad P_{t+j} = \left( \int_0^1 \mathsf{P}_{f,t+j}^{\frac{1}{1-\theta_P}} df \right)^{1-\theta_P} \tag{5}$$

where $Y_{h,t+j}$ is the amount of the output index purchased by household $h$ in period $t+j$. Household $h$ chooses quantities of $\mathsf{Y}_{f,t+j}$ to minimize the cost of producing a unit of $Y_{h,t+j}$ given the $\mathsf{P}_{f,t+j}$, and $P_{t+j}$ is the minimum cost.

To maximize profits, a firm must set its price so that expected discounted marginal revenue equals expected discounted marginal cost:

$$s_P\left(\frac{\theta_P}{\theta_P-1}-1\right)\mathcal{E}_t\left(\tilde{\delta}_{t,t+j}Y_{f,t+j}\right)=\left(\frac{\theta_P}{\theta_P-1}\right)\mathcal{E}_t\left(\frac{\tilde{\delta}_{t,t+j}W_{t+j}L^{\alpha}_{f,t+j}Y_{f,t+j}}{P_{f,t+j}X_{t+j}}\right) \tag{6}$$

Since firms are identical,

$$L_{f,+j}=L_{+j}\quad Y_{f,+j}=Y_{+j}\quad P_{f,+j}=P_{+j} \tag{7}$$

where we omit $t$ subscripts in the rest of this subsection for simplicity. Therefore, the equalities in (7) imply that the 'aggregate production function' and 'aggregate price equation' are, respectively,

$$Y_{+j}=\frac{L^{(1-\alpha)}_{+j}X_{+j}}{1-\alpha} \tag{8}$$

$$s_P\mathcal{E}\left(\tilde{\delta}_{+j}Y_{+j}\right)=\theta_P\mathcal{E}\left(\frac{\tilde{\delta}_{+j}W_{+j}L^{\alpha}_{+j}Y_{+j}}{P_{+j}X_{+j}}\right) \tag{9}$$

When $j=0$ so that period $t$ prices are set on the basis of period $t$ information, the aggregate price equation (9) can be rewritten as

$$\left(\frac{s_P}{\theta_P}\right)\frac{X}{L^{\alpha}}=\frac{W}{P} \tag{10}$$

which states that $P$ must be chosen so that the marginal value product of labor (the gross subsidy rate over the markup parameter times the marginal product of labor) equals the real wage. We assume that the government sets $s_P=\theta_P$ to offset the effect of the distortion associated with monopolistic competition in the goods market. Under this assumption, the ratio $\frac{s_P}{\theta_P}$ equals one, so it does not appear in what follows, and the implied version of equation (10) states that the marginal product of labor must equal the real wage.

## 2.2. *Households*

A continuum of 'identical' households is distributed on the unit interval, $h\in[0,1]$. With no wage contracts, households set their wages for period $t$ based on period $t$ information, but with wage contracts they set their wages for period $t+1$ based on period $t$ information. The problem of household $h$ in period $t$ is to find the

$$\max_{\{C_{h,s},M_{h,s},B_{h,s},B^g_{h,s},W_{h,s+j}\}}\mathcal{E}_t\sum_{s=t}^{\infty}\beta^{s-t}\left(\frac{C^{1-\rho}_{h,s}-1}{1-\rho}-\frac{\chi_0 L^{1+\chi}_{h,s}}{Z_s(1+\chi)}\right)U_s \tag{11}$$

subject to

$$C_{h,s} = \frac{s_W \mathsf{W}_{h,s}\mathsf{L}_{h,s}}{P_s} + \frac{\Gamma_s}{P_s} - T_{h,s} - \frac{M_{h,s} - M_{h,s-1} + \delta_{s,s+1}B_{h,s} - B_{h,s-1} + B^g_{h,s} - I_{s-1}B^g_{h,s-1}}{P_s} \tag{12}$$

$$\mathcal{C}_{h,s} = \min\left(C_{h,s}, \frac{M_{h,s}}{P_s V_s}\right), \quad M_{h,s} = P_s C_{h,s} V_s \quad \mathcal{C}_{h,s} = C_{h,s} \tag{13}$$

$$\frac{\mathsf{L}_{h,s}}{L_s} = \left(\frac{\mathsf{W}_{h,s}}{W_s}\right)^{-\frac{\theta_W}{\theta_W-1}} \tag{14}$$

In period $s$, household $h$ chooses its expenditure on the output index $(C_{h,s} = Y_{h,s})$ and its holdings of money, $M_{h,s}$, which imply a consumption realization, $\mathcal{C}_{h,s}$ Household $h$ also chooses its wage rate in period $s + j$, $\mathsf{W}_{h,s+j}$, and agrees to supply however many units of its labor, $\mathsf{L}_{h,s+j}$, firms want at this wage where the subscript $j$ takes on the value 0 if there are no wage contracts and the value 1 if there are wage contracts. In addition, in period $s$, household $h$ chooses its holdings of claims to a unit of currency in the various states in period $s + 1$. Each element in the infinite-dimensional vector $\delta_{s,s+1}$ represents the price of an asset that will pay one unit of currency in a particular state of nature in the subsequent period, while the corresponding element of the vector $B_{h,s}$ represents the quantity of such claims purchased by the household. The scalar variable $B_{h,s-1}$ represents the value of the households's claims given the current state of nature. Household $h$ also chooses its holding of government bonds $B^g_{h,s}$, which pay $I_s$ units of currency in every state of nature in period $s + 1$. Household $h$ receives an aliquot share, $\Gamma_s$, of aggregate profits and pays lump sum taxes, $T_{h,s}$.[7] All households receive an *ad valorem* labor subsidy, $s_W$. There are goods demand, $U_s$, money demand, $V_s$, and labor supply shocks, $Z_s$, that hit all consumers. We assume that the shocks $U_s$, $X_s$, and $Z_s$ have lognormal distributions.[8] We impose the restrictions that $0 < \beta < 1$, $\rho \geq 1$, and $\chi \geq 0$.[9] $\mathcal{E}_t$ indicates an expectation over the various states in period $s$ based on period $t$ information.

According to equation (11), period utility depends positively on the consumption realization and negatively on labor supply. The period budget constraint, equation (12), states that consumption expenditure must equal disposable income minus asset accumulation. According to the first equality in equation (13), the consumption realization is equal to the minimum of consumption expenditure and adjusted real balances (real balances divided by a money demand shock). It is optimal for household $h$ to keep consumption expenditure and adjusted real balances equal to one another (the second equality in equation (13)) so that the consumption realization is always equal to consumption expenditure (the third equality in equation (13)). Each household is a monopolistically competitive supplier of its unique labor input. Relative demand for labor of household $h$ is a decreasing function of its relative wage as shown in equation (14).

Substituting equation (13) into equation (11), substituting equation (14) into equation (12), constructing a Lagrangian expression with the multiplier $\eta_{h,s}$ associated with the period budget constraint for period $s$, and differentiating yields the first order conditions for household $h$ for consumption, contingent claims, and government bonds for period $t$ and for the nominal wage in period $t+j$, $j=0$ or 1:

$$\frac{U_t}{C_{h,t}^{\rho}} = \eta_{h,t} \tag{15}$$

$$\frac{\tilde{\delta}_{t,t+1}\eta_{h,t}}{P_t} = \frac{\beta\eta_{h,t+1}}{P_{t+1}} \tag{16}$$

$$\frac{\eta_{h,t}}{P_t} = \beta I_t \mathcal{E}_t\left(\frac{\eta_{h,t+1}}{P_{t+1}}\right) \tag{17}$$

$$\chi_0\left(\frac{\theta_W}{\theta_W-1}\right)\mathcal{E}_t\left(\frac{(\mathsf{L}_{h,t+j})^{\chi}\,\mathsf{L}_{h,t+j}U_{t+j}}{W_{h,t+j}Z_t}\right) = s_W\left(\frac{\theta_W}{\theta_W-1}-1\right)\mathcal{E}_t\left(\frac{\eta_{h,t+j}\mathsf{L}_{h,t+j}}{P_{t+j}}\right) \tag{18}$$

$$M_{h,t} = P_t C_{h,t} V_t \tag{19}$$

where the condition that consumption must equal adjusted real balances is repeated for convenience. The gross nominal interest rate, $I_t$, one plus the nominal interest rate, $i_t$, must be equal to one over the cost of acquiring claims to one unit of currency in every state of nature in period $t+1$:

$$I_t = 1 + i_t = \frac{1}{\int \delta_{t,t+1}} \tag{20}$$

where the integral is over the states of nature in period $t+1$. Hereafter, we refer to the gross nominal interest rate as the interest rate and omit all $t$ subscripts.

These first order conditions have implications for relationships among aggregate variables. Since households are identical,

$$C_h = C,\ \mathsf{L}_h = L,\ W_h = W,\ T_h = T,\ M_h = M,\ B_h = B,\ \eta_h = \eta \tag{21}$$

Eliminating $\eta$ and $\eta_{+1}$ using the condition that in each period in each state

$$\frac{U_{+j}}{C_{+j}^{\rho}} = \eta_{+j} \tag{22}$$

yields the 'aggregate first-order conditions for the state contingent contracts,' the 'aggregate consumption Euler equation,' the 'aggregate wage equation,' and the money market equilibrium condition:

$$\tilde{\delta}_{t,t+1}\left(\frac{U}{PC^{\rho}}\right)=\beta\left(\frac{U_{+1}}{P_{+1}C_{+1}^{\rho}}\right) \tag{23}$$

$$\frac{U}{PC^{\rho}}=\beta I\mathcal{E}\left(\frac{U_{+1}}{P_{+1}C_{+1}^{\rho}}\right) \tag{24}$$

$$\theta_W\chi_0\mathcal{E}\left(\frac{L_{+j}^{1+\chi}U_{+j}}{W_{+j}Z_{+j}}\right)=s_W\mathcal{E}\left(\frac{L_{+j}U_{+j}}{P_{+j}C_{+j}^{\rho}}\right) \tag{25}$$

$$M=PCV \tag{26}$$

When $j=0$ so that consumers act on the basis of current information, conditions (24) and (25) can be rewritten as

$$\frac{U}{PC^{\rho}}=\beta I\mathcal{E}\left(\frac{U_{+1}}{P_{+1}C_{+1}^{\rho}}\right) \tag{27}$$

$$\left(\frac{s_W}{\theta_W}\right)\frac{W}{P}=\frac{\chi_0 L^{\chi}C^{\rho}}{Z} \tag{28}$$

Equation (27) states that $C$ must be chosen so that the utility forgone by not spending the marginal dollar on consumption today equals the discounted expected utility of investing that dollar in a riskless security and spending it on consumption tomorrow. Equation (28) states that $W$ must be chosen so that the marginal return from work must equal the marginal rate of substitution of consumption for labor. We assume that the government sets $s_W=\theta_W$ to offset the effect of the distortion associated with monopolistic competition in the labor market. Under this assumption the ratio $\frac{s_W}{\theta_W}$ equals one, so it does not appear in what follows, and the implied version of equation (28) states that the real wage must equal the marginal rate of substitution.

### 2.3. *Government*

The government budget constraint is

$$\frac{M-M_{-1}+B^{g}-I_{-1}B_{-1}^{g}}{P}=G+(s_P-1)\,Y+(s_W-1)\,\frac{W}{P}L-T \tag{29}$$

where $G$ is real government spending. We impose simple assumptions about the paths of government spending, interest payments, subsidy payments, and taxes under which we can study alternative monetary policy reaction functions.[10] In particular, we assume that the government budget is balanced period by period and that real government spending is always zero, so the government budget constraint becomes[11]

$$\frac{i_{-1}B_{-1}^{g}}{P}+(s_P-1)\,Y+(s_W-1)\,\frac{W}{P}L-T=0 \tag{30}$$

We assume that the government follows a monetary policy rule in the class

$$I = \beta^{-1} P^{\lambda_P} Y^{\lambda_Y} Y^{*\lambda_{Y^*}} \bar{Y}^{\lambda_{\bar{Y}}} M^{\lambda_M} U^{\lambda_U} V^{\lambda_V} X^{\lambda_X} Z^{\lambda_Z} \tag{31}$$

where $\bar{Y}$ is a target level of output. For rules in this class, either the price level or the money supply is the 'nominal anchor;' the sum of $\lambda_P$ and $\lambda_M$ must be non-zero in order for the price level to be determined with flexible wages and prices or one-period contracts for prices, wages, or both. We derive the optimal $\lambda_j$, the ones that maximize expected welfare. We also consider some alternative values of the $\lambda_j$.

## 3. Flexible Wages and Prices

We consider four versions of our model. To establish a benchmark, we begin by considering the version with flexible wages and prices.

### *3.1. Solution*

In each version of the model six equations are used to determine the equilibrium values of the variables. With flexible wages and prices the forms of these six equations are

$$Y = \frac{L^{\tilde{\alpha}} X}{\tilde{\alpha}}, \qquad \text{(production)}$$

$$P = \frac{L^{\alpha} W}{X}, \qquad \text{(price)}$$

$$\frac{\chi_0 L^{\tilde{\chi}}}{WZ} = \frac{L}{Y^{\rho} P}, \qquad \text{(wage)}$$

$$\beta I \mathcal{E}\left(\frac{U_{+1}}{Y_{+1}^{\rho} P_{+1}}\right) = \frac{U}{Y^{\rho} P}, \qquad \text{(demand)}$$

$$I = \beta^{-1} P^{\lambda_P} Y^{\lambda_Y} Y^{*\lambda_{Y^*}} \bar{Y}^{\lambda_{\bar{Y}}} M^{\lambda_M} U^{\lambda_U} V^{\lambda_V} X^{\lambda_X} Z^{\lambda_Z}, \qquad \text{(rule)}$$

$$M = PYV \qquad \text{(money)}$$

where we have imposed the equilibrium conditions that $C = Y$ and $C_{+1} = Y_{+1}$ and where $\tilde{\alpha} = 1 - \alpha$ and $\tilde{\chi} = 1 + \chi$. With flexible wages and prices, both wages and prices are set after the shocks are known and the only expected magnitudes are in the demand equation.

The solutions for selected variables are shown in Table 1. Substituting the solutions for these variables into the equations of the model yields the solutions for the other variables.[12]

Substituting the production and price equations into the wage equation and solving yields the solution for $L$ in equation $(T1.1)$ where $\tilde{\rho} = \rho - 1$. To solve for the price level we use the method of undetermined coefficients. Suppose that $P$ takes the form given in equation $(T1.2)$. We find $\Omega$, $\omega_U$, $\omega_V$, $\omega_X$, and $\omega_Z$ by beginning with the demand equation and eliminating $Y$ and $Y_{+1}$using the solution for $Y^*$ implied by the solution for $L^*$ in equation $(T1.1)$, eliminating $P$ using the conjectured solution in equation $(T1.2)$, and eliminating $I$ using the rule equation to obtain

$$\begin{aligned} -(\lambda_P + \lambda_M)\ln\Omega - (1 + \lambda_P + \lambda_M)(\omega_U u + \omega_V v + \omega_X x + \omega_Z z) \\ = (\lambda_{Y^*} + \lambda_Y + \lambda_M)\ln\left(\tilde{\alpha}^{-1} H^{\tilde{\alpha}}\right) + \lambda_{\bar{Y}}\bar{y} + \ln\mathcal{E}(Q_1) + (\lambda_U - 1)u \\ + (\lambda_V + \lambda_M)v + \left(\frac{\lambda_X D + \tilde{\chi}(\lambda_{Y^*} + \lambda_Y + \rho)}{D}\right)x \\ + \left(\frac{\lambda_Z D + \tilde{\alpha}(\lambda_{Y^*} + \lambda_Y + \lambda_M + \rho)}{D}\right)z \end{aligned} \tag{32}$$

where lower case letters represent logarithms, $D$ is defined in equation $(T1.1)$, and

$$Q_1 = U_{+1}^{1-\omega_U} V_{+1}^{-\omega_V} X_{+1}^{-\omega_X - \frac{\rho\tilde{\chi}}{D}} Z_{+1}^{-\omega_Z - \frac{\rho\tilde{\alpha}}{D}} \tag{33}$$

If equation (32) is to hold for all $U$, $V$, $X$, and $Z$, it must be that the $\omega_j$ and $\Omega$ take on the values given in equations $(T1.4)$ through $(T1.6)$. Substituting the solution for $L^*$ and the implied solution for $Y^*$ into the period utility function and considerable rearranging yield the solution for utility. So that we can simplify expressions by using logarithms, we express utility in terms of loss, $\mathbb{L}$, by defining

$$\mathbb{L} = -\left(\frac{C_{h,s}^{1-\rho} - 1}{1-\rho} - \frac{\chi_0 \mathsf{L}_{h,s}^{1+\chi}}{Z_s(1+\chi)} + \frac{1}{1-\rho}\right)U_s > 0 \tag{34}$$

The solution for loss is given in equation $(T1.8)$. Taking expectations of equation $(T1.8)$ yields the solution for expected loss in equation $(T1.9)$.

### 3.2. *Discussion*

We are now prepared to discuss the effects of the shocks on the variables and utility. It is clear from Table 1 that our model passes the sunrise test. With flexible wages and prices, employment, $L$, and output, $Y$, the real variables that enter utility are independent of the money demand shock, $V$, and of the parameters of the monetary rule. Expected utility is independent of $\sigma_v^2$ and depends on $\sigma_u^2$ only because $U$ enters the utility function directly.

$L$ and $Y$ depend only on the productivity shock, $X$, and the labor supply shock, $Z$. The effects of a labor supply shock are easier to analyze than those of a productivity shock. The downward sloping marginal product of labor schedule, *MPL*, and the upward sloping marginal rate of substitution (of consumption for labor) schedule, *MRS*, implied by the price and wage equations, respectively are shown in the top panel of Figure 1 in logarithm space.

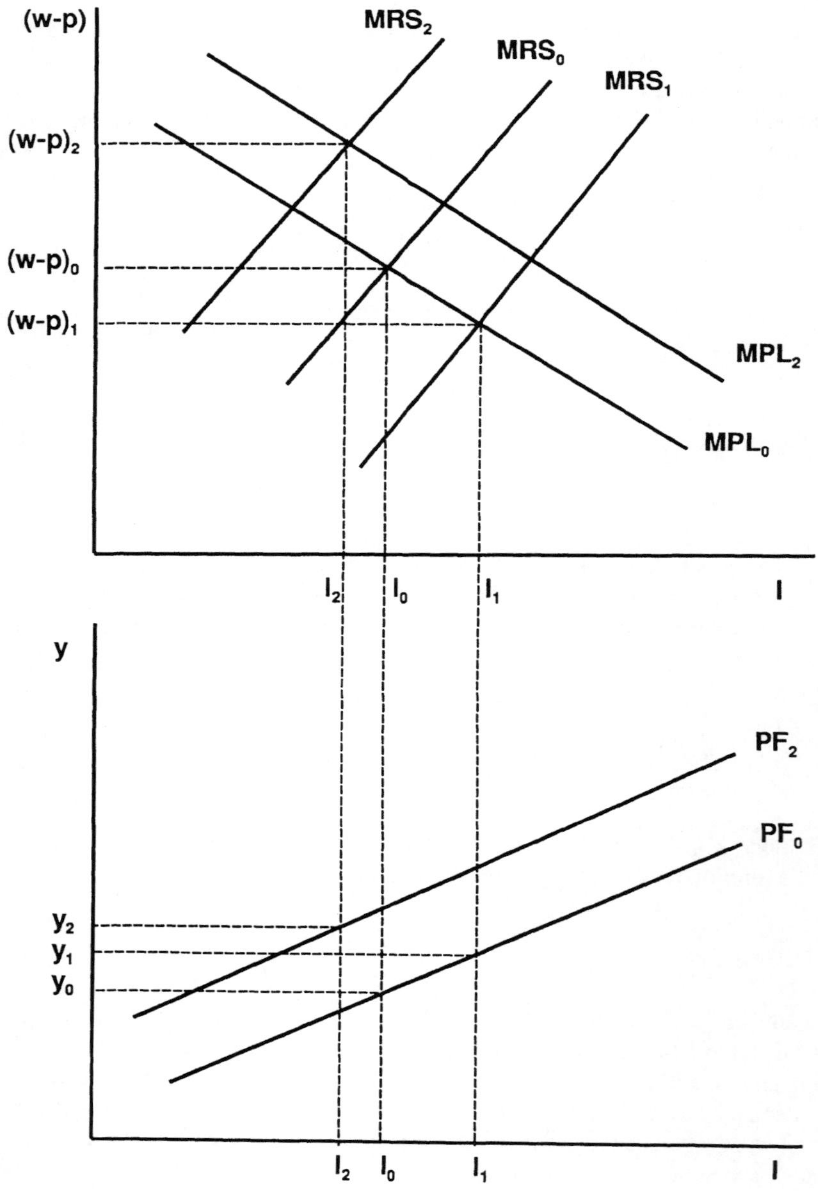


*Figure 1.* Flexible wages and prices.

*Table 1.* Flexible wages and prices.

$$L^* = H X^{-\frac{\tilde{\rho}}{D}} Z^{\frac{1}{D}}, \qquad H = \left(\frac{\tilde{\alpha}^{\rho}}{\chi_0}\right)^{\frac{1}{D}}, \qquad D = \tilde{\alpha}\tilde{\rho} + \tilde{\chi}, \tag{T1.1}$$

$$P^* = \Omega U^{\omega_U} V^{\omega_V} X^{\omega_X} Z^{\omega_Z}, \tag{T1.2}$$

$$W^* = \Omega H^{-\alpha} U^{\omega_U} V^{\omega_V} X^{\omega_X + 1 + \frac{\alpha\tilde{\rho}}{D}} Z^{\omega_Z - \frac{\alpha}{D}} \tag{T1.3}$$

$$\omega_U = \frac{1 - \lambda_U}{1 + \lambda_P + \lambda_M}, \quad \omega_V = -\frac{\lambda_V + \lambda_M}{1 + \lambda_P + \lambda_M} \tag{T1.4}$$

$$\omega_X = -\frac{\lambda_X D + \tilde{\chi}(\lambda_{Y^*} + \lambda_Y + \lambda_M + \rho)}{(1 + \lambda_P + \lambda_M) D},$$

$$\omega_Z = -\frac{\lambda_Z D + \tilde{\alpha}(\lambda_{Y^*} + \lambda_Y + \lambda_M + \rho)}{(1 + \lambda_P + \lambda_M) D} \tag{T1.5}$$

$$\ln \Omega = -\left(\frac{1}{\lambda_P + \lambda_M}\right) \ln \mathcal{E}(Q_1) - \left(\frac{\lambda_{\bar{Y}}}{\lambda_P + \lambda_M}\right) \bar{y} - \left(\frac{\lambda_{Y^*} + \lambda_Y + \lambda_M}{\lambda_P + \lambda_M}\right) \ln\left(\tilde{\alpha}^{-1} H^{\tilde{\alpha}}\right) \tag{T1.6}$$

$$\ln \mathcal{E}(Q_1) = (1 - \omega_U)^2 \sigma_u^2 + \omega_V^2 \sigma_v^2 + \left(\omega_X + \frac{\rho\tilde{\chi}}{D}\right)^2 \sigma_x^2 + \left(\omega_Z + \frac{\rho\tilde{\alpha}}{D}\right)^2 \sigma_z^2 \tag{T1.7}$$

$$\mathbb{L}^* = K U X^{-\frac{\tilde{\rho}\tilde{\chi}}{D}} Z^{-\frac{\tilde{\alpha}\tilde{\rho}}{D}}, \qquad K = \chi_0 H^{\tilde{\chi}} \left(\frac{D}{\tilde{\rho}\tilde{\alpha}\tilde{\chi}}\right) > 0 \tag{T1.8}$$

$$\ln \mathcal{E}\mathbb{L}^* = \ln K + \sigma_u^2 + \left(\frac{\tilde{\rho}\tilde{\chi}}{D}\right)^2 \sigma_x^2 + \left(\frac{\tilde{\alpha}\tilde{\rho}}{D}\right)^2 \sigma_z^2 \tag{T1.9}$$

An increase in $Z$ shifts the *MRS* schedule down from $MRS_0$ to $MRS_1$. The equilibrium real wage must fall and equilibrium $l$ must rise from $l_0$ to $l_1$. The upward sloping production function schedule *PF* is plotted in the bottom panel of Figure 1 in logarithm space. The increase in $Z$ does not affect the production function, so $y$ rises from $y_0$ to $y_1$ as $l$ rises from $l_0$ to $l_1$. An increase in $Z$ raises utility because it results in both an increase in the utility from consumption and a net reduction in the disutility of labor since we assume that $\tilde{\rho} > 0$.

Under our assumptions, an increase in $X$ increases $y$ and lowers $l$. An increase in $X$ shifts both the *MPL* and *MRS* schedules up from $MPL_0$ to $MPL_2$ and from $MRS_0$ to $MRS_2$, respectively. Under our assumption that $\tilde{\rho} > 0$, it shifts the *MRS* schedule up by more. Therefore, the equilibrium real wage must rise and equilibrium $l$ must fall. An increase in $X$ also shifts the production function to the left from $PF_0$ to $PF_2$ and by more than it shifts the *MRS* to the left because it takes more of a fall in $l$ to keep output constant than to keep households content with the same real wage. Thus, even though equilibrium $l$ falls, equilibrium $y$ rises. An increase in $X$ raises utility because it results in both an increase in the utility from consumption and a decrease in the disutility of labor.

$L$ and $Y$ do not depend on the goods demand shock, $U$, or the money demand shock, $V$. With flexible wages and prices, the model is recursive. The real variables, labor, output, and the real wage, are determined by the subsystem made up of the production, price, and wage equations. Given values of these variable, the nominal variables, the price level, the nominal interest rate, and the money supply, are determined by the subsystem made up of the demand, rule, and money equations. Neither $U$ nor $V$ enters the subsystem that determines the real variables. An increase in $U$ affects the utility of consumption and the disutility of labor in exactly the same way, so households have no incentive to change their decisions. Both $U$ and $V$ enter the subsystem that determines the nominal variables through the policy rule.

Increases in $\sigma_u^2$ $\sigma_x^2$, $\sigma_z^2$, the variances of the logarithms of $U$, $X$, and $Z$, respectively, increase expected loss.

## 4. Wage Contracts and Flexible Prices

In this section, we consider the version with wage contracts and flexible prices.

### 4.1. Solution

In this version, the price and wage equations are

$$P = \frac{L^{\alpha} W}{X}, \tag{price}$$

$$\frac{1}{W}\mathcal{E}\left(\frac{\chi_0 L^{\tilde{\chi}} U}{Z}\right) = \mathcal{E}\left(\frac{LU}{Y^{\rho} P}\right), \tag{wage}$$

The price equation is the same as in the case of perfectly flexible wages and prices, but the wage equation is different. With wage contracts, wages must be set one period in advance without knowledge of the current shocks, so the wage equation contains expectations.

As before, we solve the model using the method of undetermined coefficients. The solutions for selected variables are displayed in Table 2. The solutions for the other variables can be obtained using these solutions and the equations of the model. Suppose that solution for $L$ takes the form given in equation ($T2.1$). We find $\Xi$ by substituting the output and price equations into the wage equation and collecting terms to obtain

$$\chi_0 \mathcal{E}\left(\frac{L^{\tilde{\chi}} U}{Z}\right) = \tilde{\alpha}^{\rho} \mathcal{E}\left(\frac{U}{L^{\tilde{\alpha}\tilde{\rho}} X^{\tilde{\rho}}}\right). \tag{35}$$

Substituting in the conjectured form of the solution for $L$ in equation ($T2.1$) yields

$$\chi_0 \Xi^{\tilde{\chi}} \mathcal{E} Q_3 = \tilde{\alpha}^{\rho} \Xi^{-\tilde{\alpha}\tilde{\rho}} \mathcal{E} Q_2, \tag{36}$$

$$Q_2 = U^{1-\xi_U \tilde{\alpha}\tilde{\rho}} V^{-\xi_V \tilde{\alpha}\tilde{\rho}} X^{-(\xi_X \tilde{\alpha}+1)\tilde{\rho}} Z^{-\xi_Z \tilde{\alpha}\tilde{\rho}}, \qquad Q_3 = U^{\xi_U \tilde{\chi}+1} V^{\xi_V \tilde{\chi}} X^{\xi_X \tilde{\chi}} Z^{\xi_Z \tilde{\chi}-1},$$

Therefore, if equation (36) is to hold, $\Xi$ must take on the value in equation ($T2.3$).

*Table 2.* Wage contracts and flexible prices

$$L = \Xi U^{\xi_U} V^{\xi_V} X^{\xi_X} Z^{\xi_Z}, \tag{T2.1}$$

$$\xi_U = \frac{1-\lambda_U}{\Gamma},\ \xi_V = -\frac{\lambda_V + \lambda_M}{\Gamma},\ \xi_X = -\frac{\lambda_X + \tilde{\rho} - \lambda_P + \lambda_Y}{\Gamma} - \frac{\tilde{\chi}\lambda_{Y^*}}{\Gamma D},\ \xi_Z = -\frac{\lambda_Z}{\Gamma} - \frac{\tilde{\alpha}\lambda_{Y^*}}{\Gamma D} \tag{T2.2}$$

$$\Xi = H\left(\frac{\mathcal{E}Q_2}{\mathcal{E}Q_3}\right)^{\frac{1}{D}},\quad \Gamma = \lambda_M + \tilde{\alpha}\left(\rho + \lambda_Y\right) + \alpha\left(1 + \lambda_P\right),\quad D = \tilde{\alpha}\tilde{\rho} + \tilde{\chi}, \tag{T2.3}$$

$$\ln \mathcal{E}Q_2 = \left(1 - \xi_U\tilde{\alpha}\tilde{\rho}\right)^2\sigma_u^2 + \xi_V^2\tilde{\alpha}^2\tilde{\rho}^2\sigma_v^2 + \left(\xi_X\tilde{\alpha} + 1\right)^2\tilde{\rho}^2\sigma_x^2 + \xi_Z^2\tilde{\alpha}^2\tilde{\rho}^2\sigma_z^2 \tag{T2.4}$$

$$\ln \mathcal{E}Q_3 = \left(\xi_U\tilde{\chi} + 1\right)^2\sigma_u^2 + \xi_V^2\tilde{\chi}^2\sigma_v^2 + \xi_X^2\tilde{\chi}^2\sigma_x^2 + \left(\xi_Z\tilde{\chi} - 1\right)^2\sigma_z^2 \tag{T2.5}$$

$$\ln\left(\frac{\mathcal{E}Q_2}{\mathcal{E}Q_3}\right)^{\frac{1}{D}} = \left(\xi_U^2\Lambda - 2\xi_U\right)\sigma_u^2 + \xi_V^2\Lambda\sigma_v^2 + \left(\frac{\xi_X^2 D\Lambda + \left(2\xi_X\tilde{\alpha} + 1\right)\tilde{\rho}^2}{D}\right)\sigma_x^2 + \left(\frac{\xi_Z^2 D\Lambda + 2\xi_Z\tilde{\chi} - 1}{D}\right)\sigma_z^2 \tag{T2.6}$$

$$\Lambda = \tilde{\alpha}\tilde{\rho} - \tilde{\chi} \tag{T2.7}$$

$$W = \left(\Xi^{\Gamma}\tilde{\alpha}^{-(\lambda_Y+\lambda_M)}\left(\tilde{\alpha}^{-1}H^{\tilde{\alpha}}\right)^{\lambda_{Y^*}}\bar{Y}^{\lambda_{\bar{Y}}}\mathcal{E}\left(Q_4\right)\right)^{\frac{1}{\lambda_P+\lambda_M}} \tag{T2.8}$$

$$\ln \mathcal{E}\left(Q_4\right) = \left(\left(\frac{1}{\tilde{\alpha}\rho + \alpha} - \xi_U\right)^2\sigma_u^2 + \xi_V^2\sigma_v^2 + \left(\xi_X + \frac{\tilde{\rho}}{\tilde{\alpha}\rho + \alpha}\right)^2\sigma_x^2 + \xi_Z^2\sigma_z^2\right)\left(\tilde{\alpha}\rho + \alpha\right)^2 \tag{T2.9}$$

We can find the $\xi_j$ and $W$ by substituting the rule equation into the demand equation and collecting terms to obtain

$$UY^{-\rho}P^{-1} = P^{\lambda_P}Y^{\lambda_Y}Y^{*\lambda_{Y^*}}\bar{Y}^{\lambda_{\bar{Y}}}M^{\lambda_M}U^{\lambda_U}V^{\lambda_V}X^{\lambda_X}Z^{\lambda_Z}\mathcal{E}\left(U_{+1}Y_{+1}^{-\rho}P_{+1}^{-1}\right), \tag{37}$$

In a stationary rational expectations equilibrium with a levels reaction function $W_{+1} = W$. Imposing this restriction and eliminating $Y$, $P$, $M$, and $Y^*$ using the output, price, and money equations and the solution for $Y^*$ implied by the solution for $L^*$ in equation $(T1.1)$, respectively, and collecting some terms yields

$$\begin{aligned}
&\left(\lambda_M + \tilde{\alpha}\left(\rho + \lambda_Y\right) + \alpha\left(1 + \lambda_P\right)\right)\left(\ln\Xi + \xi_U u + \xi_V v + \xi_X x + \xi_Z z\right)\\
&\quad = -\left(\lambda_Y + \lambda_M\right)\ln\tilde{\alpha}^{-1} - \lambda_{Y^*}\ln\left(\tilde{\alpha}^{-1}H^{\tilde{\alpha}}\right) - \lambda_{\bar{Y}}\bar{y} + \ln\mathcal{E}\left(Q_4\right) - \left(\lambda_P + \lambda_M\right)w\\
&\qquad + \left(1 - \lambda_U\right)u - \left(\lambda_V + \lambda_M\right)v - \left(\frac{\left(\lambda_X + \tilde{\rho} - \lambda_P + \lambda_Y\right)D + \tilde{\chi}\lambda_{Y^*}}{D}\right)x\\
&\qquad - \left(\frac{\lambda_Z D + \tilde{\alpha}\lambda_{Y^*}}{D}\right)z
\end{aligned} \tag{38}$$

$$Q_4 = U^{1-\xi_U(\tilde{\alpha}\rho+\alpha)}V^{-\xi_V(\tilde{\alpha}\rho+\alpha)}X^{-(\tilde{\rho}+\xi_X(\tilde{\alpha}\rho+\alpha))}Z^{-\xi_Z(\tilde{\alpha}\rho+\alpha)}$$

If equation (38) is to hold for all $U$, $V$, $X$, and $Z$, then the $\xi_j$ and $W$ must take on the values given in equations $(T2.2)$ and $(T2.8)$, respectively.

### 4.2. Expected Loss

With wage contracts, the solutions for all the variables depend on the parameters of the monetary rule. In this subsection we derive the optimal rule with wage contracts and describe the effects of the shocks under that rule. Note that there is a one to one mapping from the parameters of the policy rule to the coefficients of the shocks in the solution for $L$. It is more convenient to determine the optimal shock coefficients for $L$ and then infer the optimal policy rule parameters.

The (logarithm of the) policymaker's expected loss is given by

$$\begin{aligned} \ln \mathcal{E}\mathbb{L} &= \ln K + \left(\xi_U^2 \tilde{\alpha}\tilde{\rho}\tilde{\chi} + 1\right)\sigma_u^2 + \xi_V^2 \tilde{\alpha}\tilde{\rho}\tilde{\chi}\sigma_v^2 \\ &\quad + \left(\left(\xi_X + \frac{\tilde{\rho}}{D}\right)^2 \tilde{\alpha}\tilde{\rho}\tilde{\chi} + \left(\frac{\tilde{\rho}\tilde{\chi}}{D}\right)^2\right)\sigma_x^2 \\ &\quad + \left(\left(\xi_Z - \frac{1}{D}\right)^2 \tilde{\alpha}\tilde{\rho}\tilde{\chi} + \left(\frac{\tilde{\alpha}\tilde{\rho}}{D}\right)^2\right)\sigma_z^2 \end{aligned} \tag{39}$$

The derivation of this exact expression is actually simpler than the derivation of the standard approximation.

It is more convenient to work with the deviation of the policymaker's expected loss from Pareto optimal expected loss, $\Delta \ln \mathcal{E}\mathbb{L} = \ln \mathcal{E}\mathbb{L} - \ln \mathcal{E}\mathbb{L}^*$, where

$$\frac{\Delta \ln \mathcal{E}\mathbb{L}}{\tilde{\alpha}\tilde{\rho}\tilde{\chi}} = \xi_U^2\sigma_u^2 + \xi_V^2\sigma_v^2 + \left(\xi_X + \frac{\tilde{\rho}}{D}\right)^2 \sigma_x^2 + \left(\xi_Z - \frac{1}{D}\right)^2 \sigma_z^2 \tag{40}$$

obtained by subtracting the expression for Pareto optimal expected loss in equation ($T1.9$) from equation (39).

### 4.3. Optimal Policy

It is clear from inspection that the values of the shock coefficients in the solution for labor which minimize (40) are

$$\xi_U = 0, \qquad \xi_V = 0, \qquad \xi_X = -\frac{\tilde{\rho}}{D}, \qquad \xi_Z = \frac{1}{D} \tag{41}$$

and that if the shock coefficients take on these values expected loss with wage contracts is equal to the Pareto optimal level of expected loss.

In characterizing the optimal policy rule, we assume that the policymaker adjusts the nominal interest rate only in response to the price level and the shocks:

$$\lambda_U, \lambda_V, \lambda_X, \lambda_Z \gtreqless 0, \quad \lambda_P > 0, \quad \lambda_M = \lambda_Y = \lambda_{Y*} = 0 \tag{42}$$

and that $\lambda_P$ is an arbitrary positive number. The optimal rule coefficients implied by the optimal labor coefficients are obtained by equating the expressions for the shock coefficients in equation ($T2.2$) to the optimal values of these coefficients given in equation (41) and solving for the policy rule parameters. The results are

$$\lambda_U = 1, \ \lambda_V = 0, \ \lambda_X = -\frac{\tilde{\rho}\chi}{\tilde{\alpha}\tilde{\rho} + \tilde{\chi}} + \left(\frac{\tilde{\rho} + \tilde{\chi}}{\tilde{\alpha}\tilde{\rho} + \tilde{\chi}}\right)\lambda_P,$$

$$\lambda_Z = -\frac{\tilde{\alpha}\rho + \alpha}{\tilde{\alpha}\tilde{\rho} + \tilde{\chi}} - \left(\frac{\alpha}{\tilde{\alpha}\tilde{\rho} + \tilde{\chi}}\right)\lambda_P \tag{43}$$

The model exhibits determinacy for any positive value of $\lambda_P$, so the value $\lambda_P$ can be chosen arbitrarily. Once a value of $\lambda_P$ is chosen, the values of the other policy rule parameters are determined. The policymaker should move the interest rate to exactly match any movements in $U$, but should not respond at all to movements in $V$. It should lower the interest rate if $Z$ rises no matter what the positive value of $\lambda_P$ because the marginal disutility of labor varies inversely with $Z$, so output and employment should be increased. Whether it should raise or lower the interest rate if $X$ rises depends on the value of $\lambda_P$.

An alternative way of finding the optimal rule is less direct but more elegant. If wages and prices are perfectly flexible and the policymaker follows the optimal rule for which the coefficients are given in equation (43), then for all shocks the economy is at the Pareto optimum, and the wage is unaffected. The wage result can be confirmed by substituting the expressions for the $\lambda_i$ in equation (43) into the solution for $W^*$ in equation ($T1.3$). The wage result implies that when the policymaker follows the optimal rule, the outcomes for all the variables including wages are the same no matter whether wages are preset in contracts. That is, the requirement that wages must remain constant is not a constraint that prevents attainment of the Pareto optimum. It follows that an alternative way of finding the optimal rule in the version with wage contracts and flexible prices without ever calculating the solution for that version is to find the rule that keeps wages constant in the version with flexible wages and prices.[13]

### 4.4. *Output Gap Stabilization*

If the nominal interest rate responds only to the output gap, that is, only to deviations of output from its Pareto-optimal level, so that

$$\lambda_Y = -\lambda_{Y^*} > 0, \quad \lambda_P > 0, \quad \lambda_M = \lambda_U = \lambda_V = \lambda_X = \lambda_Z = 0 \tag{44}$$

the values of the shock coefficients in the solution for labor are

$$\xi_U = \frac{1}{\Gamma_Y}, \quad \xi_V = 0, \quad \xi_X = -\frac{\tilde{\rho} - \lambda_P + \lambda_Y}{\Gamma_Y} + \frac{\tilde{\chi}\lambda_Y}{\Gamma_Y D}, \quad \xi_Z = \frac{\tilde{\alpha}\lambda_Y}{\Gamma_Y D}, \tag{45}$$

$$\Gamma_Y = \tilde{\alpha}\,(\rho + \lambda_Y) + \alpha\,(1 + \lambda_P)$$

where the subscript on $\Gamma$ indicates the special case under consideration. In this case, for example, $\Gamma_Y$ is equal to $\Gamma$ with $\lambda_M = 0$. Recall that there must always be a nominal anchor, so $\lambda_P > 0$ in $\Gamma_Y$. Clearly if $\lambda_Y = -\lambda_{Y^*} \to \infty$, the values of the shock coefficients in the solution for labor are the Pareto-optimal equilibrium values given in equation (41). That is, complete stabilization of the output gap yields the same result as the optimal policy discussed in the preceding subsection. This result makes sense because loss can be written as a function of output and shocks and because we assume that the policymaker knows the shocks and, therefore, can calculate the Pareto-optimal value of output.

### *4.5. Nominal Income Stabilization and Related Hybrid Rules*

If the nominal interest rate responds only to deviations of nominal income from a constant target value $\bar{Y}$, so that

$$\lambda_P = \lambda_Y > 0, \quad \lambda_Y = -\lambda_{\bar{Y}}, \quad \lambda_{Y*} = \lambda_M = \lambda_U = \lambda_V = \lambda_X = \lambda_Z = 0 \tag{46}$$

then the expected loss deviation is

$$\frac{\Delta \ln \mathcal{E}\mathbb{L}\mid_G^{PY}}{\tilde{\alpha}\tilde{\rho}\tilde{\chi}} = \left(\frac{1}{\tilde{\alpha}\rho + \alpha + \lambda_Y}\right)^2 \sigma_u^2 + \left(\frac{-\tilde{\rho}}{\tilde{\alpha}\rho + \alpha + \lambda_Y} + \frac{\tilde{\rho}}{D}\right)^2 \sigma_x^2 + \left(\frac{1}{D}\right)^2 \sigma_z^2 \tag{47}$$

where the superscript after the vertical bar indicates which variable is being stabilized and the subscript after the vertical bar can take on three values: $G$ for general, $C$ for complete stabilization, and $O$ for optimal stabilization.

Under complete nominal income stabilization ($\lambda_P = \lambda_Y > 0, \quad \lambda_Y = -\lambda_{\bar{Y}} \to \infty$), the expected loss deviation is

$$\frac{\Delta \ln \mathcal{E}\mathbb{L}\mid_C^{PY}}{\tilde{\alpha}\tilde{\rho}\tilde{\chi}} = \left(\frac{\tilde{\rho}}{D}\right)^2 \sigma_x^2 + \left(\frac{1}{D}\right)^2 \sigma_z^2 \tag{48}$$

Note that the more inelastic is labor supply (the larger $\chi$ and, therefore, the larger is $D$) the closer is complete nominal income stabilization to the fully optimal policy.[14]

The policy that is *optimal* within the class of nominal income stabilization policies is found by minimizing the expected loss deviation in equation (47) with respect to $\lambda_Y$. The first order condition for $\lambda_Y$ and the optimal $\lambda_Y$ and $\xi$'s are

$$0 = D\sigma_u^2 + \tilde{\rho}^2\chi\sigma_x^2 - \lambda_Y\tilde{\rho}^2\sigma_x^2 \tag{49}$$

$$\lambda_Y = \frac{D\sigma_u^2 + \tilde{\rho}^2\chi\sigma_x^2}{\tilde{\rho}^2\sigma_x^2} \tag{50}$$

$$\xi_U = \frac{\tilde{\rho}^2\sigma_x^2}{D\left(\tilde{\rho}^2\sigma_x^2 + \sigma_u^2\right)}, \quad \xi_V = 0, \quad \xi_X = -\frac{\tilde{\rho}^3\sigma_x^2}{D\left(\tilde{\rho}^2\sigma_x^2 + \sigma_u^2\right)}, \quad \xi_Z = 0. \tag{51}$$

Therefore, the expected loss from optimal stabilization of output is a positive fraction of the loss associated with the productivity shock under complete stabilization of output plus the irreducible loss associated with the labor supply shock:

$$\frac{\Delta \ln \mathcal{E}\mathbb{U}\,|_O^{PY}}{\tilde{\alpha}\tilde{\rho}\tilde{\chi}} = \left(\frac{\sigma_u^2}{\tilde{\rho}^2\sigma_x^2 + \sigma_u^2}\right)\left(\frac{\tilde{\rho}}{D}\right)^2 \sigma_x^2 + \left(\frac{1}{D}\right)^2 \sigma_z^2 \tag{52}$$

The fraction rises from zero to one as the ratio $\frac{\sigma_u^2}{\sigma_x^2}$ increases from zero to infinity.

Welfare is higher than with optimal nominal income stabilization if the policymaker completely stabilizes a combination of the price level and output in which the weights on the two variables are not equal.[15] In particular, if

$$\frac{\lambda_P}{\lambda_Y} = \frac{\tilde{\chi}}{\tilde{\rho} + \tilde{\chi}} > 0, \quad \lambda_Y = -\lambda_{\bar{Y}} \to \infty, \quad \lambda_{Y*} = \lambda_M = \lambda_U = \lambda_V = \lambda_X = \lambda_Z = 0 \tag{53}$$

then the expected loss deviation is

$$\frac{\Delta \ln \mathcal{E}\mathbb{L}\,|_O^{P,Y}}{\tilde{\alpha}\tilde{\rho}\tilde{\chi}} = \left(\frac{1}{D}\right)^2 \sigma_z^2 \tag{54}$$

The optimal hybrid policy can achieve the Pareto optimal outcomes for three of the four shocks. With only wage contracts, there are four disturbance coefficients in the solution for labor, $\xi_U$, $\xi_V$, $\xi_X$, and $\xi_Z$. When a combination of the price level and output are stabilized, $\xi_V$ and $\xi_Z$ are equal to zero no matter what the values of the rule coefficients, $\lambda_P$ and $\lambda_Y$. Zero is the optimal value for $\xi_V$, but not for $\xi_Z$, so there is some irreducible loss. The two remaining disturbance coefficients, $\xi_U$ and $\xi_X$, are independent functions of the rule coefficients, $\lambda_P$ and $\lambda_Y$, so they can be set at their optimal values by the appropriate choices of values for these coefficients. A hybrid rule can do nothing to offset labor supply shocks. The realization of the labor supply shock does not enter the solution for output and the price level because only the expectation of the labor supply equation is in the set of equations that determines the equilibrium values of these variables.

There is an alternative way of finding the optimal hybrid rule which is analogous to the alternative way of finding the fully optimal rule discussed in the subsection on optimal policy. The optimal hybrid rule in the version with wage contracts and flexible prices is the rule that would make the nominal wage invariant to demand, money, and productivity shocks ($U$, $V$, and $X$) in the version with flexible wages and prices. The solution for the nominal wage with flexible wages and prices is given in equation ($T1.3$) and with a hybrid rule the nominal wage is invariant to $U$, $V$, and $X$ if and only if the $\lambda_i$ are set at the values given in equation (53).

### 4.6. *Price Level Stabilization*

If the nominal interest rate responds only to deviations of the price from a constant target value, so that

$$\lambda_P > 0, \quad \lambda_Y = \lambda_{Y*} = \lambda_M = \lambda_U = \lambda_V = \lambda_X = \lambda_Z = 0 \tag{55}$$

then the expected loss deviation is

$$\frac{\Delta \ln \mathcal{E}\mathbb{L} \mid_G^P}{\tilde{\alpha}\tilde{\rho}\tilde{\chi}} = \left(\frac{1}{\Gamma_P}\right)^2 \sigma_u^2 + \left(\frac{\lambda_P - \tilde{\rho}}{\Gamma_P} + \frac{\tilde{\rho}}{D}\right)^2 \sigma_x^2 + \left(\frac{1}{D}\right)^2 \sigma_z^2 \tag{56}$$

$$\Gamma_P = \tilde{\alpha}\rho + \alpha + \alpha\lambda_P$$

Under complete price level stabilization, the expected loss deviation is

$$\frac{\Delta \ln \mathcal{E}\mathbb{L} \mid_C^P}{\tilde{\alpha}\tilde{\rho}\tilde{\chi}} = \left(\frac{1}{\alpha} + \frac{\tilde{\rho}}{D}\right)^2 \sigma_x^2 + \left(\frac{1}{D}\right)^2 \sigma_z^2 = \left(\frac{\rho + \chi}{\alpha D}\right)^2 \sigma_x^2 + \left(\frac{1}{D}\right)^2 \sigma_z^2 \tag{57}$$

For productivity shocks, under price level stabilization, employment and, therefore, output are more volatile than under the optimal policy. For labor supply shocks, employment and, therefore, output are less volatile than under the optimal policy.

The policy that is *optimal* within the class of price stabilization policies is found by minimizing the expected loss deviation in equation (56) with respect to $\lambda_P$. The first order condition for $\lambda_P$ and the optimal $\lambda_P$ and $\xi$'s are

$$0 = \alpha\sigma_u^2 + \left((\lambda_P - \tilde{\rho}) + \Gamma_P\left(\frac{\tilde{\rho}}{D}\right)\right)((\lambda_P - \tilde{\rho})\alpha - \Gamma_P)\sigma_x^2 \tag{58}$$

$$\lambda_P = \frac{\alpha D\sigma_u^2 + \tilde{\rho}\rho\chi\sigma_x^2}{\rho(\rho + \chi)\sigma_x^2} \tag{59}$$

$$\xi_U = \frac{\rho(\rho + \chi)\sigma_x^2}{\left(\rho^2\sigma_x^2 + \alpha^2\sigma_u^2\right)}, \quad \xi_V = 0, \quad \xi_X = \frac{\alpha D\sigma_u^2 - \tilde{\rho}\rho^2\sigma_x^2}{D\left(\rho^2\sigma_x^2 + \alpha^2\sigma_u^2\right)}, \quad \xi_Z = 0. \tag{60}$$

Therefore, the expected loss from optimal stabilization of the price level is a positive fraction of the loss associated with the productivity shock under complete stabilization of the price level plus the irreducible loss associated with the labor supply shock:

$$\frac{\Delta \ln \mathcal{E}\mathbb{U} \mid_O^P}{\tilde{\alpha}\tilde{\rho}\tilde{\chi}} = \left(\frac{\alpha^2\sigma_u^2}{\rho^2\sigma_x^2 + \alpha^2\sigma_u^2}\right)\left(\frac{\rho + \chi}{\alpha D}\right)^2 \sigma_x^2 + \left(\frac{1}{D}\right)^2 \sigma_z^2 \tag{61}$$

The fraction rises from zero to one as the ratio $\frac{\sigma_u^2}{\sigma_x^2}$ increases from zero to infinity.

### 4.7. *Output Stabilization*

If the nominal interest rate responds only to deviations of the output from a constant target value, so that

$$\lambda_Y = -\lambda_{\tilde{Y}} > 0, \quad \lambda_P > 0, \quad \lambda_{Y*} = \lambda_M = \lambda_U = \lambda_V = \lambda_X = \lambda_Z = 0 \tag{62}$$

then the expected loss deviation is

$$\frac{\Delta \ln \mathcal{E}\mathbb{L}\mid_G^Y}{\tilde{\alpha}\tilde{\rho}\tilde{\chi}} = \left(\frac{1}{\Gamma_Y}\right)^2 \sigma_u^2 + \left(\frac{\lambda_P - \lambda_Y - \tilde{\rho}}{\Gamma_Y} + \frac{\tilde{\rho}}{D}\right)^2 \sigma_x^2 + \left(\frac{1}{D}\right)^2 \sigma_z^2 \tag{63}$$

$$\Gamma_Y = \tilde{\alpha}\left(\rho + \lambda_Y\right) + \alpha\left(1 + \lambda_P\right)$$

Under complete output stabilization ($\lambda_Y = -\lambda_{\tilde{Y}} \to \infty, \quad \lambda_P > 0$), the expected loss deviation is

$$\frac{\ln \mathcal{E}\mathbb{L}\mid_C^Y}{\tilde{\alpha}\tilde{\rho}\tilde{\chi}} = \left(\frac{\tilde{\chi}}{\tilde{\alpha}D}\right)^2 \sigma_x^2 + \left(\frac{1}{D}\right)^2 \sigma_z^2 \tag{64}$$

The policy that is *optimal* within the class of real output stabilization policies is found by minimizing the expected loss deviation in equation (63) with respect to $\lambda_Y$. The first order condition for $\lambda_Y$ and the optimal $\lambda_Y$ and $\xi$'s are

$$0 = \tilde{\alpha}D\sigma_u^2 + \left(1 + \lambda_P\right)\left[\left(\rho + \chi\right)\left(1 + \lambda_P\right) - \tilde{\chi}\left(\rho + \lambda_Y\right)\right]\sigma_x^2 \tag{65}$$

$$\lambda_Y = -\rho + \frac{\left(\rho + \chi\right)\tilde{\lambda}_P}{\tilde{\chi}} + \frac{\tilde{\alpha}D}{\tilde{\chi}\tilde{\lambda}_P}\frac{\sigma_u^2}{\sigma_x^2} \tag{66}$$

$$\xi_U = \frac{\tilde{\chi}\tilde{\lambda}_P\sigma_x^2}{D\left(\tilde{\lambda}_P^2\sigma_x^2 + \tilde{\alpha}^2\sigma_u^2\right)}, \quad \xi_V = 0, \quad \xi_X = -\frac{\tilde{\rho}\tilde{\lambda}_P^2\sigma_x^2 + \tilde{\alpha}D\sigma_u^2}{D\left(\tilde{\lambda}_P^2\sigma_x^2 + \tilde{\alpha}^2\sigma_u^2\right)}, \quad \xi_Z = 0 \tag{67}$$

where $\tilde{\lambda}_P = 1 + \lambda_P$. Therefore, the expected loss from optimal stabilization of output is a positive fraction of the loss associated with the productivity shock under complete stabilization of output plus the irreducible loss associated with the labor supply shock:

$$\frac{\Delta \ln \mathcal{E}\mathbb{U}\mid_O^Y}{\tilde{\alpha}\tilde{\rho}\tilde{\chi}} = \left(\frac{\tilde{\alpha}^2\sigma_u^2}{\tilde{\lambda}_P^2\sigma_x^2 + \tilde{\alpha}^2\sigma_u^2}\right)\left(\frac{\tilde{\chi}}{\tilde{\alpha}D}\right)^2 \sigma_x^2 + \left(\frac{1}{D}\right)^2 \sigma_z^2 \tag{68}$$

The fraction increases from zero to one as the ratio $\frac{\sigma_u^2}{\sigma_x^2}$ increases from zero to infinity.

### 4.8. *Money Supply Stabilization*

If the nominal interest rate responds only to deviations of the money supply from a constant target value, so that

$$\lambda_M = -\lambda_{\tilde{Y}} > 0, \quad \lambda_P = \lambda_Y = \lambda_{Y^*} = \lambda_U = \lambda_V = \lambda_X = \lambda_Z = 0 \tag{69}$$

then the expected loss deviation is

$$\frac{\Delta \ln \mathcal{E}\mathbb{L}\mid_G^M}{\tilde{\alpha}\tilde{\rho}\tilde{\chi}} = \left(\frac{1}{\Gamma_M}\right)^2 \sigma_u^2 + \left(\frac{\lambda_M}{\Gamma_M}\right)^2 \sigma_v^2 + \left(\frac{-\tilde{\rho}}{\Gamma_M} + \frac{\tilde{\rho}}{D}\right)^2 \sigma_x^2 + \left(\frac{1}{D}\right)^2 \sigma_z^2 \tag{70}$$

$$\Gamma_M = \lambda_M + \tilde{\alpha}\rho + \alpha$$

Under complete money supply stabilization ($\lambda_M = -\lambda_{\bar{Y}} \to \infty$), the expected loss deviation is

$$\frac{\Delta \ln \mathcal{E}\mathbb{L}\mid_C^M}{\tilde{\alpha}\tilde{\rho}\tilde{\chi}} = \sigma_v^2 + \left(\frac{\tilde{\rho}}{D}\right)^2 \sigma_x^2 + \left(\frac{1}{D}\right)^2 \sigma_z^2 \tag{71}$$

The policy that is *optimal* within the class of money supply stabilization policies is found by minimizing the expected loss deviation in equation (70) with respect to $\lambda_M$. The first order condition for $\lambda_M$ and the optimal $\lambda_M$ and $\xi$'s are

$$0 = -D\sigma_u^2 + \lambda_M D\,(\tilde{\alpha}\rho + \alpha)\,\sigma_v^2 + \tilde{\rho}\,(-\tilde{\rho}D + \tilde{\rho}\Gamma_M)\,\sigma_x^2 \tag{72}$$

$$\lambda_M = \frac{D\sigma_u^2 + \tilde{\rho}^2\chi\sigma_x^2}{\tilde{\rho}^2\sigma_x^2 + D\,(\tilde{\alpha}\rho + \alpha)\,\sigma_v^2} \tag{73}$$

$$\xi_U = \frac{J}{R}, \quad \xi_V = -\frac{D\sigma_u^2 + \tilde{\rho}^2\chi\sigma_x^2}{R}, \quad \xi_X = -\frac{\tilde{\rho}J}{R}, \quad \xi_Z = 0. \tag{74}$$

$$J = \tilde{\rho}^2\sigma_x^2 + DA\sigma_v^2, \quad R = D\left(\sigma_u^2 + \tilde{\rho}^2\sigma_x^2 + A^2\sigma_v^2\right), \quad A = \tilde{\alpha}\rho + \alpha$$

The expected loss from optimal stabilization of the money supply is

$$\frac{\Delta \ln \mathcal{E}\mathbb{U}\mid_O^M}{\tilde{\alpha}\tilde{\rho}\tilde{\chi}} = \frac{\left(\sigma_u^2 + \tilde{\rho}^2\sigma_x^2\right)\sigma_u^2\tilde{\rho}^2\sigma_x^2}{R^2} + \frac{\left(\tilde{\rho}^2\sigma_x^2 + A^2\sigma_v^2\right)\tilde{\rho}^2\chi^2\sigma_x^2\sigma_v^2}{R^2} + \frac{\left(\sigma_u^2 + A^2\sigma_v^2\right)D^2\sigma_u^2\sigma_v^2}{R^2} + \frac{2\tilde{\rho}^2\left(A^2 + A\chi + \chi^2\right)\sigma_u^2\sigma_v^2\sigma_x^2}{R^2} + \left(\frac{1}{D}\right)^2\sigma_z^2 \tag{75}$$

Comparison of equation (75) with equation (52) confirms that if $\sigma_u^2, \sigma_x^2 > 0$, but $\sigma_v^2 = 0$, then the expected loss from optimal money supply stabilization is the same as the expected loss from optimal nominal income stabilization. However, if $\sigma_x^2, \sigma_v^2 > 0$, but $\sigma_u^2 = 0$ or $\sigma_u^2, \sigma_v^2 > 0$, but $\sigma_x^2 = 0$, expected loss from optimal money supply stabilization is larger than expected loss from optimal nominal income stabilization.

Although we have used our model to make clear the disadvantages of money supply stabilization, we cannot use it to evaluate claims about the advantages of this policy. In our model, all data become available simultaneously. However, in real-world economies money supply data become available more quickly than most, and it is sometimes claimed that money supply stabilization has an advantage because of this fact. In our model, the policymaker can achieve a desired value for any single variable. However, it is sometimes claimed that in real-world economies it is easier to achieve a desired value for the money supply than for some other variables.

## 5. Wage and Price Contracts

In this section we consider the version with both wage and price contracts.

### 5.1. *Solution*

In this version, both the wage and price equations are different from the case of perfectly flexible wages and prices:

$$\mathcal{E}\left(\frac{U}{Y^{\tilde{\rho}}}\right) = \frac{W}{P}\mathcal{E}\left(\frac{L^{\alpha}U}{Y^{\tilde{\rho}}X}\right), \tag{price}$$

$$\mathcal{E}\left(\frac{\chi_0 L^{\tilde{\chi}}U}{Z}\right) = \frac{W}{P}\mathcal{E}\left(\frac{LU}{Y^{\rho}}\right), \tag{wage}$$

Both wages and prices must be set one period in advance without knowledge of the current shocks so both the wage equation and the price equation contain expectations.

We solve the model using the method of undetermined coefficients. The solutions are displayed in Table 3. Suppose that the solution for $L$ has the form given in equation $(T3.1)$. We find $\Psi$ by substituting the production equation into the price and wage equations, collecting terms, and dividing the price equation by the wage equation to eliminate $\frac{W}{P}$ to obtain

$$\frac{\mathcal{E}\left(L^{-\tilde{\alpha}\tilde{\rho}}UX^{-\tilde{\rho}}\right)}{\chi_0\mathcal{E}\left(L^{\tilde{\chi}}UZ^{-1}\right)} = \frac{\mathcal{E}\left(L^{\alpha-\tilde{\alpha}\tilde{\rho}}UX^{-\rho}\right)}{\tilde{\alpha}^{\rho}\mathcal{E}\left(L^{\alpha-\tilde{\alpha}\tilde{\rho}}UX^{-\rho}\right)}. \tag{76}$$

Substituting in the conjectured form of the solution for $L$ in equation $(T3.1)$ and rearranging yields

$$\frac{\tilde{\alpha}^{\rho}\Psi^{-\tilde{\alpha}\tilde{\rho}}\mathcal{E}\left(Q_5\right)}{\chi_0\Psi^{\tilde{\chi}}\mathcal{E}\left(Q_6\right)} = 1 \tag{77}$$

$$Q_5 = U^{1-\psi_U\tilde{\alpha}\tilde{\rho}}V^{-\psi_V\tilde{\alpha}\tilde{\rho}}X^{-(\psi_X\tilde{\alpha}\tilde{\rho}+\tilde{\rho})}Z^{-\psi_Z\tilde{\alpha}\tilde{\rho}}, \quad Q_6 = U^{\psi_U\tilde{\chi}+1}V^{\psi_V\tilde{\chi}}X^{\psi_X\tilde{\chi}}Z^{\psi_Z\tilde{\chi}-1}$$

If equation (77) is to hold $\Psi$ must take on the value in equation $(T3.3)$.

We find the $\psi_j$, $P$, and $W$ by substituting the rule equation into the demand equation to obtain

$$Y^{-\rho}P^{-1}U = P^{\lambda_P}Y^{\lambda_Y}Y^{*\lambda_{Y^*}}\bar{Y}^{\lambda_{\bar{Y}}}M^{\lambda_M}U^{\lambda_U}V^{\lambda_V}X^{\lambda_X}Z^{\lambda_Z}\mathcal{E}_t\left(Y_{+1}^{-\rho}P_{+1}^{-1}U_{+1}\right) \tag{78}$$

In a stationary rational expectations equilibrium with a levels reaction function $P_{+1} = P$. Imposing this restriction and eliminating $Y$, $M$, and $Y^*$ using the production and

*Table 3.* Wage and price contracts.

$$L = \Psi U^{\psi_U} V^{\psi_V} X^{\psi_X} Z^{\psi_Z} \tag{T3.1}$$

$$\psi_U = \frac{1-\lambda_U}{F},\ \psi_V = -\frac{\lambda_V+\lambda_M}{F},\ \psi_X = -\frac{\lambda_X+\rho+\lambda_Y+\lambda_M}{F} - \frac{\tilde{\chi}\lambda_{Y*}}{FD},$$
$$\psi_Z = -\frac{\lambda_Z}{F} - \frac{\tilde{\alpha}\lambda_{Y*}}{FD} \tag{T3.2}$$

$$\Psi = H\left(\frac{\mathcal{E}Q_8}{\mathcal{E}Q_9}\right)^{\frac{1}{D}},\quad F = \tilde{\alpha}(\rho+\lambda_M+\lambda_Y),\quad D = \tilde{\alpha}\tilde{\rho}+\tilde{\chi} \tag{T3.3}$$

$$\ln \mathcal{E}Q_5 = (\psi_U\tilde{\alpha}\tilde{\rho}-1)^2\sigma_u^2 + \psi_V^2\tilde{\alpha}^2\tilde{\rho}^2\sigma_v^2 + (\psi_X\tilde{\alpha}\tilde{\rho}+\tilde{\rho})^2\sigma_x^2 + \psi_Z^2\tilde{\alpha}^2\tilde{\rho}^2\sigma_z^2 \tag{T3.4}$$

$$\ln \mathcal{E}Q_6 = (\psi_U\tilde{\chi}+1)^2\sigma_u^2 + \psi_V^2\tilde{\chi}^2\sigma_v^2 + \psi_X^2\tilde{\chi}^2\sigma_x^2 + (\psi_Z\tilde{\chi}-1)^2\sigma_z^2, \tag{T3.5}$$

$$\ln\left(\frac{\mathcal{E}Q_5}{\mathcal{E}Q_6}\right)^{\frac{1}{D}} = \left(\psi_U^2\Lambda - 2\psi_U\right)\sigma_u^2 + \psi_V^2\Lambda\sigma_v^2 + \left(\frac{\psi_X^2\Lambda + (2\psi_X\tilde{\alpha}+1)\tilde{\rho}^2}{D}\right)\sigma_x^2$$
$$+\left(\frac{\psi_Z^2\Lambda + 2\psi_Z\tilde{\chi} - 1}{D}\right)\sigma_z^2 \tag{T3.6}$$

$$\Lambda = \tilde{\alpha}\tilde{\rho} - \tilde{\chi} \tag{T3.7}$$

$$P = \left(\Psi^F\left(\tilde{\alpha}^{-1}\right)^{-(\lambda_Y+\lambda_M)}\left(\tilde{\alpha}^{-1}H^{\tilde{\alpha}}\right)^{\lambda_{Y*}}\bar{Y}^{\lambda_{\bar{Y}}}\mathcal{E}Q_7\right)^{-\frac{1}{\lambda_P+\lambda_M}} \tag{T3.8}$$

$$\ln \mathcal{E}Q_7 = (1-\psi_U\tilde{\alpha}\rho)^2\sigma_u^2 + \psi_V^2\tilde{\alpha}^2\rho^2\sigma_v^2 + (\psi_X\tilde{\alpha}\rho+\rho)^2\sigma_x^2 + \psi_Z^2\tilde{\alpha}^2\rho^2\sigma_z^2 \tag{T3.9}$$

$$W = P\Psi^{\tilde{\alpha}\rho+\tilde{\chi}+1}\left(\frac{\chi_0}{\tilde{\alpha}^\rho}\right)\left(\frac{\mathcal{E}Q_5}{\mathcal{E}Q_8}\right), \tag{T3.10}$$

$$\ln \mathcal{E}Q_8 = \left(\left(\psi_U + \frac{1}{1-\tilde{\alpha}\rho}\right)^2\sigma_u^2 + \psi_V^2\sigma_v^2 + \left(\psi_X - \frac{\rho}{1-\tilde{\alpha}\rho}\right)^2\sigma_x^2 + \psi_Z^2\sigma_z^2\right)(1-\tilde{\alpha}\rho)^2 \tag{T3.11}$$

money equations and the solution for $Y^*$ implied by the solution for $L^*$ in equation ($T1.1$), respectively, and collecting some terms yield

$$\tilde{\alpha}(\rho+\lambda_M+\lambda_Y)(\ln\Psi + \psi_U u + \psi_V v + \psi_X x + \psi_Z z)$$
$$= -(\lambda_Y+\lambda_M)\ln\tilde{\alpha}^{-1} - \lambda_{Y*}\ln\left(\tilde{\alpha}^{-1}H^{\tilde{\alpha}}\right) - \lambda_{\bar{Y}}\bar{y} - \ln\mathcal{E}_t(Q_7) - (\lambda_P+\lambda_M)p$$
$$+(1-\lambda_U)u - (\lambda_V+\lambda_M)v - \left(\frac{(\lambda_X+\rho+\lambda_Y+\lambda_M)D + \tilde{\chi}\lambda_{Y*}}{D}\right)x$$
$$-\left(\frac{\lambda_Z D + \tilde{\alpha}\lambda_{Y*}}{D}\right)z \tag{79}$$

$$Q_7 = U^{1-\psi_U\tilde{\alpha}\rho}V^{-\psi_V\tilde{\alpha}\rho}X^{-\psi_X\tilde{\alpha}\rho-\rho}Z^{-\psi_Z\tilde{\alpha}\rho}$$

If equation (79) is to hold for all $U$, $V$, $X$, and $Z$, it must be that the $\psi_j$ and $P$, respectively, must take on the values given in equations ($T3.2$) and ($T3.8$). Given the solution for $P$, the price equation can be used to obtain the solution for $W$ in equation ($T3.10$).[16]

### 5.2. *Optimal Policy and Output Gap Stabilization*

In this subsection we discuss the optimal policy with wage and price contracts. As in the case of wage contracts and flexible prices, we state the policymaker's optimization problem in terms of the labor coefficients and then infer the optimal rule coefficients. It is clear from Tables 2 and 3 that the solutions for $L$ and, therefore, the solutions for $Y$ have exactly the same form with wage and price contracts as they do with wage contracts alone with $\psi_j$, $j = U, V, X, Z$ replacing $\xi_j$, $j = U, V, X, Z$ whereever they appear. It follows that the expressions for expected loss and, therefore, the optimal values of the shock coefficients in the solution for $L$ are the same with wage and price contracts as they are with wage contracts alone. That is,

$$\psi_U = 0, \qquad \psi_V = 0, \qquad \psi_X = -\frac{\tilde{\rho}}{D}, \qquad \psi_Z = \frac{1}{D} \tag{80}$$

In characterizing the optimal policy rule, as before we assume that the policymaker responds only to the price level and the shocks:

$$\lambda_U, \lambda_V, \lambda_X, \lambda_Z \gtreqless 0, \quad \lambda_P > 0, \quad \lambda_M = \lambda_Y = \lambda_{Y^*} = 0 \tag{81}$$

and that $\lambda_P$ is an arbitrary positive number. The optimal rule coefficients implied by the optimal labor coefficients are

$$\lambda_U = 1, \quad \lambda_V = 0, \quad \lambda_X = -\frac{\rho\tilde{\chi}}{D}, \quad \lambda_Z = -\frac{\tilde{\alpha}\rho}{D} \tag{82}$$

In contrast to the results for wage contracts alone, with wage and price contracts the optimal $\lambda_j$, $j = U, V, X, Z$ are independent of $\lambda_P$. The only role played by $\lambda_P$ is to guarantee determinacy, in particular, to insure that agents can calculate the expected future price level. The contract price for the current period is set before the shocks are drawn so there can be no movements in the current price level induced by the shocks and therefore nothing for the policymaker to respond to.

With wage and price contracts, just as with wage contracts alone, complete stabilization of the output gap yields the optimal outcome and for the same reason.

### 5.3. *Simple Policy Rules*

Given one-period wage and price contracts and the list of variables we have included in the policy rule, there are really only two simple rules to consider: output stabilization and money supply stabilization. Since prices are set before uncertainty is resolved, the price level is always completely stabilized. As a consequence, stabilizing nominal income is the same thing as stabilizing output. Given the simple form of our money demand function, output stabilization and money supply stabilization have very similar implications. Stabilizing the money supply is the same thing as stabilizing output except that there is some increase in loss because shifts in money demand are not fully accommodated.

If the nominal interest rate responds only to deviations of output from the constant target value $\bar{Y}$, so that

$$\lambda_Y = -\lambda_{\bar{Y}} > 0, \quad \lambda_P > 0, \quad \lambda_{Y*} = \lambda_M = \lambda_U = \lambda_V = \lambda_X = \lambda_Z = 0 \tag{83}$$

then the expected loss deviation is

$$\frac{\Delta \ln \mathcal{E}\mathbb{L}\,|_G^{PY}}{\tilde{\alpha}\tilde{\rho}\tilde{\chi}} = \left(\frac{1}{\tilde{\alpha}\left(\rho + \lambda_Y\right)}\right)^2 \sigma_u^2 + \left(-\frac{\tilde{\rho} + \lambda_Y}{\tilde{\alpha}\left(\rho + \lambda_Y\right)} + \frac{\tilde{\rho}}{D}\right)^2 \sigma_x^2 + \left(\frac{1}{D}\right)^2 \sigma_z^2 \tag{84}$$

Under complete output stabilization ($\lambda_Y = -\lambda_{\bar{Y}} \to \infty$, $\lambda_P > 0$), the solutions for the $\psi_j$ are

$$\psi_U = 0, \quad \psi_V = 0, \quad \psi_X = -\frac{1}{\tilde{\alpha}}, \quad \psi_Z = 0. \tag{85}$$

and the expected loss deviation is

$$\frac{\Delta \ln \mathcal{E}\mathbb{L}\,|_C^{PY}}{\tilde{\alpha}\tilde{\rho}\tilde{\chi}} = \left(\frac{\tilde{\chi}}{\tilde{\alpha}D}\right)^2 \sigma_x^2 + \left(\frac{1}{D}\right)^2 \sigma_z^2 \tag{86}$$

As is clear from a comparison of equations (86) and (48), if $\frac{\tilde{\chi}}{\tilde{\alpha}} > \tilde{\rho}$, that is, if the ratio of the elasticity of the disutility of labor to the labor elasticity of production exceeds the elasticity of the utility of consumption, complete nominal income stabilization increases loss more when there are price contracts.

The policy that is *optimal* within the class of output stabilization policies is found by minimizing the expected loss deviation in equation (84) with respect to $\lambda_Y$. The first order condition and the optimal $\lambda_Y$ and $\xi$'s are

$$0 = -\tilde{\alpha} D\sigma_u^2 + \tilde{\rho}\left(\alpha + \chi\right)\sigma_x^2 + \tilde{\alpha}\tilde{\chi}\sigma_x^2\lambda_Y \tag{87}$$

$$\lambda_Y = \frac{D\sigma_u^2 - \tilde{\rho}\left(\alpha + \chi\right)\sigma_x^2}{\tilde{\chi}\sigma_x^2} \tag{88}$$

$$\xi_U = \frac{\tilde{\chi}\sigma_x^2}{\tilde{\alpha}D\left(\sigma_u^2 + \sigma_x^2\right)}, \quad \xi_V = 0, \quad \xi_X = -\frac{D\sigma_u^2 + \tilde{\rho}\tilde{\alpha}\sigma_x^2}{\tilde{\alpha}D\left(\sigma_u^2 + \sigma_x^2\right)}, \quad \xi_Z = 0. \tag{89}$$

Therefore, the expected loss from optimal stabilization of output is a positive fraction of the loss associated with the productivity shock under complete stabilization of output plus the irreducible loss associated with the labor supply shock:

$$\frac{\Delta \ln \mathcal{E}\mathbb{U}\,|_O^{PY}}{\tilde{\alpha}\tilde{\rho}\tilde{\chi}} = \left(\frac{\sigma_u^2}{\sigma_u^2 + \sigma_x^2}\right)\left(\frac{\tilde{\chi}}{\tilde{\alpha}D}\right)^2 \sigma_x^2 + \left(\frac{1}{D}\right)^2 \sigma_z^2 \tag{90}$$

The fraction rises from zero to one as the ratio $\frac{\sigma_u^2}{\sigma_x^2}$ increases from zero to infinity.

## 6. Conclusions

In this paper we construct an optimizing-agent model with one-period nominal contracts which is simple enough that we can make exact utility calculations. We evaluate alternative monetary policy rules using as a criterion the utility function of the representative agent. We focus on the two cases of (1) wage contracts and flexible prices and (2) wage and price contracts because, as we show, the outcomes in the third case, price contracts and flexible wages, are the same as the outcomes in the case of wage and price contracts for all variables except the nominal wage.

The fully optimal rule under complete information can attain the Pareto-optimal equilibrium because we assume one-period nominal contracts. We contrast the performance of the fully optimal policy with both 'naive (complete)' stabilization and 'sophisticated (constrained optimal)' stabilization of one variable or a combination of two variables. The simple rules we consider can never achieve the Pareto-optimal outcome because they imply no response to labor supply shocks. However, if there are no labor supply shocks, in a few special cases, naive and optimal simple rules are as good as fully optimal rules. Of course, in general, they are not.

A number of our conclusions regarding simple rules depend critically on the relative importance of productivity disturbances. For example, with only wage contracts, the more important are productivity disturbances, the worse are all forms of nominal income targeting and the greater the difference between the naive and sophisticated versions. Another critical parameter is the elasticity of the disutility of labor (which, of course, is inversely related to the elasticity of labor supply). For example, if the elasticity of the disutility of labor is high with wage contracts alone naive nominal income targeting performs very well but with both wage and price contracts it performs very badly.

Just how much further it is worthwhile to push the analysis of one-period nominal contract models is an open question. In this paper, we reaffirm that such models are tractable, but we show that some of their results are quite special, for example the result that if there are price contracts the existence of wage contracts is of no consequence. In Henderson and Kim (1999) we determine the effects of targeting money growth, inflation, and combinations of inflation and output on employment, output, and inflation. At a minimum, we plan to use the model of this paper to analyze the welfare implications of simple and optimal forms of these and related types of targeting.

## Appendix A

In this appendix we summarize the properties of log normal distributions that are used in this paper.

Suppose that the variable $Q$ has a log normal distribution; that is, suppose that $q = \ln Q \sim N(\mu_Q, 2\sigma_Q^2)$. Now $\ln Q^k = kq$ so $Q^k = e^{kq}$. It follows that the $E\left(Q^k\right) = E(e^{kq}) = M(q,k)$ where $M(q,k)$ is the moment generating function for $q$ and is given by

$$M(q,k) = \int_{-\infty}^{\infty} e^{kq} \left[ \frac{1}{2\sqrt{\pi}\sigma_Q} e^{-\frac{(q-\mu_Q)^2}{4\sigma_Q^2}} \right] dq = e^{k\mu_Q + k^2\sigma_Q^2} \tag{A.1}$$

*Table 4.* Price contracts and flexible wages.

$$L = \Phi U^{\phi_U} V^{\phi_V} X^{\phi_X} Z^{\phi_Z} \quad (T4.1)$$

$$\phi_U = \frac{1-\lambda_U}{F},\ \phi_V = -\frac{\lambda_V + \lambda_M}{F},\ \phi_X = -\frac{\lambda_X + \rho + \lambda_Y + \lambda_M}{F} - \frac{\tilde{\chi}\lambda_{Y*}}{FD},$$

$$\phi_Z = -\frac{\lambda_Z}{F} - \frac{\tilde{\alpha}\lambda_{Y*}}{FD} \quad (T4.2)$$

$$\Phi = H\left(\frac{\mathcal{E}Q_9}{\mathcal{E}Q_{10}}\right)^{\frac{1}{D}},\quad F = \tilde{\alpha}(\rho + \lambda_M + \lambda_Y),\quad D = \tilde{\alpha}\tilde{\rho} + \tilde{\chi} \quad (T4.3)$$

$$\ln \mathcal{E}Q_9 = (\phi_U\tilde{\alpha}\tilde{\rho} - 1)^2\sigma_u^2 + \phi_V^2\tilde{\alpha}^2\tilde{\rho}^2\sigma_v^2 + (\phi_X\tilde{\alpha}\tilde{\rho} + \tilde{\rho})^2\sigma_x^2 + \phi_Z^2\tilde{\alpha}^2\tilde{\rho}^2\sigma_z^2 \quad (T4.4)$$

$$\ln \mathcal{E}Q_{10} = (\phi_U\tilde{\chi} + 1)^2\sigma_u^2 + \phi_V^2\tilde{\chi}^2\sigma_v^2 + \phi_X^2\tilde{\chi}^2\sigma_x^2 + (\phi_Z\tilde{\chi} - 1)^2\sigma_z^2, \quad (T4.5)$$

$$\ln\left(\frac{\mathcal{E}Q_9}{\mathcal{E}Q_{10}}\right)^{\frac{1}{D}} = \left(\phi_U^2\Lambda - 2\phi_U\right)\sigma_u^2 + \phi_V^2\Lambda\sigma_v^2 + \left(\frac{\phi_X^2\Lambda + (2\phi_X\tilde{\alpha} + 1)\tilde{\rho}^2}{D}\right)\sigma_x^2 + \left(\frac{\phi_Z^2\Lambda + 2\phi_Z\tilde{\chi} - 1}{D}\right)\sigma_z^2 \quad (T4.6)$$

$$\Lambda = \tilde{\alpha}\tilde{\rho} - \tilde{\chi} \quad (T4.7)$$

$$P = \left(\Phi^F\left(\tilde{\alpha}^{-1}\right)^{-(\lambda_Y + \lambda_M)}\left(\tilde{\alpha}^{-1}H^{\tilde{\alpha}}\right)^{\lambda_{Y*}}\bar{Y}^{\lambda_{\bar{Y}}}\mathcal{E}Q_7\right)^{-\frac{1}{\lambda_P + \lambda_M}} \quad (T4.8)$$

$$\ln \mathcal{E}Q_{11} = (\phi_U\tilde{\alpha}\rho - 1)^2\sigma_u^2 + \phi_V^2\tilde{\alpha}^2\rho^2\sigma_v^2 + (\phi_X\tilde{\alpha}\rho + \rho)^2\sigma_x^2 + \phi_Z^2\tilde{\alpha}^2\rho^2\sigma_z^2 \quad (T4.9)$$

that is

$$E\left(Q^k\right) = e^{k\mu_Q + k^2\sigma_Q^2} \quad (A.2)$$

Note that if $\mu_Q = 0$, then $E(Q) = e^{\sigma_Q^2} \neq 1$ and $E\left(Q^2\right) = e^{4\sigma_Q^2}$. However, if $E(Q) = 1 = e^{\mu_Q + \sigma_Q^2}$, then $0 = \mu_Q + \sigma_Q^2$ so $\mu_Q = -\sigma_Q^2$ and $E\left(Q^2\right) = e^{2\mu_Q + 4\sigma_Q^2} = e^{2\sigma_Q^2}$. We have assumed that $\mu_Q = 0$ in order to simplify our calculations. However, we can understand why others might prefer the alternative assumption.

Now suppose that the variables $U$, $V$, and $X$ are independently and log normally distributed; that is, suppose that $u = \ln U \sim N(\mu_u, 2\sigma_u^2)$, $v = \ln V \sim N(\mu_v, 2\sigma_v^2)$, and $x = \ln X \sim N(\mu_x, 2\sigma_x^2)$. It follows that

$$E\left(U^{k_U}V^{k_V}X^{k_X}\right) = e^{k_U\mu_u + k_U^2\sigma_u^2 + k_V\mu_v + k_V^2\sigma_v^2 + k_X\mu_x + k_X^2\sigma_x^2}. \quad (A.3)$$

## Appendix B

In this Appendix we show that the solutions with price contracts and flexible wages are the same as those with wage and price contracts for all variables except the nominal wages, as can be confirmed by comparing Table 4 with Table 3. With price contracts and flexible wages the wage and price equations are

$$\mathcal{E}\left(\frac{U}{Y^{\tilde{\rho}}}\right) = \frac{1}{P}\mathcal{E}\left(\frac{WL^{\alpha}U}{Y^{\tilde{\rho}}X}\right) \quad \text{(price)}$$

$$\frac{W}{P} = \frac{\chi_0 L^{\chi} Y^{\rho}}{Z} \quad \text{(wage)}$$

Suppose the solution for $L$ takes the form given in equation ($T4.1$). To find $\Phi$ we substitute the production and wage equations into the price equation, and collect terms:

$$\chi_0 \mathcal{E}\left(L^{\tilde{\chi}} U Z^{-1}\right) = \tilde{\alpha}^{\rho} \mathcal{E}\left(L^{-\tilde{\alpha}\tilde{\rho}} U X^{-\tilde{\rho}}\right) \quad \text{(B.1)}$$

Substituting in the conjectured form for $L$ in equation ($T4.1$) in Table 4 yields

$$\chi_0 \Phi^{\tilde{\chi}} \mathcal{E} Q_6 = \tilde{\alpha}^{\rho} \Phi^{-\tilde{\alpha}\tilde{\rho}} \mathcal{E} Q_5 \quad \text{(B.2)}$$

$$Q_9 = U^{1-\phi_U\tilde{\alpha}\tilde{\rho}} V^{-\phi_V\tilde{\alpha}\tilde{\rho}} X^{-(\phi_X\tilde{\alpha}\tilde{\rho}+\tilde{\rho})} Z^{-\phi_Z\tilde{\alpha}\tilde{\rho}}, \quad Q_{10} = U^{\phi_U\tilde{\chi}+1} V^{\phi_V\tilde{\chi}} X^{\phi_x\tilde{\chi}} Z^{\phi_Z\tilde{\chi}-1}$$

If equation (B.2) is to hold $\Phi$ must take on the value given by equation ($T4.3$). Note that $Q_9$, $Q_{10}$, and $\Phi$ are identical to $Q_2$, $Q_3$, and $\Xi$ respectively except that $\xi_j$ is replaced by $\phi_j$ for $j = U, V, X$, and $Z$.

To find the $\phi_j$ and $P$ we substitute the rule equation into the demand equation:

$$Y^{-\rho} P^{-1} U = P^{\lambda_P} Y^{\lambda_Y} Y^{*\lambda_{Y^*}} \bar{Y}^{\lambda_{\bar{Y}}} M^{\lambda_M} U^{\lambda_U} V^{\lambda_V} X^{\lambda_X} Z^{\lambda_Z} \left(Y_{+1}^{-\rho} P_{+1}^{-1} U_{+1}\right) \quad \text{(B.3)}$$

Imposing the restriction that $P_{+1} = P$ and eliminating $Y$, $W$, $M$, and $Y^*$ using the production, wage, and money equations, and the solution for $Y^*$ implied by the solution for $L^*$ in equation ($T1.1$), respectively, and collecting terms yield

$$\begin{aligned}
&\tilde{\alpha}\left(\rho + \lambda_M + \lambda_Y\right)\left(\ln \Phi + \phi_U u + \phi_V v + \phi_X x + \phi_Z z\right) \\
&\quad = -\left(\lambda_Y + \lambda_M\right)\ln\left(\tilde{\alpha}^{-1}\right) - \lambda_{Y^*}\ln\left(\tilde{\alpha}^{-1} H^{\tilde{\alpha}}\right) - \lambda_{\bar{Y}}\bar{y} - \ln \mathcal{E}\left(Q_{11}\right) - \left(\lambda_P + \lambda_M\right) p \\
&\quad\quad + \left(1 - \lambda_U\right) u - \left(\lambda_V + \lambda_M\right) v - \left(\frac{\left(\lambda_X + \rho + \lambda_Y + \lambda_M\right) D + \tilde{\chi}\lambda_{Y^*}}{D}\right) x \\
&\quad\quad - \left(\frac{\lambda_Z D + \tilde{\alpha}\lambda_{Y^*}}{D}\right) z
\end{aligned} \quad \text{(B.4)}$$

where $\ln \mathcal{E}\left(Q_{11}\right)$ is given by equation ($T4.10$). If equation (B.4) is to hold for all $U$, $V$, $X$, and $Z$, the $\phi_j$ and $P$ must take on the values given in equations ($T4.2$) and ($T4.8$), respectively. The solution for $W$ is found by substituting the solutions for $L$ and $P$ given by equations ($T4.1$) and ($T4.8$), respectively, and the solution for $Y$ implied by the solution for $L$ in equation ($T4.1$) into the wage equation ($T4.10$).

## Acknowledgments

We would like to thank Jo Anna Gray, our discussant, for helpful comments and Charles Engel for suggesting that we change our specification of the objective function of firms to the current one. The views in this paper are solely the responsibility of the authors and should not be interpreted as reflecting the views of the Board of Governors of the Federal Reserve System or any other person associated with the Federal Reserve System.

## Notes

1. This assertion can be confirmed using the methods developed in Rotemberg and Woodford (1998) and imposing our assumption that subsidies are used to eliminate the output and employement distortions arising from monopolistic competition. Even when the variances of shocks are small, aproximate solutions yield incorrect welfare rankings in some models. For example, Kim and Kim (1999) show that in a model of international risk sharing a standard approximation implies that welfare is lower with a complete market than with autarky.
2. However, if prices are fixed by staggered contracts instead of by one-period contracts (or by synchronized multiperiod contracts), results depend crucially on whether wages are fixed by contracts or are flexible as shown by Erceg, Henderson, and Levin (forthcoming).
3. Even the fully optimal policy under complete information cannot attain the Pareto-optimal equilibrium if both wages and prices are fixed by staggered contracts as shown by Erceg, Henderson, and Levin (forthcoming).
4. This set includes Ireland (1997), Goodfriend and King (1997), Rotemberg and Woodford (1998), Henderson and Kim (1999), King and Wolman (1999), and Rotemberg and Woodford (1999).
5. This set includes Corsetti and Pesenti (1998), which is based on a perfect foresight model, and Obstfeld and Rogoff (1998) Devereux and Engel (1998), and the paper by Engel in this collection which are based on stochastic models.
6. That is, we assume for simplicity that there are no factors of production other than labour and no fixed costs. Kim (1998) shows that our formulation can be viewed as a model with capital in which the marginal adjustment cost for the first unit of net investment approaches infinity. Kim (1997) explores the implications of allowing for fixed costs.
7. These equal shares exhaust aggregate profits:

$$\int_0^1 \Gamma_s dh = \int_0^1 \left(s_P \mathsf{P}_{f,s} \mathsf{Y}_{f,s} - W_s L_{f,s}\right) df$$

8. That is, we assume that $u_s = \log U_s \backsim N(0, 2\sigma_u^2)$, $v_s = \log V_s \backsim N(0, 2\sigma_v^2)$, and $z_s = \log Z_s \backsim N(0, 2\sigma_z^2)$.
9. As is well known, given the form that we have assumed for the utility of consumption, as $\rho \to 1$, the utility of consumption approaches $c = \ln C$.
10. Assumptions about the paths of government spending and taxes have implications for which monetary policies are feasible and for the effects of different feasible monetary policies. For an up to date discussion of the interaction between monetary and fiscal policy and citations of other recent contributions see Canzoneri, Cumby, and Diba (1998).
11. We assume a monetary policy reaction function that implies that the expected rate of inflation, the solution for inflation in the model with flexible wages and prices when all shocks take on their mean values, is equal to zero. The analysis could be modified to allow for a nonzero expected rate of inflation. If the expected rate of rate of inflation were positive, the expected government deficit would have to be positive.
12. The properties of log normal distributions used in this paper are summarized in Appendix A.
13. Analogous logic applies in the case with price contracts and flexible wages. That is, the optimal rule with price contracts is the rule that keeps prices constant with completely flexible prices and wages. As we show in Appendix B, outcomes with price contracts and flexible wages are the same as the outcomes with wage and

price contracts for all variables except the nominal wage. Therefore, the optimal rule with wage and price contracts is the same as the optimal rule with price contracts and flexible wages.

14. This result was obtained by Bean (1983).
15. This result was obtained by Koenig (1996).
16. Of course, the solution for $W$ can also be obtained using the wage equation.

## References


Bean, C. (1983). "Targeting Nominal Income: An Appraisal." *The Economic Journal* 93, 806–819.

Canzoneri, M. B., R. E. Cumby, and B. T. Diba. (1998). "Is the Price Level Determined by the Needs of Fiscal Solvency?" Processed, Georgetown University.

Corsetti, G., and P. Pesenti. (1998). "Welfare and Macroeconomic Interdependence." Processed, Yale University.

Devereux, M. B., and C. Engel. (1998). "Fixed vs. Floating Exchange Rates: How Price Setting Affects the Optimal Choice of Exchange-Rate Regime." NBER Working Paper 6867, National Bureau of Economic Research.

Erceg, C. J., D. W. Henderson, and A. T. Levin. (forthcoming). "Optimal Monetary Policy with Staggered Wage and Price Contracts." *Journal of Monetary Economics*.

Goodfriend, M., and R. King. (1997). "The New Neoclassical Synthesis and the Role of Monetary Policy." In *NBER Macroeconomics Annual 1997* (pp. 233–283). Cambridge, MA: MIT Press.

Henderson, D. W., and J. Kim. (1999). "The Choice of a Monetary Policy Reaction Function in a Simple Optimizing Model." In A. Leijonhufvud (ed.), *Monetary Theory as a Basis for Monetary Policy*. London: Macmillan.

Ireland, P. N. (1997). "A Small Structural, Quarterly Model for Monetary Policy Evaluation." In *Carnegie–Rochester Series on Public Policy* (vol. 47, pp. 83–108).

Kim, J. (1997). "Three Sources of Increasing Returns to Scale." Finance and Economics Discussion Series 1997-18, Federal Reserve Board.

Kim, J. (1998). "Specifications of Investment Adjustment Costs in a Simple Dynamic Model." Finance and Economics Discussion Series 1998-39, Federal Reserve Board.

Kim, J., and S. H. Kim. (1999). "Spurious Welfare Reversals in International Business Cycle Model." Processed, University of Virginia.

King, R. G., and A. L. Wolman. (1999). "What Should the Monetary Authority Do When Prices Are Sticky?" In J. Taylor (ed.), *Monetary Policy Rules*. Chicago: The University of Chicago Press, pp. 349–398.

Koenig, E. F. (1996). "Targeting Nominal Income: A Closer Look." *Economics Letters* 51, 89–93.

Obstfeld, M., and K. Rogoff. (1998). "Risk and Exchange Rates." NBER Working Paper 6694, National Bureau of Economic Research.

Rotemberg, J. J., and M. Woodford. (1998). "An Optimization-Based Econometric Framework for the Evaluation of Monetary Policy." In *NBER Macroeconomics Annual 1997* (pp. 297–346). Cambridge: MIT Press.

Rotemberg, J. J., and M. Woodford. (1999). "Interest-Rate Rules in an Estimated Sticky Price Model." In J. Taylor (ed.), *Monetary Policy Rules*. Chicago: The University of Chicago Press, pp. 57–119.

# Simple Monetary Policy Rules Under Model Uncertainty

PETER ISARD pisard@imf.org
*International Monetary Fund, Washington, DC 20431*

DOUGLAS LAXTON dlaxton@imf.org
*International Monetary Fund, Washington, DC 20431*

ANN-CHARLOTTE ELIASSON ann-charlotte.eliasson@seb.se
*Stockholm School of Economics, Stockholm, Sweden*

***Abstract***

Using stochastic simulations and stability analysis, the paper compares how different monetary policy rules perform in a moderately nonlinear model with a time-varying NAIRU. Rules that perform well in linear models but implicitly embody backward-looking measures of real interest rates (such as conventional Taylor rules) or substantial interest rate smoothing perform very poorly in models with moderate nonlinearities, particularly when policymakers tend to make serially-correlated errors in estimating the NAIRU. This challenges the practice of evaluating policy rules within linear models, in which the consequences of responding myopically to significant overheating are extremely unrealistic.

## I. Introduction and Overview

This paper employs stochastic simulations and stability analysis to compare the performances of several types of simple monetary policy rules in a small model of the U.S. economy. The model, which is estimated with quarterly data for the post-1968 period, exhibits a moderate degree of nonlinearity, assumes that inflation expectations have a model-consistent component, and treats the non-accelerating-inflation rate of unemployment (NAIRU) as a time-varying and unobservable parameter. The simulation framework assumes that policymakers update their estimates of the NAIRU period by period, using their information about the macroeconomic model, and in a manner that implicitly recognizes the tendency to make serially-correlated errors in estimating the NAIRU.

The simulations and stability analysis demonstrate that several classes of rules that have been shown to perform well in linear models of the U.S. inflation process perform very poorly in our moderately-nonlinear model. These include conventional Taylor rules, as advocated by Taylor (1993, 1999a) and others; a class of forward-looking rules with a high degree of interest rate smoothing, as proposed by Clarida, Gali, and Gertler (1998); and a first-difference rule for the interest rate, as proposed by Levin, Wieland, and Williams (1999). One of the main conclusions is that rules that implicitly embody backward-looking measures of real interest rates (such as conventional Taylor rules) or too much interest rate smoothing can be too myopic to meet the stability conditions for macro models with moderate nonlinearities, particularly in a world in which policymakers tend to make serially-correlated errors in estimating the NAIRU. This finding in turn suggests, as a second main conclusion, that the propensity of economists to analyze the properties of monetary policy rules within the confines of linear models is difficult to defend as a research strategy. Linear models, in which bad policy rules affect the variances but not the means of inflation and unemployment, are fundamentally inappropriate for policy analysis because they fail to capture the fact that policymakers who allow economies to overheat significantly can fall behind "shifts in the curve" and fail to provide an anchor for inflation expectations, with first-order welfare consequences.

The paper also reports simulation results for inflation-forecast-based rules without explicit interest rate smoothing[1] and explores how their optimal calibrations vary with the degree of NAIRU uncertainty, the shape of the Phillips curve, and the nature of inflation expectations. These results support the view that optimally-calibrated simple rules can deliver attractive macroeconomic performances in small empirical macro models. Indeed, a third main conclusion is that optimally-calibrated *linear* rules in which the interest rate is a function of the inflation forecast—when applied to model-consistent inflation forecasts—can stabilize our *nonlinear* model with approximately the same welfare outcome as a strategy that explicitly optimizes the policy loss (welfare) function. However, echoing the theme of Flood and Isard (1989), we stress that policymakers face considerable difficulties in attempting to identify the true macroeconomic model and the optimal calibration for any proposed policy rule.

In recognizing the contributions of Bob Flood, it is useful to reflect on the extent to which research on monetary policy strategies has shifted focus over the past decade (Box 1). Ten years ago, the academic discussion centered on the time inconsistency problem and the issue of monetary policy credibility.[2] The rules-versus-discretion debate continued to rage, and new thinking had emerged on the roles of institutional mechanisms other than rules (e.g., independent central banks and conservative central bankers), along with reputation, as vehicles for mitigating credibility problems.[3] In this setting, Bob Flood became intrigued by the observation that central banks found it appealing to adopt simple policy rules, such as target growth rates for monetary aggregates, but to periodically modify the rules. This led to Flood and Isard (1989), which was interpreted as a contribution to both normative and positive economics.

Flood and Isard (1989) started from the premise that an optimal fully-state-contingent rule for monetary policy is not a relevant possibility in a world in which knowledge about the macroeconomic structure and the nature of disturbances is incomplete. Since simple rules (including partially-state-contingent rules) and discretion cannot be unambiguously ranked, a mixed strategy of combining a simple rule with discretion can be preferable both to rigid adherence to the rule and to complete discretion.[4] The paper showed formally that a mixed strategy under which the authorities adhered to a simple rule in "normal circumstances," but overrode the rule when there were relatively large payoffs from doing so, could increase social welfare (relative to either the case of complete discretion or the case of rigid adherence to the rule) by providing a mechanism for both enhancing credibility during normal times and allowing for flexibility when it was most needed. It was also suggested that, by establishing well-designed institutional mechanisms, society could motivate the monetary authority to

*Box 1.* Research on monetary policy: 1989 vs. 1999

**The 1989 setting**

- concern with time inconsistency
- focus on rules and other institutional arrangements for mitigating credibility problems
- interest in robustness of rules—i.e., in simple rules that perform well across the spectrum of plausible macro models

**Key points in Flood and Isard (1989)**

- Fully-state-contingent rules are not relevant possibilities in practice.
- Since partially-state-contingent rules and discretion cannot be unambiguously ranked, it seems attractive to consider mixed strategies that combine a simple rule with discretion (an "escape clause") and to establish institutional arrangements that provide incentives for policymakers not to overuse or underuse discretion.
- In evaluating a simple policy rule, it is not valid to base counterfactual historical simulations on the assumption that rational market participants would have expected the authorities to completely adhere to the rule when policymakers, had they actually been confronted with the counterfactual history, would have sometimes had incentives to deviate from the rule.

**The 1999 setting**

- consensus that simple rules cannot and should not be mechanically followed by policymakers
- notion that research can nevertheless be useful for identifying the types and calibrations of rules that are relatively attractive as guidelines for policy
- extensive reliance on stochastic simulation analysis with some attention to the robustness issue, little attention to modeling the process that the authorities use to update their information on key model parameters, and little explicit allowance for the fact that rational market participants might not find an announced rule fully credible

avoid both the overuse and the underuse of its override option. By 1990–91 such mixed strategies were referred to as "rules with escape clauses."[5]

Along with the conceptual analysis that had emerged ten years ago, a second strand of literature was oriented toward simulating and comparing the performances of different types of simple monetary policy rules in empirically-estimated models of macroeconomic behavior. A primary objective of this literature, spearheaded by McCallum (1988), was to find a simple rule that performed reasonably well across the spectrum of plausible models. Although the search for robustness seemed appropriate in the context of model uncertainty, Bob Flood recognized a serious flaw in the methodology that was typically used to evaluate how well the rules performed. In particular, as Flood and Isard (1989) pointed out, it is not generally valid to base counterfactual historical simulations on the assumption that rational market participants would have expected the authorities to adhere rigidly to a given monetary rule when policymakers, had they actually been confronted with the counterfactual history, would have sometimes had incentives to deviate from the rule. While some economies have experienced prolonged periods of stable non-inflationary growth guided by transparent and predictable monetary policy behavior, no economy is insulated from occasional strong unanticipated shocks (such as the oil price shocks of the 1970s, or the current global financial crisis) that create situations in which the pursuit of short-run economic objectives would require a departure from any simple rule that the monetary authorities might have been following, and would therefore call into question the credibility of the rule.

Compared with the situation a decade ago, the academic literature today has become more extensively dominated by simulation studies, with credibility issues no longer at center stage. The shift in emphasis has obviously been facilitated by advances in computational technology, but it also reflects changes in the practice of monetary policy along with the widespread success that the industrial countries have had in subduing inflation during the 1990s. Monetary authorities in a number of industrial countries today are pursuing strategies of inflation targeting, broadly defined to encompass objectives for both the inflation rate and output/employment. To help guide the formulation of monetary policy strategies in both the inflation targeting cases and other countries, economists at central banks and elsewhere have been generating a large volume of research that simulates and compares the performances of selected forms of simple policy rules in different macroeconometric models.[6]

For the most part, contributors to the current stream of research on monetary policy rules implicitly accept the "escape clause" notion that monetary authorities should have a certain degree of flexibility to deviate from simple rules. In particular, few economists today seriously suggest that central banks should adhere mechanically to simple policy rules. In a world in which the structure of macroeconomic relationships and the distribution of shocks is imperfectly known ex ante, central banks need to be prepared to adjust their reaction patterns, and to exercise discretion intelligently,[7] when macroeconomic behavior deviates substantially from the model on which previous reaction patterns were conditioned.

That being said, however, there remains considerable interest in analyzing how different types and calibrations of well-defined policy reaction functions would perform in hypothetical macroeconomic models, reflecting sentiment that such analysis can provide useful insights for monetary policy. Most central bankers and academic economists also believe that it is important for monetary policy to be transparent, and many have argued that the adoption of policy rules as guidelines can be helpful for communication, accountability, and credibility. Svensson (1999b) argues that this is particularly true for "targeting rules" that correspond to the first-order conditions of policy optimization problems.[8]

The recent literature on monetary rules has taken several directions (Box 2). Some researchers have sought to derive optimal rules (first-order conditions) for relatively simple macro models.[9] Others have compared the performances of different simple rules in macro models with optimizing agents.[10] Still others have looked for simple rules that exhibit robustness in performing relatively well across a spectrum of plausible macro models.[11]

A fourth approach, as reflected in the first set of simulation experiments reported in this paper, looks for insights from the somewhat different tack of exploring how the optimal calibration of simple policy rules varies with key characteristics of the macro model. This approach provides perspectives that may be useful in suggesting how policymakers should adapt the overall aggressiveness of their policy reactions, and the relative strengths of their reactions to inflation and unemployment, to the specification and parameters of the macroeconomic "model" they confront,[12] including such characteristics as the degree of NAIRU uncertainty, the degree of nonlinearity in the model, and the nature of inflation expectations.

The main conclusion from our stochastic simulations, however, relates to the robustness properties of rules that have been shown to perform well in linear models of the U.S. inflation process. In particular, we find that rules that perform well in linear models but

*Box 2.* Alternative lines of research on monetary policy rules.

**Alternative research objectives**

- identify properties of optimal rules (first-order conditions) for particular macro models
- analyze performances of simple rules in macro models with optimizing agents
- look for simple rules that exhibit robustness in performing well across a spectrum of plausible macro models
- analyze how the optimal calibration of simple rules varies with key characteristics of macro models

**Characteristics of macro models used in recent research**

- most of the models embody Phillips curves
- some assume backward-looking inflation expectations; others embody a forward- looking model-consistent component of inflation expectations
- most of the models are linear, such that policy-rule evaluation with quadratic loss functions focuses (almost) exclusively on the variances of inflation, output/unemployment, and in some cases the policy instrument (i.e., the nominal interest rate)
- some studies allow explicitly for uncertainty about key model parameters—in particular, the NAIRU—but most of these studies simply treat the implications of this uncertainty as white noise rather than extending the model to allow the authorities to update their estimates of parameters period-by-period in a model-consistent manner that mimics the policymaking process and recognizes that policymakers in reality tend to make serially-correlated errors
- almost all studies either implicitly assume that the candidate policy rules are fully credible or treat the degree of credibility as exogenous

implicitly embody backward-looking measures of real interest rates (such as conventional Taylor rules) or high degrees of interest rate smoothing, can fail to provide a nominal anchor for inflation expectations in models with moderate nonlinearities.

The analysis is developed by focusing on a small macro model in which certain key characteristics can be varied. The model resembles most of the others that have been used to analyze monetary policy rules insofar as it embodies Phillips curves as a "fixed" characteristic;[13] beyond that, the treatment of inflation expectations, the shape of the Phillips curve, and the degree of uncertainty about the NAIRU are variable characteristics.

The relevance of models that rely on the Phillips curve paradigm has been a topic of active debate in recent years.[14] Casual inference from the failure of inflation to accelerate in the United States through mid-year 1999, despite unemployment rates in the vicinity of $4\frac{1}{4}$ percent, suggests that the U.S. NAIRU may have declined over time to well below the 6 percent neighborhood in which it was thought to reside several years ago. Recent empirical work supports the view that the NAIRU for the United States has declined over the past decade, but it also suggests that a 95 percent confidence interval around the current value of the NAIRU may be as wide as 3 percentage points.[15]

Such time variation and imprecision in estimates of the NAIRU have led some economists to conclude that it is time to abandon the Phillips curve paradigm.[16] We regard this position as premature in the absence of a stronger consensus on an alternative analytic framework. It may also be noted that most industrial-country central banks continue to rely on the Phillips curve framework and to condition the nature and strength of their policy reactions on such analytic frameworks. That being said, however, a central premise of this paper is that monetary policy analysis based on the Phillips curve paradigm can be strengthened considerably by taking account of the nature of ex ante uncertainty about the NAIRU and by updating estimates of the NAIRU regularly and in a model-consistent manner—that is, by explicitly modeling the process through which the monetary authorities rationally update their estimates of the NAIRU period by period, based on new observations of unemployment and inflation along with their information about the structure of the model. This approach recognizes that errors in estimating the NAIRU tend to be serially correlated rather than white noise.[17]

In the tradition of most other recent simulation studies of policy rules, the model variants we use in this paper assume that adherence to the policy rule is fully credible; in other papers we have simulated the performances of simple policy rules under a crude but empirically-based representation of imperfect and endogenous credibility.[18] We demonstrate, however, that analysis based on the full credibility assumption is internally consistent in the following limited sense: When the macro model is well defined and known to the policymaker, when inflation expectations are either backward looking or model consistent, and when institutional arrangements motivate the policymaker to optimize over a long horizon, then the realized means and variances of inflation and unemployment are essentially independent of the loss-function parameter to which the credibility problem has traditionally been ascribed, so the announced calibration of a simple rule is time consistent. While this might be taken to justify the assumption that adherence to the announced calibration of the rule is fully credible, it does not generally imply—in a stochastic world with nonlinear behavior—that the prospect of achieving the inflation target embodied in the monetary policy rule is fully credible.

These considerations suggest that if policymakers are motivated by appropriate institutional arrangements cum reputation, credibility problems can be primarily attributed to the shortcomings of the analytic frameworks on which policies are based—that is, to the limitations of the authorities' understanding of macroeconomic behavior. By the same token, they emphasize that institutional arrangements (commitment mechanisms) alone cannot make announced policy objectives fully credible when the authorities have imperfect information about the nature of macroeconomic behavior. Thus, although a number of simulation studies have now shown that simple policy rules, when optimally calibrated, are capable of generating an impressive degree of macroeconomic stability in well-defined macro models,[19] economists should not be quick to take comfort in these results. Such findings need to be weighed against the realization that policymakers confront difficulties in trying to arrive at optimal calibrations of policy rules when the "true" macro model is not well defined, and even more so, against analysis suggesting that several rules that have been advocated on the basis of good performances in linear models perform very poorly in models with moderate nonlinearities.

The remainder of the paper is structured as follows. Section II presents the equations and estimated parameters of the base-case model, along with details on the other model variants. The model describes a closed economy and is estimated with quarterly data for the United States. It includes: short-run Phillips curves that link observed inflation rates (for the CPI and the CPI excluding food and energy) to both the expected rate of inflation and the gap between the NAIRU and the observed unemployment rate; an equation describing the behavior of survey data on inflation expectations; a description of the dynamics of the unemployment rate as a function of the real interest rate; and a model-consistent process for generating and updating estimates of the NAIRU. We consider several model variants (linear and nonlinear short-run Phillips curves paired with forward- and backward-looking inflation expectations), each of which is consistent with the long-run natural rate hypothesis. The incorporation of uncertainty is limited to simple additive uncertainty about the NAIRU and ex ante uncertainty about various exogenous shocks in an environment where all model parameters and frequency distributions of shocks are known and dynamic learning occurs only through the process of updating estimates of the NAIRU.

Section III describes the simple policy rules, the loss function, the monetary authority's behavior, and the stochastic simulation framework. We distinguish between two classes of inflation forecast based (IFB) rules: IFB1 rules, in which a forward-looking measure of the real interest rate—in particular, a measure that embodies a model-consistent inflation forecast—is adjusted in response to both the deviation of inflation from target and a measure of the unemployment gap; and IFB2 rules, in which the same measure of the real interest rate is adjusted in response to deviations of an inflation forecast from target as well as the unemployment gap. Most of our simulations involve IFB1 rules. The Monte Carlo experiments employ a conventional quadratic loss function in searching for the optimal calibrations of the simple policy rules, but we focus in addition on a longer list of performance indicators, including the standard deviations of the unemployment, inflation, and the nominal interest rate and, for the nonlinear model variants, also the means of the unemployment and inflation rates.

Section IV reports the simulation results, which are presented in two subsections, each addressing a different set of issues. Subsection IV.A describes and compares the optimal calibrations of IFB1 rules under different well-defined model variants. In particular, it explores how the optimal calibrations of these rules depend on policy preferences, the degree of NAIRU uncertainty, the extent to which inflation expectations are backward looking, and the shape of the Phillips curve.

Subsection IV.B then addresses several specific rules that have been proposed in the literature and compares their performances with the performances of optimally calibrated IFB1 rules. The additional rules on which we focus are: (i) Taylor's (1993, 1999a) conventional Taylor rule; (ii) an inflation-forecast-based rule with interest rate smoothing, as estimated for the United States by Clarida, Gali, and Gertler (1998); (iii) the IFB2 rule analyzed by Isard and Laxton (1998); and (iv) a first-difference rule for the interest rate, as proposed by Levin, Wieland, and Williams (1999). The stochastic simulation results, supplemented by stability analysis (Appendix II), demonstrate that in a world in which inflation expectations have a forward-looking model-consistent component, monetary policy guided by a myopic rule that incorporates a backward-looking measure of the real interest rate, such as a conventional Taylor rule, can be destabilizing in our moderately nonlinear model. Similarly, rules with high degrees of interest rate smoothing, such as certain calibrations of forward-looking Clarida, Gali, and Gertler (CGG) rules and the first-difference rule proposed by Levin, Wieland, and Williams (LWW), can lead to instability in our model.

Section V summarizes the key messages of the paper.

## II. A Model of the Unemployment-Inflation Process

Our model is a somewhat extended version of the framework developed in Laxton, Rose, and Tambakis (1999). It includes four estimated equations: two Phillips curves (one focusing on the CPI, the other on the CPI excluding food and energy), an equation describing the dynamics of inflation expectations, and an equation describing the dynamics of the unemployment rate. The inclusion of two Phillips curves allows us to exploit a larger data set when drawing inferences about the NAIRU. The model estimates are based on quarterly data for the United States over the period since 1968:Q1. The model is closed with a monetary policy reaction function and a model-consistent procedure for updating estimates of the NAIRU (both described in Section III). In the "base-case" version of the model, the Phillips curve specifications are convex and inflation expectations include a forward-looking model-consistent component. Other model variants include linear Phillips curves and entirely-backward-looking inflation expectations.

### A. *The Short-Run Phillips Curves*

The convex versions of our Phillips curves are broadly similar to the specification used in Debelle and Laxton (1997):

$$\pi_t = \lambda\bar{\pi}_t^e + (1-\lambda)\pi_{t-1} + \gamma(u_t^* - u_t)/(u_t - \phi_t) + \epsilon_t^{\pi} \quad (1)$$

$$\pi_t^x = \lambda^x\bar{\pi}_t^e + (1-\lambda^x)\pi_{t-1}^x + \gamma(u_t^* - u_t)/(u_t - \phi_t) + \epsilon_t^{\pi^x} \quad (2)$$

where

$$\bar{\pi}_t^e = \left(\sum_{i=1}^{N} E_{t-i}\pi 4_{t+4-i}\right)/N \quad (3)$$

Here $\pi_t$ denotes the rate of consumer price inflation during quarter $t$, measured at an annual rate; $\pi 4_{t+4}$ denotes the rate of inflation over the year through quarter $t+4$; $E_t\pi 4_{t+4}$ is the public's expectation in quarter $t$ of the rate of inflation over the year through quarter $t+4$; $\pi_t^x$ denotes the annualized rate of change during quarter $t$ of the consumer price index excluding food and energy; $u$ is the unemployment rate; and $\lambda$, $\lambda^x$, and $\gamma$ are parameters to be estimated. ($u^*$ and $\phi$ will be defined below.)

The model of how expectations influence inflation dynamics is meant to reflect a bargaining framework that is capable of generating significant persistence in the inflation process.[20] The implicit underlying assumption is that a standard contract has an $N$-quarter horizon, with one-$N$th of the contracts respecified every quarter.[21] Thus, equation (3) defines $\bar{\pi}_t^e$ as an average of one-year ahead inflation expectations that economic agents held during the $N$ quarters in which currently-prevailing contracts were written. Inflation dynamics are also assumed to depend on the lagged inflation rate, which can be viewed as a summary indicator of the strength of incentives to incur the costs of revising price or wage contracts before their specified expiration dates.

Note that the coefficients on the first two right-hand-side terms in equations (1) and (2) are constrained to sum to unity, consistent with the long-run natural rate hypothesis. We

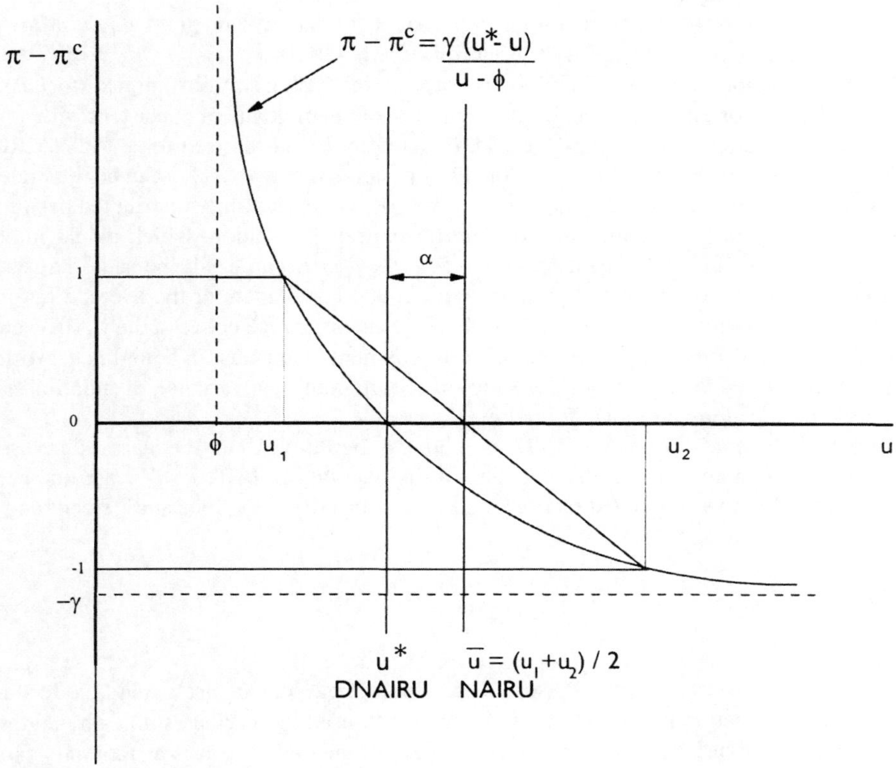


*Figure 1.* The convex Phillips curve.

refer to the sums of these terms as the core rates of inflation, $\pi^c$ and $\pi^{cx}$.

$$\pi_t^c = \lambda \bar{\pi}_t^e + (1 - \lambda)\pi_{t-1} \tag{4}$$

$$\pi_t^{cx} = \lambda^x \bar{\pi}_t^e + (1 - \lambda^x)\pi_{t-1} \tag{5}$$

Figure 1 plots the difference between observed inflation and core inflation (vertical axis) against the unemployment rate (horizontal axis). For purposes of the discussion here, we interpret core inflation as synonymous with expected inflation, so the figure can be viewed as an expectations-augmented Phillips curve. Consistent with the specification in equation (1), the short-run Phillips curve is convex with horizontal asymptote at $\pi - \pi^c = -\gamma$ and vertical asymptote at $u = \phi$. Following Laxton, Meredith, and Rose (1995), $\phi$ can be interpreted as a "wall parameter," reflecting short-run constraints on how far rising aggregate demand can lower unemployment before capacity constraints become absolutely binding and inflationary pressure becomes unbounded. The magnitude of $u^*$ corresponds to the unemployment rate at which actual inflation and expected inflation coincide, such that there would be no systematic pressure for inflation to rise or fall *in the absence of stochastic shocks*.

This corresponds to the non-accelerating-inflation rate of unemployment in a *deterministic* world. We refer to $u^*$ as the DNAIRU (deterministic NAIRU).[22]

An important point is that the DNAIRU is not a feasible stable equilibrium in a *stochastic* world with a convex Phillips curve. The average rate of unemployment consistent with non-accelerating-inflation in a stochastic world, denoted by $\bar{u}$ and referred to as the NAIRU, must be greater than the DNAIRU when the Phillips curve is convex. This can be illustrated in Figure 1 by assuming that actual inflation turned out to be uniformly distributed between plus and minus one percentage point of core (or expected) inflation, which would imply an average rate of unemployment of $\bar{u} = 0.5(u_1 + u_2)$. It can easily be seen that with a wider distribution of the actual inflation rate around core inflation, the average rate of unemployment would be even greater. The fact that the difference between the NAIRU and DNAIRU—and hence the average rate of unemployment—depends, in a nonlinear world, on the degree to which the authorities succeed in mitigating the variance of inflation has important implications for monetary policy.

Following Debelle and Laxton (1997) and others, the Phillips curve equations are estimated jointly with an equation that describes a time-varying DNAIRU.[23] We assume here that the latter follows a bounded random walk and arbitrarily set a floor at 4 percent and a ceiling at 8 percent, such that

$$u_t^* = \begin{cases} 8 & \text{if } u_{t-1}^* + \epsilon_t^{u^*} \geq 8 \\ 4 & \text{if } u_{t-1}^* + \epsilon_t^{u^*} \leq 4 \\ u_{t-1}^* + \epsilon_t^{u^*} & \text{otherwise} \end{cases} \tag{6}$$

where $\epsilon_t^{u^*}$ is drawn from a normal distribution with mean zero. We also extend the formulation of the estimation problem beyond the approach used in previous studies by adding the assumptions that the business cycle component of unemployment is a stationary (and presumably highly autocorrelated) process, $\epsilon_t^u$, and that the difference between the NAIRU and the DNAIRU is a constant:[24]

$$u_t = \bar{u}_t + \epsilon_t^u \tag{7}$$

$$\alpha = \bar{u}_t - u_t^* \tag{8}$$

If we rewrite equations (1) and (2) for heuristic purposes as

$$\pi_t - \pi_t^c = \delta_t\,[1/(u_t - \phi_t)] - \gamma\,[u_t/(u_t - \phi_t)] + \epsilon_t^\pi \tag{9}$$

$$\pi_t^x - \pi_t^{cx} = \delta_t\,[1/(u_t - \phi_t)] - \gamma\,[u_t/(u_t - \phi_t)] + \epsilon_t^{\pi^x} \tag{10}$$

where $\delta_t = \gamma u_t^*$ is a time-varying parameter, equations (6)–(10) provide a nonlinear estimation problem that can be solved using the Kalman filter technique.[25]

Table 1 reports the estimation results. The estimated parameters of the Phillips curves have the correct signs and are statistically significant. The gap between the NAIRU and the DNAIRU is estimated to be two-tenths of a percentage point. To remain consistent with these parameter estimates, the Phillips curves that are used in analyzing the linear variants of the model are calibrated as:[26]

$$\pi_t = \pi_t^c + 0.80(u_t^* - u_t) + \epsilon_t^\pi \tag{1a}$$

$$\pi_t^x = \pi_t^{cx} + 0.80(u_t^* - u_t) + \epsilon_t^{\pi^x} \tag{2a}$$

*Table 1.* Phillips curves and the time-varying NAIRU.

Estimated equations: 1/

$$\pi_t = 3.20(u_t^* - u_t)/(u_t - \phi_t) + 0.41\bar{\pi}_t^e + (1 - 0.41)\pi_{t-1}$$
$$\quad (9.39) \qquad\qquad (6.97)$$

$$\pi_t^x = 3.20(u_t^* - u_t)/(u_t - \phi_t) + 0.64\bar{\pi}_t^e + (1 - 0.64)\pi_{t-1}^x$$
$$\quad (9.39) \qquad\qquad (9.59)$$

$$\bar{u}_t = 0.20 + u_t^*$$
$$\quad (0.30)$$

$$u_t^* = u_{t-1}^* + \epsilon_t^{u^*}$$

Variables:

| | |
|---|---|
| $\pi_t$ | Percent change in consumer price index, quarterly at annual rate. |
| $\pi_t^x$ | Percent change in CPI excluding food and energy. |
| $\bar{\pi}_t^e$ | Expected inflation rate based on equation (3) with $N = 12$. |
| $\phi_t$ | Time-varying "wall parameter"—see text. |
| $u_t^*$ | Unobserved DNAIRU as estimated from the Kalman filter. |
| $\bar{u}_t$ | Estimated NAIRU. |

1/ $t$-values in parentheses.

## B. *The Dynamics of Inflation Expectations*

Within the sample period over which the Phillips curves are estimated, inflation expectations are based on the mean responses from the Michigan survey of expectations about one-year-ahead changes in the consumer price index. For purposes of the simulation analysis, however, we require a model of how expectations evolve. An important issue is the extent to which expectations are forward looking and model consistent.

The approach here, following Laxton, Rose, and Tambakis (1999), is based on an investigation of three alternative equations for explaining the historical survey data. The different specifications are described in Table 2. The first two include a forward-looking model-consistent component, $\pi 4^{mc}$, which was constructed from a proxy for the model—namely, as the fitted values of an auxiliary equation that predicts observed inflation over the year ahead using four lagged values each of the unemployment rate, a long-term interest rate, the survey measure of inflation expectations, and the inflation rate.

As can be seen from Table 2, the constrained model has almost the same fit as the basic unconstrained model and slightly outperforms the overfitted model with inflation lags. The latter result indicates that, conditional on the presence of the forward-looking proxy, the estimation prefers the lagged dependent variable to lagged data on observed inflation. This suggests that expectations are not inherently backward looking; the lags of inflation are

*Table 2.* Dynamics of inflation expectations.

Estimated equation:

$$E_t\pi 4_{t+4} = \alpha + \delta_1 \pi 4_t^{mc} + \delta_2 E_{t-1}\pi 4_{t+3} + \rho_1 \pi_{t-1} + \rho_2 \pi_{t-2} + \rho_3 \pi_{t-3} + \rho_4 \pi_{t-4}$$

$E_t\pi 4_{t+4}$ Expected inflation, CPI, one-year-ahead measure from the Michigan survey

$\pi 4_t^{mc}$ Fitted values from auxiliary regression to forecast one-year-ahead CPI inflation

$\pi_t$ Inflation, CPI, quarterly measure at annual rate

Estimation period 1968:Q1 to 1997:Q2

| Coefficient | Basic Model Unconstrained | Constrained ($\delta_2 = 1 - \delta_1$) | Overfitted, With Inflation Lags |
|---|---|---|---|
| $\alpha$ | | | 0.470 (2.3) |
| $\delta_1$ | 0.258 (3.8) | 0.261 (3.8) | 0.346 (4.5) |
| $\delta_2$ | 0.726 (10.5) | | |
| $\rho_1$ | | | −0.092 (1.7) |
| $\rho_2$ | | | −0.072 (1.2) |
| $\rho_3$ | | | 0.076 (1.2) |
| $\rho_4$ | | | 0.011 (0.2) |
| $\bar{R}^2$ | 0.743 | 0.745 | 0.732 |
| DW statistic | 2.33 | 2.35 | 2.27 |
| Residual variance | 1.08 | 1.08 | 1.03 |

Note: Figures in parentheses are $t$-statistics.

useful in explaining the expectations data only to the extent that they help predict the future, as reflected in their contribution to $\pi 4^{mc}$. The estimates also point to substantial inertia in inflation expectations, as reflected in a relatively high coefficient on the lagged dependent variable.

In light of the estimates reported in Table 2, most of our simulation analysis reflects the following base-case assumption about inflation expectations:

$$E_t\pi 4_{t+4} = 0.261\, \pi 4_t^{mc} + 0.739 E_{t-1}\pi 4_{t+3} + \epsilon_t^{\pi^e} \tag{11}$$

As alternatives, we also consider a fairly traditional forward-and-backward-looking components model with equal weights of 0.5 on the forward-and-backward-looking components,[27] along with two extreme cases in which inflation expectations are entirely backward looking and entirely forward looking. These correspond, respectively, to the following specifications:

$$E_t\pi 4_{t+4} = 0.5\pi 4_{t+4}^{mc} + 0.5\pi 4_{t-1} + \epsilon_t^{\pi^e} \tag{11a}$$

$$E_t\pi 4_{t+4} = \pi 4_{t-1} \tag{11b}$$

$$E_t\pi 4_{t+4} = \pi 4_{t+4}^{mc} \tag{11c}$$

Specification (11), which we consider more realistic than the other three, presents a case in which shocks to inflation expectations can be more persistent than under the traditional forward-and-backward-looking components model, thereby presenting a more difficult challenge for monetary policy.

### C. *The Dynamics of the Unemployment Rate*

We draw again on Laxton, Rose, and Tambakis (1999) in modeling the behavior of the unemployment rate, which reflects the influence of monetary policy as transmitted through aggregate demand. The estimated equation has the form

$$u_t = c_t + \sum_{i=1}^{2} \eta_i u_{t-i} + \sum_{i=1}^{3} \phi_i r_{t-i} + \epsilon_t^u \tag{12}$$

where

$$r_t = rs_t - E_t \pi 4_{t+4} \tag{13}$$

is our measure of the real interest rate.[28] The time-varying "constant," $c_t$, is assumed to follow a random walk to capture the combined effects of any changes in the trend levels of unemployment and the real interest rate.

Table 3 reports the fit of equation (12), which is also estimated using a Kalman filter. The lag structure is written in its final form, following testing down from specifications with longer lags.[29] The results reflect two stylized facts concerning the monetary authority's ability to control the economy. First, there are important lags between changes in interest rates and their effects on aggregate demand. Second, there is persistence in movements in the unemployment rate, implying that shocks to aggregate demand propagate into future periods. The coefficients on the unemployment lags imply some augmenting propagation, but with relatively speedy reversion to the mean.[30]

## III. The Policy Rules and Stochastic Simulation Framework

### A. *The Simple Policy Rules*

We focus on several classes of simple policy rules. Part of the motivation for focusing on simple forms of policy reaction functions is pragmatic; particularly in the nonlinear variants of our model, the task of deriving the optimal rule associated with conventional specifications of policy loss functions would be horrendous. In addition, simple classes of rules are transparent and relatively appealing to policymakers.

Most prominent among the simple policy rules that have received attention in the recent literature are conventional Taylor rules. Under Taylor rules the monetary authorities adjust the short-term nominal interest rate in response to both the deviation of the current inflation rate from target and either the deviation of current output from potential output or the deviation of unemployment from the NAIRU.[31] The conventional specification of Taylor rules, when expressed in terms of the unemployment gap, is:

$$rs_t = r^* + \pi 4_t + w_\pi(\pi 4_t - \pi^{TAR}) + w_u(\bar{u}_t - u_t) \tag{14}$$

*Table 3.* Dynamics of the unemployment rate.

Unemployment rate equation

$$u_t = c_t + \sum_{i=1}^{2} \eta_i u_{t-i} + \sum_{i=1}^{3} \phi_i r_{t-i} + \epsilon_t^u$$
$$c_t = c_{t-1} + \epsilon_t^c$$

Real federal funds rate

$$r_t = rs_t - E_t \pi 4_{t+4}$$

$u_t$ unemployment rate

$rs_t$ federal funds rate

$E_t \pi 4_{t+4}$ expected inflation over the next year from the Michigan survey

$c_t$ time-varying parameter estimated using Kalman-filtering methods

Estimation period: 1968:Q1 to 1998:Q2

| Coefficient | Estimate | $t$-ratio |
|---|---|---|
| $\eta_1$ | 1.027 | 11.6 |
| $\eta_2$ | −0.258 | 2.9 |
| $\phi_1$ | 0.010 | 0.6 |
| $\phi_2$ | 0.034 | 1.8 |
| $\phi_3$ | 0.023 | 1.2 |
| Residual variance | 0.0285 | |
| Log likelihood | −28.96 | |

where: $rs_t$ is the nominal interest rate setting at time $t$; $\pi 4_t$ and $u_t$ represent the rates of inflation and unemployment; $\pi^{TAR}$ denotes a target rate of inflation; $\bar{u}_t$ is the authorities' estimate of the NAIRU based on observed data through period $t - 1$; $r^*$ is a constant corresponding to the equilibrium real interest rate; and $w_\pi$ and $w_u$ are parameters.

Note that, in the second term on the right-hand side of (14), the inflation rate over the four quarters through period $t$ appears as a backward-looking measure of the expected rate of inflation. As discussed below, in the context of our moderately nonlinear model of the U.S. economy, the precise form of the rule suggested by Taylor (1993, 1998, 1999a) is a very myopic rule that in some situations is not sufficient to ensure stability in the inflation process.[32]

The second class of rules that we examine—which can be regarded as a class of inflation forecast based (IFB) rules that we refer to as IFB1 rules—replaces the second term in equation (14) with a model-consistent measure of inflation expectations. Specifically, IFB1 rules can be written in the general form:

$$\tilde{r}_t = r^* + \tilde{E}_t \left\{ w_\pi (\pi 4_t - \pi^{TAR}) + w_u (\bar{u}_t - u_t) \mid \Omega_t \right\} \tag{15}$$

where

$$\tilde{r}_t = rs_t - \tilde{E}_t \left\{ E_t \pi 4_{t+4} \mid \Omega_t \right\} \tag{16}$$

Here $\tilde{r}_t$ is the monetary authority's ex ante measure of the real interest rate on which aggregate demand and unemployment depend; $E_t\pi 4_{t+4}$ denotes the public's expectation at time $t$ of the inflation rate over the year ahead; and $\tilde{E}_t\{|\ \Omega_t\}$ denotes a model-consistent forecast at time $t$ based on the authorities' information set $\Omega_t$, which includes information about the model along with the observed values of the inflation rate through quarter $t$ and all other economic variables through quarter $t-1$.

Note that the IFB1 rule is specified in the form of a rule for real interest rate adjustment. Although monetary policy operates by setting the nominal interest rate, in our model (and most others) the extent to which monetary policy adjustment stimulates or restrains aggregate demand and employment depends on the real interest rate. It would thus make no sense to propose that policy be guided by a nominal interest rate rule that could not be explicitly translated into an economically reasonable rule for the real interest rate.

The IFB1 rule involves a forward-looking measure of the real interest rate. A third class of rules that has received attention in the literature, which we refer to as IFB2 rules and make a number of references to in parallel with our discussion of IFB1 rules, is defined through a simple modification of the bracketed expression in equation (15) in which the period-$t$ inflation rate is replaced by an inflation forecast.

By focusing on the deviation from target of the authorities' inflation forecast, inflation-forecast-based rules have the appealing feature of inducing the authorities to condition their interest rate settings on current information about the determinants of future inflation, given their information/assumptions about the structure of the model.[33] As we will demonstrate, the conditioning of monetary policy reactions on forward-looking inflation forecasts, rather than backward-looking inflation measures, appears to be critical to stability in moderately nonlinear models in which inflation expectations have a model-consistent component and policymakers confront an historically normal degree of uncertainty about the NAIRU.

## B. *The Policy Objective Function*

The literature on optimal policy rules has traditionally relied on quadratic loss functions that are separably additive in the deviation of inflation from target, the unemployment (or output) gap, and sometimes also the change in the nominal interest rate; see, for example, Rudebusch and Svensson (1999) and Wieland (1998). To remain consistent with this literature, we adopt an objective function in which the period-$t$ loss has the following general form

$$L_t = (\pi_t - \pi^{TAR})^2 + \theta[u_t - (u_t^* - \beta)]^2 + \nu(rs_t - rs_{t-1})^2 \tag{17}$$

where $\theta$, $\beta$, and $\nu$ are parameters and $u_t^*$ is the DNAIRU (deterministic NAIRU). For $\beta = 0$ this corresponds to the specification that it has been popular to use in recent simulation studies of policy rules. More generally, it also allows us, somewhat in the spirit of Barro and Gordon (1983a, 1983b) and Rogoff (1985), to consider cases in which the authorities' preferences with regard to unemployment are not symmetric around the DNAIRU but center on an unemployment rate below the DNAIRU (i.e., cases with $\beta > 0$), and to note how our simulation results are affected by credibility issues in these cases.[34]

### *C. The Monetary Authority's Behavior*

The monetary authority adjusts a short-term nominal interest rate period by period in accordance with a prespecified simple policy rule. We assume that its action in quarter $t$ is timed to come soon after the announcement of the observed inflation rate for quarter $t$, when the period-$t$ values of other macroeconomic variables have not yet been observed.

The monetary authority is assumed to have full information about the structure of the model and the ex ante distributions of the exogenous shocks. After observing the period-$t$ inflation rate, the central bank is assumed to update its estimates of the DNAIRU and NAIRU (i.e., resolve the Kalman filter problem defined by equations (6)–(10)) and set the period-$t$ interest rate based on an information set $\Omega_t$ that includes: the complete specification of the true model, including the process that generates the DNAIRU and NAIRU as well as the bounds on the DNAIRU; the history of all observable variables (including the survey measures of inflation expectations) through period $t - 1$, along with the inflation rate for period $t$; and the probability distributions (but not the realizations) of the shocks for period $t$ and all future periods.

Under these strong informational assumptions, the central bank knows that the exogenous shocks have independent normal distributions with zero means, and it also knows the standard deviations of the shocks (which we calibrated to reflect the unexplained variances of the dependent variables during the historical periods over which the model equations were estimated). For purposes of implementing its policy rule, it needs to solve for the expected rate of inflation that defines the level of the real interest rate in equation (16), which requires it to solve its forward-looking macro model for the expected future time paths of all the endogenous variables, since inflation expectations have a forward-looking model-consistent component. We make the assumption that the central bank follows a certainty equivalence procedure in solving the model—in particular, that it assumes that all future shocks will be equal to their expected values of zero.[35] The forecasting rule that it uses to project the path of the DNAIRU (a bounded random walk) is described in Appendix I. In solving the model, the central bank determines, inter alia, a set of projections for the entire future time paths of both its policy instrument and the rate of inflation.

### *D. The Stochastic Simulation Experiments*

Our first set of stochastic simulation experiments is oriented toward identifying the optimal calibrations of IFB1 rules, based on a grid search, under different model variants and parameterizations of the loss function. Additional simulations focus on evaluating the performances of selected calibrations of other classes of simple rules.

With regard to the first objective, we simulated the performance of the economy for a range of reaction function weights ($w_\pi$, $w_u$), with $w_\pi$ running over a grid from 0.1 to 2.0 in intervals of 0.1 and $w_u$ running from 0.0 to 2.0 in intervals of 0.1. Focusing first on the base-case model, we computed the value of the loss function under several parameterizations in order to evaluate how the monetary authorities' preferences would influence the optimal parameters in the IFB1 rule. We then considered several alternative variants of the model in order to see how specific modeling assumptions influence the optimal calibration of the

*Table 4.* Optimal calibrations of IFB1 rules. (The case of a convex Phillips curve, historically-normal NAIRU uncertainty, and 12-quarter contracts.)1/

| | Loss Function Parameters 2/ | | | Optimal Weights 3/ | |
|---|---|---|---|---|---|
| | $\theta$ | $\beta$ | $\nu$ | $w_u$ | $w_\pi$ |
| 1. | 0 | Irrelevant | 0.5 | 0.2 | 0.8 |
| 2. | 1 | 0 | 0.5 | 0.3 | 0.8 |
| 3. | 1 | 1 | 0.5 | 0.4 | 0.8 |
| 4. | 1 | 2 | 0.5 | 0.4 | 0.7 |
| 5. | 2 | 0 | 0.5 | 0.4 | 0.7 |
| 6. | 2 | 1 | 0.5 | 0.5 | 0.7 |
| 7. | 2 | 2 | 0.5 | 0.6 | 0.7 |
| 8. | 1 | 1 | 0 | 1.5 | 1.0 |

1/ Inflation expectations are described by equation (11).
2/ Loss function is $L_t = (\pi_t - \pi^{TAR})^2 + \theta[u_t - (u_t^* - \beta)]^2 + \nu(rs_t - rs_{t-1})^2$.
3/ Reaction function is $rs_t - \tilde{E}_t\{E_t\pi 4_{t+4} \mid \Omega_t\} = r^* + \tilde{E}_t\{w_\pi(\pi 4_t - \pi^{TAR}) + w_u(\bar{u}_t - u_t) \mid \Omega_t\}$.

parameters in the reaction function. In each case the hypothetical path of the economy was simulated 64 times over a horizon of 100 quarters, starting in a position with the inflation rate at its target (specifically, 2.5) and the unemployment rate at the long-run NAIRU (specifically, 6.0), and using a common set of the 64 different random drawings of the timepaths of the various shocks that enter the model. This generated 6,400 observations for evaluating the cumulative (undiscounted) loss in each case, and provided information both on the optimal calibration of the rule (conditional on the loss function parameters, particular model variant, and the grid over which we searched), its implications for a range of performance indicators in addition to the cumulative loss, and the sensitivity of the cumulative loss to the calibration of the rule.

## IV. Simulation Results

### A. *Optimal Calibrations of IFB1 Rules*

This section describes the optimal calibrations of IFB1 rules, as defined by equations (15) and (16), under different model variants and for a range of loss-function parameters.

We first focus on the case in which the behavior of inflation expectations follows our preferred model, as specified in equation (11). Table 4 reports optimal calibrations of IFB1 rules under base-case assumptions about the shape of the Phillips curve, the degree of NAIRU uncertainty, and the length of wage-price contracts. The first seven rows consider combinations of three different settings of $\theta$ (the loss attached to unemployment variance relative to inflation variance) and three different settings of $\beta$ (the strength of the short-run temptation to push unemployment below the DNAIRU) when a positive loss is attached to interest rate variability ($\nu = 0.5$).[36] Several points may be noted.

*Table 5.* Optimal calibrations of IFB1 rules under a backward-and-forward-looking components model of inflation expectations. (The case of a convex Phillips curve, historically-normal NAIRU uncertainty, and 12-quarter contracts.)1/

| | Loss Function Parameters 2/ | | | Optimal Calibrations 3/ | |
|---|---|---|---|---|---|
| | $\theta$ | $\beta$ | $\nu$ | $w_u$ | $w_\pi$ |
| 1. | 0 | Irrelevant | 0.5 | 0.2 | 0.8 |
| 2. | 1 | 0 | 0.5 | 0.3 | 0.8 |
| 3. | 1 | 1 | 0.5 | 0.4 | 0.8 |
| 4. | 1 | 2 | 0.5 | 0.4 | 0.8 |
| 5. | 2 | 0 | 0.5 | 0.4 | 0.8 |
| 6. | 2 | 1 | 0.5 | 0.5 | 0.7 |
| 7. | 2 | 2 | 0.5 | 0.6 | 0.7 |
| 8. | 1 | 1 | 0 | 1.8 | 1.1 |

1/Inflation expectations are described by equation (11a).
2/Loss function is $L_t = (\pi_t - \pi^{TAR})^2 + \theta[u_t - (u_t^* - \beta)]^2 + \nu(rs_t - rs_{t-1})^2$.
3/Reaction function is $rs_t - \tilde{E}_t\{E_t\pi 4_{t+4} \mid \Omega_t\} = r^* + \tilde{E}_t\{w_\pi(\pi 4_t - \pi^{TAR}) + w_u(\bar{u}_t - u_t) \mid \Omega_t\}$.

First,even for cases in which no loss is attached to unemployment variance (top row), the optimal calibration of the IFB1 rule places a positive weight on the unemployment gap. Thus, in setting the nominal interest rate relative to a model-consistent measure of expected inflation, authorities who condition their interest rate settings on information about both inflation and unemployment can achieve a more desirable path for future inflation than authorities who ignore information about unemployment. Second, as the relative loss attached to unemployment variance increases, so do the *relative* weights on unemployment in the optimal calibrations of these rules (compare, e.g., rows 1, 2, and 5). Third, as $\beta$ increases and the "target" unemployment rate $(u^* - \beta)$ declines, the optimal *relative* weight on unemployment increases (compare rows 2, 3, and 4 and rows 5, 6, and 7). We regard these results as intuitively very plausible and likely to prove fairly robust across both models and different classes of simple policy rules. It may be noted, however, that when we double the relative loss associated with interest rate variability by raising the setting of $\nu$ from 0.5 to 1.0, the optimal calibration of $w_u$ declines in all cases and rounds to 0.0 in cases with $\theta = 0$.

A fourth result is that the optimal weights on inflation and unemployment are inversely related to the loss attached to interest rate variability; compare rows 3 and 8. The lower is the loss associated with interest rate variability, other things equal, the more aggressive are the optimal responses to unemployment gaps and deviations of inflation from target.

As a check on the sensitivity of these results to our assumption about the dynamics of inflation expectations, Table 5 reports results comparable to those in Table 4 in all respects except for the assumption about inflation expectations. In Table 5, inflation expectations are assumed to reflect the traditional forward-and-backward looking components model defined by equation (11a). It may be seen that the four points noted about Table 4 are equally evident in Table 5.

Table 6 characterizes the sensitivity of the optimal calibrations to the degree of NAIRU uncertainty and alternative assumptions about the model. Each of the five panels corresponds to a particular choice of the loss function parameters. Within each panel, the top row corresponds to the base-case results reported in Table 4.

We noted above that the optimal weight on the unemployment gap depends on the relative loss attached to unemployment variance. Here we add an intuitive result on how the optimal reaction function parameters vary with the degree of NAIRU uncertainty. In particular, rows 2 and 3 report results for the cases in which the magnitudes of NAIRU uncertainty are, respectively, half as much and twice as great as the base-case level. These results confirm that the optimal *relative* weight on the unemployment gap is inversely related to the degree of NAIRU uncertainty.

Another finding is that the optimal weights increase (implying more aggressive policy reactions) as the length of standard wage and price contracts shortens and thereby reduces the degree of inertia in the backward-looking component of inflation expectations. This can be seen by comparing rows 1 and 5 or rows 4 and 6. Consistently, for cases in which market participants are assumed to have completely backward-looking expectations, the optimal calibrations of the IFB1 rule involve weaker policy responses to unemployment gaps than for analogous cases with partially forward-looking expectations; compare rows 1 and 7.

We expected to also find that, other things equal, the optimal policy reaction is more aggressive in model variants with convex Phillips curves than in model variants with linear approximations to the same Phillips curves.[37] This is simply because the greater the degree of Phillips-curve convexity, the higher is the inflation and/or unemployment variance that tends to be generated by shocks to the economy, other things equal. The results in Table 6 support these priors insofar as the optimal weights on unemployment are higher in the cases with convex Phillips curves than they are in the cases with linear Phillips curves (compare rows 1 and 4 and rows 5 and 6). In reflecting on this result, it may be noted, in addition, that the differences in weights across the two models is moderated by two factors: first, the forward-looking IFB1 rules, which implicitly take account of the nonlinearities in the model, are highly successful in avoiding large boom and bust cycles; and second, our convex Phillips curves are approximately linear in the region of the NAIRU.

Table 7 reports a number of relevant performance characteristics associated with a selected subset of the optimally-calibrated IFB1 rules shown in Table 6. The performance characteristics include the cumulative undiscounted losses (over 6,400 simulated observations, with a scale factor); the average rates of inflation and unemployment; the standard deviations of the inflation and unemployment rates; and the standard deviations of both the level of, and the change in, the nominal interest rate (the policy instrument). Several points may be noted.

First, for the linear model variants, the simple policy rules succeed in hitting the inflation target to a very close approximation (i.e., with an error averaging less than .015 percentage points over 6400 observations) and achieving an average unemployment rate equal to the long-run DNAIRU (i.e., the center of the band within which the DNAIRU randomly walks).

Second, as noted in Section II, for model variants with convex Phillips curves (and simulations that start with inflation on target and the unemployment rate at the long-run DNAIRU), it is infeasible to hit the inflation target on average in a stochastic environment

*Table 6.* Sensitivity of optimal calibrations of IFB1 rules to different assumptions.

| Model Characteristics | | | | Optimal Calibrations5/ | |
|---|---|---|---|---|---|
| Phillips Curve 1/ | Inflation Expectations 2/ | NAIRU Uncertainty 3/ | Contract Length 4/ | $w_u$ | $w_\pi$ |
| 1. Base Case: $(\theta, \beta, \nu) = (1, 1, 0.5)$ | | | | | |
| Convex | F | Normal | 12 | 0.4 | 0.8 |
| Convex | F | Low | 12 | 0.8 | 0.8 |
| Convex | F | High | 12 | 0.0 | 0.7 |
| Linear | F | Normal | 12 | 0.0 | 0.8 |
| Convex | F | Normal | 4 | 1.1 | 0.9 |
| Linear | F | Normal | 4 | 0.7 | 0.9 |
| Convex | B | Normal | 12 | 0.0 | 0.9 |
| 2. No Unemployment Loss and Preference for $u =$ DNAIRU: $(\theta, \beta, \nu) = (0, 0, 0.5)$ | | | | | |
| Convex | F | Normal | 12 | 0.2 | 0.8 |
| Convex | F | Low | 12 | 0.6 | 0.9 |
| Convex | F | High | 12 | 0.0 | 0.8 |
| Linear | F | Normal | 12 | 0.0 | 0.9 |
| Convex | F | Normal | 4 | 0.9 | 0.9 |
| Linear | F | Normal | 4 | 0.6 | 0.9 |
| Convex | B | Normal | 12 | 0.2 | 1.0 |
| 3. High Unemployment Loss and Preference for $u =$ DNAIRU: $(\theta, \beta, \nu) = (2, 0, 0.5)$ | | | | | |
| Convex | F | Normal | 12 | 0.4 | 0.7 |
| Convex | F | Low | 12 | 0.8 | 0.8 |
| Convex | F | High | 12 | 0.1 | 0.7 |
| Linear | F | Normal | 12 | 0.1 | 0.8 |
| Convex | F | Normal | 4 | 0.9 | 0.8 |
| Linear | F | Normal | 4 | 0.7 | 0.8 |
| Convex | B | Normal | 12 | 0.0 | 0.9 |
| 4. High Unemployment Loss and Strong Preference for $u <$ DNAIRU: $(\theta, \beta, \nu) = (2, 2, 0.5)$ | | | | | |
| Convex | F | Normal | 12 | 0.6 | 0.7 |
| Convex | F | Low | 12 | 1.0 | 0.7 |
| Convex | F | High | 12 | 0.1 | 0.6 |
| Linear | F | Normal | 12 | 0.1 | 0.8 |
| Convex | F | Normal | 4 | 1.1 | 0.8 |
| Linear | F | Normal | 4 | 0.7 | 0.8 |
| Convex | B | Normal | 12 | 0.2 | 0.8 |
| 5. No Loss on Interest Rate Volatility: $(\theta, \beta, \nu) = (1, 1, 0)$ | | | | | |
| Convex | F | Normal | 12 | 1.5 | 1.0 |

1/The convex Phillips curves are described by equations (1) and (2). The linear Phillips curves are described by equations (1a) and (2a).

2/*F*denotes partially forward-looking expectations as characterized by equation (11). B denotes completely backward-looking expectations defined by equation (11b).

3/Normal level of NAIRU uncertainty reflects sample period variances of $\epsilon^{\pi}$, $\epsilon^{\pi^x}$, and $\epsilon^{u^*}$ in equations (1), (2), and (6). Low (high) NAIRU uncertainty corresponds to variances of $\epsilon^{\pi}$, $\epsilon^{\pi^x}$, and $\epsilon^{u^*}$ that are half (twice) as large as in the normal case.

4/Length of standard price and wage contracts measured in calendar quarters; value of $N$ in equation (3).

5/Reaction function is $rs_t - \tilde{E}_t\{E_t\pi 4_{t+4} \mid \Omega_t\} = r^* + \tilde{E}_t\{w_\pi(\pi 4_t - \pi^{TAR}) + w_u(\bar{u}_t - u_t) \mid \Omega_t\}$.

*Table 7.* Performance characteristics of optimally-calibrated IFB1 rules1/.

| Model Characteristics | | | | Performance Characteristics | | | | | | |
|---|---|---|---|---|---|---|---|---|---|---|
| | | | | | Inflation Outcomes | | Unemployment Outcomes | | | |
| Phillips Curve | Inflation Expectations | NAIRU Uncertainty | Contract Length | Cumulative Loss | Mean | Standard Deviation | Mean | Standard Deviation | Standard Deviation of Nominal Interest Rate | Standard Deviation of Change in Nominal Interest Rate |
| | | | | $(\theta, \beta, \nu) = (1, 1, 0.5)$ | | | | | | |
| Convex | F | Normal | 12 | 6.90 | 2.65 | 2.17 | 6.03 | 0.54 | 2.17 | 1.06 |
| Convex | F | Low | 12 | 2.71 | 2.57 | 1.13 | 6.01 | 0.36 | 1.20 | 0.58 |
| Linear | F | Normal | 12 | 6.80 | 2.51 | 2.17 | 6.00 | 0.55 | 2.17 | 1.04 |
| Convex | F | Normal | 4 | 8.46 | 2.71 | 2.44 | 6.04 | 0.59 | 3.01 | 1.22 |
| Linear | F | Normal | 4 | 8.31 | 2.51 | 2.44 | 6.00 | 0.60 | 3.03 | 1.20 |
| Convex | B | Normal | 12 | 7.13 | 2.66 | 2.04 | 6.03 | 0.54 | 2.90 | 1.52 |
| | | | | $(\theta, \beta, \nu) = (2, 0, 0.5)$ | | | | | | |
| Convex | F | Normal | 12 | 6.02 | 2.64 | 2.17 | 6.02 | 0.52 | 2.04 | 1.01 |
| Convex | B | Normal | 12 | 6.26 | 2.66 | 2.04 | 6.03 | 0.54 | 2.90 | 1.52 |
| | | | | $(\theta, \beta, \nu) = (2, 2, 0.5)$ | | | | | | |
| Convex | F | Normal | 12 | 14.20 | 2.64 | 2.17 | 6.02 | 0.52 | 2.04 | 1.02 |
| Convex | B | Normal | 12 | 14.52 | 2.65 | 2.04 | 6.03 | 0.52 | 2.77 | 1.47 |

1/Reaction function is $rs_t - \tilde{E}_t\{E_t\pi 4_{t+4} \mid \Omega_t\} = r^* + \tilde{E}_t\{w_\pi(\pi 4_t - \pi^{TAR}) + w_u(\bar{u}_t - u_t) \mid \Omega_t\}$.

without generating an average unemployment rate above the long-run DNAIRU. For these cases, the policy rule calibrations that are optimal under the quadratic loss function—which trades off deviations of inflation from its target against deviations of unemployment from an implicit target at or below the DNAIRU—result in both above-target average inflation rates and above-DNAIRU average unemployment rates.

Third, the realized means and standard deviations of inflation and unemployment are essentially independent of the loss-function parameter $\beta$, other things equal; compare, for example, the results in the second and third panels of Table 7. Thus, under the assumptions that the macro model is well defined and known to the authorities, that inflation expectations are either backward looking or model consistent, and that the authorities are motivated to optimize over a long horizon, there may be some basis for taking comfort in the traditional assumption that adherence to a well-performing policy rule would be fully credible. As noted earlier, however, except in completely linear models such an assumption does not imply that the prospect of achieving the announced inflation target is fully credible.

Fourth, for all cases shown in Table 7—and more generally, for most cases with historically normal (or low) levels of NAIRU uncertainty—the optimal calibrations of the IFB1 rules succeed in keeping average inflation within .25 percentage points of target and average unemployment within .05 percentage points of the long-run DNAIRU. Moreover, the associated standard deviations of inflation, unemployment, and the nominal interest rate might also be regarded as attractively small. This highly attractive performance is an interesting result in light of Schaling's (1998) argument that for models with convex Phillips curves, optimal policy reaction functions are nonlinear in the observable state variables. In particular, our simulation results provide the additional perspective that when policymakers are assumed to have complete information about the structure of the model, linear IFB rules that embody model-consistent measures of real interest rates and thereby implicitly take account of the nonlinearities in the model may provide acceptably-close approximations to "optimal rules." By contrast, as is emphasized in the next section, complete information about the structure of the model would have little value if policymakers were committed to follow a conventional Taylor rule.

A fifth result, evident from simulation results not reported in this paper, is that the performances of IFB1 rules are slightly dominated by the performances of IFB2 rules, which we have described verbally in Section III.A above and characterize formally by equation (19) in Section IV.B below. But the shift from a Taylor rule to an IFB1 rule achieves a much larger gain in macroeconomic stability than the shift from an IFB1 rule to an IFB2 rule.

While the results reported in this section suggest that simple rules are capable of performing very well as monetary policy guidelines when macro models are well defined, such a conclusion does not necessarily extend to the model-uncertain environments in which monetary policy is actually conducted. At best, such inference would rest on a presumption that the monetary authorities can identify a rule calibration that comes close to achieving the performance of the optimal calibration. Moreover, a point that we find even more alarming is that economists seem to have a poor track record at identifying rules with good stabilizing properties. In particular, as the next section illustrates, a number of rules that economists have chosen to advocate on the basis of their performances in linear models of the U.S. economy perform very poorly in models with moderate nonlinearities, particularly when policymakers tend to make serially-correlated errors in estimating the NAIRU.

### *B. Perspectives on Several of the Simple Rules Proposed in the Literature*

This section focuses on the stabilizing properties of several types of simple rules that have been proposed in the literature, and compares their performances with the performance of an optimally-calibrated IFB1 rule. The additional rules on which we focus are: (i) the conventional Taylor rule advocated by Taylor (1993, 1999a), (ii) an inflation-forecast-based rule with interest rate smoothing, as estimated for the United States by Clarida, Gali, and Gertler (1998), (iii) an optimally-calibrated IFB2 rule, as analyzed previously in Isard and Laxton (1998) and Isard, Laxton, and Eliasson (1998), and (iv) a first-difference rule for the interest rate, as proposed by Levin, Wieland, and Williams (1999).

One of the key findings of our simulation analysis, supported by the stability analysis presented in Appendix II, is that in a world in which inflation expectations have a forward-looking model-consistent component, monetary policy guided by a myopic rule that incorporates a backward-looking measure of the real interest rate, such as a conventional Taylor rule, can be destabilizing in our moderately nonlinear model. A second key finding is that rules with high degrees of interest rate smoothing, such as the forward-looking rule estimated by Clarida, Gali, and Gertler (CGG) and the first-difference rule proposed by Levin, Wieland, and Williams (LWW), can also lead to instability in our moderately nonlinear model.

The specification of conventional Taylor rules has been described by equation (14) above. The CGG rules that we consider can be written as:

$$rs_t = (1-\rho)c + \rho rs_{t-1} + (1-\rho)\tilde{E}_t\{\beta\pi 4_{t+4} + \gamma(\bar{u}_t - u_t) \mid \Omega_t\} \qquad (18)$$

where $(\rho, \beta, \gamma)$ are the parameters to be chosen.[38] Note that in CGG rules the interest rate is adjusted in reaction to an inflation forecast rather than a backward-looking measure of inflationary pressures as embodied in the conventional Taylor rule.[39]

The IFB2 rule that we consider here has the following form:

$$\tilde{r}_t = r^* + \tilde{E}_t\left\{w_\pi(\pi_{t+3} - \pi^{TAR}) + w_u(\bar{u}_t - u_t) \mid \Omega_t\right\} \qquad (19)$$

where

$$\tilde{r}_t = rs_t - \tilde{E}_t\{E_t\pi 4_{t+4} \mid \Omega_t\} \qquad (20)$$

As in the IFB1 rule, $\tilde{r}_t$ is the monetary authority's ex ante measure of the real interest rate on which aggregate demand and unemployment depend; $E_t\pi 4_{t+4}$ denotes the public's expectations at time $t$ of the inflation rate over the year ahead; and $\tilde{E}_t\{\mid \Omega_t\}$ denotes a model-consistent forecast at time $t$ based on the authorities' information set $\Omega_t$, which includes information about the model along with the observed values of the inflation rate through quarter $t$ and all other economic variables through quarter $t-1$.[40] However, in the IFB2 rule the real interest rate is adjusted in response to a forecast of the annualized inflation rate three quarters ahead rather than the contemporaneous year-on-year inflation measure that is used in the conventional Taylor rule and IFB1 rule. While the assumption of a three-quarter-ahead inflation forecast is somewhat arbitrary, some experimentation suggested that such a specification was capable of producing reasonable macroeconomic stability, and of offsetting unanticipated shocks to inflation within a horizon of two or three years.[41] Nevertheless, the issue may deserve more consideration in future work.[42]

There are three potentially important differences between the CGG rule and the IFB2 rule. First, the IFB2 rule embodies information about the real interest rate on which aggregate demand depends. Consequently, with prespecified reaction-function parameters, the behavior of nominal interest rates under the IFB2 rule appears to be more sensitive to assumptions about the manner in which inflation expectations are formed by the private sector. Second, the CGG rule employs a fourth-quarter-ahead forecast of the year-on-year inflation rate while the IFB2 rule employs a third-quarter-ahead forecast of quarterly inflation (measured at an annual rate). Third, the IFB2 rule does not incorporate interest rate smoothing.

CGG provide estimates of the "Volcker–Greenspan" calibrations that best fit the post-October 1979 and post-1982 data for the United States; these estimates, in rounded numbers, are $(\rho, \beta, \gamma) = (0.7, 2.0, 0.1)$ and $(\rho, \beta, \gamma) = (0.8, 1.6, 0.9)$, respectively. CGG implicitly suggest that the "Volcker–Greenspan" calibrations have attractive stabilizing properties, and that a CGG rule with these calibrations could have avoided the stagflation that occurred in the late 1960s and 1970s. We test this conjecture by using our stochastic simulation framework to explore how well their rule would work in our model under the Volcker–Greenspan calibrations and a historically-normal degree of ex ante NAIRU uncertainty.

The final rule that we consider is a first-difference rule for the nominal interest rate, as explored by Levin, Wieland, and Williams (1999). This LWW rule can be written as:

$$rs_t - rs_{t-1} = w_\pi \sum_{i=0}^{N-1} (\pi_{t-i} - \pi^{TAR})/N + w_u(\bar{u}_t - u_t) \tag{21}$$

where we consider both $N = 12$ and $N = 4$.

Table 8 summarizes the performance characteristics of the selected policy rules in the context of our base-case model and base-case loss function parameters. Among other things, the base-case model embodies an historically normal degree of NAIRU uncertainty and recognizes that such uncertainty creates a tendency for policymakers to make serially-correlated errors in estimating the unemployment gap. In this context, both the conventional Taylor rule and the LWW first-difference rule are too myopic to satisfy the stability conditions for our moderately nonlinear model in which inflation expectations have a model-consistent component.

Some intuition for these results is provided by the following points. First, the stability conditions depend essentially on the inflationary consequences of excess demand. Second, when an economy gets into a region of significant overheating, the inflationary consequences of a marginal increase in excess demand can be significantly greater with a convex Phillips curve than with a linear Phillips curve. Third, serially-correlated errors in estimating unemployment gaps increase the likelihood of getting into states with significant excess demand. Fourth, when inflationary expectations have a forward-looking model-consistent

*Table 8.* Performance characteristics of selected rules. (The case of a convex Phillips curve, historically-normal NAIRU uncertainty, and 12-quarter contracts under loss function parameterization $(\theta, \beta, \nu) = (1, 1, 0.5)$.)

| | Performance Characteristics | | | | | | |
|---|---|---|---|---|---|---|---|
| | | Inflation Outcomes | | Unemployment Outcomes | | | |
| Rule | Cumulative Loss | Mean | Standard Deviation | Mean | Standard Deviation | Standard Deviation of Nominal Interest Rate | Standard Deviation of Change in Nominal Interest Rate |
| Conventional Taylor rules | too myopic to satisfy stability conditions (see text) | | | | | | |
| IFB1 rule1/ $(w_u, w_\pi) = (0.4, 0.8)$ | 6.90 | 2.65 | 2.17 | 6.03 | 0.54 | 2.17 | 1.06 |
| CGG rules2/ | based on cases that do not explode (see text) | | | | | | |
| $(\rho, \beta, \gamma) = (0.8, 1.6, 0.9)$ | 8.13 | 2.90 | 2.33 | 5.99 | 0.53 | 1.74 | 0.30 |
| $(\rho, \beta, \gamma) = (0.7, 2, 0.1)$ | 6.98 | 2.74 | 2.24 | 6.02 | 0.56 | 1.85 | 0.45 |
| IFB2 rule3/ $(w_u, w_\pi) = (0.0, 1.5)$ | 6.32 | 2.57 | 2.06 | 6.02 | 0.50 | 1.93 | 1.12 |
| LWW first-difference rule | too myopic to satisfy stability conditions (see text) | | | | | | |

1/Reaction function is $rs_t - \tilde{E}_t\{E_t\pi 4_{t+4} \mid \Omega_t\} = r^* + \tilde{E}_t\{w_\pi(\pi 4_t - \pi^{TAR}) + w_u(\bar{u}_t - u_t) \mid \Omega_t\}$.
2/Reaction function is $rs_t = (1-\rho)c + \rho rs_{t-1} + (1-\rho)\tilde{E}_t\{\beta\pi 4_{t+4} + \gamma(\bar{u}_{t+1} - u_{t+1}) \mid \Omega_t\}$.
3/Reaction function is $rs_t - \tilde{E}_t\{E_t\pi 4_{t+4} \mid \Omega_t\} = r^* + \tilde{E}_t\{w_\pi(\pi_{t+3} - \pi^{TAR}) + w_u(\bar{u}_t - u_t) \mid \Omega_t\}$.

component and policy reactions are not sufficiently forward looking, attempts to achieve a target average rate of inflation can put the economy through boom and bust cycles where the busts are more pronounced than the booms. And fifth, as an alternative and more extreme outcome, reliance on backward-looking or sluggish policy rules can leave policymakers so far behind "shifts in the curve" that they fail to provide an anchor for inflation expectations.

Appendix II provides an extended discussion of the stability properties of Taylor rules and LWW rules. It also demonstrates that LWW rules bear a close resemblance to price level targeting.

Instability was encountered in some of the simulations with CGG rules. Although as Table 8 indicates, reasonably good performances are delivered, on average, for those cases of random shock drawings in which the simulations do not explode, it may be noted that the first calibration of the CGG rule failed to prevent instability in 8 out of 64 simulations, and the second in 22 of 128 simulations.

These results for CGG rules, along with the analysis of LWW rules, emphasize that it would be very dangerous to constrain policymakers to always exercise gradualism in adjusting interest rates. It may be quite appropriate to associate losses with interest rate variability and to take these losses into consideration when calibrating the strength of policy reactions to estimated unemployment gaps and deviations of inflation from target. But to adhere mechanically to either an LWW rule or a CGG rule with a high degree of interest rate smoothing would be a recipe for disaster.[43]

By contrast, the optimally-calibrated IFB1 and IFB2 rules succeed in preventing instability in all 64 simulations and deliver relatively attractive outcomes for the means and variances of inflation and unemployment. By incorporating model-consistent measures of inflation expectations and the real interest rate, which implicitly takes account of the nonlinearities in macroeconomic behavior, these rules are highly successful in avoiding boom and bust cycles within our well-defined macro model, and in delivering average rates of inflation and unemployment respectively close to the inflation target and the long-run DNAIRU.

## V. Conclusions

The various simulation results reported in this paper illustrate the prospective dangers of adopting a simple policy rule as an automatic pilot for monetary policy. These dangers are reflected, among other places, in the observation that economists seem to have a poor track record in identifying rules with good stabilizing properties. In particular, several prominent types of simple monetary policy rules—rules that have been shown to perform well in linear models of the U.S. economy and that have accordingly received prominent attention in the economics literature—are too myopic to deliver macroeconomic stability in our moderately nonlinear model in which inflation expectations have a forward-looking model-consistent component.

While recognizing that simple policy rules should not be followed mechanically, many economists argue that the adoption of simple rules as guidelines can be helpful for communication, accountability, and credibility. This is reflected, for example, in the widespread attention that inflation targeting strategies have received during the 1990s. Moreover, even for advocates of discretionary monetary policies, simulation experiments and analytic studies of the properties of simple rules can provide valuable insights. In this context, two key messages of this paper are that it is very important for policymakers to calibrate their nominal interest rate adjustments on the basis of forward-looking measures of real interest rates, and that it is also important to be aware that excessive caution (interest rate smoothing) in policy reactions can be much more costly in a nonlinear world than is apparent from simulation experiments with linear models. These messages are especially relevant for a world characterized by NAIRU uncertainty in which policymakers tend to make serially-correlated errors in estimating the unemployment gap. Our analysis suggests that relying heavily on guidance from a conventional Taylor rule would lead to a repeat of the policy errors of the 1970s, independently of how the Taylor rule was calibrated.

A third message of the paper is that the propensity of economists to analyze the properties of simple policy rules within the confines of linear models is difficult to defend as a research strategy. In linear models, bad policy rules affect the variances of unemployment and inflation, but not the means: bad rules do not have first-order welfare consequences. By contrast, nonlinear models recognize that policy rules that allow economies to overheat significantly can leave policy "behind shifts in the curve," with consequences that are much more dire than simply increasing the variances of unemployment and inflation. While the nonlinearity on which this paper has focused is a moderate one associated with convex Phillips curves that are highly linear in the region of the DNAIRU (deterministic NAIRU), in reality policymakers also confront other possibly-important nonlinearities, such as nonlinearities in the response of inflation expectations (policy credibility) to the authorities' track record in hitting announced inflation targets (including asymmetry in the speeds with which credibility can be lost and regained), asymmetric hysteresis in the dynamics of unemployment, and floors on nominal interest rates.

## Appendix I. Optimal Forecasting Rules for Bounded Random Walks

As summarized by equation (6), our simulations assume that the DNAIRU follows a bounded random walk centered at 6 percent, with a floor and ceiling of 4 percent and 8 percent, respectively. The central bank is assumed to know the process that generates the DNAIRU, including the variance of the random walk and its upper and lower bounds. In each period the central bank updates its estimates of the historical path of the DNAIRU, based on knowledge of the structural model, the ex ante distributions of the exogenous shocks, and the history of all observable variables. For purposes of implementing its IFB1 or IFB2 rules, it needs to solve its forward-looking macro model, which, among other things, requires it to forecast the timepath of the DNAIRU.

The optimal forecasts for a bounded random walk depend on the upper and lower bounds, the variance of the random walk process, and the most recently observed or estimated value of the time series. Figure A1 shows optimal forecasts over horizons of 100 periods, based on different estimates of the initial value of the DNAIRU, a standard deviation of 0.12, and the lower and upper bounds of 4 percent and 8 percent. As can be seen in the figure, the optimal forecasts revert very gradually toward the long-run DNAIRU of 6 percent. Note, however, that the expected speed of convergence is positively related to the distance between the estimated initial value of the DNAIRU and its long-run value.

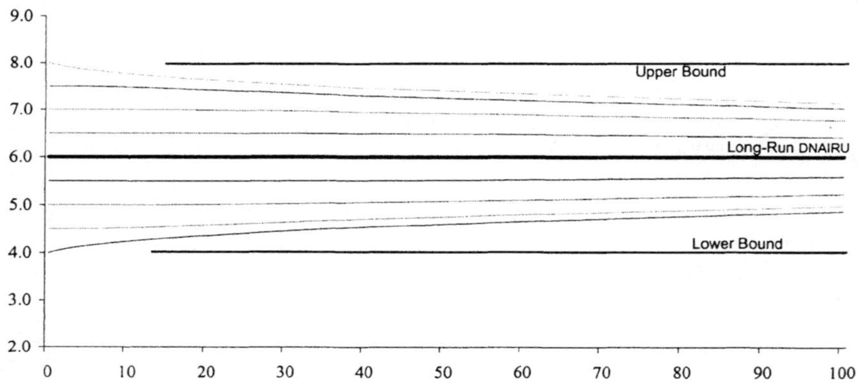


**Sources:**

Each line in the figure is derived from taking the average values over 500 simulations of a bounded random walk with a standard deviation of 0.12, a lower bound of 4.0 percent and an upper bound of 8.0 percent.

*Figure A1.* Optimal forecast trajectories of a bounded random walk.

In solving for the optimal forecast paths for the DNAIRU, we rely on numerical derivations. In particular, the paths shown in Figure A1 were constructed by averaging over 500 outcomes for each initial estimated value of the DNAIRU. For purposes of conducting the stochastic simulation experiments reported in the text, we created a grid of candidate optimal forecasts, corresponding to a grid of initial values that varied between 4 percent and 8 percent in increments of .001 percent. We then assumed that the central bank's forecast, in period $t$, of the path of the DNAIRU from period $t$ to $t + 100$ corresponded to the optimal path associated with its period-$t$ estimate of the DNAIRU for period $t - 1$.

The bounded random walk has a number of advantages over other stochastic processes that might be assumed in modeling the DNAIRU. First, it allows for quasi-permanent, or highly persistent, shifts in the underlying DNAIRU. Second, it allows us to differentiate between long-run concepts like the natural rate of unemployment, which is usually presumed to be fairly stable over time, and short-run concepts like the DNAIRU, which potentially is considerably more variable as a reflection of mismatches resulting from stochastic variability in the offer curves of workers and firms. For purposes of simplification, we have based our analysis on the assumption of a constant expected long-run DNAIRU of 6 percent, but it would be relatively straightforward in principle to vary the expected long-run DNAIRU as a function of unemployment compensation schemes, demographics, and so forth.

## Appendix II. Stability Analysis of Taylor Rules and LWW Rules

Research during the last few years has suggested that conventional Taylor rules, when appropriately calibrated, have reasonably attractive stabilization properties within a range of different macro models. Along similar lines, Levin, Wieland, and Williams (LWW:1999) have recently shown that simple rules linking the change in the interest rate to the variables that enter conventional Taylor rules have desirable properties in four different macro models.

Such favorable impressions of Taylor rules and LWW rules have not gone unchallenged, however. Christiano and Gust (CG: 1999) have been quick to point out that the stabilization properties of these rules have been evaluated almost exclusively in sticky-price IS-LM models with similar structures. CG demonstrate that in a limited-participation-rate model developed by Christiano, Eichenbaum and Evans (1998), Taylor rules or LWW rules may be dangerous, especially if the rules place too high a weight on output (or unemployment) relative to inflation.

This appendix argues that Taylor rules and LWW rules are also likely to be highly destabilizing in plausible specifications of sticky-price IS-LM models. In particular we emphasize that in contrast to their favorable performances in linearized versions of such models where overheating does not have first-order welfare consequences, Taylor rules and LWW rules tend to perform very poorly in nonlinear rational-expectations models in which myopic or sluggish policy responses can fail to provide an anchor for inflation expectations.

For each of the two classes of rules, we start by reporting the Blanchard–Kahn (1980) saddle-point stability conditions for a linear forward-looking model developed by Fuhrer and Moore (FM: 1995a, 1995b).[44] We show that both classes of rules produce saddle-point stability over an enormous range of parameter values. We then go on to argue that the stability of these rules in linear sticky-price IS-LM models with rational expectations breaks down in models that do not presume global linearity.[45] In particular, we show that in our model with moderate nonlinearities, such rules can give rise to extreme instabilities in inflation expectations and would risk a repeat of the monetary policy errors of the 1970s. As a corollary, the assumption that such myopic policy rules would be fully credible in these models is untenable, especially in cases where the monetary authorities place a high weight on output (or unemployment) relative to inflation.

### A. *Conventional Taylor Rules Generalized for Interest Rate Smoothing*

Figure B1 reports the combinations of parameter settings that lead to unique and indeterminate solution paths in the Fuhrer-Moore (1995b) model under a conventional Taylor rule that has been generalized to allow for interest rate smoothing. This rule can be written as:

$$rs_t = \rho rs_{t-1} + (1 - \rho)[w_\pi(\pi 4_t) + w_y(y_t)] \tag{B.1}$$

where: $rs_t$ is the nominal interest rate setting at time $t$; $\pi 4_t$ is the average inflation rate over the previous four quarters; $y_t$ represents the output gap in the Fuhrer–Moore model; and $\rho$, $w_\pi$, $w_y$ are parameters.[46] Note that the interest rate reaction function has been coded so

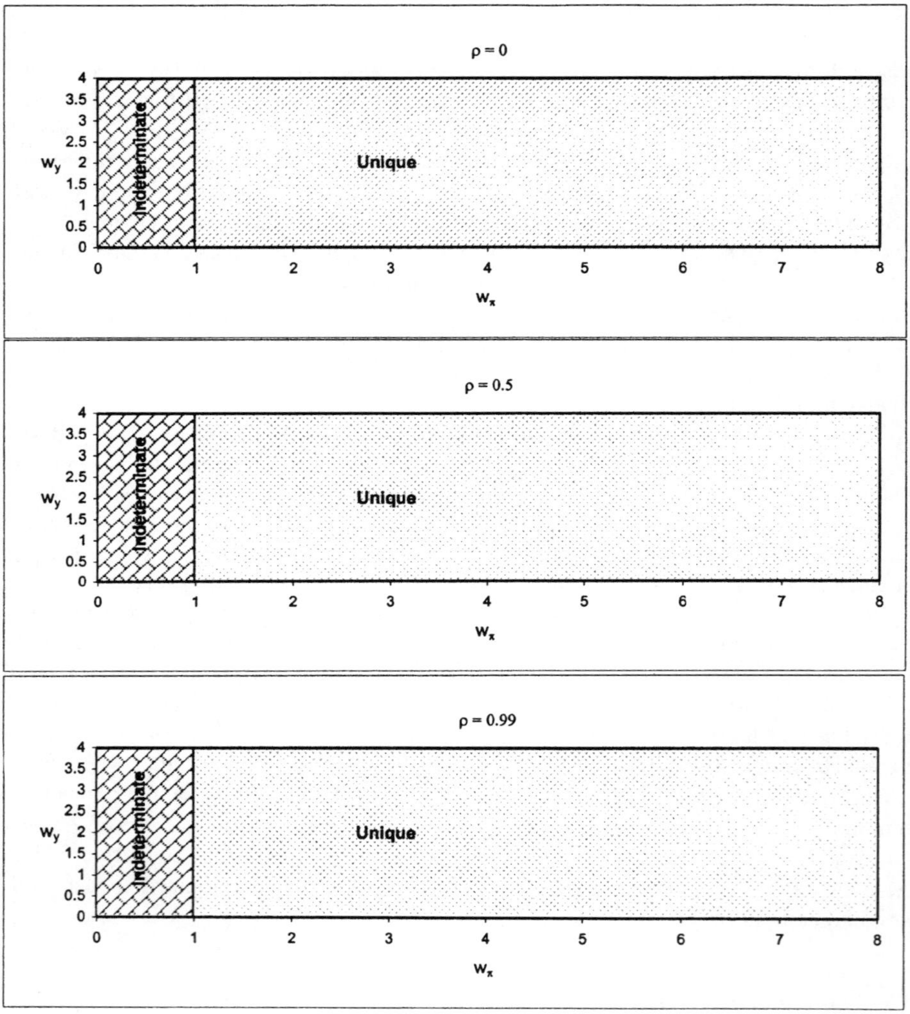


*Figure B1.* Regions of uniqueness and indeterminacy (generalized Taylor rule in Fuhrer-Moore model). Policy reaction function: $rs_t = \rho rs_{t-1} + (1 - \rho)[w_\pi(\pi 4_t) + w_y(y_t)]$.

that the parameters $w_\pi$ and $w_y$ represent asymptotic long-run responses of interest rates to the year-over-year inflation rate and the output gap.[47]

A striking feature of Figure B1 is that for a very wide range of parameter values—and independently of the speed with which monetary policy reacts to inflation and output gaps (i.e., independently of $\rho$)—the model has a stable and unique solution. Indeed, the stability properties of the generalized Taylor rule in this linear rational expectations IS-LM model are extremely simple. The only condition necessary for stability and uniqueness is that the long-run response of the interest rate to year-over-year inflation must be greater than one. Provided this condition is met, even a Taylor rule that reacts much more aggressively to output than to inflation will provide an anchor for inflation expectations in the Fuhrer–Moore model.

What is it that explains the "excessive stability" generated by Taylor rules in these sticky-price linear rational expectations models? What gives rise to stable macroeconomic behavior even when the monetary authorities respond in a very myopic way to inflation developments, or place an extremely high weight on real objectives relative to inflation objectives? Two assumptions appear to be critical here. The first is the assumption that the economy can be characterized by global linearity.[48] The second is the premise that no matter how myopic policy responses are in the short run, the private sector forms its expectations under the assumption that the monetary policy rule will be adhered to forever.

For the nonlinear model considered in this paper, which is cast in terms of unemployment gaps rather than output gaps, even moderately myopic policy rules like the conventional Taylor rule can result in explosive behavior if the economy is subjected to a significant degree of overheating. This reflects a combination of factors. Recall, first, that even moderate convexity in the Phillips curve implies that at some point the short-run unemployment-inflation tradeoff must worsen considerably when unemployment falls significantly below the NAIRU, and beyond this point a further marginal easing of monetary policy results mainly in inflation with only a very small incremental reduction in unemployment. Second, to the extent that policymakers tend to make serially correlated errors in estimating unemployment and output gaps, as reflected in our model, the probability of experiencing a significant degree of overheating is heightened. Third, when inflation expectations have a model-consistent component and rational agents possess information about the policy rule and the nonlinear nature of the expansionary effects of monetary policy, attempting to adhere to a conventional Taylor rule with a high weight on imprecise measures of unemployment gaps relative to a backward-looking measure of inflation could be conducive to wide swings or explosiveness in inflation expectations.

To sharpen quantitative perspectives, and to emphasize as well that in the region of small unemployment gaps our nonlinear model exhibits similar behavior to models that impose global linearity, consider the following. From equation (1), the direct effects of unemployment gaps $(u^* - u)$ on the annualized inflation rate in the nonlinear model are given by the functional form $\gamma(u^* - u)/(u - \phi)$, where we also assume $\phi = u^* - 4$. To simplify, define $g = (u^* - u)$ such that the direct effects of the gap on inflation can be written as $F(g) = \gamma g/(4 - g)$. Differentiating this last term with respect to $g$ leads to the expression $F'(g) = [\gamma(4 - g) + \gamma g]/(4 - g)^2$ and shows how the slope of the Phillips curve will depend on the initial state of excess demand conditions in the labor market. For example, if we linearize the Phillips curve at $g = 0$, the point where there is zero labor market tightness, and also substitute in our empirical estimate of $\gamma = 3.2$, we can see that the slope of the Phillips curve is 0.8. This estimate would suggest that a surprise of 0.1 percentage point in labor market tightness would have a direct effect on the contemporaneous annualized inflation rate of 0.08 percentage point, and hence would raise the year-on-year inflation rate by 0.02 percentage points. Such an order of magnitude of the direct impact effect

*Table B1.* Slope of Phillips curve and impact effects of surprises in the unemployment gap.

| Initial Unemployment Gap | Slope of Phillips Curve | Impact Effect of Surprise in the Unemployment Gap1/ |
|---|---|---|
| $g = u^* - u$ | $F'[g]$ | $0.1F'[g]/4$ |
| −3.00 | 0.26 | 0.01 |
| −2.00 | 0.36 | 0.01 |
| −1.00 | 0.51 | 0.01 |
| 0.00 | 0.80 | 0.02 |
| +1.00 | 1.42 | 0.04 |
| +1.6 | 2.22 | 0.06 |
| +2.00 | 3.20 | 0.08 |
| +3.00 | 12.80 | 0.32 |

1/Response of year-on-year inflation to an unanticipated shift of 0.1 percentage point in the unemployment gap.

of marginal changes in labor market tightness on year-on-year inflation is consistent with numerous studies of the U.S. inflation process based on linear models that suggest that the direct impact effects on inflation of changes in unemployment or output gaps are extremely small. Indeed, such findings have led some commentators in U.S. policymaking circles to sometimes describe the in-quarter and 1 to 2-quarters-ahead year-on-year inflation rate as "predetermined," or as effectively independent of small surprises in the degree of labor market tightness.

Although our nonlinear model encompasses this prediction in the neighborhood of zero excess demand, it also suggests that the direct impact effects of a marginal increase in labor market tightness can be much more significant when there is already substantial tightness in the labor market. To illustrate, Table B1 shows the slope of the Phillips curve, and the direct impact effects on the year-on-year inflation rate of a 0.1 percentage point change in the unemployment gap, at various initial levels of the unemployment gap. Note that the direct impact effects accelerate as the unemployment gap widens.

To appreciate how easily the inflation process can become explosive in our nonlinear model when policy follows a conventional Taylor rule, it needs to be recognized that the full effects on inflation of shocks to the unemployment gap can be much larger than the direct effects. This reflects the fact that inflation expectations have a model-consistent component and depend on the entire timepath of the unemployment gap that rational agents come to expect, given their information about the nature of the policy rule. When our Phillips curve is linearized around the NAIRU, our model satisfies the Blanchard–Kahn conditions for a Taylor rule calibrated with the weights originally suggested by Taylor (1993): $w_\pi = 1.5$, $w_u = 1.0$, and $\rho = 0$.[49] However, if we linearize the Phillips curve around a point of excess demand at which the unemployment gap exceeds 1.6 percentage points, the Blanchard–Kahn conditions are no longer satisfied. In this case, the Taylor rule is sufficiently myopic in terms of responding to inflationary pressures that monetary policy fails to provide an anchor for inflation expectations and the solutions of the model become explosive.

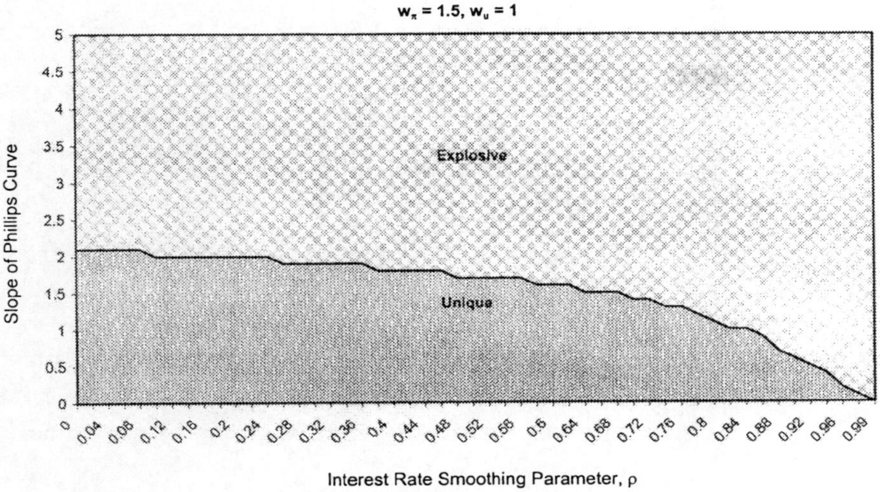


*Figure B2.* Regions of uniqueness and explosiveness (generalized Taylor rule in the nonlinear model). Policy reaction function: $rs_t = \rho rs_{t-1} + (1-\rho)[w_\pi(\pi 4_t) + w_u(g_t)]$.

As is evident in Figure B1, one of the striking features of the stability conditions for the Fuhrer-Moore model is that they appear to be independent of the degree of interest rate smoothing. This points to a general problem with linear models of the inflation process, which imply that slow monetary policy responses to information about future inflation developments only have second-order welfare consequences. Figure B2 reports the regions of stability for our nonlinear model in terms of both the slope of the Phillips curve and the degree of interest rate smoothing. For $\rho = 0$, the critical slope of the Phillips curve, about 2.2, corresponds to an unemployment rate of 1.6 percentage points below the NAIRU, as noted in Table B1. Notice that in the nonlinear model, the region of stability shrinks further if interest rate smoothing is imposed on an already myopic policy rule.

### B. *LWW Interest Rate Change Rules*

Figure B3 reports the regions of stability for the class of interest rate change rules suggested by Levin, Wieland, and Williams (LWW: 1999). In this case, the general form of the reaction function is:

$$rs_t = rs_{t-1} + (w_\pi(\pi n_t) + w_y(y_t)) \tag{B.2}$$

where $\pi n_t$ is an $n$-quarter moving average of inflation measured over the previous $n$ quarters. The top and middle panels of Figure B3 consider the two optimal rule parameterizations reported by Levin, Wieland and Williams (1999), where $n$ is equal to 4 quarters and 12 quarters; the longer lag structure on inflation was found to be optimal in a linearized version of

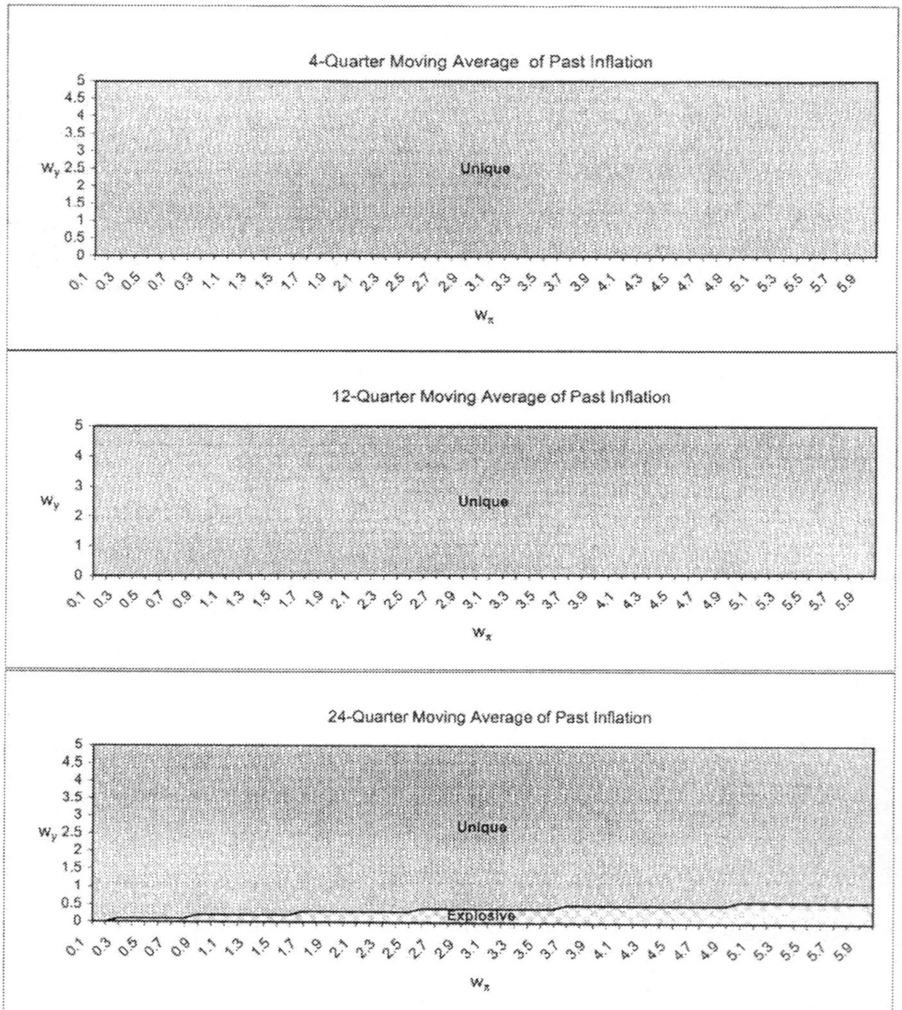


*Figure B3.* Regions of uniqueness and explosiveness (LWW rule in the Fuhrer-Moore model). Policy reaction function: $rs_t = rs_{t-1} + w_\pi(\pi 4_t) + w_y(y_t)$.

the FRB-U.S. model, while the shorter lag structure was found to be optimal in the other linear models that they included in their study. In this case again, even where there is extreme interest rate smoothing and monetary policy responds to very backward-looking measures of inflation, the linear model is stable for an incredibly wide range of weights on inflation and output. The lower panel of Figure B3 considers an even more extreme case of myopic reaction functions, where the reaction function now depends on a six-year moving average of past inflation. Here there is some evidence of instability in the model; but in contrast to the type of results found by Cristiano and Gust (1999), in this case explosiveness can arise from setting too low a weight on output.

The LWW rule has extremely poor stabilizing properties in the nonlinear model developed in this paper. First, for the model that was estimated the rule is so myopic and backward-looking that it fails to provide an anchor for inflation expectations. Second, even if one recalibrates the model to reduce the effects of overheating very substantially, an optimal parameterization of the LWW rule still gives rise to significant boom and bust cycles.

It does not seem to be widely recognized that interest rate change rules such as equation B.2 are exactly equivalent to targeting a trend change in the price level when $w_y = 0$, and result in approximate price level targeting for small values of $w_y$. To see this, consider a simple case in which the interest rate change depends solely on the quarterly change in the price level $(P)$ expressed at an annual rate:

$$rs_t = rs_{t-1} + w_\pi \pi_t \tag{B.3}$$

where $\pi_t = 4(P_t - P_{t-1})$. As initial conditions, assume that inflation is on target and the real interest rate is at its equilibrium value (i.e., in period 0, $rs_0 = rs^*$ and $\pi_0 = \pi^* = \pi^e$, where * denotes equilibrium).

Now assume that a demand or supply shock raises the inflation rate in period 1 to some arbitrary value $\pi_1$. It is interesting, and perhaps even surprising, that monetary policy governed by equation B.3 would attempt to move the price level back to the original baseline path. This will be the case, for example, if long-run neutrality holds (as LWW claim for each of the models they consider), because long-run neutrality implies that the real interest rate must return back to its initial value. But if the real interest rate returns back to control, the nominal interest rate must also eventually return back to control in some period $T$ since, by assumption, the rule is successful in moving inflation back to its initial level of $\pi^*$.

If we now sum equation B.3 between periods 1 and $T$ we obtain

$$rs_T - rs_0 = w_\pi \sum_{i=1}^{T} \pi_i \tag{B.4}$$

So $rs_T - rs_0 = 0$ implies

$$\sum_{i=1}^{T} \pi_i = 0. \tag{B.5}$$

Thus, under the assumption that long-run neutrality holds, a policy rule in the form of equation B.3 essentially amounts to a price-level targeting rule, since any shock that generates positive inflation must be offset at some point by negative inflation rates. This result obviously carries over to cases in which the contemporaneous inflation rate in equation B.3 is replaced by some finite moving average lag structure on past inflation; and even when the rule is extended to include a term in the output gap, as in the general form of LWW rules described by equation B.2, it continues to bear a close resemblance to price-level targeting.

Thus, it should not be surprising that such myopic LWW rules can generate extremely poor business cycle properties in models with strong inflation persistence and convexity in the Phillips curve.

## Acknowledgments

The views expressed are those of the authors and do not necessarily reflect the views of the International Monetary Fund. We thank Jeffrey Fuhrer, Lars Svensson, Robert Tetlow, and Volker Wieland for useful discussions and Susanna Mursula and Sarma Jayanthi for extensive research assistance.

## Notes

1. Losses associated with interest rate variability are reflected in the policy objective function, however, and thereby influence the optimal calibration of the policy reaction function.
2. Attention to the credibility problem was stimulated by Kydland and Prescott (1977) and Calvo (1978).
3. Barro and Gorden (1983a, 1983b), Backus and Driffill (1985), Canzoneri (1985), and Rogoff (1985), among others, were instrumental in advancing the analysis of these issues.
4. The arguments are further articulated in Flood and Isard (1990), which corrects a technical error identified by Lohmann (1990).
5. The terminology emanated from Persson and Tabellini (1990).
6. Recent examples of such papers were included in the programs of the NBER Conference on Monetary Policy Rules (January 15–17, 1998), the Federal Reserve Bank of San Francisco Conference on Central Bank Inflation Targeting (March 6–7, 1998), the Riksbank-IIES Conference on Monetary Policy Rules (June 12–13, 1998), the 1998 Symposium on Computational Economics at Cambridge University (June 29–July 1, 1998), and the Reserve Bank of New Zealand Conference on Monetary Policy Under Uncertainty (June 29–July 3, 1998). Earlier contributions to the inflation targeting literature include the conference volumes Leiderman and Svensson (1995), Haldane (1995), Federal Reserve Bank of Kansas City (1996), and Lowe (1997).
7. A crucial prerequisite for exercising discretion intelligently, of course, is that the monetary authorities must understand the time-consistency issue and continuously evaluate the extent to which their behavior may be affecting the credibility of their announced objectives.
8. In this context, Svensson argues that the strategy of inflation targeting can be viewed as a way of committing to minimize a particular loss function by adopting a rule (first-order condition) that involves target variables or forecasts of target variables and by implementing communication practices that allow the public to evaluate the monetary authority's performance and hold it accountable.
9. For example, Wieland (1998), Rudebusch and Svensson (1999), Svensson (1999a).
10. For example, McCallum and Nelson (1998, 1999), Henderson and Kim (1999).
11. For example, McCallum (1988), Levin, Wieland, and Williams (1999).
12. Data uncertainties, which also have implications for the optimal strength of policy reactions, are not addressed in this paper; see Orphanides (1998) for a recent exploration of this topic. On the general importance of changing the strength of policy responses when the (perceived) macro model changes, see Amano, Coletti, and Macklem (1998).
13. See McCallum and Nelson (1998, 1999) and Henderson and Kim (1999) for studies of monetary policy rules in models with optimizing agents rather than postulated Phillips curves.
14. See, for example, the Symposium comprised of Blanchard and Katz (1997), Galbraith (1997), Gordon (1997), Rogerson (1997), Staiger, Stock, and Watson (1997), and Stiglitz (1997), as published in the Winter 1997 issue of the *Journal of Economic Perspectives*.

15. Staiger, Stock, and Watson (1997).
16. For example, Galbraith (1997).
17. Other recent analyses of the implications of NAIRU uncertainty (or output gap uncertainty) include Wieland (1998) and Smets (1998), who use simple linear models with backward-looking expectations to demonstrate that uncertainty about the NAIRU (or about the Phillips-curve parameters on which NAIRU estimates depend) provides a motive for cautious policy reactions.
18. Isard and Laxton (1998), Isard, Laxton, and Eliasson (1998).
19. Williams (1999) finds that even in models with hundreds of state variables, parsimonious specifications of simple policy rules appear to be very effective in achieving stabilization objectives. See also Rudebusch and Svensson (1999).
20. The model contains important backward- and forward-looking components, as derived from the bargaining framework in Fuhrer and Moore (1995a, 1995b), but the functional form is less restrictive and is more consistent with empirical evidence that suggests that there is a small weight on the "rational" or forward-looking component of the US inflation process—for example, see Fuhrer (1997).
21. The base-case model variant assumes $N = 12$, but to explore the sensitivity of the results to the length of contracts we have also conducted simulations with $N = 4$.
22. In equations (1) and (2), the estimated value of $\gamma$ is 3.20. The estimation and stochastic simulations are based on the assumption that $\phi_t = \max[0, u_t^* - 4]$, and $u_t^*$ is always strictly greater than 4 in the actual and hypothetical data we address.
23. For discussions of the potential pitfalls associated with conventional tests for asymmetries in the Phillips curve, see Clark, Laxton, and Rose (1996) and Laxton, Rose, and Tambakis (1999).
24. The latter would be implied by constant adherence to a given policy rule. Note that equation (7) is relevant for interpreting history and updating estimates of the NAIRU, but that apart from assuming stationarity, we do not require specific assumptions about the distribution of the $\epsilon_t^u$ terms, which are not drawn directly in the simulation analysis.
25. Kuttner (1992, 1994) has applied this idea to measuring potential output. In using information about the error terms in each of the two Phillips curves, our procedure for estimating the NAIRU and DNAIRU essentially gives equal weight to the data on the CPI and the CPI excluding food and energy.
26. The simulations set $\phi_t = u_t^* - 4$, so the convex term in the unemployment rate in equations (1) and (2), based on the estimates reported in Table 1, can be expressed as $3.20F(g)$, where $g = u^* - u$. The linear approximations in equations (1a) and (2a) replace $F(g)$ with $[F'(0)](u^* - u) = (3.20/4)(u^* - u) = 0.80(u^* - u)$.
27. Estimates of equations based on the Michigan survey measures of inflation expectations suggested a weight of .6 on the model consistent component, but there was significant evidence of residual autocorrelation in the estimated equations.
28. Fuhrer and Moore (1995b) argue that longer-term interest rates are more relevant for explaining aggregate demand and unemployment. The implications of such an alternative representation of the monetary transmission mechanism might be interesting to explore as an extension of the analysis in this paper.
29. See Laxton, Rose, and Tambakis (1999) for details on the estimation.
30. The qualitative results and main conclusions of this paper do not hinge on the precise nature of the unemployment dynamics, although they clearly depend on a positive response of unemployment to the real interest rate, as well as on the existence of both lags in the response of unemployment to policy actions and a persistent component of unemployment. It might be interesting, in future work, to consider modifications of the model in which the response of unemployment to the interest rate was forward looking. It might also be interesting to treat the parameters of the unemployment equation as an additional element of uncertainty—along with the level of the NAIRU—that policymakers take into account when choosing the "optimal calibration" for a policy rule.
31. Interest in this formulation received considerable impetus from Taylor (1993), who defined his rule in terms of the output gap. Recent studies of the performance of Taylor rules can be found, for example, in Levin, Wieland, and Williams (1999) and Taylor (1999a).
32. Appendix II discusses the stability conditions for models that are based on linear and nonlinear Phillips curves and explains why the conventional Taylor rule ensures stability in models with linear Phillips curves but does not ensure stability in nonlinear models of the inflation process.
33. Different types of IFB rules have been shown to deliver reasonable economic performances over a wide range of disturbances; see, for example, Amano, Coletti, and Macklem (1998), Haldane and Batini (1999), and Rudebusch and Svensson (1999).
34. The $\beta$ parameter also provides a basis for analyzing the pros and cons of central bank transparency. As

Faust and Svensson (1998) emphasize, transparency about the central bank's objectives, by improving the accuracy of the public's information about $\beta$ (or alternatively, about the difference between $u_t^* - \beta$ and the long-run DNAIRU, $u^*$), can make it possible for the public to distinguish more accurately between the intended components of macroeconomic outcomes and the central bank's control errors, thereby making the central bank's reputation and credibility more sensitive to its actions.

35. The stochastic simulations were performed using a robust and efficient Newton–Raphson simulation algorithm that is now available in portable TROLL—for a discussion of the properties of this algorithm see Juillard and others (1998).
36. The setting $\nu = 0.5$ corresponds to the base-case value used by Rudebusch and Svensson (1999). Note also that the setting of $\beta$ is irrelevant when $\theta = 0$.
37. Recall the discussion in Section III.A on how the linear Phillips curves are calibrated.
38. Clarida, Gali, and Gertler (1998) consider specifications based, alternatively, on output gaps and unemployment gaps. The CGG rule is derived by combining the following two equations

$$\begin{aligned} rs_t^* &= r^* + \tilde{E}_t\{(\beta - 1)(\pi 4_{t+1} - \pi^{TAR}) + \gamma(\bar{u}_t - u_t) \mid \Omega_t\} \\ rs_t &= (1 - \rho) rs_t^* + \rho rs_{t-1} \end{aligned}$$

where $rs_t^*$ represents a target nominal interest rate. Thus, the constant term in equation (18) can be decomposed into $c = r^* - (\beta - 1)\pi^{TAR}$.

39. Clarida, Gali, and Gertler (1998) also suggest that it is more consistent with actual Fed behavior for the interest rate reaction function to depend upon the one or two-quarter ahead forecast of the unemployment gap rather than the contemporaneous unemployment gap. It would be interesting to further explore the stabilizing properties of CGG rules to see if they change significantly when the rule is based on forecasts of the unemployment gap rather than contemporaneous measures.
40. It may be noted here that the literature has distinguished between IFB rules that embody rule-consistent inflation forecasts, as does our IFB2 rule, and IFB rules defined in terms of constant-interest-rate inflation forecasts.
41. We did not undertake an extensive search for the optimal inflation forecast horizon but note that three quarters is roughly half the time that is generally believed to be required for interest rates to have their full effects on the economy. By comparison, Clarida, Gali, and Gertler (1998) use a four-quarter-ahead inflation forecast, while Haldane and Batini (1999) and Rudebusch and Svensson (1999) explore the performances of IFB rules with a range of forecast horizons.
42. Svensson (1999b) suggests that a two-year horizon might be preferable on conceptual grounds, reflecting his notion (perhaps inferred from models with substantial inflation inertia) that inflation expectations at shorter horizons have significant predetermined components. This suggestion seems to reflect a preference for rules that (approximately) correspond to the first-order conditions from policy optimization problems, along with the notion that such first-order conditions boil down to simpler expressions of the relationship between the interest rate and an inflation forecast when the inflation forecast is not largely predetermined.
43. In a separate forthcoming paper we argue that the high estimates of $\rho$ (and associated high $t$-statistics) that are obtained when CGG rules are fitted to historical data are probably reflections of specification error.
44. We chose this model because it was more easily accessible than the other models considered by Levin, Wieland, and Williams (1999). We are indebted to Jeffrey Fuhrer for taking the time to help us replicate some of his earlier results. The results reported in this appendix have been derived from the parameter estimates reported in Fuhrer and Moore (1995b).
45. Our line of argument in this appendix is broadly similar to the one presented in Christiano and Gust (1999), who show not only that poorly parameterized simple rules can give rise to poor simulation properties in their particular model, but also that choosing the parameters of rules on the basis of one particular class of models can give rise to indeterminacy or explosiveness in other models.
46. It is convenient here to follow Taylor (1993) in defining the rule in terms of the output gap rather than the unemployment gap. For notational convenience we have dropped the constant term in the equation by assuming that the equilibrium real interest rate and long-run inflation target are zero.
47. For example, the long-run effects of a permanent unitary change in the output gap is equal to the short-run effect, $(1 - \rho)w_y$, divided by $(1 - \rho)$.
48. Under the global linearity assumption, the estimated slope of the Phillips curve (based on post war U.S. data) suggests that unemployment gaps or output gaps have small effects on the inflation process. These small effects imply that it can be very costly, in the context of these models, to reduce inflation once high inflation expectations have become entrenched. The estimated slope also means that for given inflation expectations,

the marginal effect on inflation of an increase in excess demand is small, even when the level of excess demand is high.

49. Taylor (1993) suggested a weight of 0.5 on the output gap, which we translate into a weight of 1.0 on the unemployment gap under the Okun's Law assumption that the unemployment gap varies approximately half as widely as the output gap over the business cycle.

## References


Amano, Robert, Don Coletti, and Tiff Macklem. (1998). "Monetary Rules When Economic Behavior Changes." Forthcoming in Reserve Bank of New Zealand Conference Volume on *Monetary Policy Under Uncertainty*.

Backus, David, and John Driffill. (1985). "Inflation and Reputation." *American Economic Review* 75(3), 530–538.

Barro, Robert J., and David B. Gordon. (1983a). "Positive Theory of Monetary Policy in a Natural Rate Model." *Journal of Political Economy* 91, 589–610.

———. (1983b). "Rules, Discretion, and Reputation in a Model of Monetary Policy." *Journal of Monetary Economics* 12, 101–121.

Blanchard, Olivier J., and Charles M. Kahn. (1980). "The Solution of Linear Difference Models Under Rational Expectations." *Econometrica* 48, 1305–1311.

Blanchard, Olivier, and Lawrence F. Katz. (1997). "What We Know and Do Not Know About the Natural Rate of Unemployment." *Journal of Economic Perspectives* 11(1), 51–72.

Calvo, Guillermo. (1978). "On the Time Consistency of Optimal Policy in a Monetary Economy." *Econometrica* 46, 1411–1428.

Canzoneri, Matthew. (1985). "Monetary Policy Games and the Role of Private Information." *American Economic Review* 75, 1056-1428.

Christiano, Lawrence J., Martin Eichenbaum, and Charles Evans. (1998). "Modeling Money." NBER Working Paper 6371.

Christiano, Lawrence J., and Christopher J. Gust. (1999). "Taylor Rules in a Simple Limited Participation Model." Working Paper.

Clarida, Richard, Jordi Gali, and Mark Gertler. (1998). "Monetary Policy Rules and Macroeconomic Stability: Evidence and Some Theory." NBER Working Paper No. 6442.

Clark, Peter B., Douglas Laxton, and David Rose. (1996). "Asymmetry in the U.S. Output-Inflation Nexus: Issues and Evidence." *IMF Staff Papers* 43, 216–250.

Debelle, Guy, and Douglas Laxton. (1997). "Is the Phillips Curve Really a Curve? Some Evidence for Canada, the United Kingdom, and the United States." *Staff Papers*, International Monetary Fund 44, 249–282.

Faust, Jon W., and Lars E. O. Svensson. (1998). "Credibility and Transparency: Monetary Policy with Unobservable Goals." NBER Working Paper 6452.

Federal Reserve Bank of Kansas City. (1996). *Achieving Price Stability: A Symposium* (Kansas City, Missouri).

Flood, Robert, and Peter Isard. (1989). "Monetary Policy Strategies." *Staff Papers*, International Monetary Fund 36, 612–632.

———. (1990). "Monetary Policy Strategies—A Correction." *Staff Papers*, International Monetary Fund 37, 446–448.

Fuhrer, Jeffrey C., and George R. Moore. (1995a). "Inflation Persistence." *The Quarterly Journal of Economics* 109, 127–159.

———. (1995b). "Monetary Policy Trade-offs and the Correlation Between Nominal Interests Rates and Real Output." *American Economic Review* 85, 219–239.

Fuhrer, Jeffrey C. (1997). "The (Un) Importance of Forward-Looking Behavior in Price Specifications." *The Journal of Money Credit and Banking* 29, 338–350.

Galbraith, James K. (1997). "Time to Ditch the NAIRU." *The Journal of Economic Perspectives* 11(1), 93–108.

Gordon, Robert J. (1997). "The Time-Varying NAIRU and its Implications for Economic Policy." *The Journal of Economic Perspectives* 11(1), 11–32.

Haldane, Andrew G. (ed.). (1995). *Targeting Inflation*. London: Bank of England.

———, and Nicoletta Batini. (1999). "Forward-Looking Rules for Monetary Policy," in Taylor, 1999b.

Henderson, Dale, and Jinill Kim. (1999). "Exact Utilities Under Alternative Monetary Rules in a Simple Macro Model with Optimizing Agents," this volume.

Isard, Peter, and Douglas Laxton. (1998). "Monetary Policy with NAIRU Uncertainty and Endogenous Credibility: Perspectives on Policy Rules and the Gains from Experimentation and Transparency." Forthcoming in Reserve Bank of New Zealand Conference Volume on *Monetary Policy Under Uncertainty*.

———, and Ann-Charlotte Eliasson. (1998). "Inflation Targeting with NAIRU Uncertainty and Endogenous Policy Credibility." Forthcoming, *Journal of Economic Dynamics and Control*.

Juillard, Michel, Douglas Laxton, Peter McAdam, and Hope Pioro. (1998). "An Algorithm Competition: First-Order Iterations Versus Newton-Based Techniques." *Journal of Economic Dynamics and Control* 22, 1291–1318.

Kuttner, Kenneth N. (1992). "Monetary Policy With Uncertain Estimates of Potential Output." Reserve Bank of Chicago, *Economic Perspectives*, 2–15.

———. (1994) "Estimating Potential Output as a Latent Variable." Research Department, Federal Reserve Bank of Chicago, *Journal of Business and Economic Statistics* 12(3), 55–79.

Kydland, Finn E., and Edward C. Prescott. (1977). "Rules Rather than Discretion: The Inconsistency of Optimal Plans." *Journal of Political Economy* 85, 473–492.

Laxton, Douglas, David Rose, and Demosthenes Tambakis. (1999). "The U.S. Phillips Curve: The Case for Asymmetry." Forthcoming, *Journal of Economic Dynamics and Control*.

———, Guy Meredith, and David Rose. (1995). "Asymmetric Effects of Economic Activity on Inflation: Evidence and Policy Implications." *Staff Papers*, International Monetary Fund 42(2), 344–374.

Leiderman, Leonardo, and Lars E. O. Svensson (eds.). (1995). *Inflation Targets*. London: Centre of Economic Policy Research.

Levin, Andrew, Volker Wieland, and John Williams. (1999). "Robustness of Simple Monetary Policy Rules Under Model Uncertainty," in Taylor, 1999b.

Lohmann, Susanne. (1990). "Monetary Policy Strategies-A Correction: Comment on Flood and Isard." *Staff Papers*, International Monetary Fund 37, 440–445.

Lowe, Phillip (ed.). (1997). *Monetary Policy and Inflation Targeting*. Sydney: Reserve Bank of Australia.

McCallum, Bennett T. (1988). "Robustness Properties of a Rule for Monetary Policy." *Carnegie-Rochester Series on Public Policy* 29, 173–203.

———, and Edward Nelson. (1998). "Nominal Income Targeting in an Open-Economy Optimizing Model." Prepared for Sveriges Riksbank-IIES Conference on Monetary Policy Rules, Stockholm (June 12–13).

———, and Edward Nelson. (1999) "Performance of Operational Policy Rules in an Estimated Semi-Classical Structural Model," in Taylor, 1999b.

Orphanides, Athanasios. (1998). "Monetary Policy Evaluation With Noisy Information." Working Paper, Federal Reserve Board.

Persson, Torsten, and Guido Tabellini. (1990). "Macroeconomic Policy, Credibility and Politics." New York: Hardwood Academic Publishers.

Rogerson, Richard. (1997). "Theory Ahead of Language in the Economics of Unemployment." *The Journal of Economic Perspectives* 11(1), 73–92.

Rogoff, Kenneth. (1985). "The Optimal Degree of Commitment to an International Monetary Target." *Quarterly Journal of Economics* 100, 1169–1189.

Rudebusch, Glenn, and Lars Svensson. (1999). "Policy Rules for Inflation Targeting," in Taylor, 1999b.

Schaling, Eric. (1998). "The Nonlinear Phillips Curve and Inflation Forecast Targeting—Symmetric versus Asymmetric Monetary Policy Rules." Working Paper.

Smets, Frank. (1998). "Output Gap Uncertainty: Does It Matter for the Taylor Rule?" Forthcoming in Reserve Bank of New Zealand conference volume on *Monetary Policy Under Uncertainty*.

Staiger, Douglas, James H. Stock, and Mark W. Watson. (1997). "The NAIRU, Unemployment and Monetary Policy." *Journal of Economic Perspectives* 11(1), 33–49.

Stiglitz, Joseph. (1997). "Reflections on the Natural Rate Hypothesis." *Journal of Economic Perspectives* 11(1), 3–10.

Svensson, Lars E. O. (1999a). "Inflation Targeting as a Monetary Policy Rule," *Journal of Monetary Economics* 43(3), 607–654; forthcoming in Taylor, 1999.

———. (1999b). "Monetary Policy Issues for the Eurosystem." Forthcoming in *Carnegie-Rochester Conference Series on Public Policy*.

Taylor, John B. (1993). "Discretion Versus Policy Rules in Practice." *Carnegie-Rochester Conference Series on Public Policy* 39, 195–214.

———. (1998). "The Robustness and Efficiency of Monetary Policy Rules as Guidelines for Interest Rate Setting by the European Central Bank." Prepared for Sveriges Riksbank-IIES Conference on Monetary Policy Rules, Stockholm (June 12–13).

———. (1999a). "A Historical Analysis of Monetary Policy Rules." NBER Working Paper No. 6768; forthcoming in Taylor, 1999b.

——— (ed.). (1999b). *Monetary Policy Rules*. Chicago: University of Chicago Press.

Wieland, Volker. (1998). "Monetary Policy and Uncertainty about the Natural Unemployment Rate." Finance and Economics Discussion Paper No. 22, Federal Reserve Board.

Williams, John C. (1999). "Simple Rules for Monetary Policy." Draft.

# Comment

BY JO ANNA GRAY

The Henderson and Kim paper is part of a larger research agenda concerned with the evaluation of monetary policy rules. Among the issues addressed in the paper are several that involve aspects of the choice of microfoundations in modeling macroeconomic behavior. This discussion notes three in particular:

(i) The appropriate choice of a welfare criterion, with emphasis on the choice between the objective function of a policy maker and the utility of a representative agent.

(ii) The error that may be introduced by using approximate solutions of models rather than exact solutions that permit exact utility calculations.

(iii) The justification provided for the non-neutrality of money.

Direct evaluation of the utility of economic agents rather than indirect evaluation through the objective function of a policy maker is surely a direction worth exploring. In general, however, one cannot expect the convenience of an economy in which welfare is adequately characterized by the utility of a single group of homogeneous agents (the household sector in the Henderson and Kim paper). The introduction of multiple groups with independent economic interests (laborers, entrepreneurs, retirees, etc.) means that the choice of a policy rule will typically have distributional consequences. It follows that a single representation of utility will generally be inadequate as a metric for policy evaluation, and that retreat to a social welfare function with *ad hoc* attributes is not an unlikely outcome.

Another emphasis of the paper is exact utility calculation rather than approximate solution. In the paper's introduction, the authors suggest that reliance on approximation rather than exact solutions may produce erroneous welfare conclusions. However, the valued-added of exact utility calculation is not actually addressed in the analysis of the paper. In other work the authors have analyzed the choice of monetary policy rules using approximate solutions and so they are in a position to compare the outcomes of the two approaches. This is an exercise they promise to undertake in a future paper.

Perhaps the most ambitious modeling choice in the paper is the characterization of both firms and households as monopolistic competitors, a decision with non-trivial implications for the complexity of the paper's analysis. The motivation for the choice is to provide improved microfoundations for the wage and price rigidities assumed in the paper. But the case is blurred by several considerations. One would normally incorporate microfoundations into a model of price stickiness in order to insure that the conclusions drawn are robust with respect to the additional assumptions needed to explain the existence of price stickiness. However, the authors assume, rather than derive, one-period fixed nominal wage and price contracts. In addition, they leave unaddressed the question of whether the paper's conclusions would be any different if perfectly competitive workers and firms, rather than monopolistically competitive entities, were assumed. The reader is left to wonder if the advantages of the more sophisticated modeling approach, once they are articulated and evaluated, will outweigh the disadvantages of the more cumbersome analytics.

The decision to model firms and households as monopolistic competitors leads the authors to a second choice that is of independent interest. The authors use subsidies to eliminate the distorting effects of monopoly on resource allocation. In doing so, they also eliminate the possibility that optimal policy may involve a trade-off between stabilization objectives and other economic objectives such as Pareto-efficient resource allocation. It is natural to ask if something interesting is lost here, particularly given that exact utility calculations may introduce an interaction between stabilization outcomes and resource allocation.

Finally, does it make sense to characterize individual households as monopsonistic suppliers of labor, and to offer their monopsonistic behavior as the underlying reason for nominal wage contracts? The assumption that monopolistic competition characterizes the structure of the goods market has become widely acceptable, and one might wish to extend the assumption to the labor market in cases in which workers act as a collective (as in the case of unions, for example). The case for characterizing the behavior of individual households in this way is less obvious, and the authors may wish to offer more of their thinking on the matter in future work.

# Comment

BY LARS E. O. SVENSSON

Isard, Laxton and Eliasson (ILE) have written a fine and impressive paper, with much content. It presents an estimated empirical model of the U.S. economy, with a nonlinear Phillips curve (with both forward- and backward-looking elements) and an unobservable time-varying natural unemployment rate. Stochastic simulations and stability analysis are undertaken with alternative simple "instrument rules," that is, rules specifying the instrument as a given reaction function of directly observable or constructed, synthetic variables. Furthermore, since the natural unemployment rate is unobservable, instrument rules that involve responses to the unemployment gap (the deviation between unemployment and the natural rate) must rely on the policy-makers' estimate of the time-varying natural rate.

A number of interesting detailed results are presented. The main result of the paper, as I interpret it, can be expressed as: "Beware of simple instrument rules (especially conventional linear and backward-looking ones) as an automatic pilot for the economy." Such rules may even result in instability. So-called "forecast-based" rules, where the instrument responds to the deviation of model-consistent inflation forecasts from the inflation target, perform better than the backward-looking instrument rules when the instrument responds to the deviation between current and lagged inflation and the inflation target (in addition to responding to the estimated unemployment gap).

My discussion will focus on an intuitive explanation of why linear backward-looking reaction functions will be inferior in a non-linear model, and why a reaction function, where the instrument responds to an inflation forecast, is likely to perform better, but is not optimal.

## 1. Instrument Rules and Targeting Rules

First, however, I would like to raise the issue about how to handle practical monetary policy, given the paper's warning about the possible instability of conventional instrument rules. The paper states that it is very important for policymakers to calibrate their nominal interest rate adjustments on the basis of forward-looking measures of real interest rates. This can be interpreted as the paper advocating modified instrument rules rather than the conventional backward-looking instrument rules. However, in the real world, instrument rules are never applied mechanically. For several reasons, they are, at best, used as guidelines and benchmarks, which may illuminate the monetary policy decision but never be a substitute for a forward-looking decision framework for monetary policy. One of these reasons is the lack of a commitment mechanism, by which the central bank could commit itself to a given instrument rule. Another is the manifest inefficiency of any simple rule, and the strong incentives to deviate from it, since it relies on much less information than is efficient, including extra-model information that motivate judgemental adjustments.

Instead, as argued in Svensson (1999a, 1999b), I believe that the so-called "targeting rules," which involve a commitment to minimize a given loss function or to fulfill some (approximate first-order) condition for (forecasts of) the target variables, but allow the optimization to be done under discretion, is a more fruitful and realistic formalization of real-world monetary policy. In particular, as discussed in Svensson (1999b), I believe that "forecast targeting" (meaning selecting an instrument path such that resulting forecasts of inflation and the output gap minimizes an intertemporal loss function) rather than a commitment to a simple instrument rule is the best way of maintaining price stability. Furthermore, I believe that a generalization from "mean" forecast targeting to "distribution" forecast targeting is a practical way of handling both nonlinearity and model uncertainty in monetary policy.

## 2. A Simple Model with a Nonlinear Phillips Curve

Let me now illustrate what inflation targeting, interpreted as a commitment to minimize a particular loss function, implies in a model with a nonlinear Phillips curve, and how the resulting equilibrium can be used to illuminate the inferiority of linear backward-looking instrument rules and the somewhat better performance of a forecast-based instrument rule. I choose a simple model which can be seen as a simple variant of the more elaborate model of ILE.

Assume that the aggregate supply is given by the simple accelerationist Phillips curve

$$\pi_{t+1} = \pi_t + f(\tilde{u}_t) + \varepsilon^{\pi}_{t+1}, \tag{2.1}$$

where $\pi_t$ is inflation in quarter $t$,

$$\tilde{u}_t \equiv u_t - u^*_t$$

is the unemployment gap (where $u_t$ is the unemployment rate and $u^*_t$ is the natural unemployment rate), and $\varepsilon^{\pi}_t$ is N(0,$\sigma^2_\pi$), a normally distributed exogenous shock with zero mean and variance $\sigma^2_\pi$. The natural unemployment rate is a random walk,

$$u^*_{t+1} = u^*_t + \varepsilon^{u*}_{t+1},$$

where $\varepsilon^{u*}_t$ is N(0,$\sigma^2_{u*}$).

Nonlinearity enters in the Phillips curve via the nonlinear function $f$, which fulfills

$$f' < 0, \quad f(0) = 0, \quad f'' \geq 0.$$

Several functional forms can be used. ILE use the form

$$f(\tilde{u}_t) = -\gamma \frac{\tilde{u}_t}{\tilde{u}_t - 4}.$$

Schaling (1998) instead uses

$$f(\tilde{u}_t) = -\frac{\gamma \tilde{u}_t}{1 - \varphi\gamma\tilde{u}_t},$$

where $\varphi \geq 0$ is used as an index of convexity. For convenience, I choose a simple quadratic function that allows an (approximate) analytical solution, namely

$$f(\tilde{u}_t) = \begin{cases} -\gamma\tilde{u}_t + \varphi\tilde{u}_t^2 & \tilde{u}_t \leq \gamma/2\varphi \\ -\gamma^2/4\varphi & \tilde{u}_t > \gamma/2\varphi, \end{cases} \tag{2.2}$$

for the parameters $\varphi \geq 0$ and $\gamma > 0$. This function is continuous and differentiable. For $\varphi > 0$, it is decreasing and convex for $\tilde{u}_t \leq \gamma/2\varphi$ and constant for $\tilde{u}_t > \gamma/2\varphi$. For $\varphi = 0$, it is linear, $f(\tilde{u}_t) = -\gamma\tilde{u}_t$. Thus, $\varphi$ can be interpreted as an index of convexity and nonlinearity.

Aggregate demand is taken to be a linear function in terms of the unemployment gap,

$$\tilde{u}_{t+1} = \eta_u \tilde{u}_t + \eta_r(i_t - \pi_{t+1|t} - \bar{r}) + \varepsilon_{t+1}^{\tilde{u}}, \tag{2.3}$$

where $i_t$ is a short nominal interest rate (denoted $rs_t$ in ILE) and the central bank's instrument, $x_{t+\tau|t} \equiv \mathrm{E}_t x_{t+\tau}$ for any variable $x$ denotes the expectation of $x_{t+\tau}$ conditional on information available in quarter $t$, $\bar{r} > 0$ is the "natural" real interest rate, $\varepsilon_{t+1}^{u}$ is $\mathrm{N}(0,\sigma_{\tilde{u}}^2)$, and parameters $\eta_u$ and $\eta_r$ are positive. The natural real interest rate is the constant real interest rate that, in the absence of shocks, would result in a constant zero unemployment gap.

Assume an intertemporal loss function for the central bank,

$$\mathrm{E}_t \sum_{\tau=0}^{\infty} \delta^{\tau} L_{t+\tau},$$

where $0 < \delta < 1$ is a discount factor and the period loss, $L_t$, is given by the period loss function

$$L_t = \frac{1}{2}\left[(\pi_t - \pi^*)^2 + \theta\tilde{u}_t^2\right],$$

where $\pi^*$ is the inflation target (denoted $\pi^{TAR}$ in ILE). (I have simplified the period loss function relative to ILE by setting $\beta = \nu = 0$.)

Let me simplify further by setting $\theta = 0$ and consider "strict" inflation targeting,

$$L_t = \frac{1}{2}(\pi_t - \pi^*)^2,$$

leaving the case of "flexible" inflation targeting, $\theta > 0$, as an extension. We note from (2.1) that $\pi_t$ and $\pi_{t+1}$ are predetermined with respect to quarter $t$. By (2.3), the instrument $i_t$ affects $\tilde{u}_{t+1}$, which, in turn, affects $\pi_{t+2}$ (and later inflation rates). Since there is no cost to instrument adjustment (since $\nu = 0$), it is clear that $i_t$ should be set so as to minimize

$$\mathrm{E}_t \delta^2 L_{t+2} \tag{2.4}$$

(since $i_{t+\tau}$ for $\tau \geq 1$ can be freely used to minimize $\mathrm{E}_{t+\tau}\delta^{\tau+2} L_{t+\tau+2}$).

Since $\tilde{u}_{t+1}$ by (2.3) is linear in $i_t$, we realize from (2.1) and (2.4) that the first-order condition for an optimum can be written

$$\begin{aligned} 0 &= \mathrm{E}_t[(\pi_{t+2} - \pi^*) f'(\tilde{u}_{t+1})] = \mathrm{E}_t\{[\pi_{t+1} + f(\tilde{u}_{t+1}) + \varepsilon^{\pi}_{t+2} - \pi^*] f'(\tilde{u}_{t+1})\} \\ &= (\pi_{t+2|t} - \pi^*)\mathrm{E}_t f'(\tilde{u}_{t+1}) + \mathrm{Cov}_t[f(\tilde{u}_{t+1}), f'(\tilde{u}_{t+1})], \end{aligned} \tag{2.5}$$

(where I have used that $\mathrm{E}_t[x, y] = \mathrm{E}_t[x]\mathrm{E}_t[y] + \mathrm{Cov}_t[x, y]$). Furthermore, assuming that negligible probability mass falls in the interval $\tilde{u}_{t+1} > \gamma/2\varphi$, we have

$$\mathrm{Cov}_t[f(\tilde{u}_{t+1}), f'(\tilde{u}_{t+1})] = 2\varphi\, \mathrm{Cov}_t[f(\tilde{u}_{t+1}), \tilde{u}_{t+1}].$$

Exploiting a theorem of Rubinstein (1976),[1] we have

$$\mathrm{Cov}_t[f(\tilde{u}_{t+1}), \tilde{u}_{t+1}] = \mathrm{E}_t f'(\tilde{u}_{t+1})\sigma^2_{\tilde{u}}.$$

Using this in (2.5), I get the first-order condition

$$\pi_{t+2|t} = \pi^* - 2\varphi\sigma^2_{\tilde{u}}. \tag{2.6}$$

Thus, under strict inflation targeting with a convex Phillips curve, it is optimal to undershoot the inflation target, on average. Average inflation, the unconditional mean of inflation, will fulfill $\mathrm{E}[\pi_t] = \pi^* - 2\varphi\sigma^2_{\tilde{u}}$.

In order to determine the optimal setting of $i_t$, I need to solve (2.6) for $\tilde{u}_{t+1|t}$. We have

$$\pi_{t+2|t} \equiv \pi_{t+1|t} + \mathrm{E}_t f(\tilde{u}_{t+1}). \tag{2.7}$$

We note, in passing, that by taking the unconditional mean of (2.7), we have $\mathrm{E}[f(\tilde{u}_t)] = 0$. Since $f(\tilde{u}_t)$ is convex and $f(0) = 0$, it follows (as in ILE) that the average unemployment gap will be positive, $\mathrm{E}[\tilde{u}_t] > 0$. We can directly infer from (2.3) that the average real interest rate, $r_t \equiv i_t - \pi_{t+1|t}$, must exceed the natural real interest rate, $\mathrm{E}[r_t] > \bar{r}$.

In order to solve for $\tilde{u}_{t+1|t}$, assume that the variance $\sigma^2_{\tilde{u}}$ is sufficiently small to warrant the second-order Taylor approximation

$$\mathrm{E}_t f(\tilde{u}_{t+1}) = \mathrm{E}_t f(\tilde{u}_{t+1|t} + \varepsilon^{\tilde{u}}_{t+1}) = f(\tilde{u}_{t+1|t}) + \frac{1}{2} f''(\tilde{u}_{t+1|t})\sigma^2_{\tilde{u}} = f(\tilde{u}_{t+1|t}) + \varphi\sigma^2_{\tilde{u}}. \tag{2.8}$$

Combining (2.2) and (2.7)–(2.8) leads to a second-order equation for $\tilde{u}_{t+1|t}$. The solution for the relevant root can be written

$$\tilde{u}_{t+1|t} = g(\pi_{t+1|t} - \pi^*), \tag{2.9}$$

where

$$g(\pi_{t+1|t} - \pi^*) \equiv \begin{cases} \frac{\gamma}{2\varphi}\left(1 - \sqrt{1 - \frac{4\varphi}{\gamma^2}(\pi_{t+1|t} - \pi^* + 3\varphi\sigma_{\tilde{u}}^2}\right), & \varphi > 0 \\ \frac{1}{\gamma}\left(\pi_{t+1|t} - \pi^*\right), & \varphi = 0 \end{cases}$$

Combining the expectation in quarter $t$ of (2.3) with (2.9) results in the optimal reaction function,

$$i_t = \bar{r} + \pi_{t+1|t} + \frac{1}{\eta_r} g(\pi_{t+1|t} - \pi^*) - \frac{\eta_u}{\eta_r}\tilde{u}_t \tag{2.10}$$

$$\equiv \bar{r} + \pi_t + f(\tilde{u}_t) + \frac{1}{\eta_r} g\left(\pi_t - \pi^* + f(\tilde{u}_t)\right) - \frac{\eta_u}{\eta_r}\tilde{u}_t. \tag{2.11}$$

The reaction function can be expressed in terms of $\pi_{t+1|t}$ and $\tilde{u}_t$ as in (2.10). Alternatively, since the predetermined $\pi_{t+1|t}$ fulfills

$$\pi_{t+1|t} \equiv \pi_t + f(\tilde{u}_t) \tag{2.12}$$

(recall that $\tilde{u}_t$ is observable, since I simplify by assuming that $u_t^*$ is observable), it can be expressed in terms of $\pi_t$ and $\tilde{u}_t$ as in (2.11).

## 3. Comparing Reaction Functions

Thus, under strict inflation targeting, the endogenous reaction function in the equivalent forms (2.10) or (2.11) will result. The reaction function (2.10) is nonlinear in $\pi_{t+1|t}$ and linear in $\tilde{u}_t$. The reaction function (2.11) is nonlinear in both $\pi_t$ and $\tilde{u}_t$. We note that it is optimal to respond to $\tilde{u}_t$, even under strict inflation targeting with no weight on $\tilde{u}_t$ in the loss function, since, as emphasized in Svensson (1999a), it is generally optimal to respond to the *determinants* of the target variable(s) rather than just the target variable(s) themselves.

We can now compare these optimal reaction functions to a Taylor-type rule,

$$i_t = \bar{r} + \pi_t + w_\pi(\pi_t - \pi^*) - w_u\tilde{u}_t, \tag{3.1}$$

and the two forecast-based instrument rules examined by ILE,

$$i_t = \bar{r} + \pi_{t+4|t}^4 + w_\pi(\pi_t^4 - \pi^*) - w_u\tilde{u}_t$$

which is denoted IFB1 (inflation-forecast-based rule 1), and

$$i_t = \bar{r} + \pi_{t+4|t}^4 + w_\pi(\pi_{t+3|t} - \pi^*) - w_u\tilde{u}_t$$

which is denoted IFB2. Here $\pi_t^4 = \frac{1}{4}\sum_{\tau=0}^{3}\pi_{t-\tau}$ denotes 4-quarter inflation. Both IFB rules are somewhat simplified by the assumption that $u_t^*$ and hence $\tilde{u}_t$ are observable.

We see that the Taylor-type rule, as a function of $\pi_t$ and $\tilde{u}_t$, is quite different from the optimal reaction function (2.11), since the former is linear in both arguments whereas the latter is nonlinear. Thus, it is quite intuitive that, with a nonlinear Phillips curve, the linear Taylor rule is inferior.

Furthermore, for IFB1, the term $\pi^4_{t+4|t} = \frac{1}{4}\sum_{\tau=0}^{3}\pi_{t+4-\tau|t}$ enters. For IFB2, the term $\pi_{t+3|t}$ also enters. Since the terms $\pi_{t+4-\tau|t} = \pi_{t+3-\tau|t} + \mathrm{E}_t f(\tilde{u}_{t+3-\tau|t})$ for $\tau = 0, \ldots, 3$, are nonlinear functions of $\tilde{u}_t$, this means that the instrument becomes a nonlinear function of $\tilde{u}_t$. The resulting nonlinear function is, of course, not equal to the optimal reaction function (2.10) or (2.11), so it will not be optimal. Still, it may be closer to the optimal reaction function than the backward-looking Taylor-type rule (3.1). This seems to be the reason why IFB1 and IFB2 perform better than the backward-looking linear rule.

Furthermore, note that IFB1 and IFB2 are not reaction functions that are functions of predetermined variables only. Instead, they make the instrument a function of an endogenous model-consistent inflation forecast, which depends on the instrument rule itself and requires the solution of the whole model to be determined. Therefore, IFB1 and IFB2 are actually examples of quite complex equilibrium conditions.[2] For this reason and others discussed in Svensson (1999a), I remain sceptical about their usefulness in practical monetary policy.

## 4. An Instrument Rule Involving an Optimal Response to an Inflation Forecast

Suppose, however, that we would insist on applying an instrument rule involving a response to an inflation forecast. What could we do within the present model? First, consider the two-period inflation forecast $\pi_{t+2|t}$ as a function $\Pi_{t+2|t}(i_t)$ of the instrument, $i_t$, and the state of the economy in periods $t$, $\pi_t$ and $\tilde{u}_t$. This function is by (2.7) defined by

$$\begin{aligned}\pi_{t+2|t} &= \Pi_{t+2|t}(i_t)\\ &\equiv \pi_{t+1|t} + f[\eta_u\tilde{u}_t + \eta_r(i_t - \pi_{t+1|t})] + \varphi\sigma^2_{\tilde{u}},\end{aligned}$$

where we recall that $\pi_{t+1|t}$ is given by (2.12) and where I have used the approximation (2.8). Now, we can, of course, consider a first-order Taylor approximation to this forecast around the interest rate $i_{t-1}$ in the previous quarter,

$$\pi_{t+2|t} = \Pi_{t+2|t}(i_{t-1}) + \frac{\partial\Pi_{t+2|t}(i_{t-1})}{\partial i}\Delta i_t,$$

where $\Delta i_t \equiv i_t - i_{t-1}$. Combining this with the first-order condition (2.6) and solving for $\Delta i_t$ leads to

$$\Delta i_t = \frac{1}{-\frac{\partial\Pi_{t+2|t}(i_{t-1})}{\partial i}}[\Pi_{t+2|t}(i_{t-1}) - (\pi^* - 2\varphi\sigma^2_{\tilde{u}})]. \tag{4.2}$$

Here, we get an optimal instrument rule, which says that the optimal adjustment of the interest rate, $\Delta i_t$, should be proportional to the deviation between the *unchanged-interest-rate* inflation forecasts $\Pi_{t+2|t}(i_{t-1})$ and the adjusted inflation target, $\pi^* - 2\varphi\sigma^2_{\tilde{u}}$. Furthermore, the response coefficient is given by

$$\frac{1}{-\frac{\partial\Pi_{t+2|t}(i_{t-1})}{\partial i}} = \frac{1}{-\eta_r f'[\eta_u\tilde{u}_t + \eta_r(i_{t-1} - \pi_{t+1|t} - \bar{r})]}$$

$$= \frac{1}{\eta_r\{\gamma - 2\varphi[\eta_u \tilde{u}_t + \eta_r(i_{t-1} - \pi_{t+1|t} - \bar{r})]\}}.$$

Several comments are in order. First, the inflation forecast is *not* the model-consistent inflation forecast for the endogenous interest rate but the *unchanged-interest-rate* forecast (that is, for $i_t = i_{t-1}$). Second, the instrument rule involves the *change* in the interest rate, not the level. Third, an *adjusted* inflation target should be applied (when $\varphi > 0$ and the Phillips curve is nonlinear). Fourth, the response coefficient is *not constant* but state-dependent (when $\varphi > 0$). The response coefficient is the reciprocal of the slope of the Phillips curve for an unchanged-interest-rate unemployment-gap forecast for period $t+1$, given by $\eta_u \tilde{u}_t + \eta_r(i_{t-1} - \pi_{t+1|t})$. Finally, even if the response coefficient is state-dependent, the instrument rule is only an approximation, since it follows from a first-order *approximation* of a nonlinear function.

Clearly, the optimal instrument rule (4.2) is, in several respects, quite different from the IFB rules discussed by ILE. In a linear model (when $\varphi = 0$), the problem of the adjusted inflation target and the state-dependent response coefficient would disappear. Then, the optimal instrument adjustment is proportional to the deviation between an unchanged-interest-rate inflation forecast and the inflation target. Thus, it seems more intuitive that any response should be to the unchanged-interest-rate forecast than to a model-consistent forecast.

## Notes

1. The theorem says that, if $x$ and $y$ are bivariate normal, under some mild regularity conditions,

$$\mathrm{Cov}[f(x), y] = \mathrm{E}[f'(x)]\,\mathrm{Cov}[x, y].$$

2. Rudebusch and Svensson (1999, Appendix) demonstrate the complexity of this instrument rule.

## References

Rubinstein, Mark. (1976). "The Valuation of Uncertain Income Streams and the Pricing of Options." *Bell Journal of Economics* 7, 407–425.

Rudebusch, Glenn D., and Lars E. O. Svensson. (1999). "Policy Rules for Inflation Targeting." in Taylor (1999), forthcoming.

Schaling, Eric. (1999). "The Nonlinear Phillips Curve and Inflation Forecast Targeting—Symmetric versus Asymmetric Monetary Policy Rules." Working Paper.

Svensson, Lars E. O. (1999a). "Inflation Targeting as a Monetary Policy Rule." *Journal of Monetary Economics* 43, forthcoming.

Svensson, Lars E. O. (1999b). "Price Stability as a Target for Monetary Policy: Defining and Maintaining Price Stability." Presented at Deutsche Bundesbank's conference on *The Monetary Transmission Process: Recent Developments and Lessons for Europe*, March 26–27, 1999. http://www.iies.su.se/leosven/.

Taylor, John B. (ed.). (1999). *Monetary Policy Rules*. Chicago University Press, forthcoming.

# Comment

BY BENNETT T. MCCALLUM

Participating in this affair has helped me to recognize that my own concern for robustness in policy rule design was in part due to Bob Flood's influence. When we were together at Virginia, I would get excited about a particular analytical policy result. But every few weeks Bob would say to me: "Well, yes, Ben, but what if you make the following small change in the model?" And, of course, doing so would overturn my result entirely. So I gradually came to understand that it was not so exciting.

Peter Isard gave me the assignment of doing whatever I wanted with regard to the two papers in this session. Since I was having enough trouble in getting my own paper pulled together, I took the easy way out and decided to discuss only one—the Isard, Laxton, Eliasson paper—with apologies to Henderson and Kim.

Their paper is really a very ambitious and rather complex one. I am extremely supportive of their general approach, and of the aspect of their approach that treats the NAIRU as nonobservable and that treats output as observable only with a one-quarter lag. I have been arguing in favor of these kinds of information assumptions for several years, and more generally for the strategy of looking for simple policy rules that are reasonably effective in a variety of models, rather than looking for the "optimal policy" in some particular model. So, to repeat, I am entirely supportive of their general approach.

When I say that the paper is complex, what I have in mind is that there are several features of the model that are "nonstandard." Most prominent among these is the nonlinearity in the Phillips curve relation. Two others that I have noted are that expectational behavior is not straightforward rational expectations, but sort of a hybrid, and that the IS function, which they call the unemployment rate equation, is entirely backward looking. With respect to this latter function I have to observe, parenthetically, that this specification is not very nice theoretically, and even so doesn't work very well empirically. The largest $t$-ratio on the three lagged real interest rates in their Table 3 is 1.8. This is somewhat important, because the effects of monetary policy on both real and nominal variables in their model is transmitted entirely via these three parameters. If they were zeros, the model would just fall apart and policy wouldn't do anything to anything.

Anyhow, to get back to the main argument, it's quite notable that in their model the original Taylor rule (which responds to lagged variables) performs very badly indeed, leading to explosive behavior. Also performing very badly are variants utilized by Clarida, Gali, and Gertler (1997) and by Levin, Wieland, and Williams (1998). This finding that is presented in the paper contrasts very sharply with results reported by several authors at the NBER Conference organized by John Taylor and held exactly a year ago in Florida. These results are summarized in a recent paper by Taylor (1999), which argues that Taylor-style rules performed very well in a robust sense. So this finding is quite significant, I would say.

My main reservation about the paper is that it is not clear to me which of the nonstandard features are responsible for the very different behavior in their model and in the bundle of models presented by several authors at the NBER conference. Their exposition emphasizes the nonlinearity in the Phillips curves, but it is not entirely obvious that it is not another one of the nonstandard features that is crucial. Maybe that information is present in the paper, but I couldn't find it. So I would like to see results that shut down the nonlinearity and keep all of the other nonstandard features. And, I would also be interested in seeing how the results, especially those in the Appendix, would fare if nominal income growth were used as the target variable instead of inflation and the output gap—perhaps an expected value of nominal income growth. I don't really want to suggest that they report more results, but possibly somewhat different ones that make for a slightly clearer comparison.

I'll conclude by noting that the results in their Appendix are quite closely related to issues discussed in the paper that I prepared for this Festschrift—issues concerning regions of instability, unique solutions, and indeterminacy in these models. In that regard, I was surprised to see the left hand regions in their Figure B1 labeled as indeterminacy. I would have thought one would get explosions there from Taylor's discussion and from Peter's discussion. But additional investigation indicates that their result is correct, subject to considerations raised in Section II of my paper.

Anyhow, none of these comments represents any major complaint. Basically, I think this is an extremely interesting and valuable paper.

## References

Clarida, R., J. Gali, and M. Gertler. (1998). "Monetary Policy Rules and Macroeconomic Stability: Evidence and Some Theory." NBER Working Paper No. 6442, March.

Levin, A., V. Wieland, and J. Williams. (1999). "Robustness of Simple Monetary Policy Rules Under Model Uncertainty," in J. B. Taylor (ed.), *Monetary Policy Rules*. Chicago: University of Chicago Press.

Taylor, J. B. (1999). "The Robustness and Efficiency of Monetary Policy Rules as Guidelines for Interest Rate Setting by the European Central Bank." *Journal of Monetary Economics* 43, forthcoming.

# General Discussion

**Charles Engel** contrasted the Henderson–Kim paper with work that he had done with Michael Devereux, noting that he didn't understand how Henderson and Kim had treated the monopolistic inefficiency or their rationale for doing so. It wasn't clear to him what the Pigouvian taxes and subsidies ought to be. This was essentially a Jensen's inequality issue. Prices could be set to get the level of output to the competitive level, but this wouldn't get consumption or the expected utility of consumption to the competitive level. He and Devereux had chosen to leave the monopolistic inefficiencies in their model when evaluating policy rules, and he wasn't clear about the role that inefficiencies played in the Henderson–Kim analysis.

**Robert Hodrick** pointed out that it was difficult to explain inflation inertia in models in which price-setting behavior was characterized in terms of one-period-ahead contracts. This seemed to be a problem for both the Henderson–Kim and Engel papers, since considerable inflation inertia was clearly present in the data, as revealed, for example, in the estimation results presented in the Isard–Laxton–Eliasson paper.

**Kim** and **Henderson** responded to several questions that Gray had raised. In justifying the hassles of constructing a model that could be used to make exact utility calculations, Kim cited another paper in which reliance on approximate calculations had generated an incorrect ordering of the utilities associated with having complete and incomplete markets. In explaining what they felt was gained by introducing monopolistic competition among firms and households, they expressed the view that it was important to be able to rationalize price- and wage-setting behavior, but that the introduction of monopolistic competition didn't have major effects on the conclusions from their analysis.

In responding to Engel's request for clarification, **Henderson** explained that they had introduced subsidies that were not time varying, and that served to remove the monopolistic competition distortions for agents who made decisions under full current information. This essentially eliminated the distortions from the first-order conditions of price- and wage-setters who had full current information. Whether it completely eliminated the effects of the distortions from the general equilibrium was a deeper question, given that some agents had to set prices and wages without full current information. Henderson seemed to feel that by knocking the markup parameter out of all the equilibrium conditions, the taxes and subsidies did what they were intended to do. **Assaf Razin** suggested that this would be done perfectly if the taxes and subsidies were shock specific.

In responding to Hodrick, **Henderson** agreed with the empirical evidence on the importance of inflation inertia and indicated that he and Kim wouldn't be taking their model to the data any time soon. Henderson also applauded Svensson's approach of optimizing within classes of rules, indicating that despite the model specificity of the results, this approach can sometimes be very helpful in clarifying thinking, for example, about why certain ranges of parameter values are good or bad.

**Laxton** responded to McCallum's request for clarification on why the stabilizing properties of various classes of rules were so much different in the Isard–Laxton–Eliasson (ILE) model than in other models in which they had been evaluated. He emphasized that the other models tended to be linear with a lot of inflation persistence and very small effects of the output gap on the inflation process. Under these assumptions, bad policy rules could generate relatively high variances of output and inflation but did not lead to explosive behavior. This was illustrated by the first chart in Appendix II of the ILE paper, which focused on the stabilizing properties of a Taylor rule in the Fuhrer–Moore model, where the rule had been generalized to allow for interest rate smoothing. Laxton emphasized that the region of stability, defined in terms of the long-run responses of the interest rate to output gaps and inflation, essentially included all rule calibrations in which the long-run response of the nominal interest rate to inflation was greater than one. Moreover, this region of stability was completely unaffected by the lags in the response of monetary policy: even with extremely slow responses of monetary policy to inflation and the output gap, stability under a generalized Taylor rule essentially depended only on having a positive long-run response of the real interest rate to an excess demand shock.

**Laxton** noted that work at the Federal Reserve by Andrew Levin, Volker Wieland, and John Williams (LWW) had looked at several different linear rational-expectations models and found that a first-difference rule was superior to the Taylor rule. The ILE analysis had found that explosive behavior was hard to generate in the Fuhrer-Moore model, even under the extremely myopic policy behavior that resulted when the LWW rule was combined with an assumption that inflation expectations could be described by a three-year or six-year moving average of past inflation. By contrast, in the nonlinear ILE model, if excess demand in the economy became quite high and policy was responding to a backward-looking measure of inflation, while inflation expectations were forward looking and conditioned (in the simulation analysis) on the implicit assumption that the monetary authority was committed to its backward-looking rule, a situation could develop in which the nominal interest rate did not move sufficiently to make the real interest rate rise in response to the excess demand. This would be a situation in which the Phillips curve was shifting and monetary policy was always behind shifts in the curve. In response to a follow-up question from McCallum, Laxton noted that while the stability analysis reported in Appendix II was based on the assumption that inflation expectations were only partly model-consistent, the performances of Taylor rules and LWW rules in the ILE model became even more unstable when full weight was placed on the model-consistent expectations term.

A final set of questions from the audience was posed by **Michael Dooley**, who wondered who would actually want to use a simple policy rule and for what purpose. Why would central banks want to rely on simple rules when they could base their policy decisions on sophisticated models? And what was the logic of using simple rules as a communication device; how could credibility be increased if central banks explained their actions in terms of simple rules when they were actually basing policy on more sophisticated analysis?

Several of the authors and discussants responded. **Henderson** started by noting that there has been a long tradition of asking whether optimal policy can be closely approximated by a simple rule. He also emphasized that there is considerable disagreement in policy circles about how to describe the policy process to the public; while some people believe the public is quite sophisticated and can handle complicated descriptions, others recommend simple descriptions. In addition, he pointed to the fact that the Federal Reserve staff receives ongoing requests from the Board of Governors to analyze how simple monetary policy rules would guide the economy and to explain why the economy would behave in this way or that under these rules.

In a separate response to Dooley's questions, **Svensson** suggested that the targeting rule approach provided an answer, assuming that the authorities could clearly define the objectives of policy. The inflation targeting framework was designed to be explicit about the policy loss function and to have simple procedures so that the public could monitor whether the central bank was actually optimizing that particular loss function. **McCallum** disagreed with Svensson on the importance of a targeting rule approach and the associated emphasis on communication. Citing the Bundesbank as an example, he argued that a central bank's credibility depended on what it did, not on what it said.

# Robert P. Flood, Jr. – Bibliography

Birth Date: January 7, 1949

Degrees: B.A., Wake Forest University, 1970
M.A., University of Rochester, 1975
Ph.D., University of Rochester, 1977

Experience

Rochester Graduate Work
Concentrations in International Economics, Monetary Economics
Dissertation: supervised by Michael Mussa
*Essays on Real and Monetary Aspects of Various Exchange Rate Systems*
Research Assistant, International Monetary Research Program, London, 1975.
Assistant Professor, Department of Economics, University of Virginia, 1976–81.
Economist, Board of Governors of the Federal Reserve System, 1980–82.
Associate Professor, Department of Economics, University of Virginia, 1981–83.
Professor, Department of Economics, Northwestern University, 1983–89
Senior Economist, International Monetary Fund, 1987–present.

Editorial Work

Co-Editor, *Journal of International Economics*, 1983–87
Associate Editor, *Journal of Money, Credit and Banking*, 1983–present.
Associate Editor, *American Economic Review*, 1989–93.
Associate Editor, *International Journal of Finance and Economics*, 1995–present.
Associate Editor, *International Journal of Finance and Money*, 1995–present.
Editor, *IMF Staff Papers*, 1998–present.

Research Associations

Research Associate, National Bureau of Economic Research 1979-97.
Research Associate, Georgetown University Center for International Economic Policy.
Research Professor, Dartmouth College.

Published Papers:

"Growth, Prices and the Balance of Payments," *Canadian Journal of Economics*, May,1977.

"Exchange Rate Expectations in Dual Exchange Markets," *Journal of International Economics*, February, 1978.

"Backward Looking and Forward Looking Solutions to Monetary Models of Inflation With Rational Expectations," *Economics Letters* 1, 1978 (with P. Garber).

"An Example of Exchange Rate Overshooting," *Southern Economic Journal*, July, 1979.

"An Economic Theory of Monetary Reform," *Journal of Political Economy*, February, 1980 (with P. Garber).

"A Pitfall in Estimation of Models With Rational Expectations," *Journal of Monetary Economics*, July, 1980 (with P. Garber).

"Market Fundamentals Versus Price Level Bubbles: The First Tests," *Journal of Political Economy*, August, 1980 ( with P. Garber).

"Perfect Foresight and the Stability of Monetary Models," *Economica*, August, 1981 (with E. Burmeister and S. Turnovsky).

"Explanations of Exchange-Rate Volatility and Other Empirical Regularities in Some Popular Models of the Foreign Exchange Market," Vol. 15 supplement to *Journal of Monetary Economics*, Autumn, 1981.

"The Transmission of Disturbances Under Alternative Exchange-Rate Regimes," *Quarterly Journal of Economics*, February, 1982. (with N. Marion).

"Activist Policy in the Open Economy," A.E.A. Papers and Proceedings, *American Economic Review*, May, 1982.

"Bubbles, Runs and Gold Monetization," in P. Wachtel (ed.), *Crises in the Financial Structure*. Lexington Books, 1982 (with P. Garber).

"A Model of Stochastic Process Switching," *Econometrica*, May, 1983. (with P. Garber).

"Process Consistency and Monetary Reform: Some Further Evidence," *Journal of Monetary Economics*, pp. 279–295, 1983 (with P. Garber).

"On The Equivalence of Solutions in Rational Expectations Models," *Journal of Economic Dynamics and Control*, 1983 (with E. Burmeister and P. Garber)

"Gold Monetization and Gold Discipline," *Journal of Political Economy*, February, 1984 (with P. Garber), reprinted as Chapter 10 in R. Aliber (ed.), *The Reconstruction of International Monetary Arrangements*. MacMillan, 1987.

"Exchange Rate Regimes in Transition: Italy 1974," *Journal of International Money and Finance*, December,1983 (with N. Marion).

"Multi-Country Tests for Price Level Bubbles," *Journal of Monetary Economics* 8, 1984, pp. 329–340 (with P. Garber and L. Scott).

"Collapsing Exchange Rate Regimes: Some Linear Examples," *Journal of International Economics*, August, 1984. (with P. Garber)

"Exchange Rate and Price Dynamics with Asymmetric Information," *International Economic Review*, October, 1984 (with R. Hodrick).

"Central Bank Intervention in a Rational Open Economy: A Model With Asymmetric Information," in J. Bhandari (ed.), *Exchange Rate Management Under Uncertainty*. MIT Press, 1985 (with R. Hodrick).

"Exchange Rate Dynamics, Sticky Prices and the Current Account," *Journal of Money Credit and Banking*, August, 1985 (with C. Engle).

"Optimal Price and Inventory Adjustment in an Open Economy Model of the Business Cycle," *Quarterly Journal of Economics*, 1986 (with R. Hodrick).

"Bubbles, Process Switching and Asset Price Volatility," *Journal of Finance*, July, 1986. (with R. Hodrick)

"Real Aspects of Exchange Rate Regime Choice," *Journal of International Economics*, November, 1986 (with R. Hodrick).

"Risk Neutrality and the Spread in a Two-Tier Foreign Exchange Market," *Economics Letters*, 1987 (with N. Marion).

"Monetary Policy Strategies," *Staff Papers*, International Monetary Fund, Vol. 36, pp.612–32, 1989 (with P. Isard).

"Evolution of Exchange Rate Regimes," *Staff Papers*, International Monetary Fund, Vol. 36, 1989 (with J. Horne and J. Bhandari).

"Testable Implications of Indeterminacies in Models with Rational Expectations," *Economics Perspectives*, Spring 1990, Vol. 4, No. 2 (with R. Hodrick).

"An Empirical Exploration of Exchange Rate Target Zones," Supplement to the *Journal of Monetary Economics*, Autumn 1991,. pp. 7–66 (with D. Mathieson. and A. Rose).

"Speculative Attacks and Models of Balance of Payments Crisis," *Staff Papers*, International Monetary Fund, Vol. 39, June, pp. 357–394 (with Agenor and J. Bhandari).

"Macroeconomic Policy, Speculative Attacks and Balance of Payments Crisis," (revised version of previous paper) in F. Van Der Ploeg (ed.), *The Handbook of International Macroeconomics*, Basil Blackwell, 1994 (with R. Agenor).

"Linkages Between Speculative Attack and Target Zone Models of Exchange Rates," *Quarterly Journal of Economics*, Vol. 106, pp. 1367–1372 (with P. Garber).

"The Linkage Between Speculative Attack and Target Zone Models of Exchange Rates: Further Results," in M. Miller and P. Krugman (eds.), *Exchange Rate Targets and Currency Bands*, Cambridge University Press,1992.

"A Theory of Optimum Currency Areas: Revisited," G. Tavlas, ed., *Greek Economic Review*, 1992 (with J. Aizenman).

"Speculative Attacks and Models of Balance-of-Payments Crisis," *Staff Papers*, International Monetary Fund, Vol. 39, June 1992, pp. 357-94 (with P.R. Agenor and J. Bhandari).

"Macroeconomic Policy, Speculative Attacks and Balance of Payments Crises," in F. Van Der Phol, ed., *The Handbook of International Economics*, Basil: Blackwell Publishers, 1994.

"What is Policy Switching?," *Finance and Development*, September, 1992.

"An Evaluation of Recent Evidence on Stock Market Bubbles" in R. Flood and P. Garber, *Speculative Bubbles, Speculative Attacks and Policy Switching*. MIT Press, 1994, (with R. Hodrick and P. Kaplan).

"Exchange Rate Regime Choice," P. Newman, ed., *The New Palgrave Dictionary of International Finance*, 1994 (with N. Marion).

"Two-Tier Foreign Exchange Markets," in P. Newman, ed., *The New Palgrave Dictionary of International Finance*, 1994 (with N. Marion ).

"Issues Concerning Nominal Anchors for Monetary Policy," in T Balino and C. Cottarelli, eds., Frameworks for Monetary Stability, 1994, International Monetary Fund (with M. Mussa).

"Exchange Rate Economics: What's Wrong with the Conventional Approach?," in J. Frankel, G. Galli and A. Giovannini, eds., *The Microstructure of Foreign Exchange Markets*, NBER, University of Chicago Press, 1996 (with M. Taylor).

"Fixing Exchange Rates: A Vitual Quest for Fundamentals," *Journal of Monetary Economics*, Vol. 36, pp. 3-37, 1995 (with A. Rose).

"Fixes of the Forward Discount Puzzle," *Review of Economics and Statistics* 1996 (with A. Rose).

"Mexican Foreign Exchange Market Crises From the Perspective of the Speculative Attack Literature," in *International Capital Markets: Developments, Prospects and Policy Issues*, International Monetary Fund, August 1995 (with C. Kramer).

"Bubbles, Noise and the Trading Process in Speculative Markets," in *International Capital Markets: Developments, Prospects and Policy Issues*, International Monetary Fund, August 1995 (with T. Ito and C. Kramer).

"Collapsing Exchange Rate Regimes: Another Linear Example," *Journal of International Economics*, Vol. 41, No. 3/4, November 1996, pp. 223-234 (with P. Garber and C. Kramer).

"Economic Models of Speculative Attacks and the Drachma Crisis of May 1994, " *Open Economies Review*, Vol. 7, 1996, pp., 591-600 (with C. Kramer).

"The Size and Timing of Devaluations in Capital-Controlled Developing Countries," *Journal of Development Economics*, 1997 (with N. Marion).

"Policy Implications of Second Generation Crisis Models," *IMF Staff Papers*, September 1997, pp. 10-17 (With N. Marion).

"Reserve and Exchange Rate Cycles," *Journal of International Economics*, October 1998 (with W. Perravdin and P. Vitale).

"Self-Fulfilling Risk Predictions: An Application to Speculative Attacks," forthcoming, *Journal of International Economics* (with N. Marion).

"Perspectives on the Recent Currency Crisis Literature," forthcoming R. Dornbusch and M. Obstfeld, eds., *Essays on Honor of Robert Mundell* (with N. Marion).

"Is Launching the Euro Unstable in the Endgame," forthcoming P. Krugman, ed., NBER Conference Volume.

## Books:

*Speculative Bubbles, Speculative Attacks and Policy Switching*, MIT Press, 1994 (with Peter Garber).

## Comments and Reviews:

Review of M. Frattiani and K. Tavernier (eds.), "Bank Credit, Money and Inflation in Open Economies," *Journal of Monetary Economics*, August 1978.

Comment on W. Buiter and M. Miller, "Real Exchange-Rate Overshooting and the Output Cost of Bringing Down Inflation," *European Economic Review*, Vol. 18, 1982.

"Stochastic Process Switching and Inflation: A Comment on Real Exchange Rate Overshooting and the Output Cost of Bringing Down Inflation: Some Further Results" in J. Frenkel, ed., *Exchange Rates and International Macroeconomics*, University of Chicago Press, 1984.

Comment on W. McKibbin and J. Sachs, "Coordination of Monetary and Fiscal Policies in Industrial Economics," in J. Frenkel, ed., International Aspects of Fiscal Policy, University of Chicago Press, 1988.

Comment on K. Singleton, "Speculation and the Volatility of Foreign Currency Exchange Rates," Carnegie-Rochester Conference Volume, Vol. 26, 1987.

Comment on J. Frankel and R. Meese, "Are Exchange Rates Excessively Volatile?" NBER Macroeconomics Annual, 1987.

"Comment on Cukierman," Carnegie-Rochester Conference Volume.

Comment on R. Baillie paper, "Commodity Prices and Aggregate Inflation: Would a Commodity Price Rule be Worthwile?" Carnegie-Rochester Conference Series on Public Policy, vol. 31, 1989.

"Monetary Policy Strategies: A Correction," *Staff Papers*, International Monetary Fund (with P. Isard), 1990.

Comment on P. Krugman and M. Miller, "Why Have a Target Zone?" Carnegie-Rochester Conference Series on Public Policy, vol. 38, 1993 (with M. Spencer).

# Index of Authors